Transition Economies

This interdisciplinary book offers a comprehensive analysis of the transition economies of Central and Eastern Europe and the former Soviet Union. Providing full historical context and drawing on a wide range of literature, it explores the continuous economic and social transformation of the post-socialist world.

The book's core exploration evolves along three pivots of competitive economic structure, institutional change, and social welfare. The main elements include a detailed historical analysis of the early socialist economic model; its adaptations through the twentieth century; discussion of the 1990s market transition reforms; post-2008 crisis development; and the social and economic diversity in the region today. Always showing an appreciation for country specifics, the book also considers the urgent problems of social policy, poverty, income inequality, and labor migration.

Transition Economies will be invaluable for advanced students, researchers, and policy makers working on transition economies, comparative economics, economic development, and the economics of central Europe, as well as economic history, international political economy, and post-Soviet and Central and Eastern European regional studies.

Aleksandr V. Gevorkyan is Assistant Professor of Economics at the Department of Economics and Finance of the Peter J. Tobin College of Business at St. John's University, USA. His research covers themes in open economy macroeconomics, economic development, international financial economics, and post-socialist transition economics.

Transition Economies

Transformation, Development, and Society in Eastern Europe and the Former Soviet Union

Aleksandr V. Gevorkyan

LONDON AND NEW YORK

First published 2018
by Routledge
2 Park Square, Milton Park, Abingdon, Oxon OX14 4RN

and by Routledge
711 Third Avenue, New York, NY 10017

Routledge is an imprint of the Taylor & Francis Group, an informa business

British Library Cataloguing-in-Publication Data
A catalogue record for this book is available from the British Library

Library of Congress Cataloging-in-Publication Data
Names: Gevorkyan, Aleksandr V., author.
Title: Transition economies : transformation, development, and society in Eastern Europe and the former Soviet Union/Aleksandr V. Gevorkyan.
Description: Abingdon, Oxon ; New York, NY : Routledge, 2018. | Includes bibliographical references.
Identifiers: LCCN 2017052229 (print) | LCCN 2017056133 (ebook) | ISBN 9781315736747 (Ebook) | ISBN 9781138831124 (hardback : alk. paper) | ISBN 9781138831131 (pbk. : alk. paper)
Subjects: LCSH: Europe, Eastern—Economic conditions—1989- | Former Soviet republics—Economic conditions. | Post-communism—Europe, Eastern. | Post-communism—Former Soviet republics.
Classification: LCC HC244 (ebook) | LCC HC244 .G48 2018 (print) | DDC 330.947—dc23
LC record available at https://lccn.loc.gov/2017052229

ISBN: 978-1-138-83112-4 (hbk)
ISBN: 978-1-138-83113-1 (pbk)
ISBN: 978-1-315-73674-7 (ebk)

Typeset in Times New Roman
by Apex CoVantage, LLC

To my parents and brother

Contents

List of figures   x
List of tables   xii
Preface   xiii
Acknowledgments   xviii
List of abbreviations   xix

PART I
Introduction: the great unknowns   1

1   **The great unknowns: post-socialist economies and societies in motion**   3
    Introductory remarks 3
    Where are they on the map? 4
    Leading to the great unknowns 8
    Problem: transition? Transition from? Transition to? 11
    Conclusion 12
    Appendix 13

2   **Transition vs. transformation: what is clear and not so clear about transition economics**   15
    In search of a transition: definitions 15
    Transition vs. transformation 16
    The transformation 20
    Was it inevitable? 21
    The totality of the social and economic dynamic 26
    The dialectics of transition 29
    Conclusion 32

PART II
The planned economy   35

3   **The economic and social context at the turn of the twentieth century: from the Russian Empire to the Soviet Union**   37
    In the beginning there was . . . 37
    The emancipation of the serfs in 1861 38

The allure of early capitalism before the Russian revolution 39
Emergence of the Leninist State 43
The New Economic Policy 45
Industrialization, collectivization, debates, and the first Five-Year
    Plans 47
Initial analysis 49
Conclusion 50

 4 The war economy and post-World War II reconstruction in the USSR   53
The setting 53
Emerging transformation right before the war 54
The war economy 56
Post-war recovery in the USSR 59
More on central planning Soviet-style 64
Conclusion 70

 5 From war to wall to common market: the dialectics of the Eastern
 European socialist economy   72
The new political landscape of Europe 72
Before and around the wall: the political economy of Eastern Europe 73
Socialist economics in Eastern Europe immediately after WWII 78
A model of the common market 81
Crisis in disguise? 85
Conclusion 87

PART III
The economics of the market reform   89

 6 The socialist economic model, market socialism, stagnation,
 perestroika, and the end of plan   91
The socialist economic model 91
Market socialism or self-management 98
Right before 1985 102
The world order shaken: perestroika and the Berlin Wall 107
Macroeconomic challenges and opportunities 112
Conclusion: the end of plan 118

 7 Free market reform: liberalization, privatization, shock therapy, and
 policy misfortunes   122
Setting the stage 122
What happened during the 1990s 123
Macroeconomics of human transition 130
Conceptualizing the reform 134
Privatization 138

The shock therapy debates 147
Conclusion 154
Appendix 155

PART IV
The human transition: still happening 159

8 Poverty, income inequality, labor migration, and diaspora potential 161
Introduction 161
Poverty and income inequality 162
Labor migration 169
Diaspora and economic development 174
Measuring diaspora's effectiveness 176
Some new and not so new policy proposals 181
Conclusion: diaspora model and social costs of transition 182
Appendix 184

PART V
The roaring 2000s and the present 187

9 Contours of the new era post-transition economy: they are all different 189
The character of the new millennium 189
The "roaring" 2000s 190
Financial sector development 208
Regional integration and foreign direct investment 216
Conclusion 225
Appendix 226

10 Facing the present by knowing the past 231
Why the present 231
The macroeconomic (competitive) aspect 231
Human transition (again) 235
Institutions 241
Finding a place in the present 246
Of the future 248

References 250
Index 268

Figures

1.1	Schematic map of Eastern Europe and the former Soviet Union	5
1.2	Primary commodity dependence in CEE and FSU, % of merchandise exports	7
2.1	Transition GDP in proportion to 1990 GDP based on 2011 constant PPP $	19
2.2	Government spending in % of GDP and life expectancy in years (difference between 1995 and 1990)	20
2.3	Average GDP per capita growth rate (PPP 2011, CAGR)	27
2.4	Pre- and post-crisis growth rates (GDP pc, PPP 2011, CAGR)	28
2.5	The model of socio-economic transformation in the post-socialist economies	29
3.1	The price "scissors" of 1920s, index	46
4.1	The Soviet economy's structural transformation of the 1930s	55
4.2	Post-war estimated USSR GDP index, 1940 = 100	60
4.3	Post-war macroeconomic performance in the USSR	60
4.4	Soviet post-war industrial output, select indicators	61
4.5	Soviet administrative pyramid	66
5.1	Average shares of total investment by two primary sectors in socialist Europe, 1953–1956	80
6.1	Cross country comparative growth and GDP per capita shares	94
6.2	Sector shares in Soviet labor force, 1926–1980	96
6.3	Urban population in CEE and FSU as a share of total, 1960–1985	97
6.4	USSR GDP and industrial capacity growth, % YoY change (1975–1990)	105
6.5	Growth of labor productivity by worker, average % change	106
6.6	Real GDP/NMP dynamic in FSU and CEE, 1980–1998 (1989 = 100)	113
6.7	Employment to population ratio, percent, 1950–2017	117
7.1	Real GDP index for CIS-FSU (1989 = 100)	125
7.2	Real GDP index for CEE and the Baltic states (1989 = 100)	126
7.3	Real GDP per capita by country before and after transition ($PPP 2016)	131
7.4	Loss in real GDP per capita 1995 vs. 1989, by country, %	132
7.5	Average growth of employment, 1990–1994 and 1995–2000, % change	133
7.6	Privatization and foreign direct investment in the first decade	143
7.7	EBRD governance and enterprise restructuring index	145
8.1	Real 2000 and 2016 GDP per capita by country (1989 = 100)	163
8.2	Largest city population as a share of total urban population, %	166
8.3	Percentage share of income or consumption, EE and the FSU	168
8.4	Ratio of cumulative net migration to average population by country and decade, %	169
8.5	Personal average remittance inflows, % of GDP	171

8.6   FDI and remittances per capita, 2000–2015, USD   178
8.7   Home country-to-diaspora effectiveness approximation   180
8.8   Diaspora model, social costs of transition, and development   183
8.9A   Diaspora regulatory mechanism and Migration Development Bank   184
9.1   Average GDP growth by region, % change   191
9.2   Primary commodity prices super-cycle of 2000s, index (2005 = 100)   194
9.3   Average loss in GDP pc (PPP 2011) between 2008 and 2009, %   197
9.4   Current account as percent of GDP, pre- and post-GFC   198
9.5   Public debt in 2016 as % of GDP and % changes between 2016 and 2006   201
9.6   Average annual inflation pre- and post-GFC, %   202
9.7   Net private capital flows, Russia, USD blns, 1994–Q2 2017   205
9.8   Change in nominal official exchange rate (LCU per USD), %   207
9.9   Domestic credit to private sector as share of GDP, %   213
9.10   FDI inflows and stock in pre- and post-GFC period   220
9.11   Average number of announced greenfield FDI projects, by destination,
       pre- and post-GFC   221
9.12   EBRD index of competition policy by region and country, 2000 vs. 2014   224
9.13   Global competitiveness index ranking in CEE/FSU   225
10.1   Relative shares of CEE and FSU country groups to the world GDP, %   233
10.2   2016 GDP per capita: CEE/FSU vs. OECD, 2011 $PPP   234
10.3   Life expectancy at birth in CEE/FSU, total, in relation to 1980s maximum
       and 2000–2015 average   236
10.4   Life expectancy in CEE/FSU in the first transition decade vs. peak during
       1980–1989, male and female, years   237
10.5   World Bank Doing Business rankings, 2017   243
10.6   Word Bank Doing Business Report country-specific indicators, 2017   245

Tables

1.1	Transition economies by regional agglomeration	6
1.2	Transition economies by economic or political association	6
1.3A	Export shares by commodity group by country, 2000–2015 % of merchandise exports	13
3.1	Shares of select sectors in Russia's industrial mix	41
3.2	Russia's census data as of 1897	41
4.1	Select indicators of Soviet industrial production (1928–40) vs. first Five-Year Plan	55
4.2	USSR macroeconomic performance, 1951–1965 (average annual growth rates, %)	62
5.1	National income compared to pre-war index (1938 = 100)	79
5.2	Industrial and agricultural production index in Eastern Europe (pre-war = 100)	80
5.3	Individual country shares in the overall CMEA trade, %	83
5.4	Crude oil production by country as a share of total CMEA production, %	84
5.5	Soviet foreign trade by country groups (% of total exports and imports)	85
6.1	GDP per capita (1990 Int. GK$) cross country comparison	94
6.2	Soviet aggregate economic performance, % annual growth	103
6.3	Select data on the USSR economy, 1985–1991	114
6.4	Principles of a functioning new economic system à la "500 Days"	115
7.1	Changes to key macroeconomic indicators in the first reform years	127
7.2	Merchandise trade by direction CEE and Russia in 1980–2004 (% of total trade)	129
7.3	Liberalization and privatization reforms in CEE and FSU through the 1990s	134
7.4A	Private sector share in GDP, %	155
7.5A	Selected EBRD transition indicators	156
8.1	Selected social indicators of income inequality and poverty, period averages	164
8.2	Top ten remittances senders to each CEE/FSU region, % of total	172
8.3	Top ten remittances losers, % annual change	173
8.4	Potential diaspora stock and geographical spread for some transition economies	175
8.5A	Home-diaspora development effectiveness matrix	184
9.1	General government balance, % of GDP	195
9.2	Banking, currency, and sovereign debt crises in CEE/FSU, 1980–2008	210
9.3	Foreign banks' ownership shares in CEE and FSU as % of total banking sector	212
9.4	Exports exposure index: direction of exports, 2000–2016 average percent of GDP	222
9.5A	General government debt across CEE/FSU economies, % of GDP	226
10.1	Human and Gender Development Indexes in CEE/FSU, select years	239
10.2	Labor market indicators in CEE/FSU, 1990 and 2015	240

Preface

The true tale of the economic transition from a socialist to a capitalist economic model of Eastern Europe (EE) and the former Soviet Union (FSU) is yet to be heard.[1] The immensity of the phenomenon of the economic and social deconstruction launched at the end of the 20th century remains unprecedented. To fully absorb the complete account of the 1990s free market transition, or as this study maintains, *transformation*, requires a dialectical understanding of the totality of the region's economic history. Pulling together a collection of topics and unifying diverse specialized publications, this book is about such comprehensive interpretation of the dynamics of the CEE/FSU transformation. The discussion conceptualizes the past and the present, with some insights into the future of the post-socialist world. The entire history of the region reveals unending, broad-scale intensive change. As such, this study attempts to lay the foundation for an analytically concise and structurally sound blueprint for subsequent informed research.

Motivating this book is an attempt to penetrate the existing information vacuum around the post-socialist societies, despite the wealth of thematic academic studies. Often, aggregated in-group studies, the CEE/FSU economies are mistakenly treated as one and the same with little attention to the particulars of each independent nation state. While common tendencies across the region are discussed in this book, this is done intentionally to emphasize one of the critical conclusions of dynamic diversity in the region. That is, that just like individuals in a society, all the 29 nation states, despite perceived surface-level similarities and decades of shared political ideology, have always been and remain quite different from each other, and continue to evolve as such.

Put differently, applying a "one-size-fits-all" approach in studying the post-socialist region does not yield any practical results. This aspect of diversity, or economic variety—rooted in a legacy of social, ethnic, cultural, and economic distinctions within the perceived political union—needs more emphasis in transition economics studies. The analysis in this book treats such diversity as one of the main explanatory variables of the successes and failures of the ongoing transformation. The evolving diversity of post-socialist experiences in the CEE/FSU is also the key nucleus to any attempt to rationalize about sustainability of the new socio-economic model and its continued evolution.

For the most part, the countries of the CEE/FSU remain the great unknowns of the contemporary macroeconomic development. As such, an often lumping together of individual experiences in an abstract and disconnected aggregation of "transition countries" lacks the nuanced individuality of each case. Perhaps that is due to over-politicization of the social and economic transformations in the region inspired by legacy considerations. Perhaps the potential of newly opened consumer markets has not significantly lived up to the pre-reforms era expectations. Perhaps, it is due to the region's falling out of favor with development economists as the world grapples with four new challenges to global stability in the early 21st century: the wars on terror, primary commodities supply chains, financialization, and uncertain macroeconomic prospects at the beginning of the new technological century.

Whichever might be the case, the CEE/FSU region deserves objective attention from the commentators across policy circles, academia, and the media. Undeniably, the effect of the transformation on every aspect of human activity over the past decades has been immense. Not a stone has been left unturned since the launch of market liberalization reforms. The dynamic nature of the social transformation has not stopped since then. The realization of such dynamism, the often contradictory change within a social entity (individual household or group) is critical to the comprehensive story of post-socialist transition.

Consequently, the narrative of the book, based on a broad range of rich thematic literature, is set in a historic context that goes rather far back. This is done intentionally. History and legacy considerations play a critical role in shaping modern post-socialist societies. Numerous related themes are brought up in the discussion along the way. Anchored in historical analysis, this text attempts to develop an analytical framework around relevant key themes. Such framework becomes necessary for objective interpretation of the transition phenomenon and adequate policy work, bringing them all "under one roof" across some common tendencies but emphasizing individuality of socio-economic experiences.

Before sketching the structure of the book, a brief technical comment is due. A wide range of statistical data sources was relied upon in research supporting this analysis. The principal repositories were the databases of multilateral agencies (most importantly, the European Bank for Reconstruction and Development, World Bank, International Monetary Fund, United Nations and its agencies, Organization for Economic Cooperation and Development, Bank for International Settlements, and others). In addition, some specialized databases were utilized throughout, as cited. For example, the Total Economy Database developed by the Conference Board provided useful information on pre-1990s periods and forecasts. The Soviet-era publications of the Statistical Yearbooks of the CMEA and other statistics offered invaluable guidance to some of the intricacies of the socialist economic model. International Labour Organization's data portal offers a treasure chest of nuanced, difficult to find, data on labor markets by various aggregations. Importantly, the reader is reminded of the objective difficulties with data collection. Reading some results in a more directional, comparative way would be advisable, in some obvious situations, rather than attaching to specific values.

As for country names, this study has tried to maintain consistency generally following the World Bank's taxonomy. Throughout the text, variations on shorter names of some countries may appear as long as all versions refer to official country names in the international policy and academic publications (e.g. Slovak Republic, Slovakia, or shortened Slovak Rep, etc.).

Structurally, ten interconnected chapters comprise the text. To a large extent, the narrative follows a chronological path with two initial conceptual chapters. This appears to be necessary, if we are to develop a holistic historical view of the post-socialist transformation. It should be noted that the first two chapters offer a high-level preview of the transition–transformation dichotomy from a slightly more methodological angle than the more data and historical events driven remaining chapters. As such, Chapter 1 introduces the region and countries covered in the text. The vast post-socialist expanse that seemed monolithic not so long ago, today is clearly a diverse mix of cultures and economies: the "great unknowns" of contemporary economic development studies. Setting the stage for oncoming discussions, the chapter paves the way for preliminary conceptual debate over the distinction between transition and transformation processes in the post-socialist context.

Chapter 2 is somewhat conceptual—a required step that is intended to give the initial feel of the problem at hand—needed to provide some high-level direction on the subsequent analysis. Central to the conversation is a distinction between transition and transformation. In its take on post-transition assessment studies, the chapter raises concerns about the assumption of uniformity in policy advice at the time. From a dialectical perspective, the economic problems are intertwined with the problems of society development in general. Such approach then leads towards critical realization of a transformational category (as opposed to a relatively simplistic succession or transition) of development in the region. On that basis, and informing subsequent analysis, this chapter introduces an evolutionary model of socio-economic transformation in the post-socialist economies.

Chapter 3 dives into history by taking the repeal of serfdom in 1861 in the Russian Empire as a starting reference point. The discussion quickly moves through the economic and social context at the beginning of the 20th century and the aftermath of the Russian Revolution of 1917. Some common trends, including political change, struggles for independence, and formation of the USSR are addressed. On a more applied level, a critical evaluation of economic development in the CEE/FSU is conducted in parallel with such milestones of economic policy as the New Economic Policy of the early 1920s and collectivization and industrialization reforms of the USSR of the 1920s–1930s.

Chapter 4 continues by analytically dissecting political and economic structures of the former socialist states immediately before, during, and after World War II (WWII). The role of a strong unifying state, the five-year plans, monetary reforms, and immediate economic and social consequences as such policies spread beyond the USSR borders are all brought up in this discussion. This chapter also develops models of the Soviet economic and administrative blueprint that would influence post-WWII Central and Eastern Europe.

Chapter 5 brings the political economy context of Central Eastern Europe into the discussion. A closer look at the mixture of economic policies between the years 1961 and 1980 then follows. The period coincides with the construction of the infamous Berlin Wall. Adaptations of the planned economy, particularly in Central and Eastern Europe, are contrasted to the more rigid policies of the USSR. Topics of the socialist economic model and common market are addressed in this chapter with greater detail, some case studies, and theory. The chapter leads towards realization of a potential crisis of the expansive socialist economic model that by the late 1970s begins to show signs of technological lag.

In Chapter 6, the study moves into analysis of the complex socialist economic model and *perestroika*-connected policies. The years of stagnation being replaced by the enthusiasm of the *perestroika* reforms and the fall of the Berlin Wall led to early proposals for socialist economic reformation. With sweeping social and political transformations in the region, unprecedented economic changes, in turn inspired by a strong belief in the free market, took hold over the newly independent post-socialist states. The process was as much economic as it was political with sights of national sovereignty. However, the immediate breakup of the established planned economy's system led to devastating social and economic deterioration. In many cases, the switch from planned to market model was rather abrupt due to lack of preparedness to the reality of the shocks across the formerly socialist societies.

At the forefront of the forceful free market reforms were the issues of macroeconomic stabilization, market liberalization, and privatization reforms. However, as Chapter 7 emphasizes, the suddenness of the change and lack of institutional foundation collided with aggressive pursuit of the new policies' implementation. Despite the accumulating evidence of reforms' frequent misdirection, the debate is still ongoing touching on: macroeconomic gradualism vs. shock therapy vs. Washington consensus vs. development sustainability; output collapse vs. free market entrepreneurship; privatization and access to raw materials. It remains to be seen if the emerged macroeconomic and social foundation of the 1990s is sufficient to lead towards sustainable inclusive development in the region.

Chapter 8 argues that the human element has been integral to the post-socialist transformation. While some worsening of social conditions was expected, the unprecedented degree to which conditions deteriorated at a fast pace in a relatively peaceful revolution (by itself a contentious statement), stunned contemporary and later observers. Against the background of improving macroeconomics, a high incidence of poverty and rising income inequality persisted. This chapter also raises the problem of outward labor migration that has become a symbol of economic deterioration in the home economies and a boon to rapid development and growth of the stronger advanced economies. As a possible remedy, this chapter discusses and proposes closer attention to the diaspora potential, especially in the small, open economy development in a contemporary applied economic policy primer.

Chapter 9 steps into the modern era and reviews some of the major development patterns in the first two decades of the 21st century. Pushing off from the Russian financial crisis of 1998, this chapter discusses the latest evidence of macroeconomic development in the CEE/FSU, financial sector evolution, and regional economic alliances. Despite their relative insulation from international capital flows all CEE/FSU economies are now prone to international financial contagion, often dependent on the business cycle of their main trade partner. Events such as the 2008 global financial crisis or the 2014 devaluation of the Russian currency, uncovered core structural flaws in the transition group now advancing questions about sustainability of the established development model.

Chapter 10 is the concluding chapter that analytically summarizes previous discussions. The chapter also attempts to explore the question of final destination by focusing on the present conditions in the region with appreciation for its dynamic past. This is achieved by motivating the reader to consider three interconnected problem statements. First, how does one evaluate macroeconomic transition in the CEE/FSU on the basis of evidence presented in the book? Second, what is certain and uncertain about human transition? And third, can the painfully attained institutional gains of transition be sustained? As such, this chapter also elaborates on the three dimensions of the model introduced in Chapter 2: macroeconomic (competitive), human transition, and institutional.

The book is written in the hope of becoming a useful reference to researchers in economic history, macroeconomic development, and social policy, as well as to practitioners and policy decision makers in the economic development field, as well as those studying the transition region. In writing this book, every conscious attempt was made to verify facts across multiple sources and offer references to the most relevant literature and original research. Unfortunately, to maintain pace and conform with space limits, not all influential studies are included in this text. Yet, it is hoped that enough intellectual clues are contained here for a motivated researcher to objectively determine their independent research path.

A research monograph, the style of the book also allows for its adoption as a classroom text, one that reviews diverse thematic problems characteristic to the post-socialist region's evolution. If indeed used in class, it is hoped that this text would help advance students' in-depth knowledge of the complex, nonlinear cross-relationships among numerous factors pertinent to the diverse policy decisions shaping the CEE/FSU region's transformation. Students would have solid control of the core terminology and milestone events. Adding to academic facilities, the text may help enhance research skills and develop working familiarity of relevant economic data and sources.

Lastly, it is important to remember that discussion in this book is based on historical events that have already taken place. Therefore, any intellectual deviations that might consider outcomes different from the reality are purely abstract, albeit somewhat informed, attempts to rationalize the experience to date and orient subsequent analysis in an evidence-grounded approach.

The transition economies of the CEE/FSU are not natural experiments. They are a set of individual societies that have lived through and share some elements of common legacy. They should be studied and cannot be stereotyped, remaining unknown. From a political economy perspective, the still-firming institutional base of each country is integral to global harmony, stability, and unified actions. From a macroeconomic point of view, these are potentially some of the world's most prosperous economic powerhouses with eager consumer markets, a highly-skilled labor force, and vast spectrum of new opportunities. Ultimately, the philosophical question of macroeconomic and social development in post-socialist economies is about the direction of forward movement. Yet, equally, if not more, important is the present of the post-socialist region.

For all these reasons, and many more, the countries of Central and Eastern Europe and the former Soviet Union deserve objective, analytically-informed reading of their economic history and dynamic perspectives. It is with hope and modest ambition that this book attempts to unveil some of those intriguing foundational aspects of the evolutionary process of post-socialist transformation. If it succeeds in its goal, the analysis contained in this book may help us conceptualize in a more informed way the state of the post-socialist region's present and the path of the future.

Aleksandr V. Gevorkyan, Ph.D.
September 4, 2017
New York, NY

Note

1 Throughout the text we will use both abbreviations EE and CEE (referring to Central and Eastern Europe). The reader should consider those interchangeable for the purposes of the present analysis. In addition, for brevity the text relies on the use of the "transition region" phrase when making a general reference to the post-socialist EE and FSU countries.

Acknowledgments

This book started as an attempt to introduce a discussion on the post-socialist transformation of Eastern Europe and the former Soviet Union within the curriculum of standard macroeconomic development courses. During those interactions, and speaking on the topic in conferences, it became evident to me that for many, despite the wealth of thematic academic studies, the region in question remained, at best, a mystery, and, at worst, almost unknown. Intrigued by some narratives, my audiences asked the *hows* and the *whys* of the post-socialist transformation. Why what happened in the 1990s had actually happened? And what types of societies have emerged in place of the old? It is with those conversations in mind that I set out to work on this book with the hope of being able, at the very minimum, to help us begin to address these difficult and philosophical questions from more informed positions.

Reflecting on the work that went into this book, I am grateful to my students and colleagues for stimulating, through their queries, my interest in the post-socialist transition research. I am also indebted to my editor at Routledge, Emily Kindleysides, for her enthusiasm for the book's idea. Emily's reassurance helped me get the project off the ground and her trust in my work offered that invisible backing that a writer often unsuspectingly relies upon. I am equally grateful to Emily's colleagues, Natalie Tomlinson, Andy Humphries, Lisa Lavelle, Cathy Hurren, and Maire Harris who guided me through the manuscript preparation process. Five anonymous reviewers who expressed their strong support for my project deserve special thanks as well. Their positive reviews and constructive suggestions were essential in ensuring inclusion of some topics in the text.

I benefited from frequent discussions with my St. John's University colleagues on the topics of free market reforms and economic progress. I am also particularly grateful to Branko Milanovic, who reignited my work with his provocative questions about the future and penetrating insights into the region's historical development. I am grateful to Otaviano Canuto for his optimistic support, advice, and strong words of encouragement on my work.

In addition, special thanks goes to Lucas Bernard, Tarron Khemraj, Pierre Lacour, John Manley, and Willi Semmler. Their often precise and perceptive comments and suggestions helped me acquire a broader perspective of some key aspects related to the 1990s macroeconomic transformation and modern development challenges facing the post-socialist region. I would like to especially thank Hrant Mikaelian for his assistance with locating some difficult to find data on the Soviet period and his invaluable advice on several statistical representations. Matthew Foster graciously spent his time helping me with questions on graphics in text. I am also thankful to all colleagues with whom I discussed the project while preparing first drafts.

Above all, I am grateful to my family. My parents and my brother through their unquestioned inspiration, support, and advice, geographical and time zone separations notwithstanding, despite many challenges as work on the book progressed, kept me afloat, giving me the much-needed strength to complete this project.

Abbreviations

Country code	Country name	Country code	Country name
ALB	Albania	GDR	East Germany
ARM	Armenia	SCG	Serbia and Montenegro
AZE	Azerbaijan		
BLR	Belarus	UK	United Kingdom
BIH	Bosnia and Herzegovina	USA	United States of America
BGR	Bulgaria		
HRV	Croatia	**Organization code**	**Organization**
CZE	Czech Republic	CB	Central Bank
EST	Estonia	CPB	Central Planning Board
GEO	Georgia	EBRD	European Bank for Reconstruction and Development
HUN	Hungary	ECB	European Central Bank
KAZ	Kazakhstan	IMF	International Monetary Fund
KSV	Kosovo		
KGZ	Kyrgyz Republic	MDB	Migration development bank
LVA	Latvia		
LTU	Lithuania	NEM	New Economic Mechanism
MKD	Macedonia, FYR	NEP	New Economic Policy
MDA	Moldova		
MNE	Montenegro	OECD	Organization for Economic Cooperation and Development
POL	Poland		
ROM	Romania	OPEC	Organization of the Petroleum Exporting Countries
RUS	Russian Federation		
SRB	Serbia	UN	United Nations
SVK	Slovak Republic	UNCTAD	United Nations Conference on Trade and Development
SVN	Slovenia		
TJK	Tajikistan		
TKM	Turkmenistan	WB	World Bank
UKR	Ukraine	WDI	World Development Indicators
UZB	Uzbekistan		

Concept code	Concept	Region or Group code	Region or Group
CAGR	Compound annual growth rate		
		BS	Baltic States
EUR	EU euro		
		CEE	Central and Eastern Europe
FDI	Foreign direct investment		
		CIS	Commonwealth of Independent States
GFC	Global financial crisis		
GDP	Gross domestic product	CMEA (Comecon)	Council for Mutual Economic Assistance
ISI	Import substituting industrialization		
		EE	Eastern Europe
		EAEU	Eurasian Economic Union
MNE	Multinational enterprises		
RUB	Russian ruble	EU	European Union
SBC	Soft budget constraint	FSU	Former Soviet Union
USD	US dollar	SEE	Southeast Europe
WC	Washington consensus	USSR	Union of Soviet Socialist Republics
WWI	World War I (1914–1918)		
WWII	World War II (1939–1945)		

Part I

Introduction

The great unknowns

1 The great unknowns

Post-socialist economies and societies in motion

Human anatomy contains a key to the anatomy of the ape.

Karl Marx, *The Grundrisse*

Introductory remarks

This book is about a complex process of economic and social transformation in a relatively unknown, for Western development economists, region of Central and Eastern Europe (CEE or EE) and the former Soviet Union (FSU)—the former socialist economies.[1] One of the principal arguments of this book is that affecting every country in the region, the process of transformational change launched in the late 1980s and early 1990s is still very much ongoing. As such, the transformation has and continues to affect every fiber and foundational tenet of the existent and emerging societies, cultures, economies, and politics.

Back when it all started, the transformation process was dubbed transition from a socialist system to a capitalist, or free market-based, economy. However, from the very start things did not go as, ironically, planned. A myriad of social and political economy nuances emerged, disproving any hypothetical economic models promising a smooth slide into a new equilibrium. Confirmation of these observations may be found in the vast and very diverse academic and policy literature that the present study attempts to unify in a structured discussion.

This book is an attempt to rationalize the complexity of this massive social change that involved almost complete eradication of the old and, in turn, nurturing of the new institutions. As a result, matured societies of the region learned from scratch how to walk and read in a qualitatively new environment. Undeniably, the early years of transition took a heavy toll in terms of industrial collapse, economic structure destruction, and sharp declines in living standards across the CEE/FSU region.

A peculiar fact is that the adjustment, a term used here with a great degree of approximation, to the new market-based system was quite different across each, by now politically, newly independent state. Unfortunately, these days, more than two decades since the reforms, the actual nuances remain virtually unknown to a broad research field, epitomized by the propensity to average out some country-specific tendencies and to often disregard unique nuances.

History holds the key to understanding some of the early transition era differences and what by now has evolved in place of the old system over two decades since the launch of free-market reforms. The heterogeneity of the political and economic entities simultaneously involved in the transition process defies any formal one-size-fits-all rationalization.

Nearly 400 million people live in what today is broadly known as the *transition economies*. As of early 2015, that is roughly 100 million more than the total population of the US and approximately 100 million less than the population of the European Union (EU). This is an immensely rich and diverse region in terms of culture, arts, languages, societies, history, politics, geography, climate, and, necessarily so, economics.

Moreover, dozens of different languages and hundreds of dialects are spoken across the vast expanse of what once superfluously seemed monolithic in its form. In Russia (the largest country in territorial and economic terms) there are over 190 ethnic groups with almost 40 spoken languages.[2] And that is just based on broadly accepted historical trends. More recently, with the breakup of the Soviet Union in 1991 and human migration on a massive scale across the region, many more ethnicities and languages have emerged in the daily lives of average Poles, Russians, Kazakhs, Ukrainians, and all others.

We will deal with some of these questions, and migration in particular, a bit later. For now, let's lay out the game plan for what follows. How should one study these transition economies? Should one just focus on the mechanics of economic policy in each country that we are about to discuss? Or is it more worthwhile to look at the nuanced and often very complex differences of the societies involved? Or, as a less-prose-interested pragmatic investor would suggest, how do these countries fit in the "emerging financial markets" portfolio strategy that seems to dominate the business media these days?

Perhaps the true answer to the above lies somewhere in the middle. In this book, we will try to address some of the related issues directly with references to accumulated statistical data. Certainly, such evidence offers our study a benefit of hindsight, a privilege not enjoyed by the commentators and economists who worked on the transition reforms in real time back in the early 1990s. Yet, an objective analysis is overdue.

In the process some readers are set to uncover a whole new world of alternative economic development models. Some will refresh their knowledge of the region. And hopefully, all, upon reading this book will gain a new, more impartial, appreciation for the complexity of the social and economic transformation that is still ongoing in these post-socialist nations. Let's start with the basics: identifying the countries within the focus of this book.

Where are they on the map?

It helps when studying any particular geographical region to be able to identify it on the map. This is especially so when the analysis involves 29 newly independent nations. Figure 1.1 helps shed some light on this. Though, perhaps, not the most perfect graphical portrayal, this is the region we are studying.

Due to a range of political controversies, some of which may become relevant as we move along in our exploration, the actual borders shown in Figure 1.1 may at the time of reading be a bit more flexible than standardized maps might suggest. Clearly, the politics of independence movements, self-determination, and, the most tragic, regional wars, have and continue to affect regional administrative borders. Still, Figure 1.1, as an approximation, should be a good enough reference to start the conversation.

Geographically, the region covers all Central and Eastern Europe and the former Soviet Union countries. The region is vast, ranging from Germany's eastern borders all the way to Russia's border with Alaska; from the Arctic Ocean in the north to Afghanistan's and China's northern borders in the south.

Listing all the 29, Table 1.1 helps us sort these countries further by regional agglomeration, often come across either in the media or academic publications. In addition, references are made to the unrecognized, semi-independent nations that have emerged out of the socialist system breakup in the early 1990s.

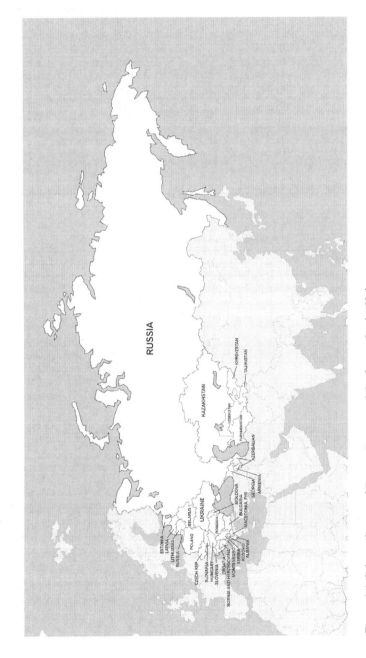

Figure 1.1 Schematic map of Eastern Europe and the former Soviet Union.

Source: modified image by MatthewFosterPhotography.com based on original image from iStock by Getty Images

Table 1.1 Transition economies by regional agglomeration

Region	Sub region	Country
Central and Eastern Europe	EU periphery	Albania; Bosnia and Herzegovina; Bulgaria; Croatia; Czech Republic; FYR Macedonia; Hungary; Kosovo; Montenegro; Poland; Romania; Serbia; Slovak Republic; Slovenia
	Baltics	Estonia; Latvia; Lithuania
	Caucasus	Armenia; Azerbaijan; Georgia
	Central Asia	Kazakhstan; Kyrgyz Republic (Kyrgyzstan); Tajikistan; Turkmenistan; Uzbekistan
Former Soviet Union	Eurasia	Belarus; Moldova; Russian Federation (Russia); Ukraine
	Unrecognized or partially recognized states	Abkhazia; South Osetia; Nagorno-Karabakh (Artsakh); Transnistria (Pridnestrovie)

Table 1.2 Transition economies by economic or political association

Agreement	Country
Commonwealth of Independent States (CIS)	Armenia (1992); Azerbaijan (1993); Belarus (1991); Kazakhstan (1991); Kyrgyz Rep (1992); Moldova (1994); Russia (1991); Tajikistan (1993); Uzbekistan (1992)
European Union (EU)	Czech Republic (2004); Estonia (2004); Latvia (2004); Lithuania (2004); Hungary (2004); Poland (2004); Slovakia (2004); Slovenia (2004); Bulgaria (2007); Romania (2007); Croatia (2013)
Eurasian Economic Union (EAEU)	Armenia (2014); Belarus (2014); Kazakhstan (2014); Russia (2014)

Note: Years of accession or agreement ratification are in parenthesis. For CIS Turkmenistan (1991) and Ukraine (1991) as associate states; Georgia (1993) withdrew in 2008.

It is also important to keep in mind that these days many of the CEE/FSU economies are either members or signatories to various regional or other multilateral association agreements. Among those, three—Commonwealth of Independent States (CIS), European Union (EU), and the Eurasian Economic Union (EAEU)—stand out as the most important ones. According to this classification, the intra-regional divisions are intensified even further, as shown in Table 1.2.[3]

At first strike, Table 1.1 and Table 1.2 present a somewhat straightforward divergent course of broad, regional (involving parts of Europe proper and spreading into Asia) integration, or disintegration, depending on one's preferences. However, perhaps, a more challenging way to analytically process this is to see a complex mix of adaptation and social evolution strategies in the region. The political and economic associations that the countries choose to join or to leave also reveal such social and political complexity.[4]

The map-view approach is instrumental to our analysis. Such an approach embodies the dialectics of the post-socialist transition: perceived unity across the space riddled with numberless divisions across terrain, national customs, and culture as well as across economic structures, social make-up and political preferences. Studying the map in Figure 1.1 for long enough and equipped with solid knowledge of the region's history, a careful observer is then set to develop a responsible understanding of the economic and political choices the countries of the EE/FSU region have dealt with since the launch of the transformational reforms over two decades ago.

Many of those choices are dictated by historical leanings, political legacy, and more often, pragmatic economic reasons. The latter may describe the effect of the smaller, in economic terms, economies seeking integration with their major trading partners versus more economically independent, relatively larger economies seeking access to competitive markets. Be that as it may, even one's basic knowledge of history should reveal the fact that we are dealing with a very diverse and unique region in economic, cultural, political, and historic contexts. History and memories of history and, more often, perceived memories of history, play a critical role. Those perceptions shape not just local traditions but also local economies, infrastructure, trade links, social norms, collective mentality, and national politics.

From an economic development aspect, the countries in our study may also be ranked based on their external performance. Figure 1.2 arranges the countries based on their average

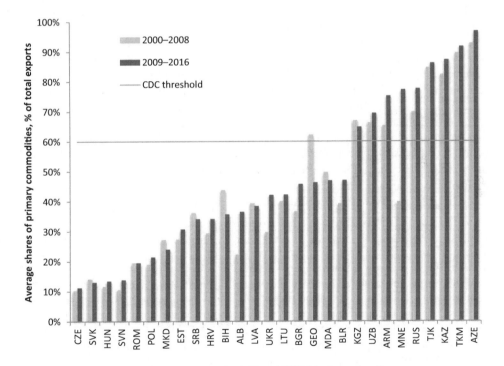

Figure 1.2 Primary commodity dependence in CEE and FSU, % of merchandise exports.

Note: commodity dependence is consistent with UNCTAD (2015) report *The State of Commodity Dependence 2014*, as the ratio of the value of commodity exports to the value of merchandise exports exceeding 60 percent threshold (solid line on the graph). Country abbreviations are consistent through the text: Albania (ALB); Armenia (ARM); Azerbaijan (AZE); Belarus (BLR); Bosnia and Herzegovina (BIH); Bulgaria (BGR); Croatia (HRV); Czech Republic (CZE); Estonia (EST); Georgia (GEO); Hungary (HUN); Kazakhstan (KAZ); Kosovo (KSV); Kyrgyz Republic (KGZ); Latvia (LVA); Lithuania (LTU); FYR Macedonia (MKD); Moldova (MDA); Montenegro (MNE); Poland (POL); Romania (ROM); Russian Federation (RUS); Serbia (SRB); Slovak Republic (SVK); Slovenia (SVN); Tajikistan (TJK); Turkmenistan (TKM); Ukraine (UKR); Uzbekistan (UZB).

Source: author's estimates based on UNCTAD Stat (2017)

ratios of the values of commodity exports to the overall merchandise exports broken down into two periods (2000–2008 and 2009–2016, with 2009 as the crisis year). This is consistent with a commodity dependence analysis conducted recently by UNCTAD (2015), when a country is considered dependent on its primary commodity exports if the above ratio exceeds 60 percent threshold. Similar to analysis in Gevorkyan (2011), some can be characterized as commodity-dependent countries (CDC) or net commodity exporters (Azerbaijan, Kazakhstan, Russia, Turkmenistan, Uzbekistan, and others). These rely primarily on energy and agricultural products exports. In another group, net commodity importers, commodity imports seem to dominate the exports.[5]

The time period chosen in Figure 1.2 coincides with the second decade of post-socialist development, which is often seen as the period of macroeconomic stabilization and relative emerging maturity in the EE/FSU. In other words, here we have information about a relatively transformed economic and industrial structure in each case. Certainly, in the present form this analysis is quite partial and trivial. Yet, to some extent, this analysis does help us draw a clear structural demarcation line. It would be important to keep this exports-based distinction in mind moving along in our journey, avoiding the common pitfall of lumping all transition economies together.

The CDC designation is significant in economic development terms. On the one hand, the CDC factor may be seen as the ultimate "resource curse" that invokes a host of associated problems of underdevelopment. On the other hand, despite the "resource curse," in the post-socialist context, there may be an opportunity to leverage the CDC position to stimulate sustained and inclusive growth.[6] Which of the two scenarios plays out in the post-socialist countries will really depend on the individual country's development path.

Informing the CDC framework, Table 1.3A of the Appendix summarizes average export shares over the period from 2000 through 2013 of each commodity group for all the economies in the sample. At the core of the external balance distinction is the logic of economic policy scaled by public spending on a range of social and infrastructure projects. Problems of balanced fiscal budget, competitive exchange rate, industrial growth, as well as macroeconomic crisis management success and accumulation of international reserves are directly related and affected by the country's dependence on primary commodity exports and imports.

Leading to the great unknowns

We will return to some specifics of macroeconomics and integration process in the post-socialist world a little later. For now, it is important to continue with setting the conceptual context for the overall discussion on transition. Two events in relatively recent history had perhaps the most profound impact on the socio-economic make-up of the region:

1   emergence in 1922 of a new political entity in Eurasia: the Union of Soviet Socialist Republics (Soviet Union or USSR); and
2   post-World War II political order that was maintained from 1945 up to the collapse of the USSR in 1991.

As a result of the first event, a whole group of countries was brought into the orbit of the formally dominant socialist political ideology and production method based on administrative state planning. The second event mentioned above, as is known from history, only reinforced the split between the ideological and economic models of the West (capitalism) and the East (communism, albeit it would be more proper to refer to the emerged system as Soviet socialism, as communist ideals were never to be achieved) in global politics.

Over the course of subsequent discussion it should become clearer exactly how the above two events transformed the transition societies. For now, suffice it to say that both have had a significant impact on much of the transition region's local political economy. In fact, by the time of market liberalization reforms and the late 1980s rise of political independence movements across the post-socialist palette, the geopolitical strife between the capitalist West and the socialist East, characterizing much of the 20th century, took a devastating toll on the transition region. In the immediate term, perceived stability, inefficiencies, and predictability of the old politically one-sided and closed economic machinery were replaced by a dysfunctional disruption of the new institutional void within new political economy frameworks and emerging alliances.

In particular, the two abovementioned external events towering over the transition economies muted many of the explicit and implicit differences in the nations involved across their history, culture, political economy, and societies, as mentioned above. Yet, through the mid-1980s up to the early 2000s this cultural multitude and diversity of economic systems was conventionally pooled into one group: *transition economies*. The question then is why, if they are so different, are they all under the same category?

Five thematic dimensions can be identified as characterizing much of the present analysis of the EE/FSU political economy. Below are brief reference points on each of the dimensions, with more contextualization throughout the text:

- history—the role of history in the region, in some cases spanning several centuries before the emergence of modern Western nation states, is critical in contributing to each country's individuality;
- culture—enriched with diverse history, geography, languages, indigenous myths, religions, as well as interactions with other cultures;
- politics—as elsewhere, here too, this arena is subject to interest groups' influence (business and old political alliances, which become a critical factor in the early market reforms period);
- economy—pre-socialist, socialist, and post-socialist structural development, where the latter is new for all and is riddled with controversies, often resulting in absorption of both the positive and the negatives of the next best alternative, capitalist, system;
- society—simultaneously the product and the maker of the political economy context, moving from predictable, defined outcomes in the pre-transition, socialist period to a host of uncertain successes and failures in the post-socialist period, now, in many cases, individually searching for a defining national path.

In practice, the above five dimensions define a formative aspect of an aspiration that is conceptually common to the region, yet, unique to each country. That is the aspiration for a national, sovereign, idea, which then as consequence shapes a distinctive political economy background in each case. The formative aspect is common conceptually because upon dissolution of the socialist polity all 29 transition economies aspired to, and to varying degrees have been successful in, establishing formal political and economic independence.

At the same time, this aspiration is individual as successes or failures in the post-socialist independence movements have relied primarily on appeals to each nation's individual history. The early years saw an unprecedented rise in national and ethnic elites. Some of the dynamic continues intensely today. Characterizing the initial national movements as unprecedented is an understatement to some degree as ethnic or religious-based divisions exacerbated, once the perceived serenity of formal internationalization in the post-WWII CEE/FSU region broke down. As some of the facts in subsequent chapters show, the political post-socialist transition was not a bloodless transition. Sadly, the region bore heavy and irreparable losses of human lives, welfare degradation, and basics of decent human existence; only to return to relative peace within some time.

Now, let us be clear here. By referencing the nationhood ideals and independent statehood we make no statement on the validity or effectiveness of any of the institutional basis that pre-existed in the transition societies.[7] We are, however, stating that for many of the 29 reforming nations their historical sovereignty offered a symbolic guide and motivation to advance reforms in the late 1980s and early 1990s. In turn, that has shaped many of the resulting economic, political, and social outcomes seen now in the post-socialist period.

In other words, early in the transition period each of the 29 new nation states pursued their individual paths of economic, social, and political reforms. For researchers of transition, the complexity of methodological and normative policy mix that such realization embodies is paramount in explaining and understanding the regional experience. Added to this historical dimension, and discussed in broader detail later, is the pre-existing economic framework and those social relations of production that characterized the socialist model. This latter observation then feeds into explaining the diversity of immediate economic outcomes in the region.

Coming back to our initial question of why, then, putting those economies into one transition category makes sense, we note the following. The countries in our investigation share a unique social experience across the greater part of the 20th century. And that is unique if one considers the time past and the scope of diverse other elements involved. That is also consistent with the map-view approach of the CEE/FSU's close proximity to each other.

Much of that shared experience is shaped by the two geopolitical events mentioned above—something that still matters in the background of the present trends. Common political platforms influenced social structures, culture, economies, morals and values, and to some extent even native languages across the CEE/FSU. A generalized characterization of the social processes that ensued on these territories can be referred to as a "top (politics)-down (society and economy)" transformation over the course of the 20th century.

And yet, there is a third event, which brings all 29 into one category. It is another collective experience shared by all CEE/FSU states, as in societies. This occurred later, towards the end of the 20th century: practically overnight the old social order that generations had grown "accustomed" to and that characterized, as stated, the entire essence of some of those societies, *was no more*. In historical terms, the economic, political, and social transformation was launched at lightning speed, between the *perestroika* in the mid-1980s, the breakup of the Berlin Wall in 1989 and the dissolution of the USSR in 1991 (and subsequent formation of the CIS).

The EBRD (2008) report offers interesting insights by systematizing its approach to the analysis of a very diverse set of countries under the general "transition" umbrella. But while the general rankings seem to be working well in the report, what is the indicative value of that ranking? For that we need to address some methodological questions first, in the next chapter. But a few words still remain to be said in this section.

Early in the reform days (end of 1980s/early 1990s) transition economies only included countries of the CEE/FSU region. Later, a few others were added and eventually the World Bank (and other multilateral organizations) adopted a geographical reference (Europe and Central Asia) for the region in focus here rather than a qualitative category of transition economies. This may in fact be a welcome sign of a conscious step towards integrating the post-socialist world in a larger context of global macroeconomic development.

Across the macroeconomic chaos and uncertainty that erupted at the time of the reform movement and collapse of the established institutional structure in the 1990s, there was much promise behind the free-market liberalization reforms. Despite a profound social and economic transformation over the past two decades, despite records of strong growth and improvements in material well-being, for some in the transition region, the long awaited post-socialist macroeconomic miracle has remained just that, a miracle that is yet to materialize.

The initial effect for the evolving societies was a massive pile-up of a complex mix of social problems. Almost instantaneously, poverty rates skyrocketed, inequality worsened, unemployment hit double digits, leading to further deterioration in human welfare. Importantly, the system of previous state-funded non-wage provisions collapsed, creating a void in place of previously existing social safety nets. For example, employment guarantees and other labor market non-wage provisions stopped functioning, as many of the former state-owned places of employment were shutting down en masse.

Many of the new institutional categories (e.g. private property, free market, entrepreneurship culture, financial credit, etc.) were either artificially introduced (in the FSU) or actively reanimated (mainly in CEE) in the vacuum of clear and predictable direction of the ongoing social change. Some (e.g. CEE) adapted faster to the new socio-economic order and with less effort than those where the state had played a larger role in the macroeconomy (e.g. FSU). The challenge was formidable yet the resolve to overcome it, while adequate in energy, lacked the institutional experience of the advanced economies.

Since the reforms, the past two decades have seen an unprecedented push for tryouts in macroeconomic restructuring and initiatives for inclusive social and economic development. Yet, rising back to the pre-reform levels of macroeconomic development and social indicators proved to be a difficult task for all. The challenge was more difficult the higher a particular country was in relative pre-transition macroeconomic comparison with its post-socialist peers (e.g. Popov, 2007a). Again, some of the social indicators reviewed later in this study reveal a more nuanced story than general macroeconomic data.

Stated differently, what once seemed known to economic theory and policy, has transformed in the CEE/FSU region, due to the historical, institutional, and economic peculiarities of the post-socialist transition period, into something unknown. Hence, the new method, paradigm shift, is needed to assess the successes and failures of transition.

Problem: transition? Transition from? Transition to?

The word transition carries a more comprehensive meaning than first meets the eye. The reference is to the process of economic development, though it is clear that when talking about development one cannot discuss economic problems in isolation from the problems of society, social relations evolution, in general. This simply means that the economic is inseparable from the human activity and reasoning aspects of development. This observation is as true for the transition region as elsewhere.

By virtue of definition, economic activity is a type of coordinated action at the root of which is some type of social interaction, in turn a function of the predominant social production mode. Now, such actions, if exercised by humans, tend to deviate from the precision of mathematical models, due to a myriad of subjective reasons, often creating an inconvenient dynamic shift in an implied equilibrium. So, from here forward we will refer to "social" as a dynamic feature that is characteristic of an evolving human behavior.

That dynamic influences our thinking, values, morals, and culture, and by extension creeps into the pure materialistic conceptions of modern-day economics and finance. Here, social is inherently economic, and economic is explicitly social. It is important to keep this in mind as we attempt to go through the chronology of events and attempt to explain them in the best possible "makes sense" way. This is the implied problem of the CEE/FSU societies and economies that is omni-present in everyday life in the political arena, economy, and routine interactions among people.

So then, what does it exactly mean when we use the word transition in application to the Eastern European and former Soviet Union economies? Well, first, transition in its simplistic view in the given context implies a transition from a planned economy to an ideally free market-driven system. From this point of view, things should be relatively easy: shut down the old state enterprise system and the old ways of coordinating production (i.e. via govern-ment contracts and orders) and open up a new shop with new rules of the game that are to be less regulated and open to free enterprise. In fact, that was exactly what was attempted across much of the CEE/FSU landscape and characterized the transition era reforms. Let's take this point as is for now and come back to it later.

Second, if we correctly follow the prescription above, do we have (or even, perhaps, do we need) a clear understanding of a) what the *planned economy* is? and b) what a *market economy* is? There are numerous models that may help us predict outcomes of imposition of either system. There are pros and cons to be argued on both sides. For example, isn't guaran-teed employment under the planned system a desirable outcome in a labor market (although the worker might have little say on the choice of allocated assignment)?

On the other hand, the opportunities within the market system, as formed in much of the developed and now post-socialist world, are indeed advantageous to personal enrichment, (albeit creating a crisis of income inequality that has mired much of the post-2008 public and economic policy debate). But then, can the theoretical models help in measuring the social element of this change? Perhaps yes, they can, and the problem here is to keep up the objectivity in research.

Lastly, the time frame over which this transition occurs must be addressed as well. How does one know and how can one confidently tell that the post-socialist transition has occurred, and occurred with a confident success rate? All three observations above are topics for numerous dissertations by interested researchers, yet, offer a good background for our discussion.

So far, we have identified some of the issues relevant to the analysis of the CEE/FSU economic and social transformation. The rest of the chapters in this study will help add some clarity and perhaps the readers might come to a common conclusion. Perhaps, each reader might take something different from the present analysis. In either case, the goal, contribut-ing and motivating an objective debate on the legacy of post-socialist transition as it informs the future prospects of macroeconomic and social transformation in the CEE/FSU region, would be achieved.

In the next chapter, we address the foundational concept of this study: the difference between transition and transformation phenomenon. Which is more characteristic of the CEE/FSU experience? Which prevails and when? A review of early scholarship on transition and proposed methodological model may help unveil some of those mysteries.

Conclusion

The time has now come to shift from "a social experiment in the making" view of the young economies of Central Eastern Europe and the former Soviet Union towards a more responsi-ble macroeconomic development approach. The latter requires accepting the fact of dynamic diversity of the region in economic, social, political, and institutional terms.

In this chapter we introduced the diverse world of the transition economies. The main purpose was to raise early awareness of how complex and multilayered the societies of the 29 nations are. The chapter briefly summarized regional economic alliances. The aspect of national sovereignty and the complex methodological normative policy mix that it invokes is paramount here. Primary are the questions of what constitutes the differences across the CEE/FSU region's economies and how one rationalizes their post-socialist experience. Despite any perceived similarities, the world is interacting with national entities that are very different and unique from all perspectives.

Appendix

Table 1.3A Export shares by commodity group by country, 2000–2015 % of merchandise exports

	Food	*Fuel*	*Metals*	*Agricultural raw materials*	*Manufactures*
ALB	5.50	12.06	13.06	5.58	63.56
ARM	17.45	4.23	31.83	1.97	43.24
AZE	3.98	88.71	0.80	0.71	5.56
BLR	8.96	30.07	0.74	2.35	54.80
BIH	6.07	9.86	13.38	7.84	57.61
BGR	12.39	11.76	14.92	1.74	55.22
HRV	11.00	12.24	3.87	3.85	68.63
CZE	3.96	3.17	1.91	1.61	88.49
EST	9.47	10.25	3.00	5.97	68.08
GEO	28.97	4.84	20.75	1.99	42.85
HUN	7.35	2.50	1.75	0.72	83.78
KAZ	4.08	66.80	13.72	0.70	14.69
KSV	N/A	N/A	N/A	N/A	N/A
KGZ	20.67	17.05	6.01	9.53	37.47
LVA	13.05	4.79	4.08	16.25	58.68
LTU	14.53	22.40	1.66	3.13	57.31
MKD	15.88	5.33	5.56	0.88	70.18
MDA	63.09	0.38	3.91	1.95	30.37
MNE	N/A	N/A	N/A	N/A	N/A
POL	9.61	4.58	4.37	1.27	79.51
ROM	5.35	7.02	4.50	2.59	79.14
RUS	2.07	61.23	6.73	2.57	18.57
SRB	19.22	2.97	15.75	3.59	62.42
SVK	4.11	5.60	2.89	1.41	85.16
SVN	3.59	3.01	4.33	1.52	87.36
TJK	4.37	3.78	58.14	12.59	21.81
TKM	0.29	86.96	0.40	9.90	9.31
UKR	15.89	7.14	7.21	1.35	67.36
UZB	N/A	18.04	10.77	N/A	34.07

Note: "N/A" refers to incomplete data.

Source: WDI, 2017

Notes

1 Throughout the text we will interchangeably use terms post-socialist or transition in reference to the economies of the CEE and FSU regions and their recent experience. Until recently, compared to other regions (e.g. Southeast Asia or Latin America) the region was relatively under-studied

within the broad field of economic development, often reduced to a collection of case study examples. Hence, our somewhat strong categorization about the post-socialist region being "relatively unknown."

2 See *Demoskop Weekly* (2014).

3 Although it would be an integral player in the socialist economic and political model in the post-World War II period up until 1989, we exclude East Germany (German Democratic Republic or GDR), which reunited with West Germany in 1990, from most of our country-level analysis that follows. For specifics on the German reunification process see Box 7.2 in Chapter 7.

4 Later, we elaborate on other dimensions to regional aggregation based on a mix of factors of geographic, political, and economic alliances.

5 For example, see Gevorkyan (2011) for the net exporter and net importer designations in CEE and FSU analysis.

6 For example, see Gevorkyan (2012) on Russia's potential for breaking the "resource curse." Also, for an excellent overview of the macroeconomic problems of commodity dependence, see Canuto and Cavallari (2012), and Brahmbhatt *et al.* (2010).

7 Clearly, these are areas of particular concern in specialized literature outside the scope of the present narrative.

2 Transition vs. transformation

What is clear and not so clear about transition economics

> The aim by itself is a lifeless universal . . .; and the bare result is the corpse which has left the guiding tendency behind it.
>
> Georg Wilhelm Friedrich Hegel, *Phenomenology of Spirit*

In search of a transition: definitions

So, what is economic transition? How did and how do the scholars of transition economics define the concept of transition? What does the term mean and why does this book insist on a transformation as opposed to *transition* as a proper characterization of what has been going on in the Eastern European and former Soviet Union economies?

First, we should find out if the definitions of each term hold any significance. According to the online Merriam-Webster Dictionary, we have the following:

Transition[1]

Noun: passage from one state, stage, subject, or place to another
Verb: to make a change from one state, place, or condition to another
— *Derivatives*: transitional or transitionary (both adjectives)

Transformation[2]

Noun: a complete or major change in someone's or something's appearance, form, etc.
— *Derivatives*: transformational (adjective)

It is clear that in the analysis of society's evolution the above polar definitions of transition and transformation, refer to two very different and complex processes. To clarify, conceptually *transition* means just that—moving or adjusting from one position or environment to another. Inevitably, the adjustment process may at first be difficult in some way but (and this is important here) the technicalities are to be worked out in the process.

The simplest way to grasp the concept of transition is by approximating it to a typical corporate setting. We generally talk about "transitioning into a role" when an employee is assigned new tasks or is promoted to a new position within a corporate managerial hierarchy. This implies the transitioning employee is somewhat familiar with his or her new duties. The adjustment requires the employee to learn quickly the basics of the new tasks or position. Once the employee has fully transitioned—and the time allowance for adjustment to a new role is minimal in the modern corporate environment—business operations, whatever those might be, are then expected to run with greater efficiency. Such is the logic of a profit-seeking enterprise, consistent with broadly accepted microeconomic assumptions.

Transformation is, on the other hand, a profoundly much more complex phenomenon. In the context of social development, transformative experience requires a complete change of the existing or dominant system of social values and norms. In an economic context, transformation refers to a 180 degree restructuring of the economy, including a movement from what may be perceived as non-competitive to what may be perceived as competitive sectors.

In the case of transformation, there always remains some degree of doubt as the final outcome, unlike in the case of transition, is not immediately known, nor can it be properly defined or adequately described accounting for every nuance. The reason for that is the inherently dialectical and complex nature of a transformational change in the context of social and economic development. No longer is there a transitioning from position A to position B. Instead, we are talking about a complete, inside-out, change of every tenet of the existing system.

So, which term then properly captures the experience in the CEE/FSU region? It is this book's position that the process of transformation (vs. simple transition) renders the only proper characterization of the massive social and economic change in the CEE/FSU countries that has been ongoing for over 20 years.

Transition vs. transformation

In terse economic terms, transition from the very start was defined as movement from a centrally planned economy to a market oriented one (e.g. Havrylyshyn and Wolf, 1999). By assumption, that suggested a change from a, implicitly backward, socialist economic model to the one comparable to advanced economies. In addition, there is an argument for comparing the transition process to a greater spread of civic liberties across the CEE/FSU region. For economists, transition to a free market-based economy suggested a host of policy measures constituting removal of price controls (liberalization), introduction and effective functioning of private ownership (privatization), competitive markets, and, as a derivation, attaining an optimal efficient solution (e.g. Kornai, 1994; Svenjar, 2001).[3]

On the surface of the argument, there is hardly any quarrel that one could raise with such prescription! Attaining efficient outcomes that require minimal to no official intervention in the economy, assuming, of course, that the attained efficiency improves the relative economic utility of all agents involved, is clearly a desirable alternative. Moreover, in what one may refer to as a social factor, the promise of the free market transition also implied attainment of higher living standards, diminishing income inequality, strict rule of law, and democratic polity relevant to the global economy map as its final destination.

But if so, then, the term transition is a misnomer, as the above-implied changes clearly are of a transformational character running as a chain reaction disruption, introducing new and nurturing, yet unknown abstract categories of social relations. This transformation has led to structurally new social forms replacing one another, albeit built upon the foundation of the prior. This is a dialectical process of change that is inherently dynamic, volatile and, unfortunately, little researched.

Typical analysis at the time (early to mid-1990s) detracted from the weight of social (and even political) factors, focusing primarily on application of macro- and microeconomic modeling. Such informed, essential, and useful analysis, however, could only be partial in bringing the full scope of the ongoing change to the discussion table.

For example, by assumption the socialist model was treated as inefficient, resulting, in economic terms, in a plethora of non-competitive sectors with lack of discipline and inadequate industrial or labor market capacity. A successful transition, then, would be seen as a shift in a standard production possibility frontier (PPF). A possible scenario could be a movement from backward and inefficient levels of production (below the PPF) to a point on a higher production possibility curve after a pre-transition shift to a competitive market outcome corresponding to the original capacity (or the original PPF).

As a general case of transition economics modeling, this is an appealing analogy, as one could rationalize an emerging competitive (or traded) goods sector replacing inefficient and below capacity working of the prior, by assumption, non-competitive sector. However, it may be too simplistic to capture the immensity of the socio-economic transformation in this particular case.

Still, in this model, the transition process concludes by the economy reaching the competitive market optimal equilibrium, which as Havrylyshyn (2013) states, the majority of economies achieved by the mid-2000s, with some exceptions. The latter are the economies identified in Chapter 1 as net commodity exporters. This suggests that Kazakhstan, Russia, Turkmenistan, Uzbekistan, and to some extent Ukraine, are instead moving away from their implicit comparative advantage positions as their economies rely on some type of raw materials exports as opposed to nurturing domestic industrial diversification leveraging, at least in the early days of transition, the remaining Soviet capital stock and high-skilled labor force. Let's come back to this observation in later chapters. We note in passing the limitation of viewing national development, in particular in CEE/FSU, from a comparative advantage perspective only. Other factors will matter, as we illustrate below, and as Amsden (2003) confirms in the cases of growth of Southeast Asian economies.

Another view on what constitutes transition and what counts as successful goal achievement may be set in the aggregate supply (AS) and aggregate demand (AD) framework. Here, there is a possibility of either demand shock deterioration or structural supply side worsening. Assuming (as some evidence suggests) consumer markets across much of the post-socialist economies, and in the FSU in particular, then any sharp deterioration in AD at the start and during the initial phase of transition could not have been a significant factor in the early economic malaise of the 1990s.

Popov (2007b) argues, instead, for supply side shocks to be a likely explanation of recession in the post-socialist economies. This would have been caused by changes in relative prices, but perhaps more profoundly, by a sharp and sudden withdrawal of a strong state from the economy. The "soft budget constraint"—a term we will come across again—was pulled out of the socialist enterprise model akin to a carpet being pulled from under one's feet.

The system's structural deterioration was one of the critical factors that exacerbated early macroeconomic transition. In turn, that has fed into some of the legacy outcomes, as may be argued based on our earlier net exporter versus net importer taxonomy. However, structural, again, implies that a correction in a particular sector or industry might do the trick of resetting things and focus is again on the competitive versus non-competitive sector. The "correction" happens by way of resources reallocation. In this, both proponents of rapid reforms and those arguing for a more gradual approach shared some unanimity, as we discover later.

At the time, the question was about the speed of reforms that would be conducive to phasing out the non-competitive sector at the rate of its fixed capital stock depreciation and as capital investment flows would go towards a competitive sector growth. In either the PPF or the AS/AD models, the focus was on getting the rules right first and then focusing on a resources reallocation exercise in an effort to achieve market efficiency (e.g. Roland, 2001a).

In his assessment of the reforms process, Roland (2001b) develops a substantive critique of the dominating role played by the Washington Consensus—a set of macroeconomic principles that formulated policy recommendations of the late 20th century and endorsed by multilateral institutions and leading economists at the time. Though it was not initially designed for the post-socialist transition reform, the "consensus" was quickly brought into the transition reforms context. Critically, the implied approach aimed at completing the reform at a fast pace by which institutions of the past had to be destroyed and replaced with new from the very foundation.[4] This coherent "clean slate" stood in contradiction to an evolutionary, institutional (or at the time of transition, gradualist) approach to the reform.

Related to the above is one of the principal concepts characterizing the transition debate: the problem of evolving institutions. Arguing along similar lines, Popov (2007b and 2000) brings up one of the key features critical to explaining the successes of the 1990s reforms movements. Namely, the role of the initial conditions in each country. According to that analysis, it turns out, despite their belonging to the same socialist economic bloc, the 29 economies were set in very different pre-market reform conditions. This pertains to structural macroeconomic aspects (private ownership, price setting, competitiveness, and entrepreneurial activity) as well as civic society.

Among the few fragile voices to point to this critical distinction were a handful of other economists arguing for gradual liberalization and state-led institutional structure (see the debate summarized in Marangos, 2004 and most prominently remarks by Arrow, 2000). This would have allowed for a smoother transition, potentially gauged to each country's specifics, on both social and economic aspects to a qualitatively new and, effectively, untested social model. Yet, the approach chosen was quite standard across the diverse palette with countries rapidly adopting market liberalization reforms, regardless of shock therapy or gradualist prescription.

In fact, Stiglitz (2003) points to there being a single prescription at the time, hinging solely on the speed of reforms. Apparently, what mattered was how rapidly the countries implemented market reforms, price liberalization, and privatization. The reform process obviously required funding procured by way of conditional loans from multilateral lending agencies, primarily the International Monetary Fund (IMF) and the World Bank (WB). The conditions pertained to the speed and the specifics of the reform process. One of these specifics was almost complete pull-out of the government from the economy—a complete turnaround from an administratively planned economy to a market-based system.

The term "shock therapy" was brought back in (from the post-WWII European reconstruction experience) in the post-socialist transformation context. It described the effect of a rapid economic reform process: a quick robust tackle that throws a system out of balance, forcing the economy to proceed along a prescribed path (recall our conversation above on market rules and efficiency). In the process, the legacy socio-economic framework is completely destroyed and it is hoped that a new system, based on private entrepreneurial activity, will spring up fast, pulling the rest of the economy up via a trickle-down effect.

We are going to be dealing with the shock therapy (also referred to as "big bang") reforms implementation as opposed to the gradualist approach a bit later in our study (Chapter 7). Here, we note that concerns with one-sided reforms implementation, raised by a visible minority of economists and social scientists, went largely unnoticed. At best, acknowledgement was given to shock therapy's "collateral damage" as in a typical big bang theory application: there would be ripples with much stardust but at the end a competitive nucleus would be formed attracting, as gravitational force, the marginal particles to add to a new formation.

In macroeconomic terms, collateral damage was assumed to be marginal and on the sidelines, as the potential reforms were to unveil the entrepreneurial and competitive potentials, leading to the Pareto optimal efficient solutions. The buzzwords of the reforms period included such loaded concepts as development, transition economics, fiscal policy, free market, growth-promoting policies, big governments, privatization, liberalization, optimal solutions, hyperinflation, monetary policy, independent banking, market failures, prudential reform, fiscal consolidation, and so on.

Unfortunately, macroeconomic and social results—subject to our further analysis— varied, significantly deviating from the intended target, to say the least. The enormity of the immediate output collapse (i.e. the structural recessions cited above and an inability to reach competitive outcomes in the PPF plane) was strikingly colossal. Figure 2.1 helps put the above discussion in perspective.

Taking the region's GDP in 1990 as a reference point (corresponding to the index level 1 on the y-axis in Figure 2.1) we express all subsequent years' GDP as proportions of that initial level. Two striking observations are immediately obvious from this exercise. First, the depth of the collapse, that is the distance by which the curve deviates below unity, is large suggesting that overall output across the region fell by close to over 40 percent. And second, is the time period required to climb back to the unity line, indicated by point A or the crossing of the vertical and horizontal lines—the transition cross.

A more straightforward explanation of the second observation is simply that it required 15-odd years for the EE/FSU economies collectively to reach their pre-transition output levels, that is, getting back to and going beyond the unity line at point A on the graph. The recovery does not seem to happen until the year 2005—a long time since the reforms and significantly past the shock therapy approach's proposed deadlines.

Subdued in Figure 2.1 are the output losses of individual countries that were significantly larger, as we discuss below. The path to recovery was neither stable nor guaranteed. The human and economic sacrifices made due to such massive output losses and due to those that were required to climb back up out of the depression pit, would run up an immeasurable toll.

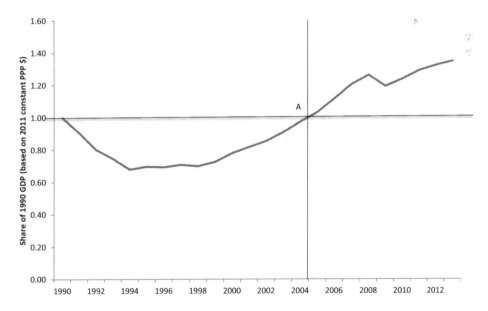

Figure 2.1 Transition GDP in proportion to 1990 GDP based on 2011 constant PPP $.

Source: author's estimates based on WDI (2017)

The transformation

Even from the brief observations above, the vast complexity of the macroeconomic collapse, its depth and lasting effects, seem impressively disappointing and disheartening. Moreover, the above also suggests a monumental societal change enormous in scope and ambition. A critical aspect that characterized the post-socialist economies of the CEE/FSU was the strong presence of the state—the government—in practically every sphere of the economic life of almost every country in the region. Government and state-owned enterprises were in charge of provision of a great variety of non-waged goods (e.g. childcare, a range of social assistance measures to a mixed sample of households and employees).

Yet, as a pre-condition for reforms and as a result of economic turnaround that did not readily produce an effective tax base to maintain government revenue flows and subsequent expenditure, early on government WDI spending dropped significantly as a share of GDP. Coincidentally, as the reforms effect was gaining full-strength, government-funded activities aside from direct involvement with the economy, for example in healthcare, education, arts, and so on, began to dissipate as budgets had to be balanced to meet the IMF/WB austerity demands. An indirect effect of the macroeconomic and structural confusion, contributing to deteriorating living conditions, adding enormous degrees of emotional stress to the population in the post-socialist countries, intertwined, in some cases, with disastrous military conflicts, led to a widespread, precipitous drop in life expectancy.

Figure 2.2 adds some factual representation comparing the levels of government spending as GDP shares and life expectancy in the years between 1990 and 1995, the latter being the symbolic middle of the reforms process. There is a clear deterioration on average (marked here and consistently through the text with the AVRG) with very peculiar individual country

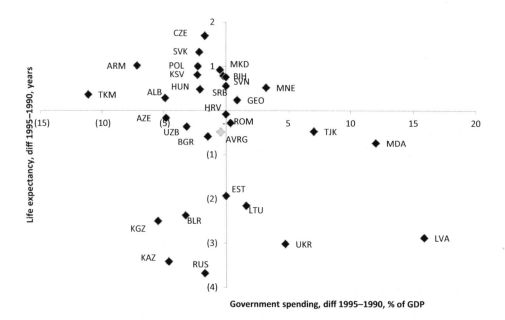

Figure 2.2 Government spending in % of GDP and life expectancy in years (difference between 1995 and 1990).

Source: author's estimates based on WDI (2017)

deviations, which can be explained by the initial preconditions that should become more obvious as we delve deeper into the region's history in the next few chapters.

And though more recent data may tell us a somewhat slightly more positive story, Figure 2.2 only reconfirms the magnitude of the social hardships and deficiencies with the economic policy reforms pushed through and imposed in the early 1990s upon the rudimentary social structures of the CEE/FS. Ironically, some of the more recent improvement has been due to the increased role of state in each country. The challenge for transition economies of the CEE/FSU is to take up proactive and innovative steps to ensure the sustainability of their improved economic performance of recent years while managing a diverse set of social issues (Gevorkyan, 2011).

It follows, then, that in this narrative, we are not simply covering a "switch" from a socialist to a capitalist system, but are uncovering and discussing a much more profound transformational change put in motion and still ongoing in the CEE/FSU region, affecting on a daily basis each country's political, social, cultural, and economic environments. To comprehend the magnitude and severity, and come up with any possible assessments of the shock it is crucial to understand the history of the region and societies. For many residents of the post-socialist countries there was no "switch". There was a step into the abyss with an expectation that things would work out along the way, which led to a massive social, institutional, and macroeconomic transformation that remains to be fully discovered, analyzed, and stabilized.

Was it inevitable?

We now come to a junction where a valid question should be asked: was the transition (from the old socialist to the new capitalist economy) inevitable? To clarify, could it have been avoided?

Before tackling some of the interpretations, we note that a short answer is "it's complicated." Conceptually, the argument for socialism's impossibility is found, most famously, in L. von Mises's *Socialism* (1951) and F.A. Hayek's *The Road to Serfdom* (2007). To them, the inevitable destruction of a system predicated on abolition of private property or competition was self-evident.

The Soviet system, however, persisted for 70 years—presenting a real-life contradiction to the inevitability of the transition process view. Considering preservation of the dominant socialist model by all means (as the Soviet system's history illustrates), as the ultimate goal, logically suggests either a limitation on or gradual depletion of the capacity for sustaining the system. And so, by the late 1970s and 1980s such objective realization necessitated an objective need for some type of change sooner or later.

At the same time, the scale and the destructive qualitative nature of the 1990s reforms were perhaps avoidable. However, this argument is only valid as an intellectual exercise, from the perspective of history. As we know, history cannot be re-done. Before drawing any conclusions, it would be instructive to review some general trends.

The coming to power in March of 1985 of Mikhail Gorbachev as the General Secretary of the Soviet Communist Party and the launch of his *perestroika* (re-building) reforms were the two landmark events associated today with the transition process. As we will see below, several mechanisms on the macroeconomic and social policy levels were put in motion. And though there was a significant accumulation of seemingly unrelated occurrences, gradually expanding to a critical destabilizing condition.

It should unequivocally be clear that at the start of the perestroika reforms following the 27th Congress of the Communist Party of the Soviet Union (CPSU) there was no intention

a) for absolute deviation from the socialist method of production to a capitalist, free market-based economy; nor b) for the eventual breakup and dissolution of either the Soviet Union or the socialist economic bloc, which included both the USSR and countries of Eastern Europe, as well as members of the Council for Mutual Economic Assistance (CMEA).

Think of this as filling a glass with water, while distracted, and not noticing how quickly the glass fills up and water starts pouring out. Something of that kind effectively happened following *perestroika* announcements on the scale of the former socialist bloc. A few examples, that we discuss in subsequent chapters, would be: the independence and labor movements in Central Europe and Eastern Europe; emergence of a well-educated and urbanized Soviet "middle class" that was stuck in jobs lacking productivity; chronic consumer goods deficits and political imports controls; on a more macroeconomic level, there were clear problems with technological efficiency of the immensely vast economic plan-system operations and cumbersome internal administration. On top of everything, as noted by several commentators, there was a critical dependence on the energy commodity markets, by which the Soviet system procured hard currency to purchase consumer and raw materials imports (including agricultural products) leveraging crude oil and natural gas export revenues.[5]

From there on, social change could have followed a range of alternative paths in the Soviet economic system. One might actually suggest that Gorbachev's rise to power was a necessary step in the evolutionary process of the USSR and the Soviet bloc. That was necessitated by the entire social reality and the economic stagnation in the immediate, to *perestroika*, decade. However, even in this case it was not exactly clear how the socialist economic model would transform.

Indeed, there is less unanimity among economists and social scientists in explaining the actual reasons for both the socialist system's longevity and the abrupt shift to capitalism. In their search for explanations, Kotz and Weir (2007) offer a multidimensional analysis. One view suggests the centrally planned economy should have collapsed due to overextension of administrative planning beyond the initial industrialization process. Chapters 3 and 4 of our text discuss the process by which the USSR underwent structural industrialization in its formative 1920s–1930s years. In less than two decades, the country accomplished industrial capacity levels comparable to the progress that previously required developed nations anywhere from 50 to 100 years.

Transposed, later, also on the CEE nations, the emerged system would lay the foundation of the socialist economic model for decades to come. It is then relatively easy to see how some early expectations speculated that the overstretched centrally planned system would crumble into pieces, as post-industrialization administrative economic control would have become ineffective and unworkable. Yet, the system persisted for another 60 years up to the 1990s free-market reforms. Consequently, a suggestion that centrally planned economy is only workable in special, smaller-scale, cases, while offering initial clues, cannot sufficiently fully explain the actual socialist economic dynamic.

Another possible explanation for the socialist model's longevity rests on a view that administrative planning might be required for massive industrialization and may remain workable at the initial stage of forming an urbanized middle class. In effect, this implies the state's role in income redistribution but critically in expanding a list of non-waged and public goods provisions to the working middle class. Those examples might include housing provisions (e.g. Khrushchev's housing programs of the 1950s), consumer goods production, infrastructure projects expansion, high-quality educational and healthcare provisions, as well as social assistance, work balance, and other social guarantees.

As the urban consumer class grows in its complexity, the centrally planned system reaches its limit and must be replaced with a more efficient competitive market construction. Otherwise, the system breaks apart leading to economic collapse. But, as Kotz and Weir (2007) note (and we find some plausible justification in this view), the economic collapse really happened in the early 1990s once the centrally planned system was completely dismantled (recall analysis in Figure 2.2 on decline in government spending as share of GDP).[6]

Other researchers (e.g. Kontorovich, 1993 and Fukuyama, 1993) suggested that the true reason behind the Soviet economic collapse and transition to the capitalist market framework was in declining legitimacy of the socialist system. For today's reader, this essentially refers to a view of outlived social norms and fading pull of the socialist ideology and implied morals. By the late 1970s and early 1980s, as the first signs of strain in the grand socialist framework became visible across the region, there was already a growing share of Soviet and CEE citizens becoming disengaged and disfranchised from the dominant political ideology of the socialist state.

A few factors may seem important here, such as, for example, strict ideological restrictions and censorship in arts and culture (in some ways, more harsh in the FSU states compared to the CEE countries located in closer proximity to Western Europe); persistence of various outdated administrative controls and checks, for example restrictive residence requirements (*propiska*), and disproportionate limits and privileges between urban and rural residents. Yet, perhaps one of the most contested contradictions was the clear divide between opportunities and living standards of the few ruling elites and the majority of Soviet citizens, toppled by chronic deficits in consumer markets. Still, the system had a wide range of functioning social guarantees and non-waged services provisions that maintained social balance (we address the problems of human transition in Chapter 8).

The above amounts to a set of contradictions, albeit critical, that, speculatively, may have been possible to resolve within a system without necessarily leading to an absolute collapse. It may be helpful to refer to a recent experience elsewhere. Consider the overall social moods in the post 2008 crisis in the advanced economies and the rise of such popular movements as Occupy Wall Street as social tensions intensify (e.g. Harvey, 2012). In this case, the financial and economic meltdown happened against the background of prevailing income distribution disparity that was only worsening (e.g. Stiglitz, 2012 on the issue of cheap credit proliferation as a way of tackling the problem of consumerism and income distribution and macroeconomic policy more generally; also Piketty, 2014; Milanovic, 2016).

However, despite some evident policy failures, as income inequality spirals higher, an outright systemic collapse was avoided backed by the involvement of strong state and monetary authorities. Instead, what seems to be evolving in the post-2008 crisis years across the world is a new social contract with government gaining a greater role in balancing social inequalities and sharp edges. Perhaps there is something to be said about the strength of the institutional base—the invisible fibers of an economy. Perhaps there may also be a strong aspect of greater global interconnection, or globalization, which offers a limited set of political economy options unlike in the situation of the early 1990s. Then, a perceived more prosperous capitalist alternative fueled the social and economic transformation.

Similarly, the Soviet political elites standing on the shoulders of over 70 years' statebuilding were concerned about the existing system's survival. Following the *perestroika* reforms, state involvement in the economy and defense spending visibly declined. Figure 2.2 in that sense is a continuation of an earlier trend. It is unlikely there was a calculated effort to dismantle the established system. Instead the "new thinking" policies may be seen as a concerted attempt to adapt the old to the conditions of the new demands, a self-progress. And the political disassociation manifested in a phenomenon of "kitchen anecdotes," as like-minded individuals disputed political themes over dinners often with an ironic sense of inability to soup up any change, by itself could not have been a sufficient enough factor leading towards systemic collapse and launching transition reforms.

Another proposition concerns the rise of nationalism and inter-ethnic and religious strife in the territory where it once seemed that ideals of internationalism, multiculturalism, and ethnic tolerance had been laid in the foundation of the very existence of the USSR and its satellites. Instead, by the late 1980s and early 1990s, in many cases the conflicts grew into prolonged and open wars affecting thousands of people, creating massive refugee and forced migration flows across the socialist map, as well as leading up to thousands of military conflict casualties. Yet, even in this case, the initial demands and intent were not a cessation from the USSR (that comes later, as conflicts matured both in social, political, and economic involvement) nor was it the breakup from the socialist economic system in favor of the capitalist.

People marched in protest demonstrations declaring slogans such as: "Lenin, Party, Gorbachev!" reaffirming their right for self-determination according to the USSR Constitution as was the case in Armenian-populated Nagorno-Karabakh Republic. In other words, the initial intent of rising nationalism was focused on restoration of the pre-USSR borders, inadvertently sparking ethnic and administrative divisions that had been effectively deep frozen by the post-1917 Russian revolution and post-1945 *realpolitik*.

There are many nuances, certainly, and it would not be possible to enumerate all factors at once. Some, but hardly all, of the related concepts and historical events will be addressed in subsequent chapters. But the above, by now, should give a relatively good idea of the social and economic conundrums in which socialist countries of the CEE/FSU were and continue to be immersed.

There was no easy exit: social and economic problems had to be resolved within the means and efforts accessible barring any external interventions. Moreover, external pressure factors, associated with the "cold war" doctrine only exacerbated domestic ideological and policy balances.

Yet, exactly "what is to be done?" as the proverbial question of this part of the world, at least since N.G. Chernyshevsky (1886), would hold. That was not exactly clear. The 27th Congress of the Communist Party of the Soviet Union, presided over for the first time by Mikhail Gorbachev, proclaimed "new thinking" across all spheres of social activity. Amidst highly idiosyncratic, to the average Soviet citizen, statements, open forum discussions proliferated tackling topics of social and economic development alternatives.

The Soviet (and broader socialist) economic system began its unstoppable dismantling. For example, state-owned enterprises were given extraordinary freedoms and discretion in management delegating some business decision-making to the effective factory managers (there were no large private enterprises at the time). A myriad of other smaller and larger adjustments conflating in one moment followed the initial *perestroika* movement. Collectively, those phenomena had put in motion the pendulum of a bigger transformative change. Exactly how it would swing, what, and how that motion would transform would surprise and shock the societies embracing the change and those watching from the outside.

As their main argument, Kotz and Weir (2007) posit that what really led to the Soviet system's political and economic demise was an internal contradiction within a system designed to deliver economic equality and benefits to all, while at the same time being controlled by a smaller group of elites and special interests. That essentially adds up to the state apparatus with no dedication to maintaining the socialist system *per se* in either its existing nor any transformed, more effective and inclusive, form. In effect, as Kotz and Weir (2007) argue, the nomenclature was not ready to give up their rent-seeking positions.

Such stance, certainly, would have been a marked departure from the Soviet system's founding conviction in the supremacy of the socialist economic and political system over an individualistic capitalist alternative. Instead, by the late 1980s, as the socialist system matured, so did the refined ideological vision and ideals. The final nail in the Soviet arrangement was hammered in, according to Kotz and Weir (2007), by the top elites' desire for perpetuation of their power hold and privileges. It follows that being materially constrained by the socialist system, the Soviet elite chose the capitalist model once opportunity appeared. Capitalism appeared as a lesser evil of an essentially redistributive alternative.[7]

One concern with such a proposition is that a political and economic turnaround would require a great degree of coordination among the elites and a conscious departure from established ideology that had bred those same elites. Instead, with the hindsight of time now, events appeared to follow a random walk, a dialectically accidental path. Yet, in their chance occurrence, the underlying social phenomena followed a blueprint tested in history for millennia: new, maturing economic and political elites struggled to sustain their gains by reforming the institutional framework of the preceding system.

So, was the transition process inevitable? Objectively, with accumulation of internal social contradictions, wearing out of the existing administrative policy mechanisms, lagging technological innovation feeding into economic stagnation of the 1980s, and other factors, a change was overdue. The perestroika reforms recognized the need for such change. However, there was hardly any intent to bring down the entire socialist economic model, as we explore in Chapter 6. Nevertheless, the *perestroika* reforms and attempts to, using a popular characterization, democratize the socialist system had also pushed the change pendulum as mentioned above. From there on, the results, one might suggest, were purely incidental.

Yet, the dialectical understanding of social evolution was stripped of the bare methodological necessities that would have made such a highly theoretical conception of any use in a practical application. The Marxian economics, the towering view in political economy of the Soviet mode, was discarded within a matter of hours. It followed then, that a theoretical view of a dynamic, that is, constantly changing in content and shape, social evolution was stuffed within the convenient confines of a proper straightjacket economic model. Most staggering, the latter existed purely on paper with no sustained success record anywhere. Still, any deviation from the emerging norms of outright liberalization, privatization, and deregulation across every component of the economy was discarded as inconsequential and, if not, was brought in line with the newly adopted standards claiming efficiency and optimality.

And so, we are talking about a collapse of the system that by external and internal pundits was perceived as one of the most sound in its foundation. The collapse was sudden, unexpected, and devastating. Interestingly, what has come out of that change in the late 1980s–1990s, after much prolonged and continued suffering, has been a world of some promise, sustainability, freedom, and *livebality*. The latter is a catch-all term, a modernized version of Sen's (1999) capability with reference to quality of living that motivates individuals' drive for self-development. And this new world is riddled with challenges of new, untried caliber.

To summarize, what really was inevitable was the economic switchover implemented in a way that required absolute turnaround within a restricted time period. Avoiding the rush there was only one requirement, which seemed to have failed to materialize. That requirement was the recognition of the differences across the 29 states' starting conditions, that is, they were all different in their economic, cultural, and social make-up.[8] It is tempting to suggest that a more gradual approach, with attention to society's nuances, would have led to more sustainable and prosperous, in the economic sense, results. Alas, history offers no chance for repeated attempts, leaving us only with an informed analysis of the past, informing the present and future objective reality.

Liveability is also a dialectical category. A random fact of attaining a certain level of comfortable living, though historical, is now an economic policy necessity. What this means in terms of future potential is highly speculative today. But the only way to form an informed and adequate opinion is through a careful and responsible appreciation of the history and all interdependent legacies.

The totality of the social and economic dynamic

Not all aspects mentioned above are fully known to us yet. The purpose of the subsequent chapters is, actually, to discover and rationalize some of those historical events illustrating the formation and eventual dismantling of the socialist economy. It is, however, clear that what unraveled following the announcement of the *perestroika* reforms was not just a transition. Instead, it was a true transformation permeating every fiber of the socialist system.[9] The end results, as implied above, were:

a)   a complete shift away from the socialist system to a market-based or mixed-type economy; and
b)   breakup and dissolution of the Soviet Union and the CMEA.

It emerges then, despite one's preferences and attitudes towards the socialist system or the Soviet system in particular, that the transition process was a far-reaching, profound, and irreversible transformation affecting more than just the economy or political lingo. In the process, new social norms, morals, values, rules, and ideals evolved. Yet, for the majority of the CEE/FSU population all that was (and some cases still is) based on frail and flimsy foundations of privatization reforms, abolition of existing social guarantees and fiscal provisions, declining standards of education, healthcare, social services, and complete chaos of forced migration and military conflicts. The 400 million citizens of the CEE/FSU woke up to a new and very different world.

The change was not a flip of a switch from low to high lights. If it ever was a flip of a switch, then it went from low to no lights for a prolonged period. In some landlocked areas, for example the Caucasus or difficult to access regions of Russia, Kazakhstan, and Central Asian republics, this analogy was factually accurate: through the rough 1990s people endured their worsening living conditions under pressures of military conflicts, staple food deficits, and energy crisis. Emerging out of such conditions was not a group of newly ranked capitalist economies, but, clearly, societies transformed.

Back in the academic discourse, the discussions remained centered on the validity, speed, and sequence of the reforms implementation, as reviewed above and below in the shock therapy debate section. It is striking that a critical application of the dominant political economy methodology appeared to be missing from the analysis of the evolving changes: the dialectics of the process was ignored.

The dialectical approach, as opposed to mechanical interpretation of the Marxian economics, suggests treatment of economic change first and foremost as a dynamic social totality. As such, early on, announcing *perestroika* reforms only in terms of new economic functioning, without building up a new, socially acceptable vision (or, in crude terms, ideology) or economic base for the transition may have set the transformation locomotive on a collision course. But, at the time, the choice was between action and no action.

Later, as economic reforms took their course in individual countries, the mechanization of economic change persisted. The Marxian model was reduced to a popular prediction suggesting socialism followed by communism with capitalism left far behind. At the same time, the task of the reforms was to ignite capitalist aspirations to a sufficient level to ensure greater levels of income and wider prosperity. So, in effect a popular misconception of one's dominant theory was transposed on the ongoing policy decision-making. It is not our aim to argue for validity or invalidate the Marxian (or for that matter any other) model. Instead, let's look at the results from a macroeconomic perspective.

Without getting much deeper into the analysis of the circumstances at the height of the market reforms (something we are dealing with in subsequent chapters), Figure 2.3 adds a broader macroeconomic spin to the story. Specifically, with rare exceptions, all 29 economies have grown at an average pace of 2 percent for the 1990–2015 period. While, perhaps, comparable to the current post-crisis growth record globally, such growth rates are insufficient to adequately patch the macroeconomic losses of the 1990s and establish a sustainable growth path going forward for the region. Perhaps, one might argue, isolating growth rates for the 2000–2015 period offers a somewhat more optimistic picture.

One is reminded of the "fat 2000s" that have characterized much of the raw materials export-driven growth in net exporters and labor migrant remittances and aid financing in the net importer nations of the region (e.g. Gevorkyan, 2011; Milanovic, 2014a). The latter point is easily verified by decomposing the 2000–2015 growth rates between the pre- and post-crisis periods of 2000–2008 and 2009–2015 as done in Figure 2.4. The stark contrasts

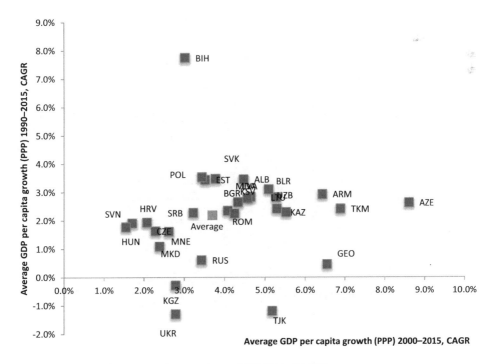

Figure 2.3 Average GDP per capita growth rate (PPP 2011, CAGR).

Source: author's estimates based on WDI (2017)

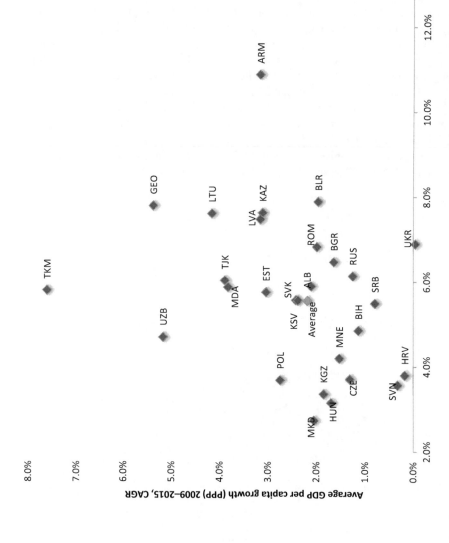

Figure 2.4 Pre- and post-crisis growth rates (GDP pc, PPP 2011, CAGR).

Source: author's estimates based on WDI (2017)

in speculative commodity exports or infrastructure projects or financial sector development motivated growth patterns of the pre-crisis 2000–2008 period stand in sharp contrast to pronounced declines in the post-crisis averages. We will return to this discussion and related question in the later chapters of this book.

For now, collective evidence on growth patterns confirms our reservations and serves to reemphasize the urgency of our exploration as we attempt to address key structural determinants of the massive transformation effort. Therefore, the current macroeconomic momentum, launched with the start of the market reforms and evolved over the past two decades, is insufficient to deal with the massive humanitarian problem of poverty, income inequality, and economic underdevelopment, in particular in the smaller countries.

The dialectics of transition

To sum up, the market liberalization reforms of the early 1990s were more than just an economic change. The impact spread beyond the competitive delimiters of macroeconomic restructuring but also profoundly affected social welfare in the, at the time, pre-dominant institutional model.[10] This story may be captured in a model of socio-economic transformation, presented in Figure 2.5 as a developmental spiral. Every new complete spiral rotation brings society in its dialectical unity of social (human) welfare, institutional, and competitive (macroeconomic) structures to a new level (of course, in a naive sense, preferably more progressive than before).

One of the principles of dialectical analysis is the evolution of the accidental and the necessary. To keep our illustration brief, consider the fact of market reforms announcement and the subsequent political actions to be that one accidental phenomenon in historical continuum. The reference to the accidental helps connect to the initially unintended event of the system's disruption against the background of the belief in the Soviet model's stability. However, dialectically, such unintended actions lay at the foundation of, and become the necessary preconditions for, any subsequent evolutionary change in the society, economy, and institutions. The process is ongoing, dynamic, and, by definition, evolutionary: one phase

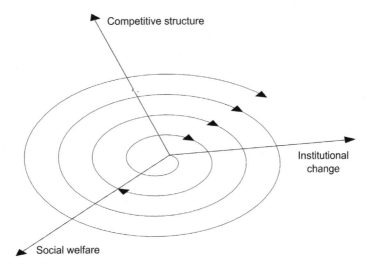

Figure 2.5 The model of socio-economic transformation in the post-socialist economies.

grows upon the preceding, adopting some and rejecting other categories of the preceding social, economic, and institutional mix.

The economic policy changes, for example the removal of state guarantees in business operations and labor markets, sets in motion social welfare forces. A simple and intuitive example would be requiring an individual to seek employment on his or her own, as opposed to a pre-assigned or guaranteed (for better or worse) appointment that was under the previous system. This in turn requires the appearance and evolution of well-functioning labor market institutions, adapted to the new socio-economic formation. Alas, in the early years of the post-socialist context it was too soon for solid institutions (if there were such) of a functioning labor market, at minimum akin to the capitalist system, to take any root in the transforming economy. In terms of job search, the previous system of state guarantees had yielded to now formalized network relations and what economists mildly refer to as rampant skills mismatching.

Figure 2.5 is a graphical depiction of the socio-economic change that relates natural progression of human society to its economic history. The problem arises when such changes are put through forcibly in haste focusing on the immediate as opposed to longer-term results and the foundation for sustained efficiency. As a result, there is not much time allocated for society and the economy to adjust to a new environment; institutions remain half-rooted and unstable. Perpetuating the push for reform (from the top policy measures without supporting the economic ground base) then exacerbates the welfare, competitiveness, and social reform conditions.

The spiral starts to spin in the opposite direction, unwinding the progress backwards, or reflects uneven changes across the three dimensions. One might argue, this has been the case in the post-socialist transition of the early 1990s. The impact was the hardest in the least prepared economies, of the so-called transitional periphery of the Balkans, Caucasus and Central Asia. As we explain in later chapters, the "least preparation" of these particular countries was in their substantially higher dependence on the centralized socialist market system and systemic political and economic, as well as military (as was in some cases), crises erupting in the early phases of independence movements. As we proceed with our narrative in the next several chapters the model captured in Figure 2.5 offers some guidance, structuring this book's focus on social and economic development.

Undoubtedly, institutions, as a collective set of norms, rules, and accepted practices in a society at a certain historical level of development, play a critical role in cementing the success of market reforms. Reflecting in the mid-2000s on Russia's economic and social change, the late Yegor Gaidar—the economist behind Russia's early 1990s reforms—devoted special attention to the role of institutions (Gaidar, 2012). In contrast to earlier work, Gaidar (2012) emphasized the gradual nature of new institutions' evolution, replacing collapsing old structures. New institutions lack a foundational tradition and progress can be very slow. This necessarily implies the gradual adaptation of the economy to the new social norms and business conduct, as the dynamic self-regenerating process of economic development takes over.

In the context of economic development, institutional improvement is routinely linked to progress in market reforms and rising national well-being (e.g. Rodrik, 2004; Acemoglu and Robinson, 2012). However, by itself, institutional progress is not the ultimate panacea to macroeconomic and business underperformance. In recent applications, the argument for gradual change and focused industrial policy has been extended to the case of Armenia in Chobanyan and Leigh (2006) and Russia in Gevorkyan (2013a) and Popov (2011). Roth and Kostova (2003) suggest that changes in corporate governance are conditioned on the overall institutional environment, emphasizing cultural characteristics and local context in transition economies.

The problem that we are trying to describe here is that the reformation period followed a naive belief that socialism was to be easily transitioned into a qualitatively-opposite in content new social and economic formation. The core notions were simplified to their static examples, removing the dialectics of the social change, and hence the logic and history out of political economy (e.g. Minasyan, 1989).[11] A dialectical interpretation that we attempt to model in Figure 2.5 then presupposes a natural, transformative, outgrowth of a consequent production mode from the prior and characteristic negation of the latter by the former.

There is an inherent interconnection across the three elements in Figure 2.5. Neither exists in isolation. Any alterations to either element necessarily affect the state of being of the other two components, analogous to the Pareto-optimal view of equilibrium. The difference from the conventional interpretation of Pareto optimality and the socio-economic transformation model is in the endogenously evolutionary nature of the Figure 2.5 model. The process does not settle into a comfortable equilibrium. At least, such is the lesson from history, which should be pivotal to macroeconomic reform and policy, something that runs as a main thread through the subsequent chapters.

This continuous evolution embodies in itself the unity of contradictory social and economic tendencies present in any given society and the much needed transformation of the accidental into necessary. In practice, abruptly cutting all ties with the past, indicates the dominance of the opposite assumption: none of that mattered.[12] Moreover, and this applies to the context of our discussion most directly, in his influential *Phenomenology of Spirit* Georg Wilhelm Friedrich Hegel states that "the actuality of this simple whole consists in those various shapes and forms which have become its moments, and which will now develop and take shape afresh, this time in their new element, in their newly acquired meaning" (Hegel, 1807, p. 7).

The intuition behind the above phrase, as it applies to the evolution of a society, is genius and simple at the same time. Indeed, witnessing the collapse of the established order in the early 1990s, the post-socialist societies moved to a new level of the transformational spiral. In turn, that level was comprised of a myriad of moments of personal, cultural, professional, academic, administrative, political, and so on, relations that stood as smaller elements of the whole. Assuming a human activity to be a purposive activity, as Hegel describes it, the emerging elements assumed new, previously unknown, shapes and context in each individual interaction. This then is transferred to an evolutionary new level, as the foundation has been set and a new set of relations emerges. Often, those interactions contradicted each other. In some dire cases, such contradictions spilled out into open military conflicts or protest demonstrations against domestic politics.

Be that as it may, the proliferation and unyielding growth of new elements, comprising one whole—a socio-economic post-socialist transformation—prevailed and continues to set the tone now even two decades since the collapse of the old system. This is an important insight that is often omitted in larger discussions, especially on economic policy. The dialectical principle must be upheld if one is to draw any lessons from the prior experience.

The immense social, economic, and political crisis that would come to characterize the 1990s decade in the countries of Eastern Europe and the former Soviet Union proved the simplistic predictions wrong. Even today, as macroeconomic situations have relatively stabilized across the landscape there is still insufficient capacity to restore pre-1990s welfare levels at a socially inclusive scale.

Conclusion

It is important when talking about economic development to keep in mind that one cannot separate technical macroeconomic problems from the problems of society, and public policy in general. This chapter has focused on unveiling the dialectical unity of the economic and social, leading towards critical realization of a transformational element (as opposed to a simplistic succession or transition) of the post-socialist region.

Applying the dialectical method, the model of socio-economic transformation in CEE/ FSU economies aptly captures the profound change of the early 1990s that is still ongoing. The key aspect is the continuous evolution and not a mechanical—reaching the destination— interpretation of the social process. For the countries in question this means, that announcing economic policy reforms and sharp reversal of established practices impacts social welfare and institutional effectiveness even before there may be any positive change in economic competitiveness.

The great economist Alexander Gerschenkron in his comments on the economic history of Russia once famously suggested that

> [a] comprehensive presentation of Russian economic history from its origins up till modern times should claim considerable interest . . . and it's in this way that students of the Soviet economy may be able to derive from the story of past centuries suggestive material for interpretation and re-interpretation of contemporary processes.
>
> (Gerschenkron, 1952, p. 146)

And so to understand what really happened, to grasp the evolutionary nature of the post-socialist transformation and its continuous impact on the societies of CEE and FSU, we turn to the history of the socialist system first. We then delve into the analysis of the post-socialist economic and social transformations in subsequent discussions. The story begins with an important historical setting in the middle of the 19th century in imperial Russia.

Notes

1 As defined in the online Merriam-Webster Dictionary. Direct weblink: www.merriam-webster. com/dictionary/transition.
2 As defined in the online Merriam-Webster Dictionary. Direct weblink: www.merriam-webster. com/dictionary/transformation.
3 We address details of these concepts in Chapters 6 and 7.
4 We return to the methodological debates again in Chapter 7.
5 Insightful on the subject are observations by Gaidar (2012, 2003) in his *Russia: A Long View*. It might be helpful to refer to our net-exporters analysis above and a similar logic developed in Gevorkyan (2011). For some of the post-socialist states, legacy economic structures have remained dominant until today suggesting much more gradual change.
6 Our more detailed discussion in Chapter 7 on the nature of the reforms and contemporary debate among macroeconomists on the direction of economic policy offers some additional insights into the complexity of the socialist model's disintegration.
7 This is consistent with the general dynamics of elites transformation through institutional environments described in Bavel (2016).
8 Ironically, such understanding would have required application of the very same political economy methodology of evolutionary, gradual transformation, built into the dominant economic theory of the region based on Marx's *Capital* (Marx, 1867).
9 Running a bit ahead of the narrative, here is a link to an informative compilation of the interactive timeline of the political and social changes inspired by the perestroika movement across the EE/ FSU. www.tiki-toki.com/timeline/entry/51634/Perestroika/#vars!date=1985-03-11_00:00:00.

10 A possible way to capture progress in those three components may be approximated by relying on a range of index proxies and other measures that have proliferated since transition reforms (e.g. EBRD Transition Index, WB Doing Business Survey, etc.).

11 We review some relevant English language literature in later chapters. Preceding some of the discussion, some of the conceptual points raised by Marangos (2004) apply here as well.

12 For more sophisticated motivation on dialectical method see Hegel (1807).

Part II
The planned economy

3 The economic and social context at the turn of the twentieth century

From the Russian Empire to the Soviet Union

> From each according to his ability, to each according to his needs!
>
> Karl Marx, *Critique of the Gotha Programme*

In the beginning there was . . .

Economic and political developments of the mid-19th century in Europe, and in the Eastern Europe and Russian Empire in particular, serve as a solid informative starting point for our analysis. In addition to inspiration from Gerschenkron (1952), there are at least two explanations for this.[1]

First, it may be argued that a study on transition economics must start with the main trigger event (either the *perestroika* launch or the fall of the Berlin Wall, depending on the scholar's choice) with, perhaps, occasional nod to some generic background observations. In fact, that appears to be the model of quite a few distinguished and quite influential texts and macroeconomic studies on CEE and FSU. However, simply summing up the socialist (pre-transition) history with a casual reference to 70 years of socialism can no longer be a sufficient institutional, social, political, and economic context for an inclusive study today, as explained on these pages.

Second, it may seem logical to look at World War I of 1914–1918 as a reference period. Why? The direct impact and the aftermath of the war had an immense influence on the subsequent formation of nation states and societies of the CEE/FSU region. It was a clear example of politics determining the economic mode across multiple national entities. In fact, there can hardly be any dispute about the fact that WWI may have started a new epoch in international political economy, as even minimal knowledge of 20th century history would suggest.

However, a series of important events took place prior to WWI. Importantly, economic and political reforms in Europe and imperial Russia led to the emergence of a new social structure of industrialists and workers. The foundation for further social stratification was set in the 19th century. Across Europe, the new societies were receptive of the socialist program appealing on a wider scale. Cutting through some of the complexities of related events, this chapter attempts to develop a more informed appreciation of the economic and political choices of the time. Appeals to pre-WWI economic circumstances would make a powerful argument later in the 20th century at the time of market liberalization reforms.

As such, the mid-19th century is chronologically close enough for one to speak of a new history, while at the same time covering the key critical historical events. The latter are the (dialectical) accidents, evolving elements of the whole, setting the necessary preconditions of the newest history and the present. In what follows, we can only offer a brief structural summary of events at the time. For more detailed analysis the reader is referred to more specialized thematic studies, some of which are mentioned here and some omitted due to space constraints.

The emancipation of the serfs in 1861

In his letter dated January 11, 1860, Karl Marx wrote to Friedrich Engels

> [i]n my opinion, the biggest things that are happening in the world today are, on the one hand, the movement of the slaves in America started by the death of John Brown and, on the other, the movement of the serfs in Russia (Marx and Engels, 1985).

There were objective reasons for such observation.

Quite broadly, by 1861 both the United States and the Russian Empire were two large political powers with lagging economic structures compared to Great Britain that led to the industrialization and capitalist transformation in Europe. For both US and Russia, economic growth, industrialization, and shifting from predominantly feudal to capitalist economic structures at the time required resolution of the problem of forced labor.

Starting in 1861, the US Civil War delivered the Emancipation Proclamation by President Abraham Lincoln in 1863. That revolutionary transformation shook the entire country politically and socially. In economic terms, those events paved the way to the broadening spread of the US model of the capitalist system.[2]

Around the same time, across the vast expanse of the Russian Empire a progressive movement was building up, advancing emancipation of the serfs and for land reforms. By the mid-1850s the old system of reactionary preservation of the established order was rendered obsolete. A new social and political design was required to stimulate economic and social change that would allow Russia to compete with industrializing Europe. Adding to the pressure for reforms were severe declines in agricultural productivity and a series of aggressive peasant revolts against landlords' brutality.

Rather than waiting for a popular revolt, Tsar Alexander II pushed for the reforms abolishing the serfdom (*krepostnoe pravo*) in his 1861 *Emancipation Manifesto*. Serfdom limited peasants' freedoms putting them in absolute dependence on the landlord (*pomeshchik*). The system had been codified, out of established order at the time, in the *Sobornoe Ulozhenie* (Law Code) of 1649 and had no provision for peasants' free movement (Moon, 2002). Any unsanctioned escapes from the landlord's territory, such as many brave attempts into the steppes to join the Cossack Hosts located around the Don River, were harshly punishable if interrupted.[3]

Following the tsar's 1861 decree, approximately 23 million peasants were granted freedoms they had not enjoyed before. Specifically, the reform allowed peasants to own property, engage in commercial trade, conduct business deals, marry, enlist in civil service, and appeal to judicial courts, all without requiring the permission of the landlord. Further, the repeal of serfdom also implied relaxation of the nominal strain over peasant mobility.

The reform, however, was a bit more convoluted as it attempted to strike a compromise between the state, landlords, and the peasants. Essentially, the land allocated to the peasants remained in the landlord's ownership, until the buyout deed. Before that happened, the peasants were considered as temporary, obligated to carry out the same tasks for the landlord as before. The reform transformed peasants' explicit dependence on the landlord to a legal concept of obligation.

Formally, buying out their land, peasants were also acquiring their full personal freedom. However, the reality was that the buyout values several times exceeded the market value of the land, in particular in non-fertile (*nechernozem*) areas. The process required the peasant to pay 20 percent of the land value directly to the landlord, while the state covered the remaining 80 percent. The peasant's obligation to the state then would extend for 49 years at 6 percent annual interest of the buyout value.

Furthermore, the concept of collective responsibility (*krugovaya poruka*) implied by establishment of the *obshchina* (community) prevented a potential freedom in relocation to the city without the community's permission. Such institutional arrangement persisted as a way of ensuring collective responsibility in paying taxes by the peasants up until 1903.[4]

As a result, a significant proportion of people stayed in their native places and continued working for the landlord but acquired some freedom in surplus distribution/allocation. They simply had no place to go, nor owned any land that they could move to and cultivate on their own. In some parts of the Russian Empire (the Baltics and Western Ukraine) the emancipation reforms were either partially or fully carried out before 1861 with less of the conditionality as in Russia proper (e.g. peasants granted their freedom). Overall, the true reform, however, would require time before being fully absorbed into the legacy of feudal realities of the time and across all provinces of the empire in Europe, the Caucasus, and Central Asia.

In a simplified reference to Karl Marx, the reform of 1861 was a bourgeois transformation that offered the Russian Empire and its provinces an opportunity for transitioning into the contemporary industrialized development mode. It certainly was one of the first scalable measures on the path of social and economic progress introduced by the state at the time. However, despite the intent, the elements of serfdom, that is, peasants still toiling the landlord's land, pulled the economy back. Lenin famously exclaimed that "[t]he year 1861 begot the year 1905" (Lenin, 1911) pointing to the desperate conditions of the peasants in post-1861 society that were complemented by the subsequent rapid industrialization.

The allure of early capitalism before the Russian revolution

It was towards the end of the 19th century that Russia entered the modern economic growth stage. By then, the initial mechanisms set forth by the 1861 reform had begun to work, setting a precedent for peasants moving to the cities taking up factory jobs and in essence monetizing relations between the peasants and landlords through redemption and land buyouts. The monetization observation is important. In general, monetary motive is one of the key characteristics of the capitalist (and industrializing) society, as opposed to the feudal in-kind exchange. Under the new conditions, monetary profits, due to the concept of liquidity and universality in exchange, commanded greater power than even the landlords' tangible assets.

The provinces in the Caucasus and Central Asia, albeit with considerable time and effectiveness lag, followed the center's transformation. Some of the Eastern European economies gained through spillover growth, either as part of the political alliance (e.g. Hungary) or due to their proximity to rapidly industrializing Germany or Italy (e.g. Czech Republic). However, for the most part they, as well as southern Romania and Bulgaria especially, remained predominantly rural with minimal industrial capacity. In this context, what was happening in Russia proper was critical, assuming robust growth, as new market and trade potentials were emerging.

The late 19th century in Europe was characterized by protectionist measures in economic policy intensified by the push for sovereignty and autonomy. The period saw slow disintegration of the Ottoman Empire, with independence struggles in the Balkans on the one hand and reactionary and oppressive actions in the Empire's eastern provinces against its Christian minorities, on the other. Positioning itself as a benefactor of the Christian world, the Russian Empire aspired to provide political protection and security guarantees to the affected communities. In economic terms, that also required a strong and sustainable industrial base to challenge potential rivals.

Witnessing the lack of domestic entrepreneurial activity (perhaps the exception being where it was based in the metallurgy and the resource-rich Ural mountains), and at the same time Germany's clear lead on the continental stage, Russia's official state embarked on a series of economic reforms aimed at strengthening the economy. Most notably, such policies included protectionist tariffs for domestic industries. The burden of heavy prices on consumer goods was mostly borne by the peasantry—the rural population.

Overall, the late 19th-century Russian Empire followed a model of forced industrialization with the state subsidizing or investing in large-scale projects, introducing new technology borrowed from abroad.[5] Count Sergei Witte played a critical role in Russia's industrial transformation, first serving as the empire's Minister of Communications (1892) and then as the Minister of Finance (1892–1903).

In transportation, to allow speedy and efficient delivery of raw and agricultural materials to the industrializing and administrative urban centers, Witte forcefully reformed the railroad network by acquiring private networks, reducing bottlenecks, and spearheading construction of the Trans-Siberian Railway in the Russian Far East.[6] There was much more than optimization of railroads. From leading trade negotiations with Germany on favorable conditions for Russia's exports, to implementing monetary reform moving Russia on to the gold standard, Witte acted with effectiveness and success. The monetary reform of 1895–1897, while stabilizing the Russian currency, being welcomed by the expanding ranks of industrialists and merchants, and opposed by the landed aristocracy, also played into development of the financial markets.

Witte's operational style and views on the role of the government in leading the initial phase of industrialization in a nascent non-capitalist society with an aim of sovereign security and economic sustainability, earned him the name of "Russian Colbert."[7] He was independent in his personnel decision often appointing to management positions based on the candidate's effectiveness rather than their aristocratic background, as had been the traditional practice.[8] Seeing commerce as one of the essential elements of capitalist development, the Russian state offered low-interest loans and other privileges to export-oriented enterprises. Of course, much of the exports were in energy and metallurgy commodities.

Due to lacking statistics, accuracy in reported growth rates is somewhat limited and varies depending on individual researcher's assumptions. Directionally, according to various estimates, industrial production between 1860 and 1990 grew sevenfold in Russia, leaving behind its European rivals (fivefold in Germany, 2.5-fold in France and twofold in England). Russia's railroad system expanded (further East) from approximately 1,000 kilometers in 1860 to 40,000 by 1916. Subsequently, proliferation of transportation links contributed to the growth of heavy industries.[9] Increased participation of foreign capital in the Russian economy provided another impetus to rapid industrial growth.[10]

In a relatively recent study, Borodkin *et al.* (2008) report a 25-fold increase in the coal production and 200-fold increase in oil production between 1870–1897. A second boom followed from 1909–1913 leading towards a more diversified economy with active private sector, commercial banking industry. Essentially, the state-led intervention at the early industrialization stage proved to be effective on a macro scale, as noted in Gerschenkron (1962) above.[11]

Table 3.1 shows approximate shares by sector in the total industrial mix at the time. The mining sector grew rapidly, while the textiles and other consumer goods sectors expanded slower but remained important for the domestic market. The agricultural sector continued to dominate the economy, despite very limited variety in grain types production and exports.

Notwithstanding the industrial (heavy manufacturing, mining, and textile production) growth over a short period of time, the sector only employed up to 5 percent of the population. This is visible also in earlier population statistics and relative urban to rural shares. As Table 3.2 clearly indicates, the majority of Russia's population as of 1897 was still employed in the agrarian sector with a small share of 10.7 percent of the urban population, which comprised the bulk of the factory labor force and government administrators.

Even with the agricultural bias in production and in terms of demographics, undergoing early industrialization, the country had to tackle the problem of migrants' adaptation to urban life and factory work—something that other countries had dealt with long before Russia. The social process was set in motion. Russia's two main cities, St. Petersburg and Moscow, saw large inflows of agricultural peasantry into the urban labor force. And it would not be until the 1880s, with the government's push for forced urbanization—especially around industrial zones in the Urals and the northwest—that the realization came for the need for a mobile and

Table 3.1 Shares of select sectors in Russia's industrial mix

Sector	1887	1900	1908
Mining	12.60	18.20	16.90
Food	24.40	18.80	18.40
Cotton and textiles	31.60	22.00	26.00
Other	31.40	41.00	38.70

Source: based on data assembled in Goldsmith (1961)

Table 3.2 Russia's census data as of 1897

	Men	Women	Total
Aristocracy	0.90%	1.00%	1.00%
Officials (non-hereditary aristocracy)	0.50%	0.50%	0.50%
Religious	0.40%	0.50%	0.50%
Honorary citizens	0.30%	0.30%	0.30%
Merchants	0.20%	0.20%	0.20%
City dwellers	10.50%	10.80%	10.70%
Peasants	76.80%	77.50%	77.10%
Cossacks	2.30%	2.30%	2.30%
Foreigners	7.10%	6.10%	6.60%
Fins (Finland)	0.00%	0.00%	0.00%
People outside official strata	0.30%	0.20%	0.30%
Not identified as part of any social group	0.10%	0.10%	0.10%
Subtotal Russian subjects	99.40%	99.60%	99.50%
Foreign subjects	0.60%	0.40%	0.50%
TOTAL	**100.00%**	**100.00%**	**100.00%**

Source: data converted into percentages from *Demoskop Weekly* (2014) based on the Russian Empire population census of 1897. Original data available online: http://demoscope.ru/weekly/ssp/rus_sos_97.php?reg=0

skilled labor force as a requirement in the nation's successful industrialization and further imperial strengthening (Moon, 2002).

By the time the empire entered the new century it had a significant and increasingly growing working class. It was this social stratum—the *proletariat*—in addition to the army recruits that the political parties of the time (*bolsheviki, men'sheviki*, etc.) targeted as critical in any political change.

The agrarian bias of the Russian economy and so much more of the peripheries necessitated the dominance of tradition in social relations. So much greater then is the significance of Count Witte's attempts, through his reforms, to pull society towards a more professional merit-based structure of production relations. But inability (or resistance by the landed aristocracy) to relinquish the past order led to the rising discontent of the peasants, signaling the weakening of the established regime.

The problem was with patchy and disorderly implementation of the reforms across the Byzantine web of interpersonal relations and vast geography. Whereas Western Europe and North America at the time exhibited relatively progressive social contracts between the ruling classes and the proletariat and peasantry, with certain individual and political right guarantees, suffrage, and protection of labor practices, such efforts were missing in the tsarist system. Still, despite their minority, it was the urban factory workers and the educated elite (primarily young students), who spearheaded the political change that was the outgrowth of the preceding economic transformation.

Sunday, January 22, 1905 went into history as Bloody Sunday and a start of the 1905 revolution. Thousands of workers in St. Petersburg marched on the Winter Palace (the official residence of Tsar Nicolas II). Their aim was to petition the tsar with political and (social) economic requests. Some of the demands included limitation of the unlimited powers of the aristocratic bureaucracy; fair workday and humane working conditions; as well as establishment of an electoral legislative body as the ultimate solution to all ills of the miserable plight of the working class.

The idea of appealing to the tsar as the last authority of trust and protection came after a series of unsuccessful strikes organized by the workers' movements at the major factories in St. Petersburg (with echoes in other industrial towns). But the political tune of the workers' demands led to the brutal repel of the peaceful march by the imperial guard. Workers, some of whom had brought their families to the march, unarmed, were shot at and hundreds died as a result of this confrontation.

The news spread across Russia and protest movements became standard in the cities at large factories but also in the army. As a result of the Revolution of 1905, the central government had to give in and release some of its powers by agreeing to a revised Constitution (that granted freedom of assembly, speech, and personal) and to the establishment of the Russian parliament (State Duma). Stolypin's reforms were aimed to deconstruct the *obschina* opening the way for individual peasant farms. This allowed richer peasants to accumulate their agricultural capacity increasing productivity. At the same time, poorer peasants were driven off the land, seeking employment in the cities. Subsidies were offered to motivate resettlement beyond the Ural Mountains, but agricultural production remained largely extensive due to rapid expansion of labor resources facing limited physical capital capacity.

What we have described above are known historical facts that fit a relatively standard pattern, so far, of industrial history across the world. Gradually, across industrializing Europe and North America, economic developments necessitated social and political change. One could say that analogous events happened at the times ancient civilizations collapsed.

In the Russian Empire, territorial and industrial growth over the 19th century required a more mobile and qualified labor force to balance the rapid discovery of significant surpluses of iron ore, minerals, and other primary resources. As an outcome of such pressures, the 1861 reforms eventually contributed to gradual formation of the working class in the most developed (and hence politically important) urban areas. Over time, the character of the labor force began to transform from modest peasantry origins into a more socially cognizant movement. Workers' early demands mimicked those of the early industrialized nations, for example those that France and Britain had to deal with approximately 50–70 years before and what US society saw in the late 19th century.

Still, by the time WWI broke out, despite massive progress in early industrialization, the Russian Empire for the larger part was an agrarian economy. One might argue that the war lent the central government an opportunity to stabilize population flows and diminish the workers' movement. The early 20th century was a time of ruthless industrial capitalism and unbounded idealism dialectically interconnected. Despite their semi-agrarian status, the countries of Central, Eastern, and especially Southern Europe were also part of the by then global capitalist system.

It was namely World War I, at the time the bloodiest and most ruthless war of the century— with the use of new destructive weapons, genocides, and political power struggles that the world unfortunately saw repeated later in WWII—that led to the emergence of new sovereign states and drew new national frontiers in Europe and Asia. The war reignited the Marxist movement (and some would correct this by referring to "ultra-Marxist") that found its fertile ground in the enormous landscape and population size of the Russian Empire.

Following the February 1917 Revolution, Tsar Nicholas II of Russia abdicated his throne. The Russian Provisional Government emerged as a compromise between the State Duma and the Executive Committee of the Petrograd Council of workers and soldiers. The new government would last for approximately six months . . .

Emergence of the Leninist State

The Russian Revolution of October 1917 is a subject of mixed controversy and will most likely remain so until the last echo of that monumental shift fades into history. It is hard to tell when this might happen: not in the near future though, since much of the present world order is a direct outcome of that event.

The revolution, which eventually elevated the Bolshevik Party to the absolute political power in the country, also resulted in Russia's abrupt withdrawal from WWI with significant territorial, political, and economic concessions under the Brest-Litovsk treaty of March 1918, including relinquishing imperial possessions of the western territories. At the time, the priority was to retain and ensure longevity of Bolshevik rule domestically. The new government withdrew all combat forces from all military fronts.[12]

And shortly after, Russia was thrown into another bloodbath of the Civil War against the *anti-bolshevik* White movement, supported by the Allied intervention. The country was torn into two camps: the "reds" and the "whites." In the periphery, the struggle intensified also as the national elites attempted to muster independence movements with short-lived successes, especially in the Caucasus and elsewhere. A detailed discussion on particular circumstances around the time is deferred to more specialized studies on the subject.[13] In our context, both the October Revolution and the start of the Russian Civil War matter as those pivotal moments that launched the 70 years of Soviet Rule and the peculiar economic system.

Lenin's first decrees (on peace, land, and on self-government) had as much political as economic impact on the newly forming society. As a result of the Decree on Peace, Soviet Russia pulled out of WWI (with consequent ramifications mentioned above). The Decree on Land abolished private land ownership, that is, announced full-scale nationalization of agricultural land. No longer could land be sold. Any damage to now nationalized property was to be punished by the revolutionary courts. All forests, rivers, roads, mineral wealth, and other resources were nationalized. The third Decree established the Council of People's Commissars assuming the highest executive power authority and leading the political groundwork for establishing the USSR.

The Russian Civil War (1918–1922) preoccupied the Bolshevik government with solving the "political" question first, rather than addressing any pragmatic economic reforms. Recall that the Bolsheviks' popularity was largely based on their appeal to the working class and the promise of rapid industrialization and technological advancement via unified cooperation. This was supposed to pull the country out of its capitalist decay and jet-speed it into the new socialist society. The problem was that Russia continued to be largely defined by its dominant agrarian sector, which was more feudal than capitalist in nature—but more on this later.

The Civil War also gave an opportunity to carry the revolution beyond the Russian border and "red" detachments were formed in Ukraine, Caucasus, and Central Asia. A pocket of determined resistance was in Russia's southern region occupied by the Cossack Hosts: by 1917 the Cossacks had their internal organization and customs figured out—a young man would be drafted in the Russian army and upon his return to the village would take over the household for the elders or others, whose turn came up to join the army. The new social order imposed by the October 1917 revolution was perceived as a threat to the old ways of running the Cossack economy and its semi-autonomous status. In the end, the Bolsheviks prevailed by force.

Back in Saint Petersburg and Moscow, to support the war effort the new government announced a policy of War Communism—requisitioning surplus (but more often the little of what remained) of peasants' produce, cattle, and even household items. This brewed an environment of distrust (again, the Cossacks' reaction is illustrative of the overall trend as the appropriation took place in Russia's southern regions) among the larger population group. Anyone with surplus grain who resisted giving it up for the revolutionary cause was labeled as an enemy of the people, turned over to revolutionary courts, and, in the best-case scenario, sentenced to years in prison.

The Bolshevik government controlled only 10 percent of the coalmines and approximately 50 percent of grain stocks in the country. By 1919, the definition of grain surplus was based on the state's need as opposed to the more logical one of what might be left over after individual household consumption. But not only grain was requisitioned. All provisions and supplies (most notably horses and cattle) were appropriated to support the front securing the success of the revolution. Mass starvation and peasant uprisings were the immediate consequences of the ill-fated policy that came on top of structural economic deprivations. Official estimates by 1921 put the numbers of starving in the range of 22–28 million people.

Simultaneously with the ongoing Civil War and War Communism appropriations, the new government advocated a determined fight against illiteracy. True to the idealism of the time, inspired as is well known by the popular interpretation of Marxism, the government announced a policy of *Likbez* (*likvidatsia bezgramotnosti* or liquidation of illiteracy). Within a short period of time, the literacy rates went from 21 percent of the total population average in the 1890s up to 57 percent in the 1920s and as much as 87 percent in 1939.[14] By then, the

Soviet Union boasted the highest literacy rates (which remained at 100% until the dissolution in 1991). Despite this promise of advancement and the established new social order of visible equality, at least in the immediate term, War Communism had the potential to lead to further disintegration.

The New Economic Policy

Perhaps realizing the antagonisms in society and the evident lagging industrial development, the Bolshevik government implemented the New Economic Policy (NEP) in place of War Communism. The policy was in place from 1921 to the summer of 1929. The NEP brought temporary prosperity to the larger masses of the now growing USSR (established in December of 1922). In retrospect, the NEP helped the Bolsheviks regain the fading trust and favor of the masses which had been eroded by prior policies. Under this new regime the official Marxist ideology coexisted with and allowed elements of private enterprise, in particular trade in agricultural markets, textiles production, and so on.[15]

The new system replaced War Communism's forced requisition with in-kind taxes that in turn by 1924 evolved into monetary obligations. The NEP essentially gave peasants freedom to distribute their surplus and produce as they desired, including selling in the local markets, as long as the minimal tax burden was covered. The state remained in control of large, heavy industry, foreign trade, and banking, though with elements of market economy management (with up to 2 percent of large industry being in private hands). Foreign capital was allowed to flow into the industrial sectors and cooperation with foreign companies was welcomed to some extent. By 1927, enterprises under foreign concessions contributed approximately 1 percent of total industrial output.

Companies in the same industry formed trusts acquiring full operational independence. Individual trusts then transformed into syndicates with high shares of market control in wholesale trade and financial operations, as well as foreign trade (with up to 82 percent of state industry by 1928 organized accordingly). By 1928, foreign trade volumes had increased by 44 percent from 1918 levels. Small-scale industries (mostly crafts but also some consumer goods production, textiles, and in particular commerce) and services were denationalized, allowing the emergence of a private sector in a pure market (if not capitalist) sense. By 1923, up to 12.5 percent of employment was in the private sector.[16]

The monetary system was stabilized with the introduction of the gold *chervonets* equivalent to the pre-revolutionary 10 rubles. The *sovznak* paper currency introduced by the Bolsheviks earlier had lost its value (and trust) feeding into hyperinflation. Introducing a gold-backed currency helped stabilize the market (an insight that was seriously debated during the early years of the *perestroika* and liberalization reforms some 70 years later). Essentially, the monetary relations that had been eradicated and seen as anti-communist just a few years before, had returned and permeated every pore of the NEP's economy spread across the vast expanse of the Soviet Union.

Some interpreted Lenin's policy as a temporary measure to revive the economy, which it did to some extent. The agricultural tax burden gradually shifted from covering all peasants, rich and poor, to a more progressive scale on middle-to-upper income peasant households. In fact, a new class in the rural areas emerged: the *kulaks* (Russian: fist) were former peasants operating private farms and seeing their fortunes grow as surplus production accumulated and relatively free exchange was introduced under the NEP. Characteristically, the *kulaks* relied on hired labor, employing largely less fortunate peasants, paying wages. The wealthy peasants' farms gained efficiency and growth. However, the momentum was not significant enough to allow for private agriculture to evolve as a strong sector of the national economy on the scale of the entire country.

Elsewhere, in rural communities of Armenia and Georgia for example, arable land and human resources were (and remain) quite scarce. Often, survival of the entire village depended on crops grown on small patches of land crossed by rocky terrain. In such situations, cooperation was inevitable and a necessary solution. It was customary for peasants to help each other, taking turns working each field. The crops were sufficient to last through the tough winter months, with not much left by the early weeks of spring the following year.

Despite the NEP's successes in stimulating private sector growth, tax collections were not sufficient to cover all the needs of the emerging socialist state. Recall that much of the country remained agrarian, based in rural areas. Hence, the main tax burden fell on the peasants. Furthermore, as agricultural retail prices remained high (see Figure 3.1) relative to manufactured goods, industrial trusts withheld some of their output to boost prices. The government opted for non-tax measures, such as forced loans and price differentials. The latter included lowering purchase prices on grain and raising prices on consumer goods. The administrative action partially explains the steep decline in agricultural prices since 1919, captured in Figure 3.1. However, one should also account for relative post-Civil War stabilization in the economy and competitive pressures on peasants (*kulaks*) bringing their produce to the urban areas in pushing down prices. Still, by late 1922 the "Scissors Crisis" emerged.[17]

The essence of the "Scissors Crisis" is captured in Figure 3.1. Towards the end of 1922, prices on domestically produced industrial goods (by some estimates at 276 percent of the 1913 levels) began to significantly outpace agricultural output prices. Prices of agricultural goods were lowered to approximately 80 percent of the 1913 level. The response was immediate: peasants withheld any grain in excess of what was sold to cover tax obligations. That effect coupled with the agricultural sector attempting to gain efficiency in production in a

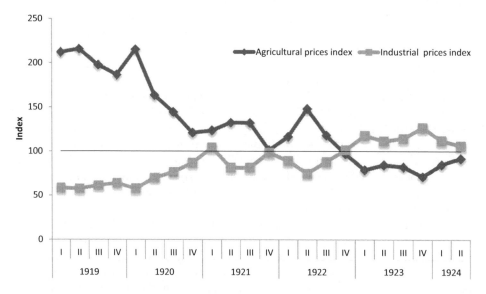

Figure 3.1 The price "scissors" of 1920s, index.

Note: derived from original data on Moscow retail prices as ratio of each sector price index to an overall index.

Source: author's estimates based on data in Appendix 7 in Vainshteyn (1972, p. 157)

new market environment, which in its turn curtailed volumes of agricultural produce to the urban areas (Harrison, 1991).

The crisis emerged in 1923 as peasants refused to purchase equipment at artificially raised prices. For policymakers, the problem was obvious: if the workers in industry were not properly fed, industrial output would collapse, eventually choking the economy. It would appear that the NEP restrained the maneuver space for centralized industrialization in the environment of fluctuating prices, especially on agricultural products.

For the time being, industrial production had to be optimized: personnel policies, efficiencies, and fixed industrial wages were introduced. Cheaper imported consumer goods were allowed and credit was restricted to domestic trusts, forcing them to bring their stockpiles to market, pushing prices down. At the same time, by 1924 agricultural prices were up again by 91 percent to 1913 levels while consumer and industrial goods prices dropped 131 percent.[18] In the end, there was no perfect price convergence (i.e. the "scissors" remained open) and agricultural surplus to urban areas continued to decline, as sector prices would continue to diverge, albeit slightly, in subsequent years.[19]

The NEP was a controversial attempt to resurrect the economy, while the socialist ideology remained dominant. In economic terms, the NEP for all practical purposes assumed the structure and character of a market economy. In 1921, Lenin insisted that the fragile balance between the socialist ideals that the USSR stood for and introduction of elements of the market economy was necessary and needed for a longer period, to enrich the general population making the "transition" to the new order of Soviet power.

In Lenin's own words, introducing the NEP was a "strategic retreat" to correct the mistakes of the past (i.e. the policies of War Communism) and reset the economy and society on a more sound and stable foundation (Lenin, 1921). To hardcore revolutionaries, it seemed as a complete retreat, instead, from the disastrous policy of the recent years, a sentiment sharply criticized by Nikolai Bukharin in his April 17, 1925 speech in defense of the NEP. His famous exclamation, "Get Rich, accumulate and grow your businesses!" served to defend the basic principle of the NEP—private property and self-enrichment as a precondition for the national economy's growth (Bukharin, 1925). A few weeks later, Bukharin was forced to withdraw his own statement.

Industrialization, collectivization, debates, and the first Five-Year Plans

By late 1929, the system of balances between the socialist production mode and pre-socialist categories (i.e. private property and individual entrepreneurship among the most visible examples) introduced by the NEP fell apart (e.g. Harrison, 1980). Much earlier it had become clear that to advance the economy further a choice had to be made between full free-market implementation or return back to the command system. Yet, the country faced a challenge of the aftermath of the industrial base destruction after the Civil War.

Even accounting for the wealthy *kulaks'* contributions, produced in the agricultural sector through market mechanisms, accumulated state revenues were insufficient to generate the required level of physical capital investments. Furthermore, the intra-party divisions on the subject intensified. In Soviet politics, this was the time of Joseph Stalin's rise to power as the heir apparent to Lenin.[20]

By the mid-1920s, the industrialization debate began in earnest.[21] The dispute seemed more about the intensity of the much-needed industrialization. Bukharin, as evidenced in his 1925 speech mentioned above, favored a gradual transition from the agrarian economic structure to the industrial one, based on the balance (*smychka*) between the then urban workers and peasants. He saw the process as an outgrowth of the NEP, arguing for allowing for imports of capital goods and moderate fixed capital accumulation. In his view, if peasants had incentives to produce and sell more of their output, the government would have sufficient resources to boost up grain exports in exchange for imported machinery. The balance was clear, as the new machinery would help make agriculture more efficient, while helping the country's industrialization effort. The evolution of the socialist economy would then be natural and without any abrupt opposition by the peasantry.

In essence, Bukharin's propositions were somewhat consistent with Lenin's original thinking behind the NEP and the entrepreneurial role of the *kulak*. However, Bukharin's views came under sharp criticism from the Bolshevik's left wing. The critique was initially led by Leon Trotsky and later joined by Yevgeni Preobrazhensky. They argued for forced industrialization as a national development strategy.

Accordingly, the first task was to develop the military complex, machinery, and heavy industries. The argument appealed to the urban factory workers whose living standards were below the 1913 levels, for which the excesses of the NEP were blamed. An intentional reinstitution of the "price scissors" was argued as a means of raising the surplus from the agrarian sector (artificially bumping up the prices of manufactured goods and lowering prices of agricultural goods; see Figure 3.1). In addition, to limit spending by workers in the agricultural sector, supplies of consumer goods directed towards rural areas were to be reduced.

Distancing himself initially from the economists' debates, Stalin used the 1928 grain crisis as an opportunity to outmaneuver without expressing his initial preferences. Eventually, the country went with rapid industrialization and collectivization (e.g. Davies, 1980). The choice was made and the first Five-Year Plan was announced in 1928. The GOELRO (State Commission for Electrification of Russia) had been in place since 1920 and set the model for the first Five-Year Plan (Gvozdetskij, 2005).

The plan implied doubling of fixed capital funds; 70 percent expansion in light (consumer goods) industry, despite obvious lack of equipment and initial capacity. In fact, Albert Vainshteyn of the Kon'ukturnyj Institute warned in 1929 about the unrealistic targets set by the proposed plan (Vainshteyn, 1929). In his note, the economist suggested lowering the rate of capital investments in manufacturing with the remainder redistributed to agriculture. That was the only way to achieve a balanced flow of accumulated savings from the agricultural sector to industry; that is, within a market-based system.

However, the administrative capacity implied by the proposition of forced industrialization opened up the doors to similarly forced collectivization as a way of diverting the needed resources to industrialization. Collectivization that brought individual agrarian households into the collective farms (*kolkhoz*) was announced in 1929. The immediate ramification was the destruction of private agricultural enterprise (fighting the *kulak* in the village) and forming in place the collective farms, *kolkhoz*. Anyone refusing to join the *kolkhozy* was branded a *kulak* and dealt with accordingly with all the severity of the time.[22]

Largely because of this abrupt economic and political turnaround, peasants retracted their products from local markets; foreign capital left the minimal industrial base put in place by the NEP. The NEP system was rapidly dismantled. Refusing to comply, peasants slaughtered livestock, burned crops, and sabotaged production. These disastrous actions left a heavy imprint on the Soviet agricultural sector up until World War II. Critically, millions of peasants perished in the 1933 famine and in the initial phases of the infamous purges, accused of being the members of the *kulak* class.

Politics dominated, and preference for heavy industry and rapid industrialization, added pressure on the peasantry and the need for the agrarian sector to integrate in the rapidly growing socialist economy. While none of the high targets were achieved in the first three Five-Year Plans, there was still a significant increase in industrial production. In the second and third Five-Year Plans, USSR industry posted stellar results. Over a short period, 10,000 industrial factories were launched. Leading by example, Aleksei Stakhanov—who mined 102 tons of coal in just six hours, which exceeded the norm 15-fold—helped launch the *sotssorevnovanie* (socialist competition) movement, inspired by people's enthusiasm and anxiety for the promise of tangible improvement in living conditions.

Rapid urbanization and the introduction of mandatory education (seven years of school in the cities) fostered the emergence of a capable industrial labor force. Foreign expertise and domestic science contributed to the enormous economic transformation. The *Gosplan* (The State Planning Committee—active since 1921) was working on various alternative capacity-building scenarios employing highly trained economists who were offered an opportunity of a lifetime of creating an economy from scratch.

Countries of Central and Eastern Europe that became part of the Soviet bloc after WWII, had to undergo similar forced industrialization and collectivization. Preference was given to the development of heavy industrial manufacture. Ironically, in view of some economists it was a true "Great Breakthrough" (to paraphrase Stalin's infamous proclamation). However, the shift to the new economic model was not a smooth transition. At an everyday level, those early years were especially hard.

Initial analysis

In this chapter, we offer just enough of a historical teaser about the early socialist model in the USSR that would later be transplanted in its own shape and form onto Eastern Europe. Clearly, such a review cannot deal with the myriad of nuances involved at each development stage described here, nor could we adequately reflect the miniscule details of the raging debates on the direction of socioeconomic policy at the time. It is hoped that the above review may be sufficient to start questioning one's understanding of the socialist model.

Was the NEP system of the USSR a type of socialism and if so, how did it differ from the subsequent model emerging in the first Five-Year Plans? To what extent did the experience of the NEP later influence the much better-known *perestroika* reforms? Was the forced collectivization, a critical necessary element of similarly forced industrialization, absolutely necessary?

It may be difficult to pinpoint a straightforward answer at the moment. Furthermore, we must remember again, there is no "if" in history. Events and social phenomena unraveled in a certain way and our task is to learn and analyze them. It is highly speculative, adventurous, and unproductive to engage in designing hypothetical scenarios without actually being directly involved in the process and without full information. Attempting to answer the above on the pages of this text is simply impossible due to space constraints, as such answers would require much longer and detailed exposition.

The magnitude of social change over a very short period, within one or two generations, must be the background against which everything is measured. The events of the late 19th and early 20th century were foundational in social, political, and economic transformation globally and in the CEE/FSU region, in particular. Those events are the basis of the later years' phenomenon of socialist, then transition, and now post-socialist economies. The discussion in subsequent chapters will attempt to provide some clarity to the above points.

By the mid-1990s, Janos (1996) identifies the following stages of economic and social development in the CEE/FSU that are applicable here:

- Leninist state (from the Bolshevik Revolution until Lenin's death in 1924);
- period of transition from Lenin to Stalin (mid-1920s to late 1929);
- Stalinist period;
- post-Stalin period;
- Gorbachev/perestroika period.

As we move through our discussion, the above categories will evolve in greater context and assume greater meaning. For now, rather briefly, we can note the following. The key aspect of the Leninist state was its idea of the global socialist revolution. The fate of the Russian Revolution of 1917 was not just about Russia's fate. The revolutionary mood was to spread elsewhere. Lenin, Trotsky, Bukharin, Plekhanov, and others, in their own selves, were true believers and revolutionaries who inspired the masses. In evident opposition to Ludwig von Mises's (1920) view on the eventual collapse of the socialist system, the Bolshevik leaders truly believed in their interpretation of the Marxian political economy.

Given such political pretext, industrialization and collectivization would become influential in pushing economic growth. The policy measures and the impact of the policies adapted in the USSR during that period would remain influential all through the post-WWII period up to more recent times, a subject of our later discussions.

In a way, it could be argued that the decisions and the socioeconomic change of the late 1920s were more significant to the subsequent development in the CEE/FSU region, as well as in global political economy and geopolitics, than the Revolution of 1917 itself. In fact, the significance was not simply in the direction of industrialization and collectivization. The true significance was in the deviation in the late 1920s economic policies from the ideals advocated at the heights of the Revolution of 1917 and during the NEP. A new and unparalleled social transformation led to creation of an equally new society that for decades remained largely isolated from the rest of the world. The economic, social, and political core framework that would evolve from that deviation would be cemented for the next 60 years as the socialist economic model.

Conclusion

This chapter has covered a long period in the Russian and later the Soviet Union's history, with direct subsequent impacts for the economies of Eastern Europe. Starting with the discussion of the 1861 repeal of serfdom as a way of setting Russia on an economic trajectory, albeit reluctantly due to the landed aristocracy's opposition, the discussion moved on to the review of the imperial government's efforts at early industrialization. Despite some visible economic progress, accumulation of political volatility and the remaining feudal system's reactionary politics exacerbated the ripple effect in Russian society, culminating in the Revolution of 1917.

The Bolsheviks' desire to establish new social order prompted a rapid unapologetic eradication of the old system, cutting any affiliation with the past. However, what had been achieved politically, turned out to be difficult to accomplish in economic terms. At an individual level, the economic foundation affected society. Much of Soviet Russia for some time remained agrarian, bound by tradition, resisting centralization, and with limited industrial capacity.

The New Economic Policy aimed to reinvigorate the USSR's economy. However, after a brief period, inflation and grain crises emerged signaling inherent contradiction between a market-based economy and the socialist ideals. One had to yield. And industrialization and collectivization followed.

The first Five-Year Plans contributed to significant industrial advancement, specifically in machinery that would continue to grow, prompting the USSR to cover the gap between the agrarian and industrialized state faster than the capitalist economies of North America and Europe before it. What mattered in this period was how industrial capacity and the new socio-economic system, shaped by the State Plan and Five-Year Plans and millions of human sacrifices, would evolve over the next 60 years. This is the subject of our subsequent chapters.

Notes

1 In addition to Gerschenkron (1952), much of the discussion in this and the following chapter is based on fundamental studies by Nove (1964), Davies (1991), and others as mentioned throughout the text.
2 On emancipation see Litwack (1980).
3 Serfdom was limited in the Cossack lands around the river Don, in the Northern territories and parts of Siberia.
4 Some informative studies looking into the detailed history of the serfdom are (but certainly in no way are limited to) Blum (1971), Zajonchkovskij (1968), Pokrovskii (1934).
5 Alexander Gerschenkron (1962) offers economic rationalization for reaping the benefits of "advantage of backwardness."
6 The railroad with some engineering reinforcements during the Soviet time and more recently is still functioning as one of the world's longest and as Russia's major transportation artery.
7 As found in Abalkin (1999).
8 Perhaps the best reference on Witte's activity and economic policy would be his own memoirs where he talks about various aspects of economic and political reform in Russia (e.g. Witte, 1921).
9 For example, see Goldsmith (1961).
10 A thorough but concise analysis is found in Gregory (1994).
11 Also see Gerschenkron (1947) for additional details on Russia's economy from late 19th century through mid-20th century.
12 In some places, such as South Caucasus (e.g. Armenia), ramifications were tragic and disastrous to the local population, where the Russian imperial troops suppressed the advancing Ottoman Empire army's and armed militia's brutality against and extermination of the Christian minorities, e.g. Hovannisian (1971).
13 One of the most influential in the scope of its discussion on the political and economic situation is the edited work in Davies (1991). But the reader is also referred to less academic, fictional, works such as B. Pasternak's *Doctor Zhivago* (1991) or M. Sholokhov's *Tikhij Don* [*And Quiet Flows the Don*] (1941), both novels being adapted as highly acclaimed films and stage productions. In both, the dichotomy of individual survival and the newly imposed collective conditions are portrayed through the turmoil of the October Revolution and the subsequent Civil War. Both are excellent depictions of the morals and tradition in Russian society (e.g. in particular the patriarchal and at the same time democratic charter of the Cossack life and customs in *Tikhij Don*).
14 Initially, the statistics reflected greater literacy rates among men than women. Also, all army recruits were able to read and at least sign their name. Data is taken from various sources but the studies found in R.W. Davies (1991) mentioned above are informative.
15 Here's a short video explaining the transition from the War Communism to the New Economic Policy www.youtube.com/watch?v=5U5duV94Ocs.
16 For detailed English language analysis of the nature and effectiveness of the NEP see Davies (1991).
17 Original data on the "Scissors Crisis" in subsequent research comes from the industrial and agricultural prices index aggregation by Vainshteyn (1972, p. 158).
18 For example, see Harrison (2008).

19 For detailed discussion on the pricing crisis and analysis of the circumstances around the "Scissors Crisis" see Harrison (1991 and 2008).
20 On the interplay of Soviet politics and economic policy, see intriguing analysis in Nove (1964).
21 For a detailed English language analysis of the Soviet industrialization debate, see Elrich (1967).
22 While the *kolkhoz* system implied that a member of the collective farm was paid out of the revenues of the *kolkhoz* (a union of individual farms), the state-operated *sovkhoz* system implied regular fixed wage payments. The *sovkhoz* system did not evolve much due to its inefficiency and costs to the state.

4   The war economy and post-World War II reconstruction in the USSR

You ask, what is our aim? I can answer in one word: Victory. Victory at all costs. Victory in spite of all terror. Victory however long and hard the road may be. For without victory there is no survival.

Winston Churchill[1]

We shape our buildings, and afterwards our buildings shape us.

Winston Churchill

The setting

In the previous chapter, we talked at length about the political and economic sequence of moving from the agrarian base of tsarist Russia to industrialization in the Soviet Union. The significance of this transformation occurring over a historically short time span cannot be overlooked. Within roughly 50 years, the territory and the population of what eventually became the USSR turned around 180 degrees in political, economic, cultural, and social respects.

In that context, one might argue that the Russian Empire's journey from 1861 to the late 1880s—a formal attempt to break with the agrarian traditional society entering the modern economic growth league—with the subsequent 1913 peak of economic activity, followed a logical and gradual institutional transformation. Indeed, the tendency was there but, as noted, the loosely coordinated industrialization had been set on shaky grounds. Deep in its core, society's institutional base changed very little. The autocracy with the vested interests of hereditary aristocracy and landlords topped by a complex web of multilayered politics, held Russia tightly connected to its agrarian roots.

The Revolution of 1917, the Civil War, subsequent nationalization, and the requisitions of War Communism sent ripple effects across every fiber of the already fragile system. The New Economic Policy, now on the scale of the newly formed USSR, was a "strategic retreat," in Lenin's words—a policy completely opposite to the advocated ideals of socialism and communism. Finally, abrupt dismantling of an emerging market system under the NEP paved the way to centrally administered industrialization. The latter was more determined, aggressive, and centrally controlled than any prior attempts at the end of the 19th–early 20th century. The agricultural sector, under forced collectivization, yet again was the only available resource that the state could lean on to carry out industrialization reforms.

Emerging transformation right before the war

It is important not to underestimate the Soviet system of economic planning that emerged in the 1930s. For the next 60-odd years, that system would play a definitive role for the USSR and Eastern European economies within the post-World War II socialist orbit. Therefore, we need to discuss the key aspects of the 1930s transformation. Again, for now, we consider events in the Soviet Union as foundational for the entire evolving socialist context.

No story of Soviet history in the 1930s can ever be complete without mentioning the Great Purge. Certainly, this vast topic is a subject for more dedicated studies, yet it is important to the overall context here. The Great Purge refers to the brutal political repression, which saw hundreds of thousands of people perish either in the Gulag forced labor camps or through execution with no or minimal trials and millions more imprisoned with lengthy sentences.[2] Millions of human destinies were destroyed. In the environment of mass terror all feared for their life. Denunciations proliferated. Even seemingly unrelated actions (e.g. scheduling teaching shifts with longer breaks), careless, or not so careless, words in friendly conversations (e.g. voicing concerns over the conformity of the Five-Year Plans with Lenin's ideals for the socialist revolution), political jokes, or, more prominently, one's position in office (e.g. a state appointed attorney) could have branded anyone as an "enemy of the people."[3]

Occasionally, economic historians fail to consider the massive negative repercussions of the purges on the fabric of Soviet society. Instead, researchers tend to focus solely on the grand industrial accomplishments of the time. In the context of this study, one cannot argue for or against such motivations. However, a student of transition economics must bear in mind the unimaginable human cost and sacrifice that accompanied the unprecedented economic transformation at the time. Perhaps, to some extent this collective knowledge of the 1930s, would later, in part, drive the fear of centralized economy among Eastern European societies in their resistance movements.

The economic transformation was indeed massive. Some estimates, for example Harrison (1985), suggest that the national income expanded by more than 60 percent during the first Five-Year Plan (1928–1932). Gregory and Stuart (1986) estimate that the Soviet economy grew on average 5.1 percent between 1928–1940 while the population rose 3.9 percent during the same period.

The structural change, attempted through forced industrialization and collectivization, was evident by the end of the decade. Figure 4.1 illustrates the sizeable transfer of the Net National Product (a Soviet statistical measure of national income) during the short ten years since the first Five-Year Plan.

The structural transformation was clearly visible in a massive drop of consumption share in the economy (from 82 percent of NNP in 1928 to 55 percent by 1937, as per Gregory and Stuart, 1986 data). At the same time, production indicators across heavy industry more than doubled and tripled within the first five years of the plan (see Table 4.1). And though the targets of the Five-Year Plans were rarely met (and validity of the statistical evidence remains a subject of ongoing debate among involved researchers), in economic terms the gains were impressive.

Table 4.1 reveals that the first plan's objectives were achieved with significant delays, in some cases two or more years past the initial target year (e.g. Latsis, 1988 offers a detailed technical analysis on this point). Still, the example of the first Five-Year Plan achievements suggests that the socialist pattern of industrialization was largely effective in redistributing resources from agricultural to the industrial sector. The evidence in Figure 4.1 also implies this happening with far greater shares of GDP than elsewhere. Of course, there were also side-effects.

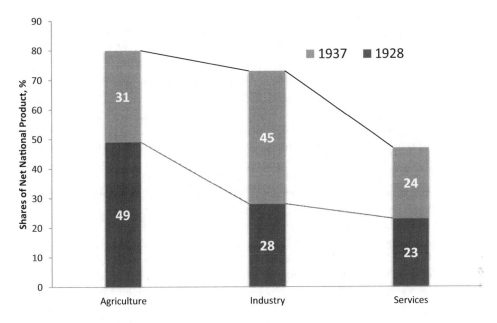

Figure 4.1 The Soviet economy's structural transformation of the 1930s.

Source: based on data assembled in Gregory and Stuart (1986)

Table 4.1 Select indicators of Soviet industrial production (1928–40) vs. first Five-Year Plan

	First Five-Year Plan target	1928	1932	1937	1940
Crude steel (mlns tons)	10.4	4.3	5.9	17.7	18.3
Electricity (blns KWH)	22	5	13.5	36.2	48.3
Cars (thousands)	100	0.8	23.9	199.9	145.4

Sources: based on data in Harrison (1985) and Latsis (1988)

Overcoming its obstacle of a mostly rural population, the USSR quickly ascended the ranks of industrialized nations that during the 1930s were dealing with the Great Depression. Gaidar (2003) argues, the economic achievements of the 1930s were possible due to a combination of three factors. These included: a) operational efficiencies of modern economic growth; b) technological advances (in particular from the core industrial nations); and c) the political environment allowing forced agricultural surplus appropriation.

While the second factor is explained by a combination of domestic scientific ingenuity, state-funded research experimentation, and imported technology, the first and the third factors are less clear. The first factor may refer to the ability to create jobs in the industrial sector, resettling workers from rural into urban or mono-factory areas. It was honorable to join the working class. Examples of Stakhanov (mentioned in the previous chapter) inspired enthusiasm and socialist competition (*socialisticheskoe sorevnovanie* or *sotssorevnovanie*) among the workers and enterprises. But by 1937, this policy of labor recruitment faced a crisis: the economy's industrial and construction capacity had yet to catch up with the planned workforce increase. In other words, while the bureaucratic machine focused on fulfilling the planned obligations on employment, the macroeconomic reality was not ready to accommodate additional labor.

Gaidar's third factor relates to the well-recognized concept of "forced savings." Drastically declining consumption levels, mentioned above, resulted due to the economy's predisposition towards capital equipment and machinery production. Heavy industry would continue to characterize the entire socialist economy through the early 1990s at the cost of consumer goods production and repressed consumption levels. By 1938, the crisis of overinvestment emerged, as planned projects were left unfinished, piling up through requirements to meet the plan. Collectively, the above factors would then lead towards lags in industrial projects completion and momentous breaks in the centralized planning system.

The impetus that the Soviet economy received from the initial drastic productive resources reallocation measures towards heavy industry began to fade by the end of the 1930s. It was clear the planned system was dealing with a major supply shock and administrative gears were running overtime to meet the plan targets. The first Five-Year Plan in that respect is indicative: the targets, continuously revised upward following political ambitions, were not to be met. This is when the planning system, under Nikolai Voznesensky, at Gosplan was put through major transformation.

The new Gosplan Director focused on industrial restoration and innovation, as well as administrative quality control and central communication.[4] Much of that capacity was dispersed during the worst years of political purges. Voznesensky emphasized personal involvement and knowledge about major projects to keep a check between reality and the plan target on paper. Finally, he also focused on long-term economic planning and national economic balance—a system that was carried over into the post-war economy of socialist central planning. In the last section of this chapter we discuss in greater detail exactly what this meant. For now, however, the reorganization, unwillingly so, offered a backbone upon which the war economy eventually emerged.

The war economy

World War II is known in the former Soviet Union as the Great Patriotic War. It is dated from the date of Nazi Germany's June 22, 1941 invasion of the USSR through the official war end date of May 9, 1945. To describe the impact of the war as devastating would be to say absolutely nothing about the catastrophic human loss and destruction in the Soviet Union. The first days, weeks, and months of the invasion were the most tragic as the Red Army was in retreat across all major front lines. There is much discussion on statistics, but historians estimate over 25 million people in Soviet losses in combat as more or less accurate. Suffice it to say that practically no family in the USSR was left untouched by the war.

In economic terms, some of the figures found in Voznesensky (1947), that Western experts have relied on, relay the story of the devastation. The productive capacity of the Soviet territory invaded by the Nazi army by November 1941 accounted approximately for between 58 and 63 percent production of steel, aluminum, coal, and pig iron, 40 percent of grain production, 41 percent of the total railway mileage, 32 percent of the factory labor force, and 40 percent of the pre-war population. Over 31,850 industrial enterprises were out of production (though not all were destroyed), corresponding to 80 percent of the industrial capacity of the USSR's European regions.

The human losses were massive, inflicting irreversible demographic pressures on the Soviet economy and society to be felt long after the war had ended. Millions who were not drafted into the army, volunteered to join the combat: women fought alongside men (though male share was far greater). In fact, in the war the Soviet Union was the only nation with all-female combat units. Estimates suggest that anywhere between eight hundred thousand to a million women served in the Red Army. Some, who volunteered for the front early, disguised their femininity by dressing up as men. Aside from what might be traditionally seen as female occupations as military nurses, radio communications specialists, or kitchen staff, the Soviet women also served, in large numbers, as military airplane pilots, snipers, tank operators, and the most fearsome: partisans who wore no uniform.[5]

Following mass scale evacuation, there was a significant population shift to the East in the early months of the war outbreak. Some data indicate that Eastern provinces of the USSR added close to one third of the pre-war population figure, with Kazakhstan seeing a 50 percent increase in its pre-war population (Nove, 1993). A rarely mentioned by-product of the war was also the immediate male deficit in the years after the war.

Those who were not fighting at the front lines were mobilized in a massive scale industrial support effort with stricter disciplinary measures, and restrictions on labor mobility and choice of employment. Dealing with obvious labor shortages (according to some estimates the civilian labor force dropped from 31 million in 1941 to just 18 million in 1942), new labor policy measures were introduced to optimize the effectiveness of the limited resources. Some of these measures included longer working days (up to three hours' increase); additional training; continuous shifts; cancellation of vacation and holiday leave, and so on.

There was another important demographic and social change that would come to shape the character of the socialist economy through to its end by the 1990s. Labor shortages, male deficit, and a desperate need for the workforce to supply the frontlines with new ammunition and all the necessary provisions, led to an immense, long-term increase in women's participation rate in the Soviet labor force.[6] The share of women in the total labor force increased from 39 percent in 1940 to 55 percent by 1945. In rural areas, the figures increased from 52 percent in 1939 to 71 percent by 1943. Despite the rise of women in the labor force and their countless, tremendous heroic contributions on the battlefields of WWII, it is important to note here that, there would be a reversal to traditional gender roles once the war was over, which Pennington (2010) attributes to more historically consistent trends (and, one might say, common at the time in other societies).

In macroeconomic terms, the war caused a drastic decline in aggregate output. On broad scale, Belarus, Ukraine, and the European part of Russia bore the heaviest burden in terms of military and civilian casualties and productive capacity destruction. The industrial planning system was readjusted through the war. Much more attention was now focused on specific, immediate, war-related projects (e.g. commissioning production of new armory, tanks, etc.). This was a step back from the grandiose national plans that characterized the 1930s, though returning after the war, albeit in a new shape. For now, the reduced scope allowed more focused effort to be dedicated to procuring a set number of materials for a limited set of users (about 30,000 materials to be procured to 120 large enterprises).

The State Committee of Defense, a newly formed political and economic state body, maintained tight control over industrial capacity mobilization and production compliance with the needs of the war orders. Ironically, the massive relocation of industrial production within the short period since the outbreak of the war, would later play a critical role in industrialization of Western Siberia and Kazakhstan in the post-war era. New infrastructure, roads, railway communication, electricity, water, and other supplies networks had to be built and rerouted from the USSR's European (Western) regions towards the East. All had to be accomplished within an unimaginably short period of time.

Towards 1943, the Red Army pushed back, regaining some of its lost territory. The drastic mobilization of all capital, human, and infrastructure resources towards the war efforts started to produce positive results. Between 1941 and 1942, the share of the whole defense sector's output from the relocated factories in the eastern regions quadrupled (from 18.5 percent to 76 percent of the country's total). Heavy industry and consumer goods output produced by the relocated factories and new capacity in the Eastern USSR also grew rapidly, while the Western part was devastated by the war (Harrison, 1985).

The evacuation of factories and productive capacities was carried out in emergency mode alongside an immense human crisis of unseen proportions. Survival of each individual factory, which had been haphazardly converted to ammunition production, was instrumental to the combat efforts due to the urgent and immediate need for supplies and military equipment at the front lines. For such reasons, decisions to dismantle and relocate the factory were often made at the very last moment (Box 4.1).

The rest of the economy was guided by an official budget and strict rationing system. The latter affected approximately 61 million urban residents in 1941, rising to close to 77 million by 1944, involving over 400,000 people in the administrative work distributing the rations (Zaleski, 1980). Helping the war effort was expenditure reallocation rising from 11 percent of national income in 1940 all the way up to 44 percent by 1943. This was achieved by diverting resources and budget outlays from consumption and investments, towards the war needs.

Box 4.1

A glimpse of the evacuation process in the first months of WWII on Soviet territory:

The evacuation of Mariupol' was ordered on 5 October [1941], and removal of the remainder of the Azovstal' and the Kuibyshev steelworks and coking plant began the next day, but the Germans entered the town on 8 October, preventing completion of the removal. From the Donbass as a whole between October and December 1941 only seventeen of sixty-four iron and steelworks were successfully evacuated. At one Ukrainian metals store over 200,000 tons of rolled metals, ingots, castings, pipes and alloys were abandoned, a quantity comparable to the entire strategic reserves of 177,000 tons of pig iron or 204,000 tons of rolled steel held at the beginning of 1941 . . .

Source: Harrison (1985, p. 72)

Consumer demand was suppressed by higher taxes (direct and indirect) with new taxes being added. Deficit financing via bond sales was critical in paying for the war effort and keeping the socialist economy intact and consistent with its core principles of central planning. Restrictive wage policies notwithstanding, average income from salaries and military pay in 1945 exceeded the 1940 levels by 2.3 billion rubles (Linz, 1985). Income in the agricultural sector derived from *kolkhoz* market sales increased as well. However, household consumption shares were significantly lower than before the war (falling from 70 percent of national income in 1940 to 57 percent by 1945). At the same time, the defense share increased from 8.5 percent of national income to 19.5 percent for the same period.

To summarize, the Great Patriotic War delivered true calamity to Soviet society and the economy. The basic challenge was, indeed, basic physical survival. At stake were the lives of many more millions, even higher than the staggering estimates of those who perished in the war. Every fabric of Soviet society was repositioned towards reverting the Nazi threat and supporting the war effort. The initial prerogative was to repel and expel the adversary from Soviet territory, and since the battle of Kursk towards strategic advance, liberation of Europe, and ultimate victory.

One might also suggest that WWII was an inhumane challenge to integrity and adaptability of the socialist economic system. The survival of the Soviet socialist state—as a political concept—was at risk many times during the war. In that respect, the system for all practical purposes survived. Behind the survival and ultimate victory, of course, was immense loss of human life and unprecedented selfless dedication of millions.

In more terse terms, it is possible to suggest two phases of the Soviet war economy (as explored in Harrison, 1985): 1) initial shock and emergency measures management aimed at rapid recovery of the capacity lost to the war; and, following the break in the course of the war, 2) expansionary phase exemplified in longer-term planning, maintaining more comprehensive balances, and coordinating the central plan across a multitude of autonomous enterprises. It is in this second phase that the foundation for the USSR recovery and economic achievements of the 1950–1960s eventually evolves. We offer a brief analysis of the post-war recovery in the next section.

Post-war recovery in the USSR

The Soviet Union emerged from World War II devastated, destroyed, and sustaining immense human losses (far greater than any other country), but victorious.[7] At the same time, overcoming immense obstacles, post-World War II economic development was rapid, dramatic, and significant in the gradually expanding Soviet bloc (a subject of our discussion in the next chapter). The widely shared, enthusiastic realization of long fought for victory, victory despite all odds and at any cost, was the backbone upon which the post-war restoration progressed, keeping pundits wondering about the USSR's rapid recovery.

Let's consider some data first. Figure 4.2 shows the evolution of the USSR's gross domestic product during and immediately after the war. Several estimates exist, and the topic of Soviet statistics is highly debated among researchers. Relying on data assembled separately by OECD (2006) and Mark Harrison (1996), we see a devastating decline in the USSR GDP following the immediate impact of the war. Estimates produced by Harrison indicate far more significant decline, close to 35 percent loss in output by 1942 compared to the 1940 pre-war levels.

We can further infer an almost immediate macroeconomic improvement after the war, and OECD's data suggest national output by 1948 reaching the 1940 pre-war levels.[8] Moreover, OECD's data also estimate the GDP per capita for the FSU in 1946 at 89 percent of its 1940 level. By 1947 it reached 99.2 percent, and was 12 percent above the 1940 level by the end of 1948.[9] We turn to some related observations on the Soviet (and EE) economy's growth a bit later.

Figure 4.3 adds to the post-war story with observations from some immediate macroeconomic performance. Again, 1940 is taken here as a base year, with index value set to 100. Given the scale of the war-related destruction, in particular in the European parts of Russia, all of Belarus, and all of Ukraine—the very regions where the majority of the pre-war industry was based—the post-war recovery was impressive.

The obvious problem, however, was the unevenness in this recovery. The difference between heavy and light industry recovery was quite pronounced. This focus on heavy (and primarily defense-related) industry would be the characteristic of the Soviet economic model

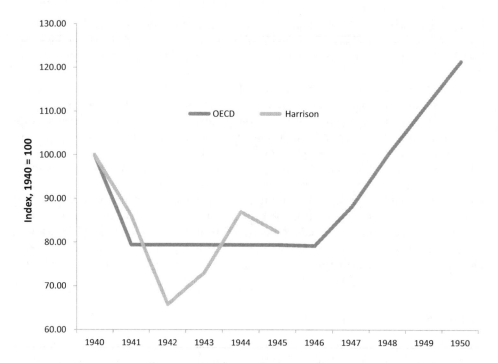

Figure 4.2 Post-war estimated USSR GDP index, 1940 = 100.

Source: estimated based on data from OECD (2006) and Harrison (1996)

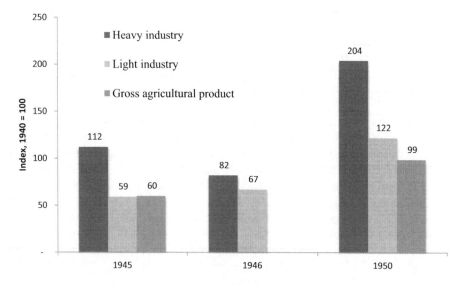

Figure 4.3 Post-war macroeconomic performance in the USSR.

Note: *index with 1940 = 100.

Source: based on data arranged from various sources in Gregory and Stuart (1986)

up until the dissolution of the Soviet Union. The country would stay on the lookout for a major war with its economic foundation ready to adapt from civilian to military production. Clearly, this would lead to a gaping lack of variety and quantity, that is, deficits, of basic consumer goods.

Agricultural production would be lagging, as shares of total investment in the sector would remain low. This also included massive-scale reconstruction of infrastructure, roads, and communications that had been totally devastated by the war. Supporting this was the recovery in the steel and energy sectors and a slower increase in grain production (Figure 4.4).

Importantly, the economic structure erected during the war and that sustained the country's needs throughout those dark years, would be gradually phased out. The State Committee of Defense was dissolved in 1945 and the new (fourth) Five-Year Plan devised with the party back in control. One of the critical milestones in post-war restoration was in late 1947 when the second Soviet monetary reform was carried out. The reform abolished the wartime rationing (stamps) system, moving to a unified price formation.

Some of the technical aspects of the reform included exchange of the old currency for the new in a ten-to-one ratio; any savings up to 3,000 rubles were exchanged at par; any balances between 3,000 and 10,000 rubles on accounts with state banks (*sberkassa*) at a rate of three old rubles for two new rubles, and finally, anything above 10,000 rubles on accounts exchanged at the rate of two old rubles to one new ruble.[10]

Conceptually, aside from dealing with war-caused inflation, the reform fitted well with the politically preferred post-war recovery view. Due to the short time frame of the reform implementation (one week) it was most disadvantageous for peasants with substantial cash holdings. It should also be noted that during the war some market economy elements were tolerated in the agricultural sector, as a political balance between the supply needs of the military front and incentivizing food production beyond the *kolkhoz* framework.[11] Many of the freedoms were reverted in the post-war recovery period, turning back to the original concept of collectivization.

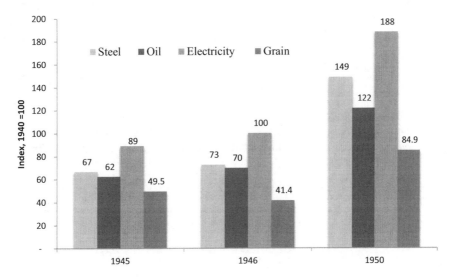

Figure 4.4 Soviet post-war industrial output, select indicators.

Note: *index with 1940 = 100.

Source: based on data arranged from various sources in Gregory and Stuart (1986)

Effectively, the reform was a type of required continuation of the forced savings policy discussed earlier in the context of Soviet industrialization. Only this time around the measures were more explicitly directed at reducing available money in circulation. As a result, spending on consumer products was further repressed and substantial funding was allocated towards heavy industry and defense sector production.

It is important, however, to emphasize not just the technical aspect of the immediate post-war years, but the human element as well. The first few years since the war were characterized by a political consolidation around the Communist party and its current leaders. Individual and collective administrative responsibility (aka discipline measures) and related controls were heightened across the country to enforce conformity and productive effectiveness (Harrison, 2011). Increasingly, people were being judged on their whereabouts during the war, those with combat experience revered and provided for by the state (e.g. higher pensions, preference in employment, housing, etc.). Perhaps most critical, was the shared enthusiasm of victory and working towards a common goal of recovery. The emerging Cold War and political confrontation with the West, only fed into that impulse.

Starting with the 1950s, the political climate had changed to a more open one compared to the prior years. In 1956, Nikita Khrushchev—rising to power following a tumultuous period after Stalin's death in 1953—delivered his famous report "On the Cult of Personality and its Consequences."[12] In his speech, the new Soviet leader denounced Stalin's policies of "political power usurpation". The speech was also the precursor of so-called Khrushchev Thaw—a relative reprieve from policies of forced mobilization in economic and political life.

The data in Table 4.2 suggest the 1950s–late 1960s was a period of strong macroeconomic growth, accounting for the massive post-war restoration effort and capital investments, that was followed by a period of industrial slowdown. The latter would seem consistent with macroeconomic dynamics, as the economy needed to absorb the available capacity, with the next logical step addressing economic diversification (a topic we address in the next chapter).

Khrushchev's attempt to remodel the Soviet plan structure, by replacing the ministries with the regional economic councils (*sovnarkhoz*) was one of the efforts to delegate more autonomy across the vast country. Though the reform did not survive Khrushchev's resignation and ministerial level of control was restored in 1965, the ten-year industrial impact was significant. The USSR advanced in all major industries in chemical, mineral, energy, and metals sectors. Some of the century's top mega-scale projects were carried out during that period, addressing the country's massive industrial and energy needs. Examples may include the Volga-Don Shipping Canal, almost 20 hydroelectric and thermal power plants, numerous industrial plants, and others.

At the same time, facing excruciating food shortages and continuing the earlier marked eastward shift of agriculture, the Soviet Union leadership advanced on an exploration of

Table 4.2 USSR macroeconomic performance, 1951–1965 (average annual growth rates, %)

	1951–1955	*1956–1960*	*1961–1965*
GNP	5.5	5.9	5
Industry	10.2	8.3	6.6
Agriculture	3.5	4.2	2.8
Services	1.9	3.5	4.4
Consumption	4.9	5.7	3.7
Investment	12.4	10.5	7.6

Source: extrapolated from data arranged in Gregory and Stuart (1986)

Virgin Lands and settlement of the vast territories in "non-black-soil" regions of Siberia and northern Kazakhstan. Initially, the project was successful in averting a major food crisis. The land sown during that time increased by 46 million hectares with 41 million, or 90 percent, as part of the Virgin Lands campaign.[13] Later, despite significant capital investment, but due to inadequate technology, inexperienced labor, poor living conditions, and the obvious limitations on crop sizes in inhospitable lands that led to crop variations, the effectiveness of the campaign faded.

On the social dimension, the project involved resettlement of approximately 300,000 young recruits, in addition to thousands of volunteers from students, soldiers, and others (Taubman, 2004). Perhaps as one of the efforts to achieving a balanced ethnic distribution, preemptively subduing nationalistic tendencies, mass resettlements involved volunteer workers of various backgrounds from different regions of the country. Only later, by the mid-1990s, would the country's diverse population mix come under pressure as the massive Soviet edifice disaggregated.

The *Corn Campaign* was launched around the same time. As before, the push was for expansive instead of intensive agricultural methods. But a combination of bad weather and high demand on labor effort (and as a result forgone work on other crops, e.g. hay, wheat) resulted in dropping yields and declining agricultural production within the first ten years. For comparison, in 1954 only 4.3 million hectares were sown to corn but by 1962 that number reached 37 million hectares (Gregory and Stuart, 1986).

An important observation, rarely brought up in literature, is due here. Some of the grand-scale projects in agriculture and industry, mentioned above, involved masses of people who otherwise might have had difficult times finding any work. Consider the post-WWII conditions in the USSR and Eastern Europe. As countries were recovering from the ruins of the war, millions of soldiers of prime working age were returning home to a new world. Pre-war infrastructure and large industrial sectors were wiped out during the war from the European (Western) part of the USSR.

Much of the industrial and scientific capacity was relocated further east as the war broke out, protecting it from the destruction and ensuring uninterrupted munitions and hardware support to the troops. Further, despite an increasingly large share of youth enrolled in the universities, the majority of the population had only basic training that did not guarantee stable employment in the more urban western areas. From a more philosophical point of view, the grand-scale projects may have those manifestations of unity between contradicting tendencies of the economic and social aspects of a historical transformation.

The 1950s–1960s also saw explosive growth in the sciences and academia. The "promotion" came not so much in monetary terms, as in political directives and regulation. We will return to problems of education again later, but some facts are worth mentioning here. One was proliferation of the higher education colleges across the Soviet Union and Eastern Europe. That too became part of the social and new economic order: completing high school a person was either to go to a factory or continue into college or university (with the exception of army draft-age men).

Though the main focus of the massive support for sciences was on engineering and technical disciplines—due to their immediate practical application in the Soviet industrial sector—equally important weight was assigned to social sciences as well, primarily: political economy and philosophy. This was also the time when the Soviets launched the first satellite (Sputnik 1 in 1957); the first man, Yuri Gagarin, orbited the Earth on April 12, 1961, which was followed by the first woman in space, Valentina Tereshkova, orbiting the Earth 48 times in almost three days starting on June 16, 1963.

Another monetary reform was carried out in 1961 with a conversion rate of ten old rubles to one new ruble. The campaign ran for three months and the initial ramifications of it were not clear. The reform was accompanied by a ten-fold reduction in all prices, incomes, taxes, savings deposits, government obligations, and so on. Resetting the ruble's gold parity, the effect was sharp devaluation of the Soviet currency: from 40 kopecks to 90 kopecks per USD1 (Bornstein, 1961). Further, contrary to the effort of keeping real incomes at the same level as before the reform, the effect turned out to be the opposite.

Due to devaluation, imports rose in prices and due to "speculation" the state-owned stores had little to offer to regular customers. In the second case, because the official prices were reduced by ten it was more profitable for the state-owned store managers to sell their inventory to the market (via speculators). As a result, the store managers were able to remit the required proceeds from the sale to the state trade regulator, while pocketing the difference from selling at the higher market price. The shortages in consumer goods and food were back again. At the same time, the revaluation coincided with a rise in Soviet energy exports that brought in hard currency revenue, that would play an instrumental role in the economy going forward.

Theoretically, the system kept a lot of people engaged both in terms of providing work to teachers, administrators, factory workers, and so on, and in terms of keeping the young population in restraint and off the streets. Such was the orderly way of life and people were so accustomed to it that rarely would one see a young, school-age man or woman wandering aimlessly around a city. At the same time, across the USSR and primarily in Russia and Ukraine, the 1960s and early 1970s saw another rise in urbanization, one of the primary indicators of advancing development.

By 1961, according to the official Soviet statistics, the urban population reached the 50 percent mark of the total population.[14] By 1980, almost 62 percent of the entire Soviet population lived in the cities. With the rise in the city population came problems of dealing with higher urban density, sustainability of infrastructure, and simple availability of housing. We will discuss some of these issues in subsequent chapters.

Following the rigid discipline of wartime which continued into the immediate post-war years, Khrushchev's tenure appears as an example of an energetic activist policy in economic development. Leaving no stone unturned, the new policies permeated the industrial, agricultural, and scientific sectors. Compared to wartime (or even the 1930s) the quality of life of ordinary citizens had improved. If not due to the living standards which, though still higher, lacked diversity of consumer goods and entailed dealing with perpetual deficits, it was due to the more tolerant political environment during Khrushchev's Thaw. But the system continued its march with core elements of the socialist planned economy solidifying and, by the 1960s, being transposed onto the economies of Eastern Europe—the subject of our discussion in the next chapter.

More on central planning Soviet-style

The so-called "classical," Soviet-type economy as a complex system of planned activity has its roots in the 1921 establishment of the State Planning Committee (Gosplan). As shown above, the blueprint was reinforced during the industrialization and collectivization programs of the late 1920s and through the 1930s. Transformed during WWII, the Soviet centrally-planned economy prevailed. After WWII, the central plan system was also adopted in socialist Eastern Europe, albeit with major alterations, as we review in Chapters 5 and 6.[15] We will reference this analysis once again in Part III of this book when we will be discussing the transformation of the socialist system into a market-based economy.

Central planning was the key characteristic of the Soviet-style economy. From a bird's-eye view, this implied the existence of a powerful administrative center issuing direct instructions to the economic entities. In this system, subordinate units could at times provide feedback. Often, the debates were made open to the general public in an effort to emulate spirited and earnest discussions of the early 1920s. However, as a rule there was little autonomy in matters of larger-scale economic policy.

This, however, is not to say there was absolutely no self-regulation. Some operational (vs. political) autonomy remained in agriculture, especially in remote regions, involving resolution of smaller issues. Still, the hold of the administrative center over the larger socialist territory was strong, solid, and seemingly unbreakable. For all practical matters, institutionally this was a centralized system with one decision-making entity. Outside of economics, in culture, academia, and other areas, "Moscow's approval" was at the same time the necessary and sufficient condition for action, tantamount to an unprecedented carte blanche for the holder of the approval.

As one can imagine, the system was immense territorially and in terms of population involvement. With the population ranging from 160 million in the late 1930s through close to 300 million by 1991 and of different social background, abilities, skills, and aspirations, the central plan system evolved as a rigid economic mechanism aimed at preserving the fundamental basics of peaceful socialist coexistence. In essence, of course, the system was designed with the aim of economic and political stability and was very limited in its capacity to adapt to new technology and social relations (e.g. Gaidar, 2003 for some of the recent commentary).

The official state effectively owned and managed the means of production, allocating as was deemed necessary resources and productive capital. The government, through its agencies, was actively engaged in the domestic economy and international trade. Ericson (1991) estimates the state's share in total final output production by 1986 to be around 88 percent of the total value (with over 98 percent control of the retail trade).

The structure of the central planning system was purely hierarchical. At the top, there was the Politburo and the Presidium of the Council of Ministers led by the General Secretary of the Communist Party. These top Party entities were in charge of drafting what today one might refer to as the development policy and strategy of the Soviet state.

Further down was the Council of Ministers, itself followed by a number of subordinate entities. Some of the most critical entities within the central planning system (but not limited to) were the following:

- Gosplan (State Planning Committee: established in 1921)—the primary agency tasked to develop, design, and implement central economic planning in the USSR in a continuous sequence of five-year plans, with targets and priorities for industries based on instructions from the political leadership;
- Gossnab (State Committee on Material and Technical Supplies: established in 1948 with precursors dating to 1917)—the key agency tasked to allocate materials and supplies to enterprises;
- Goskomtsen (State Committee on Prices: established in 1958)—the agency that regulated and established prices on industrial, consumer, and agricultural products, effectively preventing market price formation (with the exception of so-called *kolkhoz* markets);
- Gosstroi (State Committee for Construction: established in 1950)—the agency in charge of planning, management, and monitoring of the Soviet construction sector (both civil and defense);

- Gosbank (the State Bank: established in 1921)—the central bank of the USSR;
- Central Statistical Administration (established in 1918)—the central agency in charge of coordinated data gathering and statistical analysis.

Within each of the primary entities (and beyond them) were numerous subordinate agencies, sub-ministries, committees, and so on. On the all-union level, the structure was further replicated at the local hierarchies: republican, regional, *krai, oblast'*, local regions, municipalities. Towards socialist system maturity in Eastern Europe by the late 1980s, similar administrative decisions prevailed in the countries of Eastern Europe as well.

A side note: an informed reader would know, that many of the above-mentioned centralized agencies were either dissolved by 1991 or transformed into their post-socialist heirs depending on the local context of each CEE/FSU member. A traditional corporate pyramid comes to mind, helping to visualize the Soviet administrative system as we attempt to depict it in Figure 4.5. Just like a modern corporation today employs an army of support personnel to run its operations, so it was—one might say—in the socialist system, which also employed a substantial support sector.

Namely, those were the control agencies (e.g. Gossnab, State Arbitrage, Party representatives in every possible area from science to tea and coal production, etc.). The massive state apparatus dominated the economy with real production facilities and real economic activity (in terms of labor market involvement) being considerably smaller than a pyramid-view might suggest. Indeed, the Soviet state employed a considerable amount of effort in "unproductive labor" to borrow a concept from Marx, in ensuring sustainability of the system. Why was that necessary?

The answer is in the core of the planning mechanism in the Soviet-style economy. The three broad categories of plan were: 1) long-term perspective (beyond 15 years); 2) a medium-term plan (that was the Five-Year Plan); and 3) a short-term or annual plan. While initially rigid, towards the mid-1980s the first two categories focused on developing general guidelines of economic development, prioritizing certain sectors, and identifying the necessary input materials for predetermined output. The short-term plan was operational with specific targets and budget coordination.

At the same time, planning was arbitrary, based on a range of goals inspired not by the real economy's potential but largely by political ambitions and directives. A strong push for continued growth was the modus operandi that had transcended since the early industrialization

General
Secretary and
Politburo

Ministries and planning
agencies at the national and
republican levels

Regional planning and administrative
agencies (*obkom, gorkom, rajkom*)

Industrial and agricultural backbone
(local enterprises, *kolkhoz*, etc.)

Figure 4.5 Soviet administrative pyramid.

stages. The operational task for state-employed statisticians and planners was enormous. If, during WWII, the operational task was limited to a few hundred entities due to standardization of defense production and strict rationing system, things were different in the post-war period. Moreover, the earlier years (1930s–1960s) also saw a limited variety of commodities given the strongly pronounced bias towards capital goods production and heavy industry growth.

By the mid-1980s the Soviet Union was producing over 24 million products with tens of millions of various production and processing operations involved (Ericson, 1991). The central plan gave specific instructions regulating production in terms of units for each factory, plant, and enterprise. Research institutes (armies of engineers) received specific instructions on products or production methods to be designed and/or simplified to ensure sustainable mass production.

Box 4.2

It should be clear that this system involved constant communications of the center with the regional entities that were in charge of executing these instructions. Here's a typical example:

> It begins with a series of directives from the highest authorities, outlining goals and tasks. Gosplan interprets these preferences, together with information about past performance and the current state of the economy derived both from the reports of subordinates and the efforts of independent monitoring organizations like Gosbank, Gossnab, Peoples Control, and so on, and produces a set of "control figures" that set targets and priorities. These control figures are elaborated in increasing detail down the administrative hierarchy, eventually becoming specific targets and commands to operational subordinates . . .

Source: Ericson (1991, p. 15)

But the industrial plan directives were based on outdated information (an obvious contradiction between operational and longer-term plan exercises). As a result, local enterprises requested financial and capital assistance from the center, henceforth revealing to the central planners the real situation in the economy. Yet even this would be distorted for the fear of unfavorable representation of the management's work and potential, hence managers losing their jobs.

Requests for extra financial assistance or materials were not automatically granted. In fact, this continuous dearth of intermediate capital goods entering the production process became the true manifestation of the inefficiencies and pitfalls in the existing system. So, the local enterprises were pushed back to rely on their own resources and "fulfilling" the plan. In cases when the situation hit a real roadblock and came to a virtual standstill, those enterprises were salvaged by the state and continued running. More often than not, a power struggle between local factory management and party officials would ensue. Sometimes, the bailout (to use modern terminology) would result in a management turnover, while saving the jobs of non-management personnel.

Two aspects are important here. First, the plan was drafted initially as a five-year plan with the implicit goal that all involved should aim for higher than targeted realization. There were also sub-plans—annual forward outlook—that adjusted slightly depending on the real situation in the economy. The national plan had to be submitted and reconfirmed by the General Secretary, Politburo, and the Presidium of the Council of Ministers. After that it would become a complex set of binding instructions to the involved ministries and entities that in turn had to oversee the plan's fulfillment.

The second important aspect was that the plan was devised in unit measures with a primary focus on tangible goods production, and little regard to the services sector. In other words, for example, there was an explicit minimum requirement of how much poultry and bread a collective farm in a certain region had to produce. The plan then accounted for how and where this produce was to be distributed, lasting a calculated number of days.

Similarly, another example: a heavy industry truck producer (factory A) was to produce 100 trucks in a year. For that it required 400 tires, which were to come from another factory B located miles away (and in fact, often, in a different republic altogether). The parts were expected to reach factory A at a certain time in a certain package, departing from factory B. It is relatively straightforward to continue the analogy by adding factories C, D, E, and so on where other components of a final truck were manufactured. In many ways, this model is not so far-fetched from modern multinational enterprises (MNEs) constituting global value chains (GVC), described in Milberg and Winkler (2013). However, the difference is in the MNEs' profit motive (and as such detached from national origin) supply chain as opposed to the unit-based national economic model of the Soviet socialist system. In the latter case, attachment to the origin of manufacturing was critical in the entire edifice of a fair socialist economy resulting in guaranteed local employment and attempting to limit industrial concentration, as far as was possible, in a particular region.

Perhaps, surprisingly to many, despite the central plan, individual factories routinely had to take proactive measures on their own to ensure economic survival, uninterrupted investment funds flows, and lavish non-waged allocations (e.g. dedicated childcare resources or resort facilities by the Black Sea, etc.). All this required establishing good relations and dealing directly with individual ministries. As such, frequent business trips to the central ministries in Moscow by the top-tier and mid-level managers from the regional factories were common. The ministry had the authority to effectively revise the operational plans, breaking them down to individual enterprise production targets and reallocating investment funds based on discretion and proven connections with the core group of factory decision-makers, usually led by one individual.

As such, the central plan was a complex web of interlinked and interknitted production relations across the entire Soviet geography. Those relations were broad, generic, abstract, and very much personal, often dependent on individual preferences, at the same time. Clearly, this is hardly an example of an economic system that could fit standard macroeconomic modeling under perfect competition assumption. Synchronizing the myriad of supplies with the no less great quantity of needs across various industries and specific factories was an immense undertaking.

And here, one last point on central planning is worth mentioning. There was a seemingly absolute lack of consideration for money. Material balances were expressed in unit volumes in large-scale input–output matrices based on prior years' data (as we mentioned above, often outdated). Prices were centrally determined and changed once every five or ten years. Such inflexibility guaranteed easier control of the massive system, facilitating central price setting.

Since prices were centrally imposed and did not react to typical market changes they did not accurately reflect product scarcities, production inefficiencies, or changes in tastes.

In most cases, regular consumers had no other choice but to buy what was offered at the prices offered. If they did not make the purchase, other consumers in a similar situation might then take the product off the shelves, in other words there were very few substitutes to domestically produced consumer goods. Money played a secondary role in the system and monetary flows were primarily needed for non-state economic interaction. For all practical purposes, the planning system (with producer and consumer physical units plans) seemed more like a well-administered barter economy.

It should now be obvious why the state needed to employ so many highly-skilled individuals in the "system support" areas. By the mid-1980s, the plan and associated operations evolved into complex statistical and econometric exercises that required full-time employment of dedicated resources. The Soviet plan strived to maximize all available capacity, implying pressure in performance faced with limited resources and clear administrative rationing of resources.

With today's hindsight, we may conclude that the system was not just complex and cumbersome but potentially unsustainable in the presence of slow growth and redundant production. Still, the system functioned as it mobilized scarce resources and devoted those to grand-scale projects. Commentators often cite Gerschenkron's (1962) "advantages of backwardness" in support of such transformations in the Soviet system. It is undeniable that impressive industrial capacity was built from scratch and while the rest of the world was trying to pull out of the Great Depression, the Soviet Union reported high growth results and immense advances in natural resources exploration, construction, transportation, metallurgy, and so on.

Clearly, those achievements cannot be enumerated separately from the grander-scale degree of human suffering during the 1930s purges and during WWII. But, even if we attempt to set that, humanitarian, aspect aside and follow an industrial development-focused view, we should also note that the eventual convergence to (and some might argue consequent decoupling from) the advanced capitalist economies condition did not occur on a broad scale and did not necessarily achieve the sufficient levels that would have guaranteed the system's survival. In other words, while it is appropriate to cite Gerschenkron's "backwardness" in application to the Soviet experience, in particular immediately after WWII, there are problems with extending this development story beyond that.

Critical to sustaining post-WWII levels for the Soviet Union as well as for Central and Eastern European economies was their inability to modernize and introduce new technology in their production processes on the large scale achieved by the late 1960s.[16] A technological transformation was apparently needed. Perhaps history might have taken a different path. A similar formidable challenge seemed to have been tackled with greater success by China within the socialist political model.[17] One might ponder the question whether, namely, such a modernization attempt motivated Gorbachev's mid-1980s *perestroika* initiatives.

Moving ahead, it would be safe to say that, at its start, the *perestroika* movement did not aim at abolition of socialism or the planning system in principle. Instead, the aim (just like with the directional purpose of the long-term central plan) was to preserve the existing political system though with an economically critical review and subsequent adaptation to the realities. There was rich intellectual effort spearheading the process. Yet social history, its evolution, and individual contrasting tendencies across national groups and economic entities in the countries of former Soviet dominion played out a different scenario.

Conclusion

To conclude our discussion in this chapter, several observations appear as foundational for the present analysis. First, surviving World War II and coming out of it as the major victorious power, the Soviet Union solidified its political position externally and domestically. At the time, the Great Victory—a testament to the nation's combat heroism—was also the victory of the survival of socialist ideals, reconfirming the resolve of moving forward with centralized economic activity.

The first five years since the war required continued mobilization of human and physical capital resources, as the country (which by now would be more than just Russia proper) was literally rising out of the ruins. For post-war Soviet citizens, dealing with temporary problems of food scarcity or communal apartment sharing with others, due to a dearth of housing units, was little compared to the horrors the people had survived in the war. This strong feeling of national unity and patriotism explained much of the enthusiasm, now, in the post-war reconstruction campaigns.

In that context, Khrushchev's denunciation of the prior epoch was unexpected and shocking. Objectively, it may be argued it was a necessary step to advance a new paradigm of socialist development that at the time involved some regional autonomy and grand-scale infrastructure, industrial, agricultural, and energy projects. Much of what was created at the time still powers the economic structures of the former Soviet satellites.

Following WWII, the central planning system was transplanted, with major adaptations, to the by now socialist economies of Eastern Europe. The Soviet Union, in the meantime, would see a peak of its industrial development through the 1960s. Chapter 5 deals with these topics and introduces the CEE region more directly into our discussion.

Notes

1 From Winston Churchill's First Speech as Prime Minister to House of Commons on May 13, 1940. See full speech here: www.winstonchurchill.org/resources/speeches/1940-the-finest-hour/blood-toil-tears-and-sweat.
2 Estimates based on archival information oscillate around the figure of 1–1.6 million people. See, for example, Rosefielde (2010) and Getty *et al.* (1993).
3 An example of a comprehensive English language study on the topic is that by Conquest (2008).
4 For a dedicated, detailed discussion see Harrison (1985).
5 For indicative examples of insightful discussions on the role of Soviet women in World War II, see Campbell (1993), Petrova (2016), Pennington (2010).
6 Linz (1985) draws attention to this fact early in the English language literature on the impact of WWII on the Soviet Union.
7 We intentionally avoid any superfluous comparisons between the combat contributions and losses of the USSR and those of the Allied Forces in World War II. Such debates do not relate directly or indirectly to the main content of the discussion in this study.
8 Also see discussion and estimates in Davies (1998).
9 Data for Eastern Europe is not readily available. Calculation is based on OECD (2006).
10 For additional details see, e.g. Alexandrov (1949), Nove (1993).
11 It is interesting to note how these early policies would later on lead to the rural areas residents' perception of their role as workers, as opposed to more autonomous farmers or landowners, e.g. Petrick *et al.* (2013).
12 See Khrushchev, N. 1956. Secret Speech Delivered by First Party Secretary at the Twentieth Party Congress of the Communist Party of the Soviet Union, February 25, 1956. Full text in English available: http://legacy.fordham.edu/halsall/mod/1956khrushchev-secret1.html.
13 For early estimates, see Durgin (1962).
14 Data from *SSSR v tsifrakh v 1963 godu* [USSR in numbers in 1963]. 1964. Moscow: Statistika.

15 This section benefits largely from an excellent analytical capture of economic planning in Ericson (1991). Additional references may be: Ellman (1990), Kowalik (1990), Grossman (1990), and Nove (1986).
16 A clear-cut empirical analysis of this argument is found in Vonyo (2017).
17 Comparison to the experience of China can hardly be at par here. The latter benefited from a complex mix of domestic and external conditions, leaving this discussion outside the scope of the present research (e.g. see collection of studies on China's economic evolution in Barandt and Rawski, 2008).

5 From war to wall to common market

The dialectics of the Eastern European socialist economy

> We were behind the 'iron curtain' at last!
>
> Ethel Snowden, *Through Bolshevik Russia*

The new political landscape of Europe

In the immediate aftermath of World War II it became quickly apparent that a new political landscape was in place. On March 5, 1946 at Westminster College in Fulton, Missouri, USA, one of the world's most prominent statesmen, Sir Winston Leonard Spencer-Churchill, former prime minister of the United Kingdom, delivered his fateful speech defining the new post-World War II global order. In Churchill's words "[f]rom Stettin in the Baltic to Trieste in the Adriatic an iron curtain has descended across the Continent."[1] The ramifications of the new geopolitical divide would drive much of the economic and social developments discussed in the remainder of this book.

For the generations to follow, the "iron curtain"—that Ethel Snowden had actually announced already in 1920—seemed to have been cemented in Churchill's worldview.[2] The new contours of great powers' spheres of influence emerged out of the uneasy reality of the post-WWII arrangement among the victorious Allies.

The big political background was changing by the hour in the post-WWII world. Back in 1947, roughly a year after Churchill's remarks, *Foreign Affairs* published "The Sources of Soviet Conduct" by George F. Kennan. The article served as an intellectual backing to the by then evolving "Truman Doctrine"—a policy of containment by the western bloc of the expanding socialist influence (Kennan, 1947). The contradictory aspects of the political mosaic of the time require a dedicated analysis and, hence, are outside the scope of this book.

Briefly, on the ground, following the Potsdam Agreement, Germany was split into two: the East, that stayed in the Soviet control zone (in 1949 forming a German Democratic Republic or East Germany) and the West (later the Federal Republic of Germany or West Germany) that remained within the UK, US, and French, or collectively the Western, control zones.[3] Berlin, despite territorially being wholly within East Germany, was divided into two: East Berlin (in the Soviet zone) and West Berlin (under the UK, US, and French joint control). The infamous Berlin Wall would go up in 1961 (a bit more on this below).

And so, by the late 1940s, Europe (and effectively the world) was divided. The border running between East Germany and West Germany delineated the division. To the east the Soviet Union dominated the socialist bloc, while to the west the alliance of France, UK, and US, dominated by the latter, defined the capitalist model. The bipolar world would prevail and epitomize global politics and economics up until 1991, the year of dissolution of the Soviet Union. Sadly, history would record this as the Cold War period.

Before and around the wall: the political economy of Eastern Europe

The above-mentioned geopolitical divisions had direct effects over the Central and Eastern European (CEE) countries. It is helpful to briefly reflect upon some of the pertinent facts in the context of post-socialist studies. The subsequent shift towards the socialist model was not as automatic as perhaps common stereotype might hold. And much of the "small" country dynamics, as opposed to "big" geopolitical centers' initiative, played an important role at the time.

Preceding modern telecommunication technologies by several decades, political alliances and nations' destinies were settled in a rather short period of time. Initially, driven by the strength and popularity of the domestic anti-Nazi resistance movements, the social order in the CEE countries in the few months immediately after WWII presented a mixed alternative to either strictly capitalist or strictly socialist models. Perhaps contrary to today's layman's view, "prior to 1947 Stalin had no overall blueprint for expansion, nor a single uniform policy to be applied throughout the area," according to the archival work by Geoffrey Swain and Nigel Swain (Swain and Swain, 1993, p. 28).

On the contrary, the period between 1945 and 1948 saw a popular rise in homebred communist movements competing alongside other political parties. Writing in his influential *Central and Eastern Europe, 1944–1993*, Ivan T. Berend (1996), adds to the analysis in Swain and Swain (1993) on the initial reluctance of the Soviet administration to force the so-called "sovietization" of the CEE. Yet, as political events on both sides escalated, by 1949 the CEE countries moved formally within the Soviet domain.

The new world order followed quite a dialectical, though fast-paced, pattern in its evolution. The dissolution of the Austro-Hungarian Empire and the Russian Revolution of 1917, as the new Soviet government annulled czarist treaties on territorial divisions, led to independence across the CEE states initially with rising coalition governments, including communists (for a brief moment in 1919 there was even The Hungarian Soviet Republic). Yet, rather quickly as socio-economic pressures mounted and national elites struggled for political control, self-determination movements produced autocratic regimes across the CEE, persisting through the end of the Second World War. In that narrative, the first Czechoslovak Republic became a notable exception. There, the democratic coalition (of five political parties that became known as *Petka*), led for the most part by the country's first president Tomas Masaryk, endured up until the 1938 occupation by Nazi Germany.

Through WWII across the CEE the rise of the domestic National Fronts, modeled as national–democratic coalitions, rested upon solid grassroots resistance against the Nazi threat. The popularity of the coalitions, primarily led by the socialists, as Berend (1996), Swain and Swain (1993), and numerous other experts attest from extensive archival work, persisted immediately after the war. In turn, such popular support and the democratic nature of initial political engagements acted as critical internal factors for subsequent socialist (as opposed to capitalist) economic and political tilt in the region. Certainly, the Red Army remaining in parts of Europe after 1945 (e.g. in Poland as a bridge into East Germany as well as in Hungary and Romania to link with the military base in Austria) was a strong external factor supporting local communist movements in the background of big country geopolitics. However, no less, if not more, dominant, was the role played by domestic politics in each country in sealing the fate of post-war Eastern Europe.

The many varieties of socialism in Central and Eastern Europe

By 1949, as the West–East geopolitical divisions had become apparent, the Soviet economic, social, and political model began to be transplanted onto Central and Eastern Europe. Again, despite the initial gradualism, things progressed rather quickly, especially where Soviet-backed socialists gained the ultimate majority of votes. In this context, Albania and Yugoslavia appeared as two exceptions to the general flow. The strong authority of the domestic national fronts in choosing the political course characterized both countries. At the same time, while nominally adhering to the broader socialist ideals, Albania and Yugoslavia attempted to establish autonomous ties with Moscow, leading to the eventual "splits" in mutual relations (Swain and Swain, 1993 offer excellent analysis of the relevant circumstances). It is worth providing a brief overview of the Yugoslavian case.[4]

Yugoslavia, led after WWII by Josip Broz Tito—a charismatic statesman, rising out of the resistance movement with unprecedented authority sustaining him at the head of the government up until his death in 1980—rather quickly settled in its own development path.[5] Partially due to such autonomous decisions and partially due to Tito differing from Stalin's vision for the post-war socialist system, the infamous "Tito–Stalin" split erupted.

Box 5.1

Cominform, or the Communist Information Bureau, was the official international political forum for the national communist parties. Established in 1947, the organization solidified the post-World War II geopolitical split. The Soviet Union, clearly, played the dominant role in setting the agenda and direction of the conference. Ironically, it was the Yugoslav communists who expressed strong initial passion for the organization as a political vehicle. Following the Tito–Stalin split, Yugoslavia in 1948 was expelled from *Cominform*. The organization was dissolved in 1956, partially as the Soviet Union, by then led by Nikita Khrushchev, attempted to reconcile with Tito.

In an article based on archival work, Perovic (2007) argued that Tito's own territorial and political ambitions over the Balkans (post-war Albania and Greece) had been the root cause of worsening relations between the two leaders and, effectively, between Yugoslavia and the Soviet Union. In turn, that led to Yugoslavia's economic and political semi-alienation from the Eastern bloc (by 1948 Yugoslavia was expelled from the *Cominform* citing the country's pro-capitalist tendencies; see Box 5.1), while solidifying the *sovietization* of Eastern Europe. That sets Yugoslavia's dynamic as a critical illustration of the deep-rooted differences across the CEE/FSU despite perceived similarities.

Formally, Yugoslavia maintained political neutrality, which in Tito's words suggested "not taking" sides while not implying passivity (e.g. Lees, 2010). The neutrality also meant that, while formally socialist, Yugoslavia maintained its autonomous foreign policy, a "luxury" not enjoyed by the Soviet republics until 1990s independence. As a dividend of such independent policy, foreign visitors to Yugoslavia were allowed to travel freely, while the country's citizens enjoyed the privilege of traveling abroad—something that though nominally possible, was in practical terms rare across the socialist bloc and in the USSR in particular.

Over the years, Tito's administration relaxed some of the other internal controls over society and economy; including a broader religious tolerance. Moreover, dealing with problems of post-war recovery, Tito used his early distancing from the Soviet Union to obtain US financial assistance via the Economic Cooperation Administration (ECA)—the same agency that administered the Marshall Plan for Western Europe.

Despite some direct contacts, Tito maintained Yugoslavia's neutrality principle, avoiding clear-cut alliances with the West or the Soviet bloc.[6] His push for the Non-Aligned Movement, which brought under its banner socialist states across the world, played an important role in challenging the Soviet socialist model globally, on the one hand, and, it might be argued, contributed to political instability in the Eastern Europe states on the other. The Yugoslavian economic model was a distinct alternative to the Soviet framework.

Yet, before one derives a view of Yugoslavia as a bastion of freedom, it is only fair to recall the authoritative and tightly controlling nature of the country's political system. As Ivan T. Berend observes, while Tito was successful in resisting Stalin, and leading, what one might refer to as, the unique, Yugoslav socialist system, much of the country's success and stability relied on three key interlinked foundational blocs. These were: "Tito himself, his communist party, and his federal army" (Berend, 1996; p. 293). Yugoslav federalism, stitched across this multiethnic society, began to dismantle shortly after Tito's death in 1980. And, as both Berend (1996) and Bilandzic (1986) observe, Tito's personality was the strongest pillar in this federative construct.

By the mid-1950s, the rumbles of political discontent began to spread across Eastern Europe. Granville (2004) refers to the Hungarian Uprising (Revolution) of 1956 as "the first domino," as in the first major crisis in the Soviet bloc requiring military intervention and a crucial manifestation of contradiction within the socialist system of the early post-war years. The political crisis, as the early Hungarian leaders adopted a post-war straightjacketed political system emulating repressive Soviet policies of the 1930s, was also inflamed by economic difficulties at the time. Ironically, Khrushchev's Thaw and attempts to liberalize engagement across the socialist states served as fertile background for people questioning the adaptations of the socialist system in the EE societies.

Happening over the course of two weeks, the student uprising in October 1956, quickly spreading across the country, led to a temporary collapse of the pro-Soviet government in Hungary. The new government declared possible withdrawal from the Warsaw Pact (see Box 5.2), which might have been the decisive trigger in changing the Soviet leadership's negotiation tactic: reverting from initial concessions to forceful suppression (see Swain and Swain, 1993 also on Yugoslavia's complex role during the crisis).

From an economic perspective, to some extent, it was the idealized view of the Yugoslav workers' self-management system (discussed in Chapter 6) that partially inspired the protests in Hungary. This would suggest that the ultimate goal of the uprising was a modernized version of socialism, consistent with the humanitarian ideals, as opposed to an existent set of ideological constraints. However, in the end, perhaps as a reaction to the forceful response from Moscow, a politically anti-socialist (and by implication, anti-Soviet) sentiment became pronounced.

Box 5.2

The *Warsaw Pact* or the *Treaty of Friendship, Co-operation, and Mutual Assistance* (WP) was signed on May 14, 1955 in Warsaw, Poland by Albania, Bulgaria, Czechoslovakia, the German Democratic Republic, Hungary, Poland, Romania, and the USSR. The agreement, triggered by West Germany's accession into NATO, implied military cooperation among the member states. It may also be argued that the WP was a military extension to the COMECON agreement among the socialist states (see

Box 5.3). The rationale behind the WP was to maintain common defense capability across the socialist states. Clearly, the Soviet Union played an overwhelmingly dominant role in the agreement. It is not surprising then that the Warsaw Pact was dissolved on July 1, 1991 as the independence movements across the EE/FSU gained momentum. The emergence of the Warsaw Pact, as a counterweight to NATO and the West, solidified the bipolar world of Cold War geopolitics. The dissolution of the WP, at the time, proclaimed a new era of hope for global cooperation and sustained peace.

Sources: Crump, L. 2015. *The Warsaw Pact Reconsidered: International Relations in Eastern Europe, 1955–1969.* Oxford: Routledge; United Nations. 1955. *Copy of the Treaty of Friendship, Co-operation, and Mutual Assistance.* UN Treaty Series, No 2962. Available online: https://treaties.un.org/doc/Publication/UNTS/Volume%20219/volume-219-I-2962-Other.pdf.

A parallel between the tragic events in Hungary and the protest of a few months before in the same year in Poznan, Poland is inescapable. In Poland, although on a significantly smaller scale than in Hungary, workers at one of Poznan's factories protested against poor working conditions and requirements for higher productivity without adequate pay increase. Following some period of negotiations, the army forcefully subdued the riot, albeit with significantly lower casualties than in Hungary. It is important also to point out that squeezed between the USSR and East Germany (the latter yet with unclear destiny of its own at the time) the Polish leadership attempted gradual reformation of the socialist system as opposed to outright protest. Such stance would eventually work out as a stronger starting foundation ahead of the 1990s economic reforms.

Overall, the Poznan events and the Hungarian Revolution of 1956 had put in motion the social and political wheels that eventually produced tangible deviations from the economic and political system characteristic of the Soviet model in Eastern Europe. A long-term result was that much of Eastern Europe achieved some relative (to the FSU) freedoms and concessions in macroeconomic policy. The Warsaw Pact acted as a control mechanism against any cardinal political dissent from the socialist path, as such preserving the post-war geopolitical status quo.

Yet, socialist Europe would not remain the same: some now aspired for greater individualism in foreign policy (e.g. Romania and, clearly, Yugoslavia), others set course on economic reforms under a tight political umbrella (e.g. Hungary and Poland), still others either maintained or reinforced their firm political control and top-down management (e.g. Bulgaria, Czechoslovakia, and East Germany).

East Germany

In such context, East Germany followed the third scenario, masterfully utilizing its position as a small, yet crucial, ally to the Soviet Union. As Harrison (2003) observes in *Driving the Soviets up the Wall*, Walter Ulbricht—the General Secretary of the Socialist Unity Party of Germany commanding the executive power in the country at the time—was the key political figure resisting the Soviet government's proposals for moderate domestic and foreign policy reforms. In fact, as the events of 1956 unfolded first in Poland and then in Hungary, Ulbricht remained silent, bearing the course of a socialist hardliner and discouraging his more open-minded opponents' attempts at liberalization. Similar restraint and estrangement evolved in relations with the West and West Germany (Federal Republic of Germany or FRG). And here we arrive at what appears to be a historical conundrum.

The popular view would have us believe that the impediment to early reunification between East and West Germany was Soviet domination and the Warsaw Pact obligations. Though existence of both is undisputable, archival records (first unveiled to researchers in the early 1990s), add a new twist to an established interpretation. The arguments laid out by Steininger (1990) and Walko (2002), writing separately about a decade apart from each other, on the *Stalin Note* and East German politics, are informative.

The *Stalin Note* was a formal proposal presented by the USSR to the Western allied powers in March of 1952, advocating reunification and neutralization of Germany. This might seem quite at odds with the infamously established superpower dynamic narrative. However, in fact, the original note had a series of follow-ups in the same year. Picking up the relay after Stalin's death and emerging out of internal political strife, Khrushchev then pushed forward with his efforts to pacify the Cold War disagreements, arguing for the possibility of peaceful coexistence and tolerating alternative approaches to socialism. Despite the seeming goodwill and amicable intentions, neither the original *Stalin's Note* nor the later-declared Khrushchev's efforts succeeded: the West (the allied coalition and the FRG) rejected the proposals.

As might be expected, interpretations have varied. For example, Steininger (1990) suggests that the ultimate rejection of the *Stalin's Note* was an opportunity lost to patch up relations between the West and the Soviet Union.[7] Walko (2002), on the contrary, questions Stalin's sincerity, implying foul play by the Soviets. The East and West rapprochement at the time did not take place. Clearly, the topic calls for more detailed reading and research to which the reader is invited to follow up on the sources herewith.

Bringing new archival evidence to the debate, Harrison (2003) advances a possible reasonable explanation for the failure of the early German unification attempts. As has been observed above, the Soviet policy towards GDR was anything but clear-cut absorption within the socialist system. Yet, the small country *realpolitik*, as leaders from Yugoslovia's Tito, Poland's Gomulka, to GDR's Ulbricht, and elsewhere held on to their powers and voting rights in the collective socialist project, may have been the decisive, and veiled, phenomenon. As such, Harrison argues, in the spirit of solidarity and assuming greater responsibility for the stated socialist ideals, the Soviet Union had to often enact second choice, at best, policies demanded by its smaller EE allies.[8]

On the flip side, Konrad Adenauer, West Germany's charismatic Chancellor at the time, perceived the Soviet move (i.e. the *Stalin's Note*) to be aggressive. Adenauer's priority in office was to establish strong ties with the West, fortifying the FRG first within the global capitalist economy, before considering a possible reconciliation with East Germany. Back then, West German skepticism was fueled by distrust in the possibility of effective reconciliation with its East brethren while the overall socialist system still persisted.

To sum up, four critical factors played against the idea of German unification in the mid-to late 1950s. The first, undeniably, was the mutual distrust as the political, economic, military, and cultural gap between the Soviet Union and its Western allies widened. The second factor was the small ally dependency speculation role played by, most notably, East Germany against the Soviet Union. With softer Khrushchev in power, Ulbricht was relentless in his opposition to concessions to the West or liberalization. The third, was a similar scenario played out by West Germany against its allies. And finally, the fourth factor was the influence exerted by strong China's stance on Khrushchev's government to adopt a hardline approach for the common socialist cause and in opposition to the capitalist model, as the 1950s Sino-Soviet rift was worsening.

The Berlin Wall

If the above narrative might read as a perplexing web of international politics, it is because it was precisely such. Adding insult to injury, Berlin's dual status—where socialism met capitalism—was quickly discovered by East Germans and other Eastern Europeans. Thousands of people crossed from East into West Berlin (and recall that for a long period of time it was common to see workers living in the East section and commuting by public transportation to the West for work) as a gateway to ultimate immigration to the western countries.

Considering that many of the events described above were happening almost simultaneously, with the socialist bloc's cohesion and security questions on the line, and Ulbricht's continuous pressure for East Germany's effective seclusion, the Soviet leadership decided to approve the construction of the infamous Berlin Wall. Despite the multitude of factors involved and despite the Soviet's opposition to the entire idea, the preferences and political manipulation of East Germany's leadership prevailed. To borrow and paraphrase from Harrison (2003), the Soviets were finally driven up the wall.

Construction of the wall began in August 1961 and modifications were added through the years up until eventual demolition in 1989.[9] The world would never be the same again from the moment the wall went up.[10] The wall became the symbol of two competing social orders: capitalism and socialism, each mutually exclusive.

As is often the case with symbols, the Berlin Wall made a profound and lasting impression on nations across the world. For Western culture and those in capitalist economies, the Wall became a sign of "oppression of freedom," while for the socialist bloc in the EE/FSU, and scattered sympathizers across the world, it was the first defense against encroachments of the "immoral" and "exploitative" capitalist system. Sadly, the Berlin Wall became also a symbol and a herald, at least to some extent, of reversal of the liberalization process across the EE/FSU that many expected to continue following Khrushchev's Thaw.

Politically, the subsequent tightening of social freedoms (e.g. East Germany and Romania) or reactionary views as social development outpaced economic foundations (e.g. Czechoslovakia and Poland) led to the tragic events of 1968 in Prague. In turn, that marked the rise of a new, more informed reformist movement, with Poland's *Solidarność* at the forefront. From a political economy perspective, the significant aspect of the popular uprisings in Poland and Hungary in 1956, Prague in 1968, and later across socialist Europe, was their definitive influence on the structure of the socialist economy and shaping of economic relations in the respective countries.[11] Let's move on to the economics of CEE's post-WWII integration within the socialist bloc.

Socialist economics in Eastern Europe immediately after WWII

WWII left Eastern European economies in ruins: the devastation was disproportionately greater than in Western Europe. At the same time, the destruction was comparatively less than it was in the eastern parts of the USSR (Belarus, Moldova, Russia, and Ukraine, to be specific). It is estimated that the CEE's GDP losses accounted for anywhere between 25 percent (Czechoslovakia) and up to 50 percent (Poland and Yugoslavia) relative to the pre-war period. In such circumstances, for the Soviet socialist model to win East European hearts, not by force but by manifesting the system's declared humanitarian superiority, a robust economic recovery plan was much needed.

It should come then as no surprise that the Soviet model of the late 1920s–1930s was introduced in Eastern Europe. The Marshall Plan was out of the question as per, already addressed, political preferences, though Czechoslovakia flirted with the idea in July of 1947 and we have already mentioned Yugoslavia's attempts to gain Western assistance (for discussion see Swain and Swain, 1993, Chapter 5 in particular). By the early 1950s, with the Soviet-type Five-Year Plans initiated, the EE as a group achieved its pre-war output levels. In fact, with minor exceptions, the majority of the countries outpaced national income levels on macro and per capita scales (see Table 5.1).

It may by now be self-evident that the Soviet-styled recovery was characterized by three key elements:

- nationalization of private assets;
- agricultural reform; and
- rapid industrialization (with emphasis on heavy industry).

The agricultural reform was modeled on the Soviet *kolkhoz* experience. The duality of EE collectivization transpired through peasants' staunch opposition to the reform, on the one hand, and the socialist planners' attempt at a careful balancing act, slowly winning the popular mood, on the other. Compared to the reform in the USSR, agricultural collectivization in the EE took a slow turn. In many cases, the percentage of collectivized agricultural land would not reach the 50 percent mark until 1957 (e.g. Czechoslovakia). In some cases, agricultural land was predominantly privately owned (e.g. Poland or Yugoslavia).[12]

Still, with the exception of Czechoslovakia and parts of East Germany, the majority of the EE countries were largely agricultural at the time. Seen as more progressive, creating value in Marxian terms, the industrialization of each country became a top policy priority. As students of economic development learn from other examples, for example in Latin America, industrialization, in its ideal form, should contribute to an economy's growing self-sustainability. From that perspective, the progress achieved in a short period of time in the EE, given the challenges of post-war recovery and lacking a significant industrial base, was quite impressive:

> the heritage of productive capacity created during the war, shifts in territory, the composition of reparations deliveries, the high demand for producers' goods for reconstruction, and the momentum being gained for rapid industrialization towards the end of the period resulted in faster growth for means of production . . . than for industrial consumer's goods.
>
> (Brus, 1986a, p. 627)

Table 5.1 National income compared to pre-war index (1938 = 100)

	Total		
	1948	*1949*	*1949 per capita*
Bulgaria*	107.5	122	108
Czechoslovakia**	98	113	138
Hungary	85	116.5	115
Poland	105.5	118.5	166
Romania	70	90	88

Source: adapted from Table 22.15 in Brus (1986a)

Note: *, ** pre-war years 1939 and 1937, respectively.

Table 5.2 reflects the relative effects of the recovery efforts in both industrial and agricultural sectors by country. The industrial gains were obvious. Agriculture was seen as a necessary sector supporting industrial growth, consistent with the earlier Soviet industrialization model. The initial gains, reflected in Table 5.2, set the stage for even stronger growth through the early 1950s.

Zauberman (1964) estimated EE's share of gross capital formation to gross national product (service-sector inclusive) to reach record levels (e.g. 44 percent for Czechoslovakia and close to 50 percent for Poland in 1953). By the 1960s as Kornai (1992) reports, the EE averaged 35 percent ratio of gross investment to GNP as opposed to 25 percent in Western Europe. These figures were unprecedented for Central and Eastern Europe at the time.

Much of the dedicated investment, as during the immediate post-war years, continued to be directed into industry (with clear emphasis on heavy vs. light industry). According to the data assembled by Brus (1986b) and represented here in Figure 5.1, the average share of investment in agriculture at 13 percent of the total capital formation was drastically below the 46 percent

Table 5.2 Industrial and agricultural production index in Eastern Europe (pre-war = 100)

	Industrial		Agricultural	
	Pre-war year	*1949*	*Pre-war year*	*1949*
Albania	1938	415	1937–1938	113–119
Bulgaria	1938	227–248	1934–1938	87–96
Czechoslovakia	1937	112–127	1934–1938	80–88
Hungary	1938	137–154	1934–1938	85–94
Poland	1938	148–177	1934–1938	77–97
Romania	1938	114–117	1934–1938	86–96
Yugoslavia	1938	167–287	1934–1938	88–93

Note: *, * *pre-war years 1939 and 1937, respectively.

Source: adapted from Tables 22.16 and 22.17 in Brus (1986a)

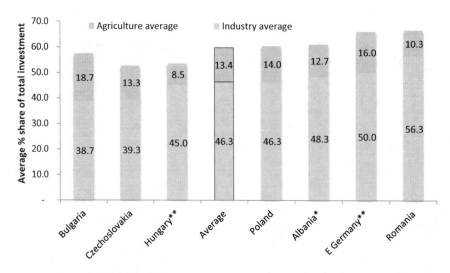

Figure 5.1 Average shares of total investment by two primary sectors in socialist Europe, 1953–1956.

Notes: ranked by shares of industrial investment; *data for 1953 are from 1950; **no 1956 agricultural data.

Source: adapted from Table 24.2 in Brus (1986b)

going towards the industrial sector. The above trends continued through the 1960s, with even the least developed economies of Southern Eastern Europe rapidly expanding their industrial output.

The usual disclaimer warning on veracity of statistical data applies. A careful reader would have noticed by now that in a preemptive effort to satisfy a critic's curiosity and limit speculation about reporting inadequacies, we have, so far, relied mostly on generally recognized literature for our data needs. And while specific data points may certainly be different depending on the choice of primary source, profound directional shifts in national economies were clearly visible across Central and Eastern Europe immediately after WWII.

The post-WWII economic upturn in the CEE was unprecedented for the region in any period prior to that. At the same time, the form and nature of the instituted program, when contrasted with similar efforts during the 1930s in the USSR, were somewhat smoother. Importantly, the industrialization of Eastern Europe was characterized by greater relative tolerance of diversity in national economic models compared to the Soviet uniform experience. Of course, the CEE's economic model autonomy was valid only to a certain degree: strict control over the sequence and general focus of the industrialization process was maintained by the presiding elites in each EE country.

By the 1960s, the CEE factory managers gradually adopted the operational mode of their Soviet peers: pushing for lower plan targets while simultaneously raising purchase quotas for incoming raw materials. However, the complexity of the system's administration, more challenging with factories' geographical distance from the planning center, did not permit for flexible, efficient optimization. The system relied on the quality of information on factory needs transmitted by the managers.

Even with daily updates (though monthly, quarterly, and annual reporting was more prevalent) the central system's micromanagement techniques had limited success. Efficient managers were not exactly favored, but those focused on expanded production were supported by the planning center. As in the USSR, the focus of the CEE planned system, was on expansive industrial production. As such, factories competed for resources, in a system that Kornai (1979a, b) described as resource-constrained. Here factories operated with a soft budget constraint, which implied a bail-out by the center in case of insolvency.[13]

A model of the common market

Stitching together the newly emerging socialist economic bloc of the USSR and Central and Eastern Europe was the Council for Mutual Economic Assistance (CMEA or COMECON; see Box 5.3 for definition), a post-WWII political and economic organization established in 1949. Ideological aspects aside, over time the CMEA served a practical purpose in the broader socialist economic construct, which included non-European members as well.

The mechanics of the CMEA

Nominally aimed at providing economic assistance and by derivation promoting regional integration within the socialist market, the CMEA gained its greater operational capacity during Khrushchev's tenure in office. The early patterns of intra-socialist bloc trade resembled a comparative advantage-like exchange. In this fragile balance the USSR mainly exported raw materials of all types (crude oil, coal, iron ore, cotton, agricultural products, etc.) in exchange for the higher-quality CEE's machinery, steel products, and consumer goods, primarily from Czechoslovakia, GDR, Hungary, and Poland. From Bulgaria and Romania, the USSR imported agricultural products in exchange for machinery, equipment, and energy exports. Cut off from trade in high-technology products with the West, due to the trade embargo imposed by the latter, the CEE leveraged this socialist market to advance individual countries' industrial development.[14]

In terms of integration, according to Zwass (1989), the total share of CMEA trade in CEE's exports reached up to 61.4 percent as of 1950, with individual shares ranging between 54.1 percent for Czechoslovakia and 91.8 percent for Bulgaria. These shares would stay relatively stable up until the dissolution of the CMEA, with non-European members being the most dependent on intra-bloc exchange. For Cuba and Mongolia, trade with the CMEA accounted for up to 86.1 percent and 94.4 percent of exports and 80.7 and 97.5 percent of imports, respectively.[15]

The CEE countries' national development models counterbalanced the evolving international socialist economic system. While more advanced Czechoslovakia, Hungary, or GDR, saw CMEA as an opportunity to strengthen their industrial and technological advantage, specializing in capital-intensive production, the weaker Bulgaria and Romania pushed for greater autonomy. The latter two objected to the comparative advantage dictated status of raw materials suppliers, emphasizing investment in heavy industry development. Often such economic disputes led to political contradictions within the CMEA and a search for capital investments from other sources (e.g. Romania's loans from the International Monetary Fund and the country's push for and eventual success in building the Galati steel-mill).

Box 5.3

CMEA (also *Comecon*) or The Council for Mutual Economic Assistance was an economic organization of socialist states led by the Soviet Union. Established on January 18, 1949 the CMEA was a response to the integration movements in Western Europe and a socialist alternative to what eventually had become the European Economic Community and the Organization for Economic Cooperation and Development (OECD), early predecessors of today's European Union. The CMEA's declared goal was economic cooperation, development, and integration in the socialist economic space. The CMEA's founding members (Bulgaria, Czechoslovakia, Hungary, Poland, Romania, and the USSR) were later joined by others (Albania, Cuba, GDR, Mongolia, Vietnam) and observers (Afghanistan, Angola, Ethiopia, Finland, Iraq, Laos, Mexico, Mozambique, Nicaragua, North Korea, South Yemen); Yugoslavia maintained an associate status. The status differentiation impacted the degree of integration of an individual member country with the common socialist market. Comecon was dissolved in 1991 as the European socialist bloc disintegrated.

Sources: Encyclopedia Britannica. *Comecon*. Online: www.britannica.com/topic/Comecon; Zwass, A. 1989. *The Council for Mutual Economic Assistance: The Thorny Path from Political to Economic Integration.* Armonk, NY: M.E. Sharpe.

Effectively, the CMEA's nominal political interdependence was offset by individual policies for economic self-sustainability and independence, resulting in bilateral (as opposed to integrated) trade. Among individual countries, there was neither an integrated common plan nor the means to enforce economic compliance on such a large, politically diverse scale. Further, Zwass (1989) notes that bilateralism was a transitory phenomenon in post-WWII Western Europe, preceding broader integration. However, in the East it evolved in a more

Table 5.3 Individual country shares in overall CMEA trade, %

	1970	1975	1980	1985
Bulgaria	6.3%	6.0%	5.9%	6.7%
Czechoslovakia	12.2%	9.7%	9.0%	9.3%
Cuba		4.3%	3.4%	3.9%
GDR	15.4%	12.7%	11.5%	12.0%
Hungary	7.8%	6.9%	9.3%	9.6%
Mongolia	0.3%	0.3%	0.3%	0.4%
Poland	11.7%	13.5%	11.1%	8.9%
Romania	6.2%	6.3%	7.4%	5.1%
USSR	40.1%	40.3%	42.1%	44.1%

Source: author's calculations based on data from *Statistical Yearbook of the CMEA 1986*

permanent mode with intra-industry trade dominating much of the later years' exchange, with the exception of some specialized monopolies (e.g. Hungary in production of buses or Czechoslovakia in electric trams). Political aspects aside, the economic reason for CMEA bilateralism may have also been due to the non-convertibility of the national currencies and subsequent initial technical impediments to the CEE's access to Western markets, lacking as it did a foreign exchange (e.g. Eichengreen, 2008 for more background).

In fact, trade with the developed Western economies barely averaged 25 percent of the total volume for the CEE and USSR combined, even in 1985, long after surpassing initial developmental challenges. Within the group, Hungary had the largest share (34%) of trade volume with the West, with Bulgaria having the smallest (12%).[16] Evidently, the CMEA provided a guaranteed source of consumer and industrial demand for exports with relatively unchanged individual country shares in the overall exchange (e.g. Table 5.3), explaining the high intra-council trade volume shares. Combined, the Soviet Union, GDR, Poland, and Czechoslovakia accounted for 75.2 percent of the overall CMEA exchange between 1970 and 1985.

Prices and the subsidy debate

In such an environment, the "transferrable ruble" was established as the unit of account and official settlement currency within the bloc. The conversion rate to Western currencies was approximated to the Soviet ruble. The International Bank for Economic Cooperation (IBEC), established in 1963, coordinated a payment system among the country members.[17] This was necessary as trade in hard currency within the CMEA was minimal. The result was a phenomenon of balanced trade, by which what really mattered was a country's overall trade balance as opposed to a bilateral deficit. The latter would be adjusted by shifting future targets on hard (high in demand) and soft (low in demand) goods. Achieving trade balance was pivotal since bilateral trade was derived as part of each country's national economic plan integrated under the CMEA umbrella.

Prices in the CMEA, negotiated at mutual meetings, were determined on the basis of five-year averages of world prices. In practice, the price-setting mechanism benefited producers of capital-intensive goods (consumer products, machinery) and pushed down the terms of trade of raw materials exporters. As a result, the terms of trade of the Soviet Union, due to a large share of energy and raw materials exports, dropped by nearly 20 percent between 1958 and 1970, according to Hewett (1974).

On the latter point, in their seminal study Marrese and Vanous (1983) found that the USSR was providing an effective subsidy to the CEE by underpricing energy exports relative to potential gains in the Western markets, in particular after the 1970s oil shocks. According to these studies, the policy amounted to Soviet exports (i.e., crude oil) being priced at a hefty discount vis-à-vis machinery imports from CEE. The discount was greater than the structurally similar exchange in the Western markets (even with correction for the lower quality of CEE's export output) would suggest.

Once empirically verified, a "subsidy debate" ensued in the Western academic literature (e.g. Brada, 1988; or Desai, 1986). It seemed puzzling why the USSR, a political and economic power in the region, agreed to such pricing to its own detriment. The typical argument at the time saw hardly any economic rationale (especially given higher oil prices in the global markets through the 1970s) in such a policy. Furthermore, as a result of the earlier mentioned push for industrialization and self-sustainability among the smaller CEE economies, the CMEA market was saturated with similar manufactured goods exports of various types. That should have brought relative prices down. And the USSR effectively maintained a monopoly on energy and other raw materials within the European socialist economic bloc (excluding Romania, which followed the USSR in per capita crude oil production; see Table 5.4).

Moreover, the energy subsidy (to give a phenomenon a name) was not distributed evenly. Czechoslovakia and GDR received the greatest concessions, followed by Bulgaria, Hungary, Poland, and then Romania. Clearly, political economy considerations here superseded the actual trade flows.

Brada (1988) details some scenarios explaining the generous subsidies, as the least trusted ally (e.g. autonomy-minded Romania) received the least. At the same time, the CMEA provided a sense of security and guaranteed market, and hence some economic and social stability for the CEE's national political elites while Western economies, though growing, experienced typical business cycle bouts. Taken together, cheap raw materials and guaranteed demand for domestic output, provided a strong explicit economic incentive to the CEE's industrial producers and individual national plans.

The system was structurally fragile, growing in its complexity of overlapping national plans, lacking transparency in intra-bloc trade, and burdened by the individualistic development preferences of its members. By 1991, the CMEA disintegration became equally politically motivated just as its creation had been in 1949. And still, the collapse of the CMEA status quo was as abrupt as the collapse of the Soviet Union and socialist system all together. The entire hierarchy of national political leadership lost its economic backbone, yielding control to new political and economic forces.

Table 5.4 Crude oil production by country as a share of total CMEA production, %

	1970	1975	1980	1981	1982	1983	1984	1985
Czechoslovakia	0.6%	0.3%	0.2%	0.2%	0.2%	0.2%	0.2%	0.3%
Cuba	0.8%	0.9%	0.9%	0.9%	1.8%	2.5%	2.6%	3.0%
Hungary	8.0%	6.7%	6.3%	6.2%	6.2%	6.1%	6.2%	6.5%
Poland	0.6%	0.6%	0.3%	0.3%	0.2%	0.2%	0.2%	0.2%
Romania	28.1%	24.1%	17.1%	17.2%	17.1%	16.9%	16.8%	16.2%
USSR	61.9%	67.5%	75.1%	75.2%	74.4%	74.2%	74.0%	73.8%

Note: data from Table 40, p. 112, per capita production.

Source: author's calculations based on data from *Statistical Yearbook of the CMEA 1986*

With discussions on the effectiveness of the council ongoing, the CMEA offers an insightful example of politically motivated regional economic integration with one important caveat. The industrial foundation forged in the countries of Central and Eastern Europe over the post-WWII period through 1991 would come to help them through the 1990s transition ensuring smoother, relative to the USSR, transformational shocks and paving the way to economic integration with yet another, bigger, regional project of the European Union.

Crisis in disguise?

Outside of the CMEA, and broader global socialist realm, the Soviet Union maintained trade connections with capitalist economies and developing countries (see Table 5.5). As the countries of the CEE developed stronger contacts with Western counterparts, the share of CMEA trade for the Soviet Union gradually declined. For the USSR, the 1990 total trade turnover in this category dropped 10.9 percent from its 1989 level, by official estimates, due to declining global prices on energy and food, and declining volumes of exports.

At the same time, and as clearly visible in Table 5.5, the Soviet Union expanded its trade with the rest of the world. Among the capitalist countries, the Soviet Union traded the most with (unified) Germany, Italy, Japan, and then the UK and the USA. Energy resources and military equipment drove much of the Soviet exports. Imports were heavily weighted towards agricultural products (approximately one third) and deliveries of machinery, equipment, and industrial technology.

Expanding trade with developing countries, starting with the late 1960s and early 1970s, might be seen as a form of economic compensation sought by the Soviet economy as the most developed members of the CMEA increasingly pushed for economic breaks with the socialist market (e.g. see next chapter's discussion on market socialism and economic autonomy in Hungary and Yugoslavia). Here, Soviet trade with India (rivaling China) would play a leading role (averaging about 2.0 percent of Soviet total foreign trade share) up until the late 1980s. However, in addition to physical trade exchange, there also was another dimension to the dichotomies of the socialist economic exchange: financial.

By the mid-1970s, the model of expansive industrial growth resulted in limited improvements to the living standards of an average citizen. Instead, industrial production was largely for industry's own consumption with equally limited contributions from the CMEA exchange. Consumer products were missing, shortages were common and intensified by the late 1970s–early 1980s.

Table 5.5 Soviet foreign trade by country groups (% of total exports and imports)

	1950	*1960*	*1970*	*1975*	*1980*	*1985*	*1990*
Socialist countries	81.1	73.2	65.2	56.3	53.7	61.2	50.4
of which with CMEA	57.4	53.1	55.6	51.8	48.6	55.0	43.8
Industrial capitalist countries	15.0	19.0	21.3	31.3	33.6	26.7	38.0
Developing countries	3.9	7.8	13.5	12.4	12.7	12.1	11.6

Notes: data on socialist countries includes China, Cuba, North Korea, Vietnam, and Yugoslavia. Data for 1990 excludes GDR from the CMEA post-German reunification, and includes with West Germany in the industrial capitalist countries group.

Sources: author's calculations based on official Soviet foreign trade statistical publications, *Foreign Trade of the USSR for 1922–1981*; *Foreign Trade of the USSR in 1986*; and *Foreign Economic Relations of the USSR in 1990* (Foreign Trade Statistics 1982, 1987, 1991)

For many Central and Eastern European CMEA members, advancing industrial modernization by way of technology imports from the West was perceived as the next optimal policy
step. Unable to pay for those imports with non-convertible national currencies, the CEEs
stocked up increasing foreign debt obligations, as exports did not provide for sufficient compensation leverage for imports. Much of the financing came from Western European commercial banks, with early estimates reporting up to $40 billion of CMEA debt in 1976 to the
West (Weintraub, 1977). Yet, the effort built on reliance on cheap Soviet energy imports as
backbone and the CMEA as the primary market for their output, turned out largely unsuccessful. By the late 1970s, the early signs of the CEE's exacerbating debt situation became
visible to the outside world.

With limited immediate revenue growth from new modernization projects and bouncing
off stagnant Soviet economy, by the 1980s Hungary, Poland, Romania, and Yugoslavia (the
most prominent cases) had to turn to the West (i.e. the IMF, Paris Club, and the BIS) for help
with their foreign debt repayments. The price of the problem was staggering for its time,
context, and complexity.

Poland owed $25 billion in external debt at the end of 1980 to Western governments and
over 500 foreign commercial banks. At the same time, Romania owed $300 million to the
International Monetary Fund, with $1 billion owed to foreign banks by late 1981 and rising.
In Romania, debt repayment was achieved by reduction in domestic consumption. That debt
was repaid in 1989, a short time before popular revolts and the execution of Nicolae Ceaus-
escu, a long-serving General Secretary of the Romanian Communist Party. Hungary—"the
crown jewel of the CMEA"—owed $10 billion in foreign debt that was largely short-term.
Yugoslavia borrowed heavily from the IMF with debt obligations reaching the $20 billion
mark by late 1982.[18]

Those early bailouts of Eastern European governments would become the prelude, as
the IMF report qualifies them, to the larger debt crisis in Latin America (Boughton, 2001).
Debt service accounted for anywhere between 40 to 70 percent of foreign currency earnings
in Hungary and Poland (Berend, 2009). Notably, for much of the Soviet period the USSR
remained a structural creditor to the CMEA group, for example coming to Poland's rescue
with hard currency enabling the latter to keep up with its repayment to foreign lenders but
in exchange having larger shares of Poland's manufactured exports directed to the USSR.

Still, each case in the CEE was unique in structure and various accompanying circumstances (and certainly deserves a separate chapter if not a dedicated longer study outside
of strict space confines of the present notes). For example, some reports estimated up to
50 percent of Poland's $6 billion debt (of the overall $16 billion indebtedness) to West German banks to be explicitly or implicitly guaranteed by the German government (e.g. Eichler,
1986; Tagliabue, 1982). The largest four creditor banks accounted for approximately 23 percent of overall exposure by the West German banks.

In Romania, even with the IMF-coordinated bailout, fears of the 1981 contagion from
the political crisis in Poland (by then the *Solidarność* movement was gaining full force) and
retreating foreign banks' operations prevailed, leading to the country's loss of external credit
lines and further deterioration of the economy, even with subsequent accords with the Paris
Club lenders. In Yugoslavia, mounting debt pressures and authorities' (post-Tito) attempt to
implement austerity measures on the economy, similar to the efforts in Romania and Poland
a few years earlier, resulted in rising domestic deficits and in further exacerbating social
instability. On the other hand, in Hungary the bailout, at least from the capital account point
of view, turned out to be relatively fruitful as the country was able to negotiate a bridge loan
with the Bank for International Settlements (BIS) while completing its application for stand-
by agreement with the IMF.

Finally, as hard currency export revenues decreased following declines in energy prices in the mid-1980s, the Soviet Union ran up its foreign debt balance significantly also. After the breakup of the USSR, overall external debt inherited by Russia in 1991 amounted to $66 billion with only $2.25 billion in combined foreign exchange and gold reserves (Boughton, 2012). At the time, few could have predicted Russia's 1998 impeding default on its obligations. Early in the reforms process, even assuming debt obligations of the former Soviet republics, now independent countries, and settling claims with its counterparts from Central and Eastern Europe, Russia in early 1991 was invited into the world's top multilateral associations, procuring swift IMF assistance with repayments in exchange for implementing rigid economic policy reforms.

However, we are running ahead of our timeline. It is now time to draw brief conclusions on the above discussion. We will resume the rest of the narrative, starting with individual efforts in market socialism in the CEE, in the next chapter.

Conclusion

So what does one make of the above historical analysis of Central and Eastern European transformation within the socialist economic model? There may be at least three lessons for contemporary economic historians and development economists to take from this. First, the path of Central and Eastern European societies into the Soviet socialist realm was anything but uni-linear, in contrast to descriptions that discard much of the historical context around post-WWII dynamics. Consider the early popularity of the socialist parties in post-WWII Europe in general and in Yugoslavia or Poland more specifically. The ultimate result, though, was dictated by much more burdensome geopolitical pressures giving rise to unique adaptations in the case of each country.

Second, once within the broader CEE-socialist construct it was apparent that diversity persisted. There was even less uniformity among the Eastern European countries than the term "socialist" might have suggested to the casual observer. Consider, for example, the emergence of local Communist Party elites and their strong hold on power, with immediate ramifications for social and economic development, as the examples with early Germany's unification or Hungary's political crisis illustrate.

In economic terms, the Soviet Union's effort to win Eastern European hearts by delivering fast and robust economic upturn was an important foundational factor of the post-WWII social and political dynamic. Nevertheless, high growth rates across the board were not sufficient to guarantee the CEE's full self-sustainability. The preference for heavy industry growth (including defense) according to complex multinational trade coordination effectively implied extensive growth as opposed to intensive growth. Combined with individual country tendencies for self-sufficiency, repetitive industrial production, lack of technological innovation, and surging external debt stocks, economic tensions inevitably led to the social and political disruptions of the 1980s. Yet, importantly, each case was quite unique, formulated by a complexity of economic preconditions and political aspirations of the contemporary elites.

And finally, the critical lesson is that the story is not over. Collapse of the CMEA in 1991 did not result in immediate improvements in living standards. On the contrary, bypassing immediate surges in economic activity (mainly influenced by temporary ability to attract external capital flows), all countries of the CEE and FSU experienced sharp declines in employment, productivity, and output, and worsening health, education, and other social indicators—a phrase that does not begin to describe the severity of the human crisis of the post-socialist transition.

At the time of writing in mid-2017, the aftershocks of the early 1990s disintegration are still rumbling through the economic and political tenets, to varying degrees, across the post-socialist societies. In the next section we will turn directly to the problems explaining the circumstances in the immediate pre-transition period (the *perestroika* reforms) and accompanying macroeconomic policy discussions and outcomes of the time.

Notes

1 The full transcript as well as a video clip of Winston Churchill's speech may be found in his "The Sinews of Peace" speech available from The Churchill Centre online www.winstonchurchill.org/resources/speeches/speeches-of-winston-churchill/120-the-sinews-of-peace.
2 Ethel Snowden was a UK human rights activist who in 1920 visited Russia. Subsequently her critique of the trip was reflected in her book *Through Bolshevik Russia*. It was once her travel group had found themselves situated in the post-revolutionary Petrograd that she exclaimed that "[w]e were behind the 'iron curtain' at last!" (Snowden, 1920, p. 32).
3 The Potsdam Agreement was quite critical to the forthcoming East and West political, social, cultural, and economic division. These days much of the archives and transcripts are available online; for example, see here for English language www.pbs.org/wgbh/americanexperience/features/primary-resources/truman-potsdam/ and here, with slightly more detail on individual conversations, for the Russian language versions www.hist.msu.ru/ER/Etext/War_Conf/berlin.htm.
4 This is not to imply that Albania's defection from Soviet-styled socialism lacked importance but to emphasize, without taking up much space, the existence of deep-running contradictions exemplified in Yugoslavia's independent stance vis-à-vis the Soviet Union.
5 On Yugoslavia's post-war transformation, see Bokovoy *et al.* (1997).
6 For a detailed overview of Yugoslav and US interactions in the post-WWII period, see Lampe *et al.* (1990).
7 Consistent with the opportunity lost view is the analysis by Loth (2004).
8 It is doubtful a similar strategy and explanation would directly apply to the case of the Soviet republics. Those existed in a uniquely different environment as opposed to the EE countries. The differences as we see through this text were profound in domestic politics, foreign policy (its effective non-existence in the FSU smaller states), economics, and culture. Nevertheless, as the plethora of territorial disputes in the post-Soviet world through the 1990s indirectly suggests, the big power play within FSU relied significantly on the relative proximity and political respect [recognition] that smaller republics' long-serving leaders enjoyed with the central authorities.
9 For a brief and informed guide, see Hope Harrison's commentary in Harrison (2014).
10 Alas, it is a phrase that one might find repeated too often on the pages of this narrative given the volatile character of the profound social waves in the CEE/FSU history.
11 For a dedicated analysis of social and political movements in socialist Europe, see, for example, Stibbe and McDermott (2006).
12 See Brus (1986b) Table 24.5 for precise distribution of collective farms and collective and state-owned farms as shares of total agricultural land by EE country.
13 The theme was later developed in a more general context in Kornai *et al.* (2003).
14 There is no need to replicate at length international trade statistics that are already reported in detail from synthesized Western and Soviet sources in the earlier studies. For a good summary, see, for example, Statistical Appendix in Lavigne (1999).
15 *Statistical Yearbook of the CMEA 1986 [Statisticheskij ezhegodnik stran chlenov SEV 1986].* Moscow: Finansy i Statistika.
16 Ibid. p. 303.
17 The bank is still in operation with a mission of promoting international trade among member states, including Bulgaria, Czech Republic, Mongolia, Poland, Russia, Slovak Republic, and Vietnam. See, for example, http://en.ibec.int.
18 These figures vary depending on time frame. For example, Berend (2009) brings up $20 billion in debt for Hungary, and $42 billion for Poland over a longer period of 1970–1989. Our estimates for Hungary, Poland, and Romania are from Boughton (2001); for Yugoslavia, see OECD (1990).

Part III
The economics of the market reform

6 The socialist economic model, market socialism, stagnation, perestroika, and the end of plan

The whole is greater than the sum of its parts

Aristotle, *Metaphysics*

The socialist economic model

The historical juncture shaping the context of this chapter offers us an opportunity to briefly reflect on the socialist economic system from the evidence accumulated up to this point. It is hoped that by now our reader has developed a better-informed understanding of the massive scale of the post-WWII system with all its vastness of pre-history and contemporary complexities. In fact, the distinct symbioses of Eastern Europe's and the former Soviet Union's political, social, cultural, and historical aspects of the evolving macroeconomic constructs by the mid-1970s allowed commentators to speak about the individuality of the socialist economic model.

At the time, it was common in the academic studies of socialist economics to develop arguments in terms of factor markets equilibrium, efficiency, capacity utilization, growth convergence with the developed West, and, inevitably, structural backwardness. Depending on the case at hand or country addressed in a specific study the early pioneers of socialist economic research attempted also to construct independent estimates of economic growth, living standards, inflation, and other indicators based on the data available from the official Soviet, CMEA, or other sources. Those early estimates remain quite informative today in the analyses of the pre-perestroika era macroeconomic and social phenomena in the CEE and USSR (e.g. Vonyo, 2017).

The core determinants

Commenting on the transition experience of Russia, Yegor Gaidar in the first chapter of his *The Economics of Russian Transition* offers a compelling analysis of the key determinants of the socialist model (Gaidar, 2003). In an abridged version, for the purposes of our narrative, the key elements included:

- Paramount role of state ownership (nationalization as reviewed in previous chapters) of means of production and natural resources.
- A centralized management hierarchy on a national scale coordinating economic processes with minimal (to non-existent) role for a private market system. Objectively, one should note that agriculture would remain the "most privatized" sector of the socialist economy with a three-tiered system comprised of state farms, collective farms, and

private sector. Still, according to data in Gregory and Stuart (1986) and confirmed in official Soviet statistics, for the period 1950–1985 the private sector in the USSR averaged barely around 3 percent of total agricultural activity.

- Absolute political control and dominance of one ideology. The communist goal, at least as it was understood by an average person, promised greater rewards in the future in exchange for backbreaking work and limited consumption in the present.
- At the same time, the socialist model did achieve remarkable declines in income inequality and developed a system of non-waged support provisions as a critical social safety net (we review some elements of that in Chapters 8 and 9).
- Finally, the macroeconomic backbone of the socialist model was the focus on import substituting industrialization (ISI). The result was significant progress in developing the capital-intensive manufacturing sector, while leaving agriculture largely labor-intensive. However, to the extent that the model was successful it would be emulated in Latin America and attempted in India (see Box 6.1).

A closer analysis of these five characteristics raises several questions. At least two are critical to our exploration. Did the socialist economic model result in any early successes in capturing Western intellectuals' attention and being emulated elsewhere? Was the model sustainable in the long run?

Thinking through the first question, one must necessarily recall the origins of economic growth in the socialist system. Coinciding with the time when the capitalist world entered the Great Depression of the late 1920s–1930s, the USSR was speeding ahead in its industrialization reform by accumulating national savings and directing investment towards heavy industry. This allowed the Soviet Union (and later the CEE) to overcome the fundamental obstacle of market-led inertia in summoning investment funds for profound all-scale industrialization, as observed by Gaidar (2003). Objectively, success was achieved at the cost of lowering the living standards of those employed in agriculture, condemning the sector to remain labor-intensive for decades to come.

Box 6.1

Import substituting industrialization (ISI)—a macroeconomic development policy aimed at replacing manufactured imports with domestically produced goods. Related to the infant industry, ISI focuses on achieving domestic industrial sustainability and diversification with subsequent entry into the global markets leveraging low domestic labor costs. List (1841) was one of the first to analytically assess the infant industry policy across Western Europe and North American economies. Following the industrialization in the USSR, economists from Latin America advocated for ISI policies as an assurance of economic stability and prosperity. Variants of ISI—involving to varying degrees nationalization, tariffs, subsidization of nascent industries, dual exchange rates, etc.—were tried, among others, in Argentina, Brazil, Ecuador, Mexico in Latin America; Nigeria, Ethiopia in Africa; Japan, South Korea, and Taiwan in Asia. Only the latter group, in Asia, succeeded in achieving tangible and sustainable structural changes advancing those economies in the global trade system. Unfortunately, for the majority of others, unable to generate sufficient revenues due to small domestic markets and defaulting on sovereign debt, ISIs were scrapped by the 1990s. Nevertheless, the concept of structural diversification remains a dominant motivational factor in macroeconomic development policy as the examples of socialist Europe and the USSR illustrate.

Sources: Agénor, P.-R. and P. J. Montiel. 2008. *Development Macroeconomics*. 3rd ed. Princeton, NJ: Princeton University Press; List, F. 1841. *The National System of Political Economy*. Various editions; Prebisch, R. 1959. Commercial Policy in Underdeveloped Countries. *American Economic Review*, 49(2): 251–73.

Transplanted onto Central and Eastern European economies, the Soviet "economic miracle" continued to evolve along the ISI paradigm. Essentially, this meant a closed economy with an insignificant proportion of consumer goods exports. The CMEA assumed the proxy of external market for the CEE and USSR economies. Importantly, the centralized feature of the socialist system predicated maximum resource utilization (e.g. consider full-employment policy of no idleness), paradoxically, perhaps, very much along the lines of neo-classical economics. For the CEE in the first decades, just as for the USSR through the 1930s, there was tangible improvement in living standards across the board.

While true, the preceding statement should be taken with some degree of caution for three reasons. First, one may recall the social and political costs of Soviet industrialization of the 1930s. Those facts should not be taken lightly. Second, as has already been mentioned, industrialization resulted in net disadvantage to the agricultural sector. Finally, in the CEE the new model arrived with policies of nationalization, curtailing private markets. In some places (as reviewed in Chapter 5) the contradiction between social relations and the top-down imposed policy for rapid output growth led to public discontent and, at least two prominent large-scale conflicts (Hungary in 1956 and Czechoslovakia in 1968).

The macroeconomics of the socialist model

It is possible to illustrate early success of the ISI policy in terms of changes in gross domestic product per capita. Figure 6.1 puts the socialist economic development proposition in a comparative perspective with the capitalist economies. In the post-war period the socialist economies (excluding Germany) averaged 3.5% CAGR growth in GDP per capita with 1980 GDP per capita tripling from 1950 levels. Moreover, in terms of overall volume of industrial, mining, and agricultural production, the USSR was one of the leading nations, second only to the USA.

Leveraging the initial industrialization push, Yugoslavia, Bulgaria, and Romania outperformed the bulk of the socialist group adapting the central planning policies to their national economies. However, while political economy, demographics, territory, and economic incentives played a role, paramount to the explanation of the CEE's growth in per capita income levels would be the region's significantly backward starting conditions vis-à-vis the West and rapid push forward post-WWII. The latter is easily verified with GDP per capita data from the Maddison Project assembled in Table 6.1.

The fact that the CEE and USSR countries were devastated by the war is integral to understanding the significance of the 1950s–1970s growth performance. This is visible in the relatively low post-war levels of income per capita as per Table 6.1. The expansive model of industrialization, effectively carried out by individual CEE nations with massive resources

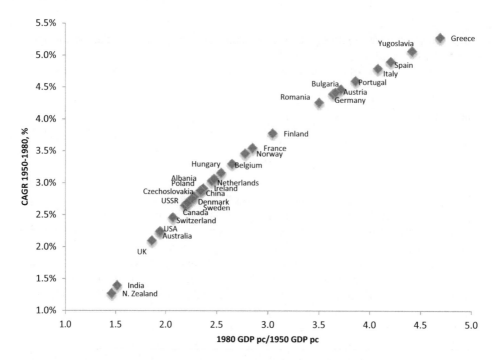

Figure 6.1 Cross country comparative growth and GDP per capita shares.

Note: Japan was an outlier with 7.0 share of 1980 GDP pc/1950 and 6.7% CAGR; socialist average was 2.9 and 3.5% while capitalist economies (incl. Germany) were 2.8 and 3.3%, respectively.

Source: extrapolated from the Maddison Project (2013).

Table 6.1 GDP per capita (1990 Int. GK$) cross country comparison

	1950	*1960*	*1970*	*1980*	*1985*
Albania	1,001	1,451	2,004	2,347	2,413
Bulgaria	1,651	2,912	4,773	6,044	6,226
Czechoslovakia	3,501	5,108	6,466	7,982	8,367
Hungary	2,480	3,649	5,028	6,306	6,557
Poland	2,447	3,215	4,428	5,740	5,660
Romania	1,182	1,844	2,853	4,135	4,159
Yugoslavia	1,428	2,370	3,945	6,297	6,279
USSR	2,841	3,945	5,575	6,427	6,708
Austria	3,706	6,519	9,747	13,759	14,752
Belgium	5,462	6,952	10,611	14,467	14,977
Denmark	6,943	8,812	12,686	15,227	17,384
Finland	4,253	6,230	9,577	12,949	14,522
France	5,186	7,398	11,410	14,766	15,530
Germany	3,881	7,705	10,839	14,114	15,140
Italy	3,172	5,456	9,367	12,927	14,010
Netherlands	5,996	8,287	11,967	14,705	15,283
Norway	5,430	7,204	10,027	15,076	17,320
Sweden	6,739	8,688	12,716	14,937	16,189
Switzerland	9,064	12,457	16,904	18,779	19,586
Ireland	3,453	4,282	6,199	8,541	9,306

	1950	*1960*	*1970*	*1980*	*1985*
Greece	1,915	3,146	6,211	8,971	9,316
Portugal	2,086	2,956	5,473	8,044	8,306
Spain	2,189	3,072	6,319	9,203	9,722
UK	6,939	8,645	10,767	12,931	14,165
Australia	7,412	8,791	12,024	14,412	15,638
New Zealand	8,456	9,465	11,189	12,347	13,664
Canada	7,291	8,753	12,050	16,176	17,582
USA	9,561	11,328	15,030	18,577	20,717
Japan	1,921	3,986	9,714	13,428	15,331
China	448	662	778	1,061	1,519
India	619	753	868	938	1,079

Note: data in Geary–Khamis dollars.

Source: extrapolated from the Maddison Project (2013)

provided by the USSR, achieved gains in income per capita up to a certain point (approximately, mid-1970s). The role of the CMEA as the guaranteed outlet for the region's exports was in that sense definitive. Comparing average shares of employment in agriculture and change in GDP per capita, Vonyo (2017) confirms empirically that CEE economies achieved relatively high growth levels despite their initial structural deficiencies as a result of the postwar reconstruction effort.[1] Still, imported machinery and technology from the West, paid for by the earlier procured loans from the IMF, World Bank, and western commercial banks, while coming up against lack of production quality and low labor productivity, helped put the CEE ahead of the USSR in consumer goods and durables production.

Overall, the view expressed in Vonyo (2017) undermines an earlier established opinion that the socialist economic model ran out of steam due to exhaustion of the extensive growth model which was unable to absorb agricultural labor. Ofer's (1976) analysis of the key determinants of the socialist model alludes to this latter opinion.[2] In that analysis, a large share of agricultural employment was part of the central planning equilibrium. This reasoning may be credible considering the socialist central plan goal to maximize production across sectors, setting higher targets with each plan, and as such, providing a dependable estimate for resource utilization.

Later, Ofer (1987) estimated that by 1980, 26 percent of the Soviet workforce was employed in the agricultural sector (Figure 6.2). That represented a sharp decline from the 1950 highs of 54% but still lagged behind developed countries' shares (15% in agriculture, 36% in industrial production, and 50% in services as of 1980). Partially, the decline may be attributed to the central plan's tendency to establish non-agricultural sector production facilities in rural areas with limited capabilities for extensive agriculture. Still, Vonyo (2017) argues that only by 1989 were some Eastern European economies able to reduce agricultural employment share to the levels of the Western economies, achieved by the latter 1950s. This brings us to the next point.

Urban living standards were, by definition, higher than rural. In a centralized economy provision of reliable infrastructure, basic necessities, and other public goods enjoyed by urban dwellers was centrally regulated and as such was a government's burden. Hence, in the central planning equilibrium à la Ofer (1976), despite urban growth, maintaining a balance between urban and rural population proportions was a cost-effective exercise. That process accounted for coordination of all industrial and agricultural inputs and outputs within the comprehensive national plan.

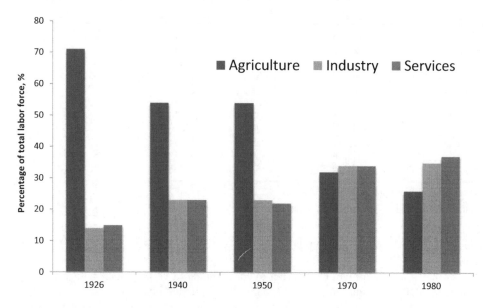

Figure 6.2 Sector shares in Soviet labor force, 1926–1980.

Source: extrapolated from Ofer (1987)

In this context, Figure 6.3 unambiguously paints a positive story of the post-WWII social-ist economic development. In addition to income growth, another measure of economic development is often associated with growing urbanization.[3] Shares of urban population skyrocketed from 39.8 percent in 1960 to average 54.7 percent of total population by 1985, according to World Bank data.

In a general case, the developmental push comes from the productivity differentials between urban and rural sectors. Either unregulated or centrally planned, cities tend to absorb more productive capital-intensive (and skill-intensive) sectors. The typical path is one of large rural-to-urban labor force migration in the early stages of development providing the necessary boost in human capital. Once urban economies begin to grow in size, productiv-ity rises (due to technological efficiency gains, knowledge spillovers, industrial clustering, and decreasing transportation costs), leading to further expansion. Assuming growth in the number of urban settlements, the impact becomes sizeable on the national economy scale.

The distribution along the trend line in Figure 6.3 deserves our attention. First, note that all countries saw their urban population shares rise from the 1960 lows (on the horizontal axis), by 1985 (on the vertical axis). Even those with high shares at the start sustained an increase in urban residents (with minor decline only in Turkmenistan). Second, those with the highest urbaniza-tion rates above or on the trend line would come up on top in terms of relative income per capita growth gains. Third, countries below the trend line seemed to be saddled with either dispropor-tionately dominant agricultural or natural resource mining sectors (e.g. Albania or Kazakhstan), both remaining labor-intensive in the socialist economic model. Finally, there may also be a par-tial cultural element as mostly Central Asian countries with strong traditional family and rural ties remain below the trend. However, this latter argument is somewhat speculative yet probably warrants a dedicated research question for anthropologists and development economists.

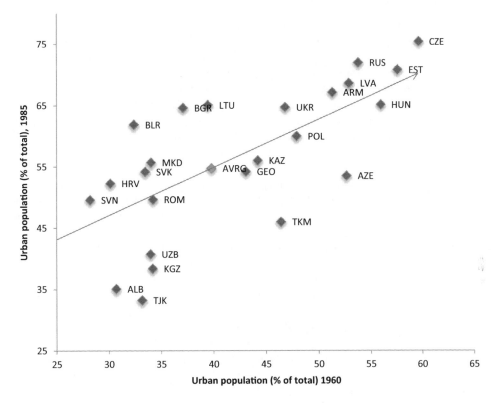

Figure 6.3 Urban population in CEE and FSU as a share of total, 1960–1985.

Note: Kosovo and Serbia omitted due to lack of data availability.

Source: author's estimate based on WDI (2017)

Furthermore, in addition to rising urbanization, the socialist economies saw a significant decline in the shares of urban population concentrated in the largest cities. Again, according to the same data source (WDI, 2017), those shares declined on average from 28.9 percent of total urban population in 1960 to approximately 27.3 percent by 1990, and rising by 2015 to 29.2 percent. This precipitous (given demographic dynamics) decline in the indicator up until the market reforms adds to the overall argument of relative living standard gains in the socialist economics.

The quick rise in the share of urban population in the largest cities in the post-socialist period of the 1990s should be seen as the absolute opposite dynamic undoing the, albeit relatively small, economic gains and stability of post-WWII growth. In this, later, period of market reforms, economic crisis, deprivation, collapse of the established industrial capacities, and of social safety nets resulted in massive migration towards the capital (or large) cities in each country. This process of migration is a subject of our analysis in the upcoming chapters. However, the observation leads us to the second question posed earlier and on which we next comment briefly.

A comment on sustainability

Given this high-level evidence, was the socialist economic model sustainable? Janos Kornai—a celebrated scholar of socialist and transition economics—offers his critique and categorical response in his *The Socialist System* (Kornai, 1992). In his opinion the socialist system, in the form that transcended through the decades into the 1980s, was not sustainable. His specific criticism refers to the first three characteristics of the socialist economy given by us above: state ownership, central plan hierarchy, and political ideology.

Kornai (1992) develops a logical argument illustrating that once administrative policy measures are employed to support a failing enterprise (soft budget constraint) or provide investment, or any other type of material guarantees, in the absence of competitive market pressures, the bureaucratic factor takes over the process. It becomes difficult, if not impossible, to weed out inefficiencies in production processes or stimulate competitive pricing dynamics and the process repeats itself continuously. Hence, the administrative skeleton of the socialist economic model evolves to further solidify in everyday operations, slowing the economy down and preventing the private market to take root.

In an empirical contribution (with conclusions consistent with Vonyo, 2017), Popov (2007c) suggests that the fragility of the socialist system was due to inability of the centrally planned economy to regenerate a sufficient rate of reinvestment in its productive facilities. He states that the "task of renovating physical capital contradicted the short-run goal of fulfilling planned targets" (Popov, 2007c, p. 49). As such, the option was for more expansive growth instead of investment in upgrading existing capacity.

In an empirical simulation, Popov (2007c) finds that the centrally planned economy needed a big push every three decades or so as old capital stock became obsolete. While reminiscent of Kondratieff long waves, in the specific case of the CEE/FSU, this finding meant, according to Popov (2007c), that to be successful, introduction of market reforms in the Soviet Union should have started in the 1960s, which would have marked 30 years since the industrialization push of the late 1920s and 1930s, as we reviewed in the preceding discussions.[4]

Without getting too far ahead, one could suggest that the overall institutional framework characterizing the socialist economic system from the 1950s up until the late 1980s was quite rigid, with initial successes and later disappointments. Before continuing this subject, it is helpful for us to turn to the obvious deviations from the established socialist economic model. Socialist on the surface but self-managed in internal operations, the economic systems evolving through the 1960s in some of the CEEs would often be referred to as market socialism.

Market socialism or self-management

Reaching the heights of industrial output unseen in some of the advanced economies (impressive, even, in the mid-2010s), by the early 1960s the CEE nations grappled with the effects of fading, expansive investment-led growth and lack of modernization capacity (Vonyo, 2017). Coming up on top of the Soviet-styled model, some countries, depending on political institutional flexibility, began to modify the rigid plan system. The result was a phenomenon, loosely referred to as "market socialism"—effectively, a system that would be socialist at the top, political, level and market-driven in the broad economy.

The idea of market socialism is often attributed to Oskar Lange's response (Lange, 1936) to Ludwig von Mises's (1920) critique of the socialist system (von Mises had commented on the "war communism" policy that we addressed in this book earlier). Was the market socialism model to offer the better of the two extremes: capitalism and socialism? The concept gained much prominence in the Western literature with debates extending beyond the purview of socialist economics and speculating about modifications of market socialist-type models in the developed capitalist economies.[5]

Theoretically, market socialism implied a system in which the state retained ownership of capital goods and means of production, while allocation of resources was left to a more efficient market mechanism (Brus, 1990). Stated differently, as the state controlled key strategic industries and natural resources, households were free to decide what and when to consume and what jobs to take. Competitive market pressures determined consumer goods prices and employment wages, while profits and wages comprised national income.

The Central Planning Board (CPB)—or some analogous entity—was to be the market maker, in today's terms, setting prices on goods in the sectors where there were no markets, that is, capital goods and production inputs. As such, hypothetically, enterprises would be motivated to develop an optimal mix of factors of production, minimizing expenditure. However, that was the precise critique of socialism coming from the Austrian economists: assuming capital goods prices were calculated, how would factor managers be incentivized? Excessive state, administrative, involvement would have been inevitable. But Oskar Lange saw the concern with bureaucratization of economic life in market socialism to be similar to the monopoly power in a capitalist system, where the former would potentially be curtailed through a regulatory mechanism. However, in market socialism, any tilt to economic power centralization would be resolved through an open process with society's active participation.

When he was appointed to lead the Economic Council in Poland in 1956, Oskar Lange emphasized incentives to factories by shifting greater controls over routine operations to them. He argued for more enterprise autonomy in investment decisions, through that freeing central authority capacity to be directed towards long-term planning. Despite some initial success, the model eventually fell through. With new autonomy but without any efficiency controls, enterprise managers pursued a strategy of "limitless investment."

The latter was characterized by an implied bailout of a failing enterprise by the state when growth slowed down. This was a natural derivative of the socialist contract between the state and society: guaranteed employment and maximum capacity utilization. In such a framework, shortages became inevitable as resources promised in administrative directive were in practice limited and over-stretched across the entire system. The phenomenon became known as soft budget constraint (SBC).[6]

New, massive construction projects would break ground, alas, not to be completed for several years, if at all. The early reformation of the socialist system in Poland ended by the late 1950s, with the only tangible achievement of stopping agricultural collectivization and reestablishing private farms. Factory managers lost their autonomy over investment decisions as these were shifted back to the center.

Variations on market socialism

Following rapid post-war recovery, living standards improved in East Germany (GDR) restoring on aggregate to pre-war levels by the mid-1950s. The government scaled back on food rationing and emphasized consumer durables in the output targets reducing the weight of producer goods. Following West Germany's exit from the bilateral trade agreement in 1960, a New Economic System was announced. In this model, factories were granted greater autonomy in their production decisions and those with profits in excess of their own targets were to retain 60 percent of the surplus. The latter was to be distributed as employee bonuses and use to invest in capital goods. However, just like in Poland before, the soft budget constraint dynamic prevailed in East Germany as well.

At the core was the inherent contradiction between profit-led incentives and state plan fulfillment. The state prioritized continuous industrialization at the expense of consumer goods production—a sector where profits were earned at a faster pace motivating enterprise resources reallocation. Because of the implied guarantees, a la SBC, industrial sectors prioritized by the government eventually began to face a shortage of investment funds. Subsequently, the government scaled back reforms by 1970 with factory-level guidelines reintroduced, productivity bonuses curtailed, and price-setting autonomy eliminated (see discussion in Swain and Swain, 1993).

Perhaps, a form of market socialism that indeed worked and offered motivation of a model to citizens of other CEE countries, was in Yugoslavia. Estrin (1991) offers an insightful review of the Yugoslavian case which he, more aptly labels as self-management market socialism. Could it be that a rare case of socialism had been working? Be that as it may, the Yugoslav case was reminiscent of the New Economic Policy in the 1920s in the USSR.

Emerging from the early 1950s political falling-out with the USSR, the Yugoslavian reforms of the socialist model aimed to further establish the country as an independent socialist state. In practical terms, the state pursued a larger developmental strategy. Nationalization was viewed as a necessary means towards ultimate economic self-sufficiency but not the goal itself. Private enterprise development drove the economy and, as Berend (2009) notes, was dependent on foreign trade, prompting stronger integration in the world economy.

The national plan was only indicative, providing information and a framework for coordination of individual enterprises. The state did not engage in direct reallocation of resources, aside from support to backward regions. The mixed economic system was a means to further socialization of the production mode that would involve workers in an active decision-making role in the process, culminating in self-management across multiple layers of the economy and social life. In Yugoslavia, it was a gradual process that stretched into the late 1970s, unlike short-lived instances in Poland or the GDR, as mentioned above.

Helping achieve a greater participatory role by creating employee-run enterprises, were worker-managed boards that controlled the distribution of factory surplus. Clearly, workers' direct engagement with the production process and the competitive aspect of final output distribution, acted as a strong incentive to sustained labor productivity and quality of final output, as well as improved working conditions. Nevertheless, while theoretically sound, in practice, this led to an apparent contradiction of design: there was no clear distinction in ownership rights. Workers' ownership in the enterprise ended with change of jobs—hence long-term capital investment decisions faced an obvious roadblock due to an apparent conflict of interests (Brus, 1990). Facing the possibility of enterprise shut-down due to inefficiency or competitive pressures, firm employees would tend to allocate greater profit shares towards the compensation pool—a short-term strategy undermining long-term growth.

As market tendencies gained strength, firms increasingly sought alternative investment funds. This would ultimately require a functioning banking system. However, the latter would not be sustained given the political realities of the time. A strong banking system implies not just economic self-sufficiency, but de facto political independence that spurs a chain reaction among others. Overall, while workers (and enterprises) effectively held control over their destinies, inability to resolve key contradictions involving short-termism by workers' councils and lack of openness in the banking sector limiting privately available investment funds, among others, led to relatively modest gains in the Yugoslavian economy compared to other CEE countries.

As the Yugoslav economy accumulated high debt of almost $19 billion by 1979 (OECD, 1990), while export-led growth failed to pick up, economic growth declined, unemployment shot up, and inflation began to rise. Brus (1990) suggests that while the principle of self-management was not the subject of debate at the time, the contradiction of property rights and workers' incentive prominently featured in public discussions. Opinions ranged from those who considered that the market was not given an adequate chance to those who argued against excessive "marketization" that made planning inefficient.[7]

Still, is it enough, as Estrin (1991) asks, to discard the case for a mixed economy (in support, of course, of the free-market model)? Probably not, for one must understand the specific aspects of Yugoslavia. Those aspects relate to the country's federal structure with strong will for autonomous decision making in the republics. All that became increasingly apparent following Tito's death in 1980 and relaxation of his unifying role of central political leadership. Reforms of the late 1980s added more layers of social and economic difficulties. Problems of income distribution (inter-sector, inter-region, inter-enterprise) quickly arose with their explosive potential across the country

Hungary launched its New Economic Mechanism (NEM) in 1968. The reform program was clearly outside the rigid confines of the "mainstream" command economy. The Hungarian experience differed from that of Yugoslavia in a few respects. First, it set aside the issue of self-management. Second, there was a difference in treatment of plan versus market relationship. While adhering to the principal of central planning, Hungarian methods in attaining social balance and market equilibrium were quite different (e.g. Eichengreen, 2008).

There were no obligatory, rigidly-defined plan targets for enterprises to comply with. Enterprises were freed from the typical hierarchical administrative structure and were offered a free float with self-regulation. Profit was the main criterion and source of workers' benefits and enterprise self-finance. Yet, though prices (money) now assume a new role, unprecedented in the post-WWII socialist economic model, not all prices were allowed to fluctuate (most "important" ones were kept fixed by the state). There were less obstacles in private-to-state interactions.

The key aspect of state (Plan Board) involvement shifted from pure administrative directives to providing guidelines on general provisions in terms of a) macroeconomic framework, including decisions on income distribution; b) rules of the game for enterprises, with coordination of efficiency checks and incentives, merging regional interests on production with national goals; and c) fiscal, monetary, and pricing policies that supported (a) and (b). Such reforms approximated the Hungarian economy to a capitalist model of the time.

There was a difference, of course, and it was that there still existed a "socialist" plan. As firms competed for workers and pushed for increasing investment borrowing from state banks the curse of the soft budget constraint surfaced in Hungary as well. The State plan would be thrown off course as wages rose unexpectedly due to the labor market squeeze. Nevertheless, with beneficial "capitalist" features also came the evils of the true capitalist structure: exposure to volatility in international trade and capital flows.

For example, as advanced economies in Western Europe—a destination for some Hungarian exports—were hit by the oil crisis of the 1970s, that had immediate ramifications for Hungary's foreign trade as exports declined due to drop in demand for Hungarian exports.[8] By early 1970, some of the core enterprises were brought back within the government's direct control. A critical analytical effort was put in motion to review the original reforms. As a result, by the early 1980s there was a strong preference to move beyond just product market and expand the economy into the "capital market." At the same time, the labor market regulation had to be relaxed also. In effect, new proposals amounted to a gradual move towards a "fully-fledged market socialism" model, away from the mixed model of central planning with regulated market mechanism. This was to be done while the center still held control over infrastructure investment and financial institutions.

Setting the initial conditions for the future?

To the extent that information on self-management and market socialism reforms filtered through censorship across the CEE, local societies were motivated by prospects of autonomy and the promise of improved welfare. By 1981, the *Solidarity* movement in Poland pushed for a wide-ranging design of self-managed market socialism reforms, which were opposed in earnest by the ruling apparatus.[9] For the Soviet Union, the concept will become relevant only at the time of mid-1980s *perestroika* reforms.

It is nevertheless interesting to note that irrespective of those deviations from the socialist economic model's blueprint there was little, if any, change in official political doctrine as (the contemporary interpretation of) Marxism and socialist ideas remained the dominant guiding paradigms. Still, even piecemeal introduction of macroeconomic reforms across the CEE led to gradual origination and accumulation of market-like tendencies leading to a phenomenon of evolving new methods of organizing societies and economic activity. More directly, the variations on the pan-socialist plan, coupled with aggressively pursued ISI policies and structural adaptations of market socialism, had irreparably altered the rigid foundations of the socialist economic model, making the eventual integration with its opposite, capitalist, model by the early 1990s easier for some CEE economies than for those in the FSU.

In practical terms, the market socialist-type methods would become cardinally opposite to contemporary socialist teaching. In the end, the post-socialist societies came to an open, dialectical contradiction between production relations and the production mode. Paradoxically, despite decades of efforts to nominally attain the opposite, now, in the environment of consumer goods deficits (felt most strongly in the USSR) the separation of producers from ownership of means of production was most pronounced.

One had to yield to the other, which would necessarily lead to a new social contract and institutional formation.[10] In this regard, the *perestroika* reform may be viewed as a necessary step (or attempt) towards balancing and resolution of the contradiction that had been at the core of the socialist economic model. In a politically tightly-knit, constrained environment, the change would have to come from within the system's nucleus.

Right before 1985

Towards the early 1980s, the socialist economy was characterized by an insurmountable effort in national plans coordination, sustaining adequate living standards, and effectively subsidizing key growth sectors. Over time, growth rates and per capita incomes declined, infrastructure required repairs, and quiet social discontent proliferated. In history, the period from the late 1970s up until the *perestroika* reforms of the late 1980s would become known as the period of *zastoi* (or stagnation) in the principal economy of the socialist economic model, the USSR.[11] The expansive model of growth needed urgent technological modernization if it were to be sustained. That necessarily would have required relaxation of controls on private economic activity and, importantly, opening up to trade with the West.

However, attempting reforms of the industrialized socialist economy, as Gaidar (2003) noted, had proven difficult to accomplish. That gave way eventually to political destabilization early on as was the case in Czechoslovakia (for specifics, see Brus, 1986b) and later Poland. In this reasoning, Gaidar parallels Kornai's views, mentioned above, on institutional impediments to comprehensive reform of the bureaucratic system, which entails a broad range of social and economic institutes. In that sense, reforms to the original socialist model appeared to be most successful in places where the import-substituting industrialization dynamic had not had sufficient time to fully settle in and transform the economy. In addition to the earlier cited examples of Yugoslavia and Hungary, one could add China of the late 1970s and Vietnam of the mid-1980s as successful attempts at such a reform of the original socialist economic model of heavy industry prioritization.

Broadly speaking, in the Soviet economy consumption goods rationing and cuts in household durables production resulted in consumer deficits in the early 1980s. Obtaining basic necessities was increasingly difficult, as endless queues of consumers would stretch along the shopping centers. Often, economic circumstances worsened with geographical distance from major industrial and administrative centers. In addition to its devastating social impact, the war in Afghanistan was another enormous financial and logistical burden as funds were diverted towards defense spending.[12] While on paper high macroeconomic indicators seemed unchanged, the real economy was coming to a stalemate.

By the late 1970s, macroeconomic performance in Eastern Europe and the USSR began to lag behind the early successes.[13] Table 6.2 underscores the structural flaw of the Soviet economy's reliance on natural resources exports. Also, visible from Table 6.2 is Ofer's (1976) point on lack of services sector development. As oil prices declined following the mid-1970s shocks, the USSR struggled to make up for the declining hard currency earnings needed to finance grain imports, as the CEE satellites turned to the world market for competitively priced resources.

Growth in agriculture declined as the sector lacked the necessary technological upgrade and extensive land use was becoming insufficient to meet the demands of the growing population and various international aid commitments. By the early 1980s, the sector was no longer seen as a resource for industrial growth. Instead, it was effectively subsidized with typical organization of employment as with any state factory (e.g. Harrison, 1996). On a larger scale, a paradox evolved (in fact starting with the late 1960s–early 1970s as the Virgin Lands resources had been exhausted). By the 1980s, the USSR, one of the richest and largest countries in terms of natural resources and agricultural lands, imported grain from its ideological opposites in the capitalist West (e.g. Gregory and Stuart, 1986 and Gaidar, 2003).

The period was characterized by major spending boosts on large projects, a legacy of the earlier industrialization initiatives. The Baikal Amur Mainline (BAM) construction

Table 6.2 Soviet aggregate economic performance, % annual growth

	1966–1970	1970–1975	1976–1980	1981–1982	1984
GNP	5.2	3.7	2.7	2.1	2.6
Industry	6.3	5.9	3.4	2.4	4.2
Agriculture	3.5	−2.3	0.3	1.8	0
Services	4.2	3.4	2.8	N/A	N/A
Consumption	5.3	3.6	2.6	1.8	4.3
Investment	6	5.4	4.3	3.2	2

Source: US Congress, as presented in Gregory and Stuart (1986)

was one of such typical mega-projects re-launched by the USSR in 1974 (original start was in 1923). The BAM was to become the key transportation link connecting the European part of Russia with the Far East, stretching over 4,300 kilometers (or 2,672 miles). It was up to the *Komsomol* and enthusiastic volunteers to lead the construction. However, putting a railway line across permafrost, swamps, and virgin woods required major capital investments adding to the already severe economic strain. The problem was not whether the project was needed, but the timing of such major diversion of, by then, scarce investment funds, technology, and labor resources away from the needs of the maturing economy.[14]

Harrison (2002) raises a point on the controversies of statistical data research and availability. Not only were there discrepancies between the Soviet official data and Western estimates, but within the Western academic and policy community itself, disagreements were abundant. An alternative set of national income and industrial growth rates was developed by a group of economists following announcement of *perestroika* reforms (Shatalin *et al.*, 1990).

One could argue that, despite the abundance of statistical data arrived at by various methodologies, the directional trends were quite clear. Figure 6.4 helps us visualize the rapid declines of the early 1980s in the Soviet macroeconomic performance, with a momentous rise following short-lived, and sometimes radical, measures to instill workplace discipline and replenish investment funds by curtailing some of the earlier introduced management flexibility (Kontorovich, 1986 on workplace discipline). However, even despite the mega projects, for example the BAM, the downward trend was inescapable, seen by Gaidar (2003) as ominous of the structural flaws of a resource-based economy running out of steam.

To add to the statistical view, Figure 6.5 tells a comparative story of falling labor productivity in the FSU and CEE starting in the late 1970s–early 1980s. Here, the need for modernization and shift to a more intensive production mode is clearly visible. Once leading, the high-growth, post-war recovery, socialist economic model's moment began to gradually fade. In contrast, Western Europe (including the UK) and the US maintained comparatively higher productivity per worker growth rates. This comes on top of the already established higher income base, widening the socialist–capitalist development gap further. The situation was most dire in the economically backward Central Asian republics of the USSR, where average labor productivity growth declined by 1.5 percent for the 1981–1985 period, declining 8.3 percent in 1991 compared to the year prior.

Standardization was one of the possibilities of attaining economies of scale while reducing costs associated with massive infrastructure projects and easing pressures on the central planners tasked with routine social and economic management. For example, in public residential construction, the standardization effort led to creation of uniform street blocks, neighborhoods, if not towns, across the massive expanse of the USSR. The typified residential construction projects led to some popular anecdotes. The most prominent would be a Soviet romantic comedy film of 1976 *The Irony of Fate, or Enjoy Your Bath! (Ironiya sudby, ili S lyogkim parom!)*.[15]

In the film, the main character, thinking he was on his way home finds himself in someone else's apartment in Leningrad, which he entered using the key to his own apartment with exactly the same layout and located at exactly the same building number and street name . . . only in Moscow. The romantic encounter with the woman living in the Leningrad apartment would take up the rest of the film, but practically every Soviet citizen and

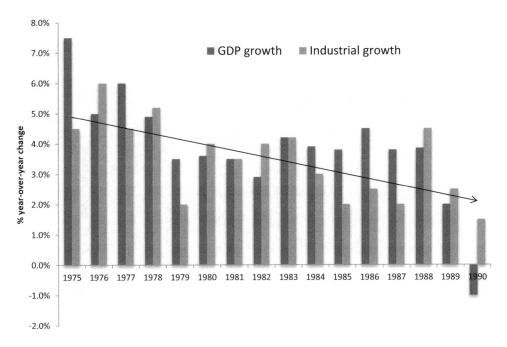

Figure 6.4 USSR GDP and industrial capacity growth, % YoY change (1975–1990).

Source: extrapolated from Shatalin *et al.* (1990)

those in Eastern Europe (the actress who played the role of the main heroine was Polish), recognized the very much familiar living conditions and other minute details of the socialist routine. This sense of uniformity was a peculiar feature of the socialist economic (and social) construct.

Meanwhile, with the compulsory education system, the number of students in USSR universities soared 74 percent between 1970 and 1980 (with similar increases in the CEE). Research institutes proliferated and academic activities were heavily subsidized by the government (data is from Kal'yanov and Sidorov, 2004). Healthcare, education, child-care, and other non-waged services were state-sponsored and nominally accessible to everyone. In many cases, large industrial factories (by definition, state-owned) provided their employees with access to subsidized amenities, leisure facilities, hospitals, kindergartens, and so on. At the time, the range of social guarantees of the socialist economic model would seem unprecedented on the global scale.

Still, the years of *zastoj* (or stagnation), as the late 1970s to mid-1980s became known, were taking their toll. By the mid-1980s the soft budget constraint had assumed its own dynamic. State enterprise directors expected and counted on state bailouts, subsidies, and other measures to balance their (enterprises) inefficient operations. The situation was going from bad to worse, as responsibility and accountability for actions were weakening. One expected someone else (i.e. the state) to pick up responsibility for what had to be done. Numerous cases of negligence and just indifference towards productive assets and mostly absence of incentive to improve performance, became widespread. In the meantime, enterprise directors

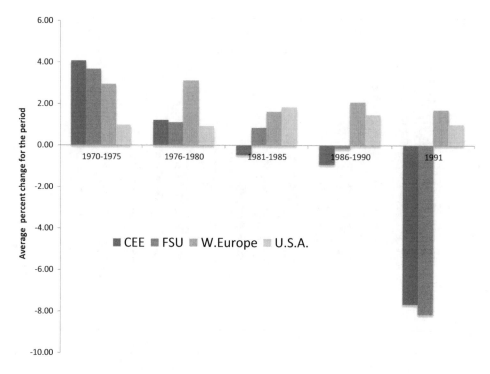

Figure 6.5 Growth of labor productivity by worker, average % change.

Notes: due to data availability, estimates prior to 1980 for FSU included Russia only; for CEE included Albania, Bulgaria, Czechoslovakia, Hungary, Poland, Romania; Western Europe also includes figures for the UK.

Source: author's calculations based on data from The Conference Board Total Economy Database (TCB, 2017)

competed with each other for local, republic-level, or federal investment funds and other resources shares.

Gradually, the political elites of the USSR were becoming more focused on domestic challenges, relaxing administrative controls over the political dynamic in Central and Eastern Europe. The social component, as in daily interactions among people, their views on current events as well as aspirations for the future, began to change. In the CEE, as the aged political leaders stepped down, the new pro-independence and economic reform movements gained popularity. In the Soviet Union, the naive idealism of the 1920s, replaced by the fear of the 1930s, principled determination of 1940s, and the relaxation of the post-war period, was now being replaced with critical revaluation of the entire socialist path, alongside cynical attitudes to the official machine.

Related to our conceptual explorations in Chapter 2, Harrison (2002) expresses hope that prior to *perestroika*, the collapse of the USSR was still preventable. Intensified centralization of the production process, enforcement of the work discipline, and resumption of control over state property in the few years before the *perestroika* reforms, all gave hope for the Soviet system's sustainability (e.g. Kontorovich, 1986). However, attention, even in the USSR (yet still lagging behind the West and Eastern European levels), towards consumer goods production starting in the 1970s, required reorientation of the entire factory space architectural layouts and plan exercises. Unfortunately, the hardening over the years of the ISI-centric institutional framework built on heavy industry emphasis was neither flexible enough nor adequately prepared for such a change.

The world order shaken: perestroika and the Berlin Wall

In hindsight, the launch of the *perestroika* movement in 1985 in the former USSR signified a fundamental break with the socialist economic model of the past. Though Mikhail Gorbachev was credited with initiation, the original research into modernizing Soviet economic activity had been put in place a few years before his announcements. The early motivation came as the Soviet system faced dangers of collapse, disintegration, and worsening external debt crisis. Still, Gorbachev's abstract ideas of *perestroika* and *glasnost'* found their dialectical realization in the very concrete dismantling of the Berlin Wall of 1989. The evolving socialist system disintegration, following *perestroika* and collapse of the wall, was practically unstoppable.

Conceptualizing perestroika

It might be surprising to learn that the end goal of the *perestroika* reform was not disintegration but strengthening and preservation of the socialist economic model. In politics, Gorbachev (1987) spoke about "more socialism, more democracy, and new thinking." In economic terms, the hope was to launch wide-scale industrial modernization and reorganization, boosting competitiveness with each Soviet republic and providing an integral link in the overall system.

Reminiscent of the 1920s *New Economic Policy* and inspired by the approximations to market socialism in Yugoslavia and Hungary, the reforms of the mid-1980s encouraged the creation of small private cooperatives and entrepreneurship. Practically all factories, with the exception of a few strategic ones in the defense sector, were encouraged to seek their own sources for operating capital, yet still fulfill state orders (*goszakazy*), with an option of selling any extra output in the market.

From society's point of view, Gorbachev-initiated conversations on new thinking and *glasnost'* were a breath of fresh air for the urbanized, highly-educated, and increasingly informed about the outside world population. There were several notable moments. For instance, The Beatles—the band that changed the Western world generations before—was finally allowed beyond the Iron Curtain. To many, it was this cultural moment that truly shook the foundations of the deeply-rooted socialist institutions of the past (e.g. Woodhead, 2013).

Media, art, culture, trade unions, politics, international relations, economics, established social orders, society's norms, and morals: absolutely everything was affected by the increasingly obvious message coming from the top: glasnost' (openness) about everything. One of the critical elements of such behavior was the initially uncomfortable introduction of open debates about the Soviet Union's legacy and specifically Stalin's Purges. As a sign of high intellectual capacity, heated debates on the topic would be carried out in the colloquiums of local and national newspapers and magazines.

At the same time, numerous previously imposed bans on various publications or artwork deemed anti-socialist at the time, as well as restrictions on travel and international communication, began to be lifted. The famed Soviet dissidents—Andrei Sakharov and Yelena

Bonner, Aleksandr Solzhenitsyn—were returning from exile and actively joining the rising plurality in political discussions.

The Soviet Union gradually opened up to the rest of the world as early Gorbachev–Thatcher–Reagan summits were broadcast via satellite television. The world held its breath in anticipation. Mikhail Gorbachev was the first of the Soviet leaders to be accompanied by his wife, Raisa Gorbacheva, on foreign trips. Through her direct support for her husband's political role and her active engagement in a range of development, cultural, and social projects in the USSR and internationally, Mrs. Gorbacheva maintained the visible public profile of the First Lady of the Soviet Union. That was both unknown to the Soviet public before and surprising to the Western world.[16] All the signs were that this highly-educated, urbanized, and socially active Soviet society with a (natural or self-grown) sense of moral responsibility was in search of its future path.

Various public discussion forums were launched becoming increasingly open every day. The mood was reminiscent, to some in the older generation, of the naive mass enthusiasm of the early years following the 1920s NEP. Unlike in those years, the environment of the mid-1980s now allowed for, if not multiparty representation, non-party affiliated organizations and individuals to participate in the Soviet government (Lapidus, 1991 and Nove, 1993). In essence, there was a developing cardinal break with the institutionalized models of the past. In the social sciences, *perestroika* was viewed as advancement with a strong idealistic bias, as the quote from a famous Soviet economist Abel Aganbegyan suggests:

> perestroika is a revolutionary process of transformation in society. The restructuring of our society is the fate of the people, the question of its survival, its further existence
>
> (Aganbegyan, 1990, p. 1)

The economics of perestroika

Perestroika was supposed to turn the economy 180 degrees from a shortage economy of "producers rule supreme" into an economy "based on satisfying social needs, where producers strive for the fulfillment of the demands of consumers" (Aganbegyan, 1990, p. 2). The deficit economy required enormous resources to sustain it. And factory managers were becoming innovative. In some industrial centers, especially where the lion's share of economic activity was tied to one big employer, for example in Togliatti, factory managers became de facto economic governors of the region. The region's administrative and political resources had to be dedicated towards guaranteeing a factory's survival, as it provided the largest share of guaranteed employment in the region. One might easily interpret such arrangements as yet another manifestation of Kornai's soft budget constraint mentioned earlier.

Perestroika reforms were to focus on technological progress and connect advances in sciences with real, consumer-led, as opposed to defense project-focused, enterprise. To that end, abandoning the administrative system was supposed to free up the limited resources in the market. Defense spending was cut abruptly, with the exit of Soviet troops from Afghanistan. A range of international agreements was reached to contain any threats of nuclear crisis, freeing up resources for the domestic economy and guaranteeing better borrowing terms. Still, these semi-free market reforms were introduced under the somewhat similar and accustomed flare of equality and fraternity among all socialist workers, groups, societies, countries. In this environment of common property there is no need to divide borders and/or compete with other regions, nations, and so on.

As is typical with any political campaign anywhere in the world, promises were made. For example, full employment was within the reach of *perestroika* reforms. Industries were to be reoriented towards society's needs (e.g. doubling investments in new housing, wage increases to teachers, medical personnel, etc.). New plans foresaw future intensive development, increasing efficiency, and better-quality production instead of simple capital goods reproducing growth. With technological innovations, labor productivity was to pick up (we have ample evidence of the opposite happening as documented in Figure 6.5). Finally, the bureaucratic system was to yield to more efficient elements of market socialism (we are reminded of Kornai's critique of deeply institutionalized administrative capacities, mentioned in the previous sections).

Some tangible policy measures were in fact adopted. In the rigid framework of the Soviet socialist economic model described so far, those policy innovations would become profound and unhesitatingly characteristic in setting in motion the pendulum of change.[17] Specifically, three critical laws were passed in the 1986–1987 period:

- Law on state enterprises—permitting individual enterprises to draw their own budgets and enter into joint venture corporations with foreign counterparts.
- Law on cooperatives—permitting individual entrepreneurs to establish private cooperative firms.
- Law on individual labor activities—effectively legalizing individual entrepreneurial activities of small business scale.

At the same time, a new banking system was being formed, at the rate of one bank a week (Aganbegyan, 1990). Still, the state bank kept tight control over banking activity and financial flows (e.g. cross border payments)—the regulatory situation would change radically by the mid-1990s. Nominally, enterprises were now allowed to access foreign markets and conduct trade in foreign currency. But there was a requirement to exchange foreign currency profits back into rubles at the state bank's rate. In practice it was not to the enterprises' advantage to report any foreign transactions.[18]

Academic studies welcomed *perestroika* as a revolutionary event, but also pointed to a few general problems (Aganbegyan, 1990; Gaidar, 2003; Mau, 2003).[19] For example, while the new principles were introduced, the legacy of the old ways of doing things was omnipresent. Dialectically, one might argue for a merged and more sensible outcome. In social phenomena there is room for both the logic of a charted course and the accidental. Which of the tendencies prevails in this unity of contradictions is often impossible to predict. It was apparent there was lack of agreement on the course of the reforms at the very top level. Just like any corporate restructuring, here too, no better method was discovered to deal with the issue than to replace old functionaries with new appointees, with minimal adjustments to the institutional processes (e.g. Mau, 2003).

Across the country, enterprise managers had been granted greater autonomy, as long as state orders were fulfilled. Yet, at the same time, enterprises were being taken off the state books and were to generate investment funds from sales beyond the state order targets (economic accounting or *khozraschet*). However, in the conditions of fixed prices and a rudimentary financial system, inventory supplies were diverted. Unable to effectively self-manage (one must also take into account the quality and usefulness of the end product to the rest of the economy bar state order fulfillment), enterprise managers sought ways of working things out privately on the ground. Final and intermediate goods as well as services were obtained rather than bought. The situation often led to establishment of barter exchange.

The market discipline, akin to a typical competitive framework, was initially missing, partly due to managers' reluctance to push through personnel decisions for fear of negative social outcry. At the same time, support via soft budget constraint was not conditioned by enterprise efficiency. Hence, there really was no strong incentive for an enterprise to restructure in face of potential competitive pressures. Ickes (2001) also notes that decentralization led to loss of control over wages, as enterprises sought to contribute profits to higher wage funds.

This was the self-destruction mechanism, so to speak, in action and very similar to the self-management fiascos of Yugoslavia and Hungary before. Prices on food staples, fixed by the state, did not rise immediately. There was no real acceleration in production and the situation led to the monetary overhang (or repressed inflation). Hence, there was no real market to spend available money on. As a result, prices on existing goods began to rise. In the Soviet Union the situation led to the extremes of rationing and food cards.

The state's response to this was to establish artificial controls over wage growth and increase investment in capital goods production. To afford these programs and prevent further large deficit spending the central government attempted to cut down fiscal expenditures by laying off employees from all government levels (municipal and up), reshuffling the structures of the mega-ministries, and other spending cuts. Moreover, government spending was financed out of deficit through monetary emission, which added to wage inflation. The push was to eliminate deficits within a two- or three-year period by saturating the economy with food and consumer goods. Only after that was it planned to allow retail prices on food staples to float freely.

Perception and assessment

It is clear today, that a characteristic feature of the early reforms was their ad hoc and inconsistent nature.[20] Some reforms would seem ill-informed today despite their well-intended designs. For example, consider the 1985 anti-alcoholism campaigns in the USSR. The typical old-time focus on "overachievement" of plan targets, while accomplishing reduction in alcoholic drinks production also led to the thousands of hectares of precious vines and vineyards that had been nurtured for decades before to be cut down.

The negative impact on agricultural sectors in Armenia, Georgia, and Moldova, as well as part of Southern Russia, was immediate and unforgiving. At the same time, as legal alcoholic drinks evaporated from the store shelves, bootlegging and homemade alcohol production proliferated, often leading to massive poisoning incidents. The trust of society in the new reformist movement was shaken not because it was no longer possible to buy vodka in stores, but because of the universal brand of distrust that was put onto people irrespective of their background, as Medvedev (2008) argues in his detailed study of major events in the last years of the Soviet Union.[21]

Despite all this uprooting, the initial sense of *perestroika* reforms was of yet another reorganization that the Soviet system had been through several times before (on reorganizations, see Harrison, 2002). The West considered the reforms to be a sign of an internal crisis, which would, of course, be resolved via ax and iron measures of the system. For the Soviet leadership, *perestroika* also was to be an adjustment, perhaps uncomfortable, but a mere adjustment to a different economic system, preserving the overall guiding objective of "communism after socialism." From a philosophical point of view this was an ironic conundrum into which the "true followers" of Marx stepped, by negating the very concept of social cognition and institutional evolution propagated in *Das Kapital*.

Box 6.2

There were two disastrous events that shook the world in the period between initiation of the *perestroika* movement and collapse of the USSR. The first was the Chernobyl (Ukraine) nuclear plant disaster on April 26, 1986. This was an immense human, psychological, and environmental tragedy of unprecedented proportions. Hundreds of people (first responders to the tragedy) died, while thousands were evacuated and several villages razed to the ground due to contamination; and an estimated five million more people may have been affected over parts of Belarus, Russia, Ukraine, and Europe. The economic costs of physical equipment losses, liquidation of the accident, and containment ran up to USD 20 billion in the first year and up to USD 80 billion of indirect expenses (Medvedev, 2008).

The second event was the massive earthquake in Armenia on December 7, 1988 killing over 25,000 people and injuring scores of thousands more. The town of Spitak in northern Armenia was mostly destroyed. Other cities, Gyumri (then Leninakan) and Vanadzor (then Kirovakan), were heavily hit as well, with structural damage remaining up until today, as some people remain living in shelters. Unlike in the case of Chernobyl, where special military brigades with massive specialized equipment against nuclear fallout were quickly mobilized to contain the tragedy, recovery in Armenia's earthquake zone was heavily criticized for poor organization, lack of coordination, and deterrence of western help. Prolonging and deepening Armenia's humanitarian crisis in the immediate years after the earthquake, were economic collapse and military conflict, marked by a (still remaining) blockade from Turkey and Azerbaijan. Collectively, those factors gave rise to one of the first large-scale humanitarian catastrophes in post-socialist space, creating a phenomenon of refugees and forced migrants. Sadly and heartbreakingly, there would be other tragic episodes that followed elsewhere in the FSU and CEE in years to follow.

Additional sources

- IAEA dedicated website on the Chernobyl nuclear accident. Available online: www.iaea.org/newscenter/focus/chernobyl.
- IAEA. 2006. *The Chernobyl Forum: 2003–2005.* Austria: International Atomic Energy Agency.
- Armenian National Survey for Seismic Protection. *Spitak 1988 Earthquake.* Available online: www.nssp-gov.am/spitak_eng.htm.
- Najarian, L. M. *et al.* 1996. Relocation after a disaster: Posttraumatic stress disorder in Armenia after the earthquake. *Journal of the American Academy of Child and Adolescent Psychiatry*, 35(3): 374–383.
- On migration, see Chapter 8.

On the ground, especially following the collapse of the Berlin Wall in 1989, events progressed quickly, ad hoc and, often, marked with violence. It is, yet, another paradox that some early observers of the transition process considered the collapse of the socialist system as peaceful. Perhaps that was an apt depiction of the power transition—*Velvet Revolution*—in Czechoslovakia and elsewhere in Central Europe (e.g. Sebetsyen, 2009). However, it was not how the breakup with the old system happened elsewhere. From Kazakhstan of 1986, Nagorno Karabakh and Estonia of 1987, to Moldova, Georgia, Abkhazia, Latvia, Chechnya, Kosovo, Serbia, and Romania, of later years, the eventual economic and political disintegration of the Soviet socialist system was by no means peaceful, nor bloodless (also see Box 6.2).

Those previously dormant conflicts, either subdued by the administrative and military controls of a once solid system or by the relative economic equality of the larger population shares, erupted across the map with human death tolls in the dozens of thousands and physical devastation that still echoes in the region. The political fallout of those conflicts hastened the collapse of the same system that stitched post-WWII Europe together.

While each conflict is certainly different and must be evaluated not in comparison to others but on its own "merit", the spread of nationalism and ethnic tensions offers two important insights applicable to our analysis. First, the socialist system of the CEE and FSU was inherently fragile, sewn by idealized concepts of internationalism and borderless societies, yet contradicting reality. Second, the central authorities' treatment of each conflict unveiled the inadequacy of the contemporary, centralized governance model. Inability of the central authorities to proactively respond to the sharpening political and economic divides across interest groups and disinterest in intervening to preempt conflict escalation, seen as minor disturbance, accelerated the processes of further systematic disintegration.

Some of the negative aspects, which we may have somewhat overemphasized, may lead to a temptation to judge the *perestroika* reform as failure to modernize the Soviet economy. After all, the end result was absolute disintegration of the socialist economic model. However, on balance, first the objective conditions internally and externally necessitated some type of top-down reformation. Second, administrative and legislative reorganization proved inadequate in adjusting the tilt of the underlying institutional structures of the economy.[22] Perhaps more time was indeed needed. Third, the major achievement of *perestroika* was that at the time, the reforms brought the socialist societies to the point of no return toward greater openness, autonomy, and development potential.

Macroeconomic challenges and opportunities

By 1990, the early optimism of the *perestroika* era yielded to grim reality. Across the board living standards had declined compared to 1989 levels (see Figure 6.6). Deterioration in basic living conditions, rising uncertainty of employment, as enterprise pushed for more market-oriented operations, as well as gradual falling through of the socialist system's famed safety nets, fed into greater separatist discontent (now, openly expressed in large demonstrations filling city plazas) and an even greater push for political and economic autonomy within the USSR and from the CEE countries. The socialist contract was becoming increasingly unstable and began to crumble.

Collectively these socioeconomic factors gave rise to new economically empowered interest groups that mobilized efforts to gain control over nominally state-owned assets now on the *khozraschet* system. In turn, those of the functioning enterprises were not set to produce competitive output to offer in the international markets. At the same time, there was oversupply of redundant produce in the domestic economy. Facing declining global prices for oil, the Soviet government borrowed internally via debt and monetary emission, virtually bringing the country to "the edge of bankruptcy" (Shatalin *et al.*, 1990, p. 23). The real economy grew at much slower pace. Any nominal wage increases were almost immediately offset by rising inflation.

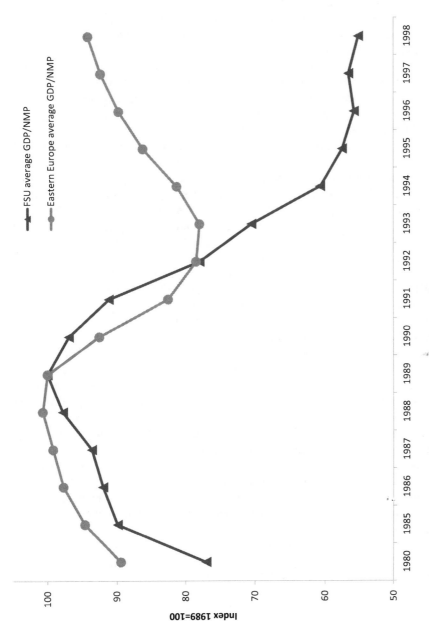

Figure 6.6 Real GDP/NMP dynamic in FSU and CEE, 1980–1998 (1989 = 100).

Notes: for details see methodological explanations at source, UN ECE Economic Survey of Europe 1999 No. 1. Table B.1. NMP=net material product—a measure of national income similar to GDP excluding services sector, which was minimal in the Soviet economic structure.

Source: extrapolated from UNECE (1999)

Inability to sustain consistent investment flows in manufacturing rendered monetary growth groundless, further localizing emerging socioeconomic contradictions. Consumer goods and durable goods deficits became rampant and seemed incurable. Prices spiraled in the parallel markets (read: shadow economy) and emptying of shelves in official markets persisted. Chronic shortages became standard and public discontent was widespread. There were spontaneous protest meetings and other demonstrations against rising prices and unemployment, requiring state guarantees and protection against factory owners, and so on.

The macroeconomic situation in the USSR at the time is well captured in Fischer's (1994) review of the reforms process (see Table 6.3). The data clearly shows continued deterioration of productive capacity, rising debt burden, and real wage suppression. It was becoming increasingly clear that loosening of controls had assumed its own, evolutionary, motion. At the same time, any reversal of granted freedoms would have politically devastated the political edifice of the entire system.

In 1990, the Soviet government sponsored a comprehensive analysis of the economy and development of pragmatic solutions that would help revert the country's (USSR) downward path. The official transformational blueprint became known as the *500 Days Program*. The state's intended focus was of a gradual nature, as there were concerns about immediate and worsening social negative impacts. The government still played an important role and as Kornai (2001) hinted, it was an important role to be considered before going full speed ahead with economic transformation.

Stanley Fischer (1994, p. 235) describes the timing of the *500 Days* program as "extraordinarily ambitious—and unrealistic." To him, the sequencing of reforms was off (privatization was to happen before price liberalization). However, to the authors of the program, privatization revenues helped balance the budget and absorb the money overhang. That would have reduced inflationary pressures once prices were liberalized. In contrast, as evident from Fischer (1994), the Western plans focused more on currency convertibility and opening of the trade and capital accounts, and external capital flows.

The program offered forced but gradual transition away from the socialist mode of production, characteristic to the late USSR, to a more market economy-driven one. It is important to reiterate that this program was adopted and was supposed to be applied on the scale of the entire diverse Soviet economy. The core principles of the proposed program are summarized in Table 6.4. The premise was to achieve economic freedom of every citizen while establishing a sound foundation for an efficient economic system.

There was no dearth in alternative proposals to the model of economic transformation. Despite open discussion and public debates the government could not settle on one approach. By then though it was clear that *perestroika* involved more than just a simple adjustment within the socialist economy. The process of economic change evolving into social transformation had been put in place.

Table 6.3 Select data on the USSR economy, 1985–1991

	1985	1986	1987	1988	1989	1990	1991
GNP growth	0.8	4.1	1.3	2.1	1.5	−4	−13
Gross investment growth	3	8.4	5.6	6.2	4.7	−2.5	−6
Budget deficit/GDP (%)	2.4	6.2	8.8	11	9.5	8.3	20
Real wage	−0.5	−1.5	−0.5	2	1	−6	−15

Source: abridged from Fischer (1994)

Table 6.4 Principles of a functioning new economic system à la "500 Days"

Principle	Description
Maximum freedom of economic agent	Critical social role of talented and skilled citizens in leading free economic activity.
Full responsibility of the economic agent	Private property is foundational and definitive in the rights and obligations of economic agents.
Competitive pressures among suppliers	Key factor stimulating economic activity, diversity and higher quality of consumer products, cost efficiencies and competitive pricing.
Price liberalization	Markets work only when prices are determined freely with little-to-no state intervention.
Proliferation of free market relations	A more efficient system, as opposed to centrally administered, to allow for increased mobility of labor, goods, and financial resources. Non-market sector (education, defense, partially healthcare, science, and culture) remains.
Economic openness	Consistent integration with the world economy and access to global markets by any economic agent.
Social guarantees by state	State at the local and republics levels to guarantee social stability, providing opportunities for descent employment and assisting those in need.
State's withdrawal from the economy	The state cannot interfere with the market aside from its regulatory, administrative role, non-waged goods provisions.

Source: based on Shatalin *et al.* (1990)

This was a once in a lifetime chance for the official entities to take charge by responsible guidance on the economy and to absorb the social shockwaves of spreading ethnic conflicts and other political instability. Yet the official state went from one political and economic program to another with no strong commitment to any scenario. The solution to all problems was often the political one—reshuffling the government cabinet. Common to the overall trend, uncertainty had replaced the predictability of the past decades, disturbing every fiber of the CEE and FSU societies.

After one such cabinet change (January 14, 1991) the new administration took a conservative stance on questions of privatization and liberalization. Blaming "non-labor" activity, foreign bank speculation, and other "non-productive" activities, an ill-famed monetary reform of early 1991 was pushed through. The money bills exchange reform was to be completed within a three-day window. Exchange was only the equivalent of a monthly pay with some bank accounts being frozen for the period of reform duration (with some families receiving compensation on their accounts only now, in the mid-2010s). Due to the lack of smaller denominated banknotes, pensions and other social support payments were stopped. The "initiative" hit hardest the common citizens who had their savings not at *Sberbank* but at home, as most households did, despite deadline revisions by the state.

Immediately after the money bills exchange the Soviet government tried to reintroduce price reforms, which raised prices but did not remove price controls. More activity was pushed into the "grey economy." Prices went up at least three times from 1990 levels. As people lost their savings, more social discontent brewed and attitudes towards the official state worsened.[23] The undeclared purpose of monetary reform was the removal of the monetary overhang, that is, reducing excess liquidity accumulated by households.

The price reform was followed by introduction of the official ruble–dollar convertibility. In 1990, the exchange rate was 0.6 Soviet rubles per one US dollar, by 1991 it was 1.7 rubles, and by 1992 (already in Russia), the ruble dropped to 193 per one dollar. In contrast, a "competitively" determined exchange rate in the foreign currency exchange by then was at 340 rubles for one USD in the grey markets. The year 1992 was also the time when the former Soviet republics, now independent, either set their currency rates or opened up their foreign exchange markets. Hyperinflation kicked in, as the government and central bank attempted to boost liquidity by printing more money. At the same time the state agencies were given a free hand in investigating the economic activity of nominally private enterprises, in an effort to root out non-market behavior and the "grey economy" sector.

The damage of disorientation in the midst of reforms was felt. A peculiar aspect about the specifically Soviet economic system was its designed interconnectedness across various industrial sectors. In fact, in regions (e.g. the mountainous republics of Armenia and Georgia) where typical extensive agricultural growth was not possible, the centralized system created numerous smaller-scale industrial assembly factories, providing full employment as per the socialist ideals. With the weakening center and push for greater enterprise autonomy, those centers of employment began to scale back resulting in massive layoffs. The remnants of past glory stand today as abandoned factory spaces dotting the vast map of the FSU.

The socialist system effectively guaranteed full employment with university graduates usually being assigned to a predetermined post. This certainly sometimes worked against the young specialist's wishes, as the assignment could have been in remote or rural regions. There were formal ways to resolve this but the bottom line was that the system offered employment with guaranteed income with implied stability of job security. In addition, with the socialist emphasis on gender equality, both the CEE and the USSR economies had large proportions of women in the labor force. The end result was sustained up until the 1990s high employment to population ratio compared to the capitalist competition (Figure 6.7).[24]

Accounting for demographic growth, Figure 6.7 is instructive in many ways for our analysis. First, relevant to the *perestroika* period, there was a clear break in the employment situation in the CEE and FSU right around 1989–1991. The decline seemed unstoppable. Second, the losses were immense, to such a degree that on average the region is yet to reach the heights of prior decades. Third, there is an interesting picture in the employment to population ratio growth from the USA where more labor force participation increased in the mid-1960s and was further boosted in the early 1990s with skilled emigration from the CEE and FSU. In more recent years, there are clear signs of strain right around the 2008 global economic crisis, with effects felt most severely in the CEE and FSU. We return to the discussions on the labor market in the next part of our analysis. For now, we note some evidence of gradual decay in social stability and of structural change on the 1989–1990 threshold.

Rising prices in April of 1991, unemployment, sharp declines in exports, organized crime, and a clear systemic crisis of all institutions collectively exacerbated low living standards. Towards the end of 1991, the Soviet economy had GDP falling at least 20 percent compared to the year before and fiscal deficit rising to almost 30 percent of GDP. The Soviet republics refused to pay back taxes to the central government, initiated separate negotiations with the G-7 and international multilateral institutions, and actively began to implement their own economic measures not necessarily aligned with the Union's program.

By December 1991, Gorbachev, who earlier in August 1991 had been practically removed from office in a *coup d'état* averted largely by the rise of Boris Yeltsin, had given up all hopes of preserving the Union even in a decentralized form. Inept economic policy, disorientation in implementation, and lack of appropriate preemptive action against social tensions in

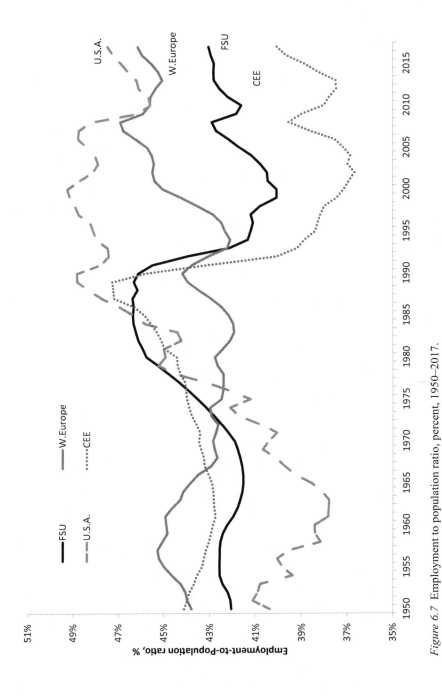

Figure 6.7 Employment to population ratio, percent, 1950–2017.

Note: Western Europe includes figures for the UK.

Source: author's calculations based on data from Conference Board, Total Economy database (TCB, 2017)

the presence of ongoing deformation of old tenets, which the old guard seemed to discard, pushed the socialist model out and effectively ended the history of the Soviet Union and socialist Central and Eastern Europe.

Conclusion: the end of plan

In this chapter we have reviewed some facts on macroeconomic and social developments in the CEE and FSU during the period of the mid-1970s through the late 1980s. Despite the visible social stability and functioning social safety nets all through the stagnation period, Gaidar (2003) argues that by 1985 the USSR had lost its financial maneuvering capacity. Hard currency revenues needed to finance technology and consumer imports dropped following declines in debt repayments from other countries. Domestic economic conditions were only superficially stable. The country depended largely on the world market for natural resources and opportunities to borrow at low interest. In Gaidar's opinion, the drop in global oil prices and subsequent decline in earnings, as the Soviet economy had mostly exhausted opportunities for low-cost surface oil extraction, set the preconditions for change. The static model of the earlier years, while reproducing the general form of the socialist economy did not result in structural efficiencies, as noted above.

In such an environment, Gaidar (2003, 2012) argued there were three possible scenarios: 1) ending the barter exchange system with Eastern Europe and effectively dissolving the socialist bloc; 2) ending food imports, but in the meantime, while technologies are developed and adjustments are being made to reach sustainable production levels, cities would have been brought to starvation; 3) option of choice–let things continue as they are but increase borrowing in the international markets. As history has shown, the third scenario played out. It has proven to be the most calamitous for the USSR and eventually for the entire European socialist economic model.

Astrophysicists might liken the collapse of the Soviet Union to a burst of one of the suns in the universe. The gravity of a stellar body pulls the planets around it. The lasting effect of the USSR was exactly this in the post-WWII world order. Once the foundations were shaken, the dynamic process aimed at separation from the union, largely driven by the local elites, gained full force. The two tangible push forces were the 1985 *perestroika* reforms and the 1989 collapse of the Berlin Wall, but the motions were simmering within the system for quite some time before that. This chapter has addressed some of those tendencies.

The world would not be the same (yet) again. The central plan system has ended. The socialist economic model built with the USSR as the ultimate resource backbone stopped in its operations.

Today, with the hindsight of history and new research emerging on other regions' experiences, it is clear that the 1990s disintegration followed a political blueprint tested in history since the early Mesopotamian civilizations. Namely, the elites (or those newly arising interest groups) struggled to retain economic power as the strength of the pull from the center began to weaken. The new interest groups would be empowered, and often politically connected, more ambitious entrepreneurs. In the socialist context, once in power, the new groups acted to protect their positions by building new business and political alliances with other equally strong groups, domestically or internationally, or rallied societies, ready for change, to nationalistic and populist slogans.[25]

The political elites, consisting of either newly elected or incumbent communist party leaders, across the USSR republics and CEE moved swiftly to ascertain their controls over local industrial and infrastructure capacities. The processes of disintegration in Eastern Europe unraveled exceptionally fast. The popularity of new pro-independent movements led by educated young intellectuals and union leaders was immense. As such, in Hungary, Poland, or Czechoslovakia, unlike the USSR, there was little need for prolonged public discussion on the appropriateness of market reforms. In the CEE the question was not to liberalize prices or to pursue privatization. Instead, the questions were about how fast one could reasonably have all market reforms pushed through necessary legislative hurdles.

Earlier experiments with market socialism in the CEE had left their footprint, leaving Eastern European societies in somewhat better shape than those in the USSR ahead of market liberalization reforms. By 1986, Hungary had a need to enact a bankruptcy law and launched a two-tier banking system by 1987 allowing private commercial banks to operate. Local governments, cooperatives, and enterprises set up the latter. Early in the process, some banks were able to bring capital from the West. Already in 1988 Hungary benefited from IMF assistance, albeit for instituting the infamous austerity program.

With the fall of the Berlin Wall in 1989, East Germany was reunited with West Germany and began the gradual and painful process of integration into a far more advanced bigger economy. The initial shock came with the shutdown of redundant and inefficient enterprises relative to the production process in West Germany. However, as a result there was an initial rise in unemployment and worsening of living standards in the East, to be partially offset by surplus from West Germany. In either case, GDR's 'transition' was unique in as much as the country did not experience the worst of the transition shocks that were yet to come to other CEEs and republics of the FSU. GDR went from the Soviet protectorate right into the West German political and economic domain.

In Czechoslovakia, following initial inertia, reform programs began to appear in 1990. Of all the CEE and smaller FSU republics, this country, aside from East Germany, was more industrialized with relatively competitive consumer and household goods production (e.g. glass). The country largely escaped the severe and degrading supplies shortages experienced in the FSU and a smooth political transition, on which we have already commented, went into the history books as a model of system change.

The federal structure of Yugoslavia cracked as hyperinflation hit in 1989 despite a seemingly stable period before that. A stabilization program was implemented and consisted of wage controls, monetary tightening, prices liberalization, budget cuts, and opening of the economy with currency convertibility. The program failed due to political disagreements. Economic malaise, which was worsening by day, eventually gave rise to disastrous ethnic conflict and war for all practical matters.

The relatively backward, compared to CEE peers, Albania, Bulgaria, and Romania, would stay on the central plan course until 1992. Subsequently, reforms stumbled either due to lack of capacity or inadequate political will. It would take several attempts before those economies began to shift from the socialist economic model, first to a mixed, and later capitalist market-based one.

By the end of the 1991, for all practical purposes, there was no more centralized socialist economic system in Europe or Central Asia. The Baltic states of Lithuania, Estonia, and Latvia left the USSR in the summer of 1991. In December, the remaining Soviet republics (except for the Baltics and Georgia), all newly independent nations, formed the Commonwealth of Independent States (CIS). It is tempting to view the CIS as a transient stage between the tightly integrated and controlled Soviet Union system and full independence of the post-1991 breakup.

And while the new framework provides some standardization across a range of areas, from air travel and cargo shipments to development aid, the old trade links were severed.

New diplomatic contacts had to be established. New regional blocs would emerge. There was no center or anyone from a ministry from Moscow to sanction a financial bailout or to re-direct investment from one republic to another based on party or personal preferences.

Each of the newly formed 29 countries of Central and Eastern Europe and the former Soviet Union was now on its own. The CMEA framework had crumbled. Each country had to start from scratch to build its own foreign and domestic policies, find trade partners, procure adequate investment, and negotiate with multilateral agencies to sustain the reforms momentum. In the process, the period between 1990 and 2000 would prove to be one of the most disastrous in peacetime history in terms of self-inflicted economic and social pains. The human aspect of transition would prove to be perhaps the most difficult of all, as we argue in the next part of this book.

The old system of socialist ideology, sustained economic growth, and collective social responsibility was gone. Now, the absolute opposite, capitalism held the promise of prosperity, freedom, and acceptance in the world. This was the end of the socialist plan . . .

Notes

1 Here, Francis Spufford's *Red Plenty* (Spufford, 2010) comes to mind as an eloquent manifestation of the, at the time, shared belief in the economic and social superiority of the socialist model. Crisscrossing history with fiction this novel reflects the enthusiasm of the 1950s–1960s with strong growth across industries, science, culture, education, infrastructure, etc.

2 Also see an impactful analysis of the Soviet economic growth model in Ofer (1987).

3 For example, see informative discussion in Spence *et al.* (2009).

4 Of course, extending the 30-year threshold logic, one might wonder about the course of events then in the 1990s, had the 1960s seen a more intensive capital investment. On Kondratieff waves, socialist cycles, and capitalist economy cycles, see Bernard *et al.* (2014).

5 The list of relevant publications would also include an informative attempt to merge socialist ideals (e.g. greater equality in income, status, provision of basic human needs) within a context of industrialized economy, e.g. Grand and Estrin (1989).

6 Soft budget constraint (SBC) was a term developed by Janos Kornai (e.g. Kornai, 1979a and 1979b; Kornai *et al.*, 2003; Maskin, 1996; etc.) to describe shortage economics of CEE countries. In this situation, an economic agent—enterprise—is no longer bounded in its activities to a fixed budget and is able to procure a state subsidy or a loan to remain afloat. The practice contradicted a competitive market principle by which inefficient enterprises would declare bankruptcy. A somewhat related dynamic has resurfaced during the GFC of 2008–2009 with widespread government-sponsored bailout programs across a diverse group of countries.

7 Property rights would be the ultimate institutional contradiction of the socialist economic model of the CEE/FSU region. The contradiction would remain unresolved until the liberalization reforms of the early 1990s. For more on the critical aspects of clear delineations of ownership in the socialist economy, see earlier cited discussion in Kornai (1992).

8 Hungarian share of exports to the capitalist world was the highest (approximately 32.6% of the total in 1983 according to the official CMEA statistics; also see Table 5.3 for indirect confirmation) in the CMEA.

9 For a detailed analysis of economic reformation, see Brus (1986c).

10 See Kornai (1991) on early analysis of market socialism and ownership rights contradictions.

11 The literature on the topic is vast, with contributions from contemporary researchers, mostly focused on developing accurate statistical sets for cross-country comparisons, to more recent works evaluating conceptual and analytical underpinnings of the socialist model. As directional references, but by no means exclusive guides since alternatives are many, the following readings may be useful: Sakwa (1999), Brown (2009), Bacon and Sandle (2002), Shatalin *et al.* (1990), and Gaidar (2012).

12 Some elaboration on this and other aspects of Brezhnev's tenure can be found in Thatcher (2002). For alternative estimates on defense spending and its impact, see Kotz and Weir (1997).

13 Also see Harrison (2002) for insightful critique on the 1970s–1980s, stagnation era, macroeconomic analysis, and statistics.
14 For unabated critique of the BAM project, see Ward (2001).
15 See film's IMDb's page online: www.imdb.com/title/tt0073179/.
16 For example, see official biography (in Russian), Raisa Gorbacheva at The Gorbachev Foundation. Available online: www.gorby.ru/gorbacheva/biography/.
17 On further reorganizations, see Åslund (1988).
18 On the early efforts of ruble convertibility, see Holzman (1991).
19 For some, problems with *perestroika* were associated with unsuccessful attempts to adjust a socialist state to a post-industrial model, e.g. Rosser and Rosser (1997).
20 One of the direct, yet constructive, critiques would be from Gaidar (2012); also see Fischer (1994).
21 For this and other insights from one of the insiders to policy decisions of the time, see Medvedev, R. (2008).
22 For additional conceptual discussions on *perestroika* reform, see Hewett (1988) and on precursors' attempts to reform, see Mau (1996).
23 We review some of the specific indicators in the next chapter. More detailed data by country is available from the UN/ECE Common Database. Available online: www.unece.org/ead/pub/991/991_xt.html#appendixb.
24 Some discussions on the Soviet labor market may be found in Nove (1986).
25 For institutional inconsistencies and the role of political and business interest groups in transition economies, see Dale (2011). For broader, non-unilinear analysis of economic history, role of political elites, evolving market structures, and case studies from other regions, see Bavel (2016).

7 Free market reform
Liberalization, privatization, shock therapy, and policy misfortunes

All happy families are alike; each unhappy family is unhappy in its own way.

Leo Tolstoy, *Anna Karenina*

Setting the stage

'Wind of Change' was a song performed in 1991 by the Scorpions—a German rock band from Hanover. The song captured, perhaps most accurately, despite evident economic disruption, the early jubilant mood of hope and progressive change steadily engulfing post-socialist societies of the late 1980s–early 1990s.[1] Inspired by the band's trip to the Soviet Union, the song's lyrics spoke of the progressive social movements and revolutionary transformation of the time. The official video included documentary clips of peace demonstrations across the world, the first friendly meetings of Soviet and Western leaders, dismantling of the Berlin Wall, and other scenes of hope and reconciliation. Resonating in every corner of the globe, the song became a top hit on international music charts almost instantaneously.

In the policy and academic circles it was understood that a move from the socialist economic model to a new free market-based system would not have been without some hardship. Theoretical economics offered reassurance to wavering political elites prepared for initial minor macroeconomic setbacks. Irrespective of any challenges, the general sense of naivety of the grand expectation, dictated the onset of a new, perceived as progressive, social and economic order. Nobody disagreed with Sir Winston Churchill in regard to the character of democracy as a social system, alas omitting his full disclosure that there was hardly any objectively perfect political [social] formation.[2]

Lacking the refinement of theoretical visions of the early 20th century, the actual political and social model of socialism in CEE and the USSR was inevitably riddled with many structural flaws, grown over the years. From the earlier discussion, there should be no difficulty in picking some of the self-evident controversies, for example the enormity of central planning and rudimentary financial system. But to the extent that such judgment leads to subjective conclusions, a related discussion is beyond the scope of the present narrative.[3]

For better or worse, the CEE/USSR socialist model featured engagement of relatively uniform political and economic measures. The interim result, as discussed above, was rapid post-WWII recovery, industrial base development in previously agrarian economies, attainment of higher literacy standards, and rapid upward social mobility, as well as provision of sustained social guarantees across the board. As reviewed in Chapter 6, some of those achievements began to lag behind Western standards. Political and economic measures aside, the problem was partly also due to the diverging starting levels between the developed West and developing socialist economies.

However, uniformity in the socialist standard evolved into apparent uniformity of perception of mutual interconnectedness at the society level, even if somewhat on the surface and even where ideology played a weaker role (e.g. Hungary) or macroeconomic policies differed substantially from the core model (e.g. Yugoslavia). To some degree, there was a perception of uniformity—sameness—from within the socialist "family" (even despite the social protest movements). That also seemed to be a common perception for many outside observers of the "socialist bloc".

The *perestroika* reforms and the fall of the Berlin Wall ended the uniformity perception. And the market transition reforms of the early 1990s carried the social transformation forward. Once the non-existence of such uniformity of the socialist experience, despite all perceptions to the contrary, was unveiled, the shock to the societies and elites of the CEE/USSR and, perhaps most dramatically, to Western observers and economic advisers, was difficult to immediately absorb.

Now, as market liberalization reforms unraveled through the 1990s, a gloomier outlook of degrading living standards, immense human stress, and national disintegration of the transition process replaced the elation from the "Wind of Change." And it was at that very moment that the elusive path of shared socialist destiny ended and, paraphrasing Leo Tolstoy, each formerly socialist family became unhappy in its own, very unique, way.

What happened during the 1990s

By the early 1990s, countries in Central and Eastern Europe (first) and (then) the former Soviet republics, after dissolution of the USSR in 1991, launched their market transition reforms. Professional economists from every corner of the world quickly engaged in a massive, unprecedented research effort advising the new governments and multilateral organizations on macroeconomic transition policies. In many ways, the 1990s would signify the "golden age" of theoretical economics and applied macroeconomic policy prescriptions.[4] The topic of the post-socialist transition earned its rightful mention in economics textbooks. And today there is no lack of dedicated thematic publications of all forms on the free market transition topic: journal articles, policy briefs, edited and authored research monographs, blogs, and so on.[5]

At the time, though, recommendations streaming from the International Monetary Fund, the World Bank, and from a broad range of professional economists advocated a steadfast, resolute, and rapid approach to reforms. The focus was on the trio of market liberalization, macroeconomic stabilization, and privatization reforms. If all was to be done right, market reforms were to be introduced quickly and proactively sustained. The pace of reforms mattered and faster was preferred to slower. In the most radical of scenarios, a "shock therapy" (or "big bang") type of reform promised faster and sound transition . . . at least when theoretically modeled (more on that later in this chapter).

The critical mass of private entrepreneurial activity would eventually arise. Reforms sequencing was a high-level exercise in economic policy with far-reaching practical implications. Institutional development was expected to spring into action from the efficiency of the market-oriented foundations. Once all was settled, a transition to a new order would have occurred, leaving the rest to the good fortunes of the free market.[6]

In Chapter 2, we offered some early conceptual thoughts on *perestroika* and the subsequent market reforms in the region. We introduced our reader to some elements of the transition debate, largely based on post-initial reforms literature. We also emphasized the contradicting nature of the reforms and of the concept of transition at the time.

In this chapter, we extend the conversation to new, country-specific evidence on macroeconomic performance. At that more individual level, drastic declines in social welfare, competitiveness, and institutional erosion (recall Figure 2.5 in Chapter 2) become more pronounced, calling for a cautious interpretation. Paraphrasing Tolstoy, once again, indeed, they were "unhappy in their own way."

It is happening

We start with Figures 7.1 and 7.2 that offer a bird's-eye view, first, by country group (Table 7.1 clarifies country-regional group designations). Both figures help visualize changes in the real GDP index derived from the Conference Board Total Economy Database (2017) from 1989 to 2017. Figure 7.1 reports on the former Soviet Union (FSU) and Figure 7.2 on Central and Eastern Europe (CEE) and the three Baltic states (BS). Setting the 1989 GDP as the baseline, we note a dramatic collapse in output across all regions during the initial years of transition (early 1990s), with varying subsequent improvement.

The initial output declines may have been expected considering the breakup of the traditional trade links across CMEA and retraction of guaranteed demand for industrial output (e.g. Fischer and Gelb, 1991; Blanchard and Kremer, 1997). Hardly anyone expected a collapse of such drastic magnitude and such slow recovery to the pre-reform levels across the board (Calvo and Coricelli, 1993).[7]

Regional details in Figures 7.1 and 7.2 reveal a geographic bias as well: things deteriorated rather quickly and at a greater scale the further East one went from the Berlin Wall. The CEE and BS economies bounced back to pre-reforms levels much faster than the CIS-FSU group. For this latter cluster, recovery to 1989 levels did not occur until approximately the early 2000s. Output declines were massive and protracted. It is clearly seen from Figure 7.1 that transition reforms-induced recession lasted several years in the weakest of the CIS economies, often referred to as transitional periphery in the Caucasus and Central Asia.[8]

Those "major negative surprises," as Gomulka (1992, p. 369) referred to them, amounted to more than just dramatic losses in output. Initially discussed in the context of the early market transformation in Poland (see Box 7.1), four problems characterized the entire early process of transition across the board: 1) severe and prolonged recession; 2) hyperinflation and skyrocketing unemployment; 3) delayed administrative and institutional restructuring; and 4) lack of foreign direct investment. Attempting to remedy the worsening conditions on the ground with further austerity (adopting modern terminology here) barely worked.

Expanding on the above, Table 7.1 adds more concrete country details within each regional group. The Baltics, previously part of the USSR, are shown here as part of the EU-8. The latter is comprised of the eight CEE economy's members of the European Union (EU) as of 2004—when the Czech Republic, Hungary, Poland, Slovak Republic, Slovenia, Estonia, Latvia, and Lithuania were admitted. For the purposes of comparison, we keep Bulgaria and Romania admitted to the EU in 2007 and Croatia in 2013 in the Southeast Europe group and return to the European integration process discussion a bit later. The Central Asian former Soviet republics are grouped as Central Asian CIS.[9] The Republic of Georgia is kept in the Caucasian CIS and Ukraine is part of the European CIS for the purposes of comparison only.

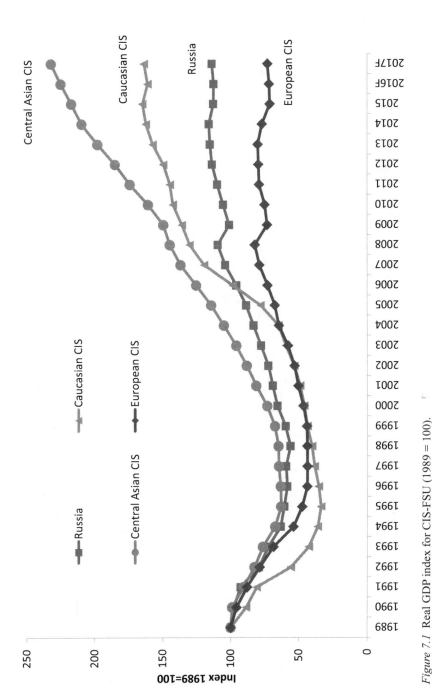

Figure 7.1 Real GDP index for CIS-FSU (1989 = 100).

Notes: derived from total GDP at 2016 price level with updated 2011 PPPs. Data for 2017 refers to preliminary estimate; F = forecast or preliminary data.

Source: author's calculations based on data from The Conference Board Total Economy Database (TCB, 2017)

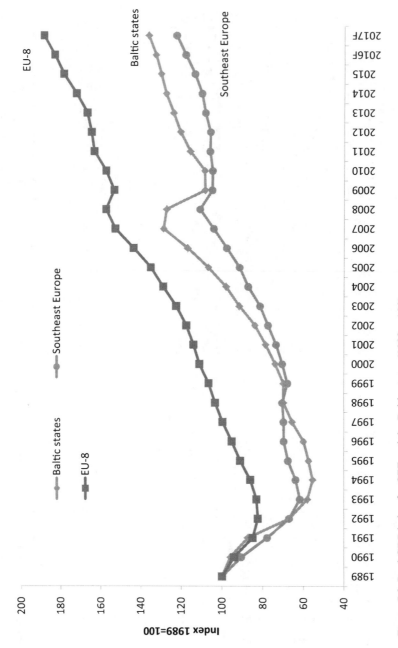

Figure 7.2 Real GDP index for CEE and the Baltic states (1989 = 100).

Notes: derived from total GDP at 2016 price level with updated 2011 PPPs. Data for 2017 refers to preliminary estimate; F = forecast or preliminary data. Baltic states are shown separately for illustration; also included in EU-8.

Source: author's calculations based on data from The Conference Board Total Economy Database (TCB, 2017)

Table 7.1 Changes to key macroeconomic indicators in the first reform years

Regional Group	Country	Worst annual GDP growth decline	Max annual inflation rate (1992–2000)*	Loss in industrial output**	Year when 1989 GDP level was recovered***
EU–8	Czech Rep	–11.6 (1991)	10.6 (1998)	–21.9 (1991)	1996
	Estonia	–14.1 (1992)	89.8 (1993)	–3.9 (1999)	2002
	Hungary	–11.9 (1991)	28.3 (1995)	–18.3 (1991)	2002
	Latvia	–32.1 (1992)	243.3 (1992)	–9.0 (1999)	2005
	Lithuania	–21.3 (1992)	410.2 (1993)	–9.9 (1999)	2005
	Poland	–9.7 (1990)	45.3 (1992)	–25.4 (1990)	1995
	Slovak Rep	–14.6 (1991)	13.4 (1994)	–19.3 (1991)	1996
	Slovenia	–8.9 (1991)	32.9 (1993)	–0.8 (1999)	1997
Southeast Europe	Albania	–28 (1991)	226 (1992)	–41.9 (1991)	1999
	Bosnia & Herzegovina	–30.8 (1993)	83,327.6 (1992)	–92.2 (1993)	1998
	Bulgaria	–10.9 (1990)	1,058.4 (1997)	–20.2 (1991)	2006
	Croatia	–21.1 (1991)	1,494.7 (1993)	–28.5 (1991)	2006
	Macedonia, FYR	–10.2 (1990)	126.6 (1994)	–17.2 (1991)	2007
	Romania	–16.2 (1991)	255.2 (1993)	–25.3 (1992)	2005
	Serbia & Montenegro	–30.8 (1993)	95.6 (1996)	–37.3 (1993)	<1989
European CIS	Belarus	–11.7 (1994)	2,221 (1994)	–14.6 (1994)	2003
	Moldova	–30.9 (1994)	39.2 (1999)	–27.7 (1994)	<1989
	Ukraine	–22.9 (1994)	4,734.9 (1993)	–27.3 (1994)	<1989
Russia	Russia	–14.5 (1992)	874.6 (1993)	–20.9 (1994)	2007
Caucasian CIS	Armenia	–41.8 (1992)	3,373.5 (1994)	–48.2 (1992)	2005
	Azerbaijan	–23.1 (1993)	1,662.2 (1994)	–30.4 (1992)	2006
	Georgia	–44.9 (1992)	162.7 (1995)	–45.8 (1992)	<1989
Central Asian CIS	Kazakhstan	–12.6 (1994)	1,877.4 (1994)	–28.1 (1994)	2004
	Kyrgyz Rep	–19.8 (1994)	37 (1999)	–36.9 (1994)	2008
	Tajikistan	–32.3 (1992)	38.6 (2001)	–25.4 (1994)	2012
	Turkmenistan	–17.3 (1994)	NA	–24.7 (1994)	2002
	Uzbekistan	–11.1 (1992)	1,550.0 (1994)	–6.7 (1992)	2001

Notes: *annual % change in consumer prices; **worst annual loss and year; *** <1989 refers to GDP below 1989 level as of 2017. Inflation is defined as per source as consumer prices (annual %). Loss in industrial output is based on real gross industrial output annual change over preceding year, as per UNECE (2004), Appendix Table B.4.

Sources: derived from WDI (2017) for GDP trends and UNECE (2004) for the remaining data

Box 7.1

The Balcerowicz Plan was a macroeconomic reforms program proposed in 1989 by Poland's Deputy Prime Minister at the time, Leszek Balcerowicz. Dubbed "shock therapy," the plan was somewhat similar to the *500 Days* program in the USSR. Poland's blueprint would serve as practical guidance for domestic market reforms in the CEE and FSU. Poland's immediate positive macroeconomic results led to policy debates on the benefits of shock therapy and to a flurry of academic publications.

Effectively, there were four key parts to the plan. First, macroeconomic stabilization was engaged with fiscal austerity as its pillar (including enforcing tax collections, raising interest rates, and removing any soft budget constraint protections). Second, most prices and economic activity were liberalized by January 1990, stimulating rise in private enterprises and breaking the implied support for state-owned companies. Third, restrictions on foreign trade and investment were lifted as the national currency became convertible. Finally, structural alterations were pushed through. The last measure included early small-scale privatization, foundation of capital markets, and new pro-market legislature on privatization, tax codes, and corporate bankruptcies.

Curtailing hyperinflation and achieving early fiscal balance, conditions of the IMF's and World Bank's financial backing, were early gains of the plan. Private business activity sprang up inspired by the enthusiasm of the perceived break with the socialist past. Consumer goods shortages were eliminated as trade with Western Europe began.

However, those gains were short-lived. Very soon the social costs of the reform became evident and turned out to be significantly greater that had been expected. As inefficient state-funded enterprises shut down, private job growth was inadequate to compensate for the losses. Structural unemployment went up (in 1993 reaching 16.4 percent of the labor force), GDP declined, and industrial production collapsed 25.4 percent in real terms between 1989 and 1990, as CMEA links were severed. The mood quickly changed from enthusiasm to criticism of the government's policies.

As the country pulled through in later years, it is often stated that Poland's shock-therapy reforms paved the way to economic stabilization and future growth. However, it is also likely that in the haste to push the reforms in fear of political reversals, the point of no return to the old system may have been crossed. As such, the new government had no other option but to hold the course and persevere with subsequent hardships, motivated by reaching the end goal of a fully market-driven economy.

Additional reading

Adam, J. 1999. Transition to a Market Economy in Poland. In Adam, J. *Social Costs of Transformation to a Market Economy in Post-Socialist Countries.* New York: Palgrave.

EBRD. 2000. Transition Report 2000. London: EBRD.

PBS. 2000. Interview with Leszek Balcerowicz. Available online: www.pbs.org/wgbh/commandingheights/shared/minitext/int_leszekbalcerowicz.html.

The Warsaw Voice. 2009. Balcerowicz Plan: 20 Years On. Available online: www.warsawvoice.pl/WVpage/pages/article.php/21501/article.

According to the most recent data, following price liberalization and removal of centralized controls, Georgia saw the worst decline in annual GDP growth rates by 45 percent followed by Armenia by 41.8 percent, both happening between 1991 and 1992. In both cases, the volatile political situation, military conflicts, and economic devastation (in Armenia's case compounded by ongoing recovery from the devastating earthquake of 1988) led to years of recession, outward migration, poverty, and underdevelopment (e.g. Gevorkyan, 2015). At the same time, hyperinflation reached previously unimaginable levels, for example in Bosnia and Herzegovina, Ukraine, Armenia, Belarus, Croatia, Bulgaria, and others. Only the highest annual inflation rates are reported in Table 7.1. In most cases, hyperinflation was sustained over several years in a row.

Industrial output fell by over 80 percent in Georgia, 74.2 percent in Albania, 70.6 percent in Uzbekistan, and elsewhere as shown in Table 7.1. While one might suggest that the fall in industrial output was due to growth in the service sector (as we indicated in previous discussions, the socialist economy's service sector was minimal), there is no evidence that would support such a statement in the early reform years, especially in the CIS group. Most likely to blame would be a practically instantaneous collapse of the established socialist market system that stitched together the formerly socialist economies. Disorientation in the economy and society progressed quickly.

Overall, GDP levels would not return to the 1989 levels until late 1990 and in many cases not until the mid-2000s (note Armenia, Bulgaria, Croatia, Romania, and others). In several cases, such as Georgia, Moldova, Serbia and Montenegro, and Ukraine, GDP levels are yet to come back to pre-reform levels at the time of writing in 2017. Elsewhere, Popov (2007a) suggested that in such cases macroeconomic distortions across transition samples might have been more severe and extensive.

Common market breakup

The breakup of the CMEA and forceful shift away from a centralized production system also resulted in disruption to the established trade patterns. In relative terms, there was a strong shift by Eastern European countries (led by EU-8) from trade with former socialist economies, as can be inferred from data in Table 7.2. That was compensated by a greater shift towards trade with Western Europe, with European Union integration prospects in sight.

Furthermore, breakup of the common market also meant disappearance of the guaranteed demand for domestic industrial output, which further exacerbated already severe recession across the region. Based on our earlier discussions, for CEE there was little sense in continuing trading in similar standard manufactured commodities. Yet another phase of the comparative advantage-like trade scheme was evolving. Only this time, it was driven largely by Western European firms jumping on the opportunity of sudden access to a skilled, educated, and lower-cost labor force as well as industrial infrastructure.

The pattern was slightly different in the FSU. The largest economy, Russia, gradually transitioned into global energy markets, while still retaining a significant role in the broader intra-CIS market. Smaller economies, Armenia, Bulgaria, Georgia, and Moldova, saw massive industrial output collapse as the common market shut down with subsequent

Table 7.2 Merchandise trade by direction CEE and Russia in 1980–2004 (% of total trade)

Region	1980	1990	1995	1999	2000	2004
Exports from Eastern Europe to:						
Eastern Europe and CIS	48.5	38.1	28.6	20.8	20.7	23.2
Developed market economies	35.7	49.5	62.6	73.4	73.1	71
Developing economies	15.8	12.4	8.8	5.8	6.2	5.8
Exports from FSU (Russia, after 1991) to:						
Eastern Europe	34.5	21.8	16.8	17.8	20	15.6
Developed market economies	42.2	49.5	60.6	57.8	55.6	56.7
Developing economies	23.3	28.7	22.6	24.4	24.4	27.7

Source: adapted from UNECE (2004)

Note: *Eastern European CMEA members. Also see methodological note at source.

de-industrialization and a mass exodus of the skilled labor force due to migration. As we discuss later, for many smaller economies the ability to draw foreign direct investment (FDI) would remain a challenge all through the 2010s, leaving the smaller economies significantly dependent on trade with their larger neighbors.

Macroeconomics of human transition

Even with equal macroeconomic disruption shock, higher pre-transition GDP made it more difficult to climb back up to pre-reform levels. Figure 7.3 offers such a comparison of pre-transition (1989) to a mid-point (1995) in transition in purchasing power parity dollars. According to The Conference Board Total Economy (TCB, 2017) data, in 1995 none of the CEE/FSU economies were able to recover to pre-transition living standards (measured by GDP per capita).

The difficulty in restoring previously higher income levels might be due to the pre-transition environment in each specific economy. As one might recall, the socialist model was characterized by active and sustained fiscal provisions in non-waged goods as well as guaranteed demand for output and consequently stable income at individual levels. Now, during transition, the fate of individual countries seemed to depend on its industrial structure but also the relative degree of the economy's involvement in common trade, dependence on the socialist market aggregate demand, and reliance on any administrative subsidies.

On the latter, recall the earlier mentioned widespread practice of ministerial discretion in investment funds allocation in the context of "soft budget constraint". Roland and Verdier (1999) formalize this argument by effectively directing their attention to the drying up of investment fund flows during the transition period, which in turn precluded sustained growth of production across sectors. In other words, disruption in trade links, decline in investment fund allocation, and protracted capital depreciation exacerbated the inertia of falling output as firms sought new capital infusions. This seems to be a more plausible, practical, explanation of what exactly happened. The explanation is particularly relevant to the countries of the former Soviet Union. In that sense, simply blaming stalled politics and inability to push reforms implementation aggressively enough or inertia of state-owned enterprises, would serve at best only as partial explanation .[10]

Further, Figure 7.3 is intentionally set up in levels to emphasize the underdevelopment problem, especially among transitional periphery states, in monetary terms. It is also possible to see in Figure 7.3 the relative positions of countries within each region relative to each other. For example, Georgia's GDP per capita is significantly higher than Armenia's in 1988 but both effectively end up at the same level by 1995. Likewise, strengthened by its industrial output and agricultural subsidies, Ukraine had larger 1989 GDP per capita than Belarus, both declining to almost the same level by 1995.

There were no gains in per capita income between the years of 1989 and 1995 for any of the CEE/FSU economies. If anything, as Figure 7.4 confirms, it is more appropriate to talk about the relative scale of disintegration and macroeconomic disruption immediately following the market reforms launch. The observation of declining GDP per capita (especially in the smaller economies such as Armenia, Georgia, Moldova, Tajikistan) is particularly disconcerting, even adjusting for population losses due to massive migration out of those countries since the early 1990s (a topic of our discussion in Chapter 8).

In relative terms, the 1995 GDP per capita for the smaller countries was significantly below the 1989 level. Between the two periods, losses amounted to 74 percent of the initial

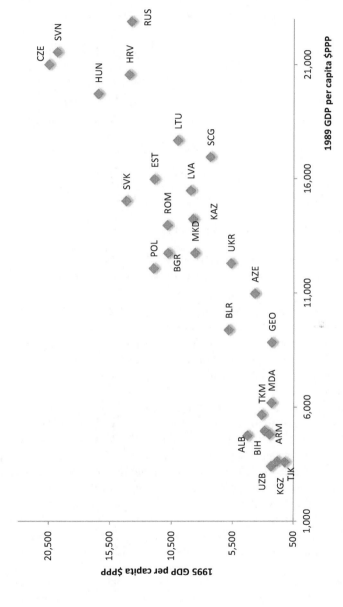

Figure 7.3 Real GDP per capita by country before and after transition ($PPP 2016).

Note: SCG stands for combined Serbia and Montenegro value as per the source data availability.

Source: author's calculations based on data from The Conference Board Total Economy Database (TCB, 2017)

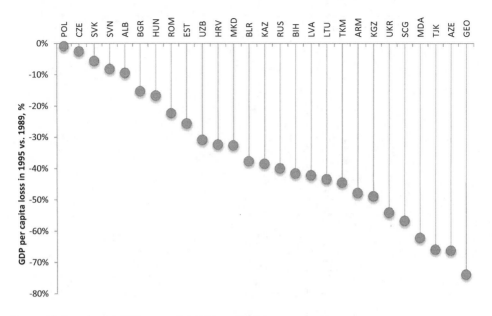

Figure 7.4 Loss in real GDP per capita 1995 vs. 1989, by country, %.

Notes: The loss is estimated as a percent share of the dollar-value difference between 1995 and 1989 levels; SCG stands for combined Serbia and Montenegro value as per the source data availability.

Source: author's calculations based on data from The Conference Board Total Economy Database (TCB, 2017)

levels in Georgia, 66 percent in Azerbaijan and Tajikistan, 62 percent in Moldova, 57 percent for Serbia and Montenegro combined, and so on.

At the same time, some, particularly those in the EU-8 group, with higher initial per capita incomes appear to be relatively better positioned compared to others (see Figure 7.3 levels). Quite a few were able to hold on to their pre-transition positions relatively better. Poland's loss in 1995 was barely 1 percent of the 1989 level and for Czech Republic, Slovakia, and Slovenia, losses did not exceed 10 percent of the 1989 base. Hardly any more convincing data may be needed to suggest that the difference in starting conditions played a critical and definitive role in the varying experiences of the post-socialist transition across the economies of Central and Eastern Europe and the former USSR.

So far, much of our discussion has revolved around aggregates, omitting essential intra-country distributional aspects. In fact, problems of income inequality within each CEE/FSU economy would rise to the top of the economic development agenda by the mid-1990s and are central to any sensible interpretation of the reforms process. We turn to that discussion in subsequent chapters. However, some early intuition can already be picked up from the above discussions. Reporting average changes in employment growth, Figure 7.5 adds another dimension to the evolving story of human transition.

By now, the pattern in Figure 7.5 should be familiar: the weakest, less industrialized, and more dependent on central government's allocations have seen some of the largest drastic declines in employment growth of the first half of the transition period (if we assume the latter to be bounded by the 1990–2000 time period). Some of the EU-8 countries (e.g. Hungary, Slovenia, Estonia, etc.) seem to also have suffered significant declines in employment growth but unlike the FSU or Southeast European economies, the former were able to either restore positive growth or minimize the losses.

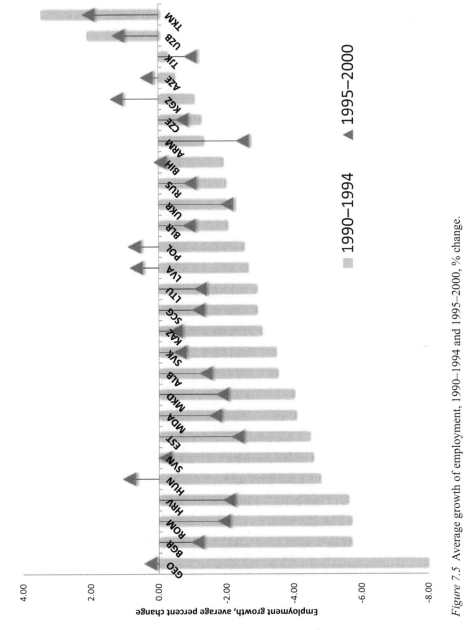

Figure 7.5 Average growth of employment, 1990–1994 and 1995–2000, % change.

Source: author's calculations based on data from The Conference Board Total Economy Database (TCB, 2017)

Conceptualizing the reform

Helping us put the above facts in a more conceptual context, Table 7.3 summarizes some key facts about market transition reforms by country. The timeline is based on regular updates from annual *Transition Reports* published by the European Bank for Reconstruction and Development (EBRD). EBRD, established in 1991, is a multilateral international financial institution supporting market-oriented transition in CEE and the FSU by providing lending to a range of development and entrepreneurial projects.[11]

Table 7.3 Liberalization and privatization reforms in CEE and FSU through the 1990s

Regional Group	Country	Liberalization	Privatization	Reform Type	Significant integration and other events around year 2000
Southeast Europe	Romania	1990	1991*	Shock therapy	WTO membership in 1995
	Bulgaria	1991	1994 / 1996*	Shock therapy	EU accession negotiations in 2000
	Albania	1991	1995*	Shock therapy	WTO membership in 2000
	Bosnia and Herzegovina	2000	1998*	Gradual	Banking law in 2000
	Croatia	1991	1992 / 1998*		WTO membership in 2000
	Macedonia, FYR	1992	1993	Gradual	EU Stabilization & Association Agreement negotiations in 2000
	Serbia and Montenegro	2000	1997	Shock therapy	UN economic sanctions lifted in 2001
EU-8	Hungary	1968	1990	Gradual	OECD membership in 1996
	Poland	1990	1990 / 1993	Shock therapy	Membership of WTO in 1995 and of OECD in 1996
	Czech Rep	1991	1992* / 1994*	Shock therapy	EU accession negotiations in1998
	Slovak Rep#	1991	1992*	Shock therapy	Membership of WTO in 1995 and of OECD in 2000
	Slovenia	1989–1994	1993	Gradual	First Eurobond in 1996
	Estonia	1992	1992	Shock therapy	EU accession negotiations in 1998
	Latvia	1992	1994	Shock therapy	WTO membership 1999
	Lithuania	1992	1991*	Shock therapy	IMF stand-by agreement in 2000
European CIS	Ukraine	1994	1994*	Shock therapy	Floating exchange rate in 2000
	Belarus	1995	1994*	Partial	FX trade liberalization in 2000
	Moldova	1992	1993*		94% of state collective farms privatized by 1999

Regional Group	Country	Liberalization	Privatization	Reform Type	Significant integration and other events around year 2000
Russia	Russia	1992	1993*	Shock therapy	First Eurobond in 1997/financial crisis in 1998
Caucasian CIS	Armenia	1995	1991–1994*	Shock therapy	WTO membership in 2003
	Azerbaijan	1992	1997*	Partial	State property ministry in 2000
	Georgia	1991–1992	1993 / 1996*	Shock therapy	WTO membership in 2000
Central Asian CIS	Kazakhstan	1994	1994	Partial	In 1999 first sovereign bond issue in CIS since the Russian crisis
	Kyrgyz Rep	1992	1997*	Gradual	Customs union with RUS, KAZ, & BLR in 1997
	Tajikistan	1992 / 1996	1996	Partial	By 2000 majority of state-owned cotton ginneries sold by auction
	Turkmenistan	1996	1997	Partial	Ten-year plan adopted in 1999
	Uzbekistan	1994	1996	Partial	Two exchange rates (budget and inter-bank) unified in 2000

Notes: see Box 7.1 for discussion on East Germany (GDR); # Slovakia adopted gradual reforms after breakup of Czechoslovakia in 1993; *voucher privatization; Liberalization refers to "most prices liberalized" as per EBRD; Privatization: includes legislature, implementation, small and large entity. In cases of two dates: phases of significant reforms. The timing depending on specific research focus may vary from what appears here.

Sources: derived from Roland (2000) and EBRD Transition Reports EBRD (2000, 2001, 2002, 2003, 2004)

In Table 7.3, we report the starting or completion years of the two integral reforms: market liberalization and privatization. A move to market-based foundations required the establishment of a radically different production mode to central plan (see Box 7.1, for example). Relinquishing state control over price setting was one of the few cornerstone elements of the transition. Closely related was denationalization, that is, privatization, of previously state-owned enterprises.

Privatization often started with small state-owned enterprises, gradually absorbing the larger ones (either via auctions or shares, vouchers, distribution). We address some of the specifics of the privatization process in the next section. From these broad strokes a range of more specific reforms followed: for example, liberalization of domestic markets, pressure to open capital accounts, raising interest rates, freeing up prices, and so on.[12]

With greater initial economic and political autonomy, reforms took off rather early in Hungary and Poland, as we can see from Table 7.3. Others followed right after, largely following in the footprints of these first movers (see Box 7.2 for discussion on East Germany's path). Yet, the top runner in Eastern Europe had already moved forward in the process. Economists opened up to discussion of reforms, sequencing and fine-tuning complex social and economic adjustment much like conducting a routine car tune-up (e.g. Fischer and Gelb, 1991 and Bruno, 1992).

A decisive signal came with the launch of forceful market reforms in Russia, certainly the core economy in the region. Russia's transition policies in many ways offered initial guidance, if not a blueprint, to the smaller economies in the FSU that attempted to replicate some of the early liberalization measures and privatization patterns. Still others, in particular those in Central Asia and Southeast Europe, had a delayed start to their reforms. In many of those latter cases, the scale of reforms was only partial, retaining many of the administrative controls over economic activity with the central government.[13]

Additionally, the Reform Type column in Table 7.3 helps navigate across three descriptive variants of reforms: shock therapy, gradual, and partial. The second and the third are often lumped into one "gradual" category due to some commonalities in macroeconomic results. However, there would be a significant difference between a common understanding of "gradual" and "partial" reforms in the social or political context.

Emphasis on diversity of the group

While we expand our discussion on the dichotomy of shock therapy and gradualism below, the difference with which the path was adopted by individual countries often meant difference in the severity of the crisis as unexpected negative surprises continued to surface through the reforms period. The contradictory aspect about shock therapy was in the divergent macroeconomic performance outcomes when two, seemingly similar, countries adopted it (e.g. Poland and Armenia). Clearly, the similarity was elusive and if any, mainly referred to the legacy political aspect and less to the macroeconomic structure, as results in the figures and tables provided in this chapter so far would suggest.

The diversity of the CEE/FSU group is further heightened by the difference in their relative achievements by and around the year 2000—in the first ten years since the reforms. Here, the EU-8 group stands out as over-achievers, especially if one might suggest treating all 29 post-socialist economies as equal.

Suffice it to say that the fact that Poland or Hungary were admitted into the highly selective OECD group in 1996, securing WTO membership a year before, and ahead of the rest of the group, suggests, all political sub-context aside, a much stronger macroeconomic foundation following the initial reforms process. Elsewhere, Slovenia would issue its first Eurobond in 1996 and the Baltic states, unlike their former Soviet counterparts, made steady progress towards global trade integration. At the same time, progress, if one considers international recognition as such, was slow in Central Asia and parts of Southeast Europe.

Box 7.2

Following the internal political crisis in the German Democratic Republic (GDR) and after the fall of the Berlin Wall in November 1989, the reunification process with West Germany gained momentum. GDR's transition was by far the smoothest when compared to the rest of the post-socialist CEE and FSU landscape. Monetary and economic unification began in 1990 and soon the currency, laws, and institutional foundation of West Germany were transposed onto East Germany. Political union followed.

As some of the evident cultural barriers were relatively manageable, while others were not,* in macroeconomic terms there was a glaring gap between lower capacity and living standards in the GDR compared to West Germany. The GDR's real GDP dropped 35 percent between 1989 and 1991 and industrial production growth declined by 33 percent between 1990 and 1991. However, both resumed growth from 1991 onwards. Similarly, East Germany's GDP per capita was estimated to be at 40 percent of West Germany's in 1991, rising to 61 percent through the 1990s.

As integration continued, East Germany's lower labor productivity and wages, accompanied by higher unemployment rate, compared to the West, persisted. The mighty professional trade unions of West Germany feared that depressed wages in the East might send wrong incentives to producers looking to save on labor cost. At the same time, the West German producer associations had legitimate concerns about foreign competition exploiting the opportunity of moving their production to a low-cost region of, by now, developed economy. As a result, at the cost of rising unemployment, wages in the East were brought up based on skill to 80 percent of the West's levels, yet productivity was still barely half of that in West Germany. This has hardly changed, rising to 83 percent as observed by Brenke (2014), while unemployment has stayed persistently high (peaking at 21 percent by 2005 and declining to 12 percent in 2014 compared to just over 6 percent in 2014 in West Germany).

Massive public investment and subsidies went from West Germany into the infrastructure of East Germany, also introducing social protections, e.g. insurance system and unemployment benefits, which helped stem rising migration from East to West and stabilize living standards. Early privatization efforts stumbled due to the multi-stakeholder negotiation process, partly due to GDR's adoption of the most radical variant of the socialist economic model as discussed in Chapter 5. In the end, unfortunately, there was no perfect convergence of the same growth path or living standards between East and West Germany, though sharp disparities have evened out.

* Some obvious and minute cultural differences and similarities between West and East Germans, as well as some reflections on ordinary citizens' political beliefs, fears, and dedication are aptly captured in the 2003 film *Good Bye Lenin!* See: www.imdb.com/title/tt0301357/.

Sources: Brenke (2014); Sinn (2000); Von Hagen, Strauch, and Wolff (2002); also see Hans-Werner Sinn's personal website for additional readings www.hanswernersinn.de/en/topics/GermanUnification.

Structurally and institutionally, these results reconfirm our initial views on the definitiveness of the unique pre-transition conditions in each case. Legacy of self-management mechanisms, relatively diversified industrial base, market socialism, and persistence of private small businesses, especially in agriculture (e.g. Poland as discussed in Chapter 6)—all were essential contributing factors to these early successes.

In academic and policy literature, the starting macroeconomic conditions were mentioned in passing as professional economists engaged in more theoretical derivations. Effectively, the underlying assumption was that in each case the economy was being built from the ground up.[14] In fact, the legacy social and economic structures would in many cases prove to be strong and more steadfast than some of the transition era proposals. Before proceeding, let's briefly tackle the question of privatization and its institutional discontents.

Privatization

At the onset of the new market system in the post-socialist region, privatization was "the most difficult and novel" of the three policy imperatives. The other two were liberalization and macroeconomic stabilization, to which we have referred in the preceding sections.[15] This mutually underpinning triumvirate embodied the essentials of macroeconomic reform at the time, or so it seemed.

Prior to the transition, there was virtually no private sector in the CEE and FSU economies (with few minor exceptions; see Table 7.4A of the Appendix). Hence, privatization was broadly understood as a transfer of state-owned property into private hands and encouraging new private enterprises. It should be possible to see that privatization would profoundly restructure the post-socialist economies and societies. Questions of property rights, corporate governance, operational and managerial efficiency, competitiveness, and others came to the forefront. Therefore, the reform was pivotal to the success of the entire transformational movement.

Initiating the privatization process in CEE/FSU

From a practical standpoint, there were two privatization components: small-scale and large-scale enterprises privatization. In the process, small-scale privatization was launched and accomplished rather early across most countries. Laws on small-scale privatization were adopted and enacted early on. The reforms went particularly well in countries with existing traditions of private or cooperative ownership (e.g. Hungary, Poland, and parts of former Yugoslavia). That included (but were not limited to) such small operations as retail stores, minor units in the hospitality sector and household services (e.g. barber shops or shoe repairs), some small-scale transportation facilities, and so on.

For the most part, small-scale privatization was carried out by auctions. Those auctions were not open to foreigners. However, early on, across CEE and the FSU, local residents would formally appear in paperwork as nominal owners, in reality being proxies for and financed by foreigners. That situation often led to contradictory results, where domestic proxies would exercise their nominally legal right of ownership and push or discredit their foreign partners out of the agreement. This was particularly common in the case of land privatization.[16]

In Hungary and Poland, small firms were sold to de facto managers who had been leasing the firms from the state prior to transition—a manager–employee buyout (MEBO) strategy of sorts. Milanovic (1991) observes that spontaneous transfers of state property into private ownership started early in Hungary (1988), Poland (1989), and by 1990 in Yugoslavia. If the sale was delayed, managers could have waited until the lease agreements expired. But the state was in a rush to drop the extra balance.[17] Privatization of residential apartments by the primary residents (e.g. in the FSU those with the relevant *propiska*), was another important aspect of the reform. Though a cooperative ownership was known in the FSU since the *perestroika* initiatives, for most urban dwellers owning an apartment, this was a novelty that required adjustment

Medium- and large-scale privatization of industrial and service enterprises would turn out to be the most difficult component of the reform. Countries' approaches varied without one standard template. The process required a sophisticated legislative basis and dedicated investment of political will in institutional foundations. Fischer and Gelb (1991) point to the need for corporatization, corporate restructuring, as the state-owned enterprises were saddled with old debts and, in most cases, required physical capital upgrades.

Much of the inspiration for the privatization reform and its speedy execution came from the earlier experiences in the UK, where Prime Minister Margaret Thatcher had presided over an impressive campaign of industrial denationalization, and elsewhere. However, with hindsight, now, the proposal for aggressive privatization campaigns in CEE and the FSU seemed to be out of tune with the post-socialist institutional and structural realities. Whereas in the UK it was estimated that roughly 20 large companies had been privatized over a ten-year period and in Mexico there were 150 entities privatized in six years . . . Hungary had approximately 2,000, Poland anywhere from 7,500 to 8,400 enterprises, and Russia approximately 50,000 enterprises (and comparable numbers for others) that were to be privatized in a timeframe of a few short years.[18] Early on, Fischer and Gelb (1991) noted that worldwide only roughly 1,000 firms had been privatized between 1980 and 1987; also suggesting that privatization in the post-socialist environment might continue for years.

Early warnings

The earlier mentioned Kornai's *The Socialist System* (Kornai, 1992) offered a balanced conceptual framework for the privatization reforms. In a simplified interpretation, Kornai viewed the socialist system as characterized by property rights contradiction: the workers had no claim on the final product. As such, while the system was nominally socialist, with means of production and final output belonging to society, the workers had minimal representation and participation in the decision-making processes at all levels (with earlier discussed Yugoslavia's self-management being the closest but imperfect approximation to full representation).[19] As such, privatization should have resolved the key contradiction of the system. In practical terms, this would have meant having industrial and service sectors operating, once in private hands, at higher efficiency and producing higher-quality final goods and services, consequently contributing to tax revenue collections.

For Kornai, there was one important caveat in this prescription. Rather than being quick and rushed, privatization had to be focused on finding a "good owner" first and foremost.[20] The point was not to simply "hand out" property but to find a new owner who would invest to develop the assets further. Elsewhere, Kornai (2000) summarized two distinct views on privatization at the time: a) "organic development" and b) accelerated privatization. The two were distinguished by the varying speed of transition. However, it is not difficult to suggest that adoption of either a measured (first) or haphazard (second) approach would also lead to opposite policies and reform outcomes.

In the first case, privatization was not the end goal itself. Instead, the private sector was expected to grow ("organically") over time as economies matured. In other words, privatization reform, per se, was not a sufficient condition of successful transition. This was an evolutionary approach with private property rights guarantees and contracts enforcement being introduced in phases as markets matured. Note that none of that was even remotely familiar to the societies in transition at the time, especially in the FSU, where as we have described before, the institutional framework differed from CEE.

In the gradual approach, the focus was on advocating sales of state enterprises to outsiders and finding core investors (e.g. Estonia, Hungary, and later Poland). This was contrary to simply giving out shares to citizens (e.g. voucher privatizations in Czechoslovakia and Russia) or selling to enterprise managers. Regarding the latter, virtually no CEE/FSU country escaped the perennial "insider" privatization effects, albeit with varying depth (e.g. Dale, 2011).

In Kornai's second case, the view that "reforms must be pushed before there may be any chance for return of socialist governments" (paraphrasing a common refrain in academic work at the time) prevailed. As such, the focus was on elimination of state ownership by all means possible and as fast as possible. The majority of academic publications in the early 1990s, as well as the World Bank's own policy advice, supported this approach (e.g. Nellis, 2002).[21]

A loose interpretation of the Coase theorem offered theoretical grounds in the post-socialist case.[22] The popular view held that it did not really matter who the initial private owners would be, because the market would push inefficient owners/managers out of business forcing them to sell assets to the more ambitious and effective managers among the rising entrepreneurs. The market would reach its optimal outcome. Privatization had to proceed fast and on a mass (as opposed to case by case) scale to achieve greater efficiency (Lipton and Sachs, 1990b).

Of course, one might raise a valid question as to how a typical new entrepreneur was to raise sufficient financial resources to bid for the failing enterprises? In the midst of macroeconomic transformation of the early days, the banking system and capital markets, known to the average person today, were inexistent, their development being piecemeal and rudimentary.

Explaining the logic of speedy movement, Fischer and Gelb (1991), among others, posited that fast privatization would lead to "a rapid and irreversible shift to private production" (p. 99). Those benefits would then outweigh any costs, such as reduced government revenues from asset sales. Fast privatization would then prevent formation of any interest groups that could have potentially subverted the privatization process and unfairly gained a larger share in the enterprise.

Once fast privatization was completed and efficiencies realized, higher tax revenues would then offset any potential initial losses to the state. Unfortunately, things did not really work out as hypothetical scenarios had it. Practically in every country, insider or other noncompetitive ownership schemes skewing the optimal equilibria solutions accompanied privatization.[23]

The mechanics of mass privatization

In terms of mechanics, there were three ways in which medium and large privatization was administered: direct sales (auctions), asset giveaways (e.g. via vouchers and certificates), or via manager–employee buyouts. A fourth, but minor, method was restitution, primarily in CEE and attempts to reconcile in East Germany.[24] Though it mostly related to the rights on land and in some cases formerly religious organizations' property, restitution was not quite an effective mechanism, leading to unending debates within and across countries, delaying the rest of the reform.[25]

All countries experimented with variants of all three privatization methods, but some were primary. A common feature was almost immediate removal of any barriers (even reasonable ones in strategic raw materials sectors) to private ownership (e.g. Milanovic, 1991). There was generally a welcome attitude in societies towards the privatization process and its potential benefits.

According to the EBRD (1999) Transition Report, manager–employee buyouts (MEBO), by which the businesses were sold to groups of de facto managers and employees, comprised the primary means of state-owned enterprise privatization in Albania, Croatia, FYR Macedonia, Romania, Slovenia, Belarus, Turkmenistan, Ukraine, and Uzbekistan. In these schemes, managers would retain majority control (often buying out privatization vouchers from the factory workers at nominal cost) over the enterprise. This was an example of insider, non-competitive, privatization. The problem with the insider approach is that it frequently resulted in collusion between the now technically private owners and local or national governments, dragging with it the problem of soft budget constraint.

Others, for example Bosnia and Herzegovina, Czech Republic, Lithuania, Armenia, Azerbaijan, Georgia, Kyrgyz Republic, Moldova, Russia, and Tajikistan opted for voucher (or certificates) privatization. Initially, seemingly optimal, voucher (or coupon) privatization also led in many cases to dubious results. The most well-known examples in literature are the cases of the Czech Republic and Russia.

Privatization in Czechoslovakia

The Czech Republic in 1992 was the pioneer of voucher privatizations. For a nominal fee, citizens could obtain vouchers and had an option to invest in a public company or investment funds (Investment Privatization Funds or IPF) that managed investment. The IPFs campaigned to attract funds promising risk diversification and positive returns. The government played an important role, defining the property rights.[26] According to some estimates, up to 70 percent of Czech citizens (e.g. Nellis, 2002) deposited their vouchers in investment funds in the first wave of privatization (1993). As such, the average citizen had claims on the shares of the pooled fund but not the actual enterprise.

The initial results from Czech's privatization were overwhelmingly positive. Unemployment was low (and lower than in Hungary and Poland) and growth seemed stronger than in the neighboring peers. The Czech results were encouraging to the degree that World Bank staff—learning on the job, as Nellis (2002) reports in the internal evaluation study—recommended voucher privatization to the transition economies, especially in the FSU area. As far as the Czech Republic was concerned, transition to the free market was declared over by the mid-1990s.

The euphoria ended in 1997 when the Czech GDP growth rate dropped nearly 40 percent and subsequently remained depressed (Nellis, 2001). A careful analysis of Czech privatization revealed that investment funds turned out to be the dominant owners in the end, pushing out any minority shareholders (ordinary citizens for whom the privatization was launched in the first place). This led to a high concentration of economic power. The funds, often owned by domestic banks, were poorly regulated. Special interest groups, more concerned about asset stripping (tunneling) than restructuring for efficient production, quickly took advantage of the situation.

The banks continued to roll over loans to the companies owned by the same investment funds that the banks owned, despite the poor financial performance of private firms. Public dissatisfaction with privatization was on the rise as voucher investments failed to realize tangible profits. Problems emanating from the still inadequate legal system (under which much of that activity was still deemed legal) and rudimentary financial market delayed the needed restructuring as firms were unable to raise new capital, reorganize, or attract managerial talent. The conflict of interest was obvious, to the point that the OECD in its report considered Czech's voucher privatization to be an obstacle to efficient corporate governance and restructuring.[27]

By the early 2000s the government moved in aggressively to address these problems, adopting much of the required legislature and enforcing new regulations on investment funds. Most of the commercial banks were privatized. Also, by 2000, privatization of large utilities enterprises was launched. Relying on voucher privatization, Slovakia and Lithuania would experience similar problems to the Czech Republic.

Privatization in Russia

Russia was another notable case of voucher privatization, following immediately after the Czech privatization's initial success. Russian citizens received a voucher of 10,000 rubles in value that could be used to acquire direct ownership in an enterprise that was being privatized. In just two years, thousands of enterprises were privatized and converted into corporations. As Nellis (2002) states, the World Bank was there at every step of the process.

By itself, the voucher's nominal value was minor, but vouchers were publicly tradable and those with means were buying them. Lacking the administrative capacity to wrestle often-powerful factory bosses, the government offered chunks of cheap shares to the enterprise managers and employees. Company managers, often exercising their executive authority, called for staff meetings during which companies were transformed into joint stock enterprises. Various schemes were designed, all consistent with contemporary legislature that would retain a certain portion of company stock within employees control while auctioning off the remainder. The vouchers were used extensively and a large number of state enterprises were privatized by the vouchers' expiration date in mid-1994. A second phase of privatization would then follow after 1997, mainly by competitive auction sales of state enterprises.

In either case, and especially in the vouchers scheme, the factor of insider (or "spontaneous") privatization was quite important. Most notoriously it led to the infamous "loans for shares" mechanism, leaving a scar on Russia's economy for years to come. In the mid-1990s setting, domestic commercial banks, those that had been established by then and often controlled by various interest groups, provided financial loans to the Russian government accepting shares in state enterprises as collateral. Lack of transparency of the process was rampant (e.g. Lavigne, 1999).

As history has it, unable to repay on debts the government was caught between a rock and a hard place. By the mid-1990s, a massive transfer, via questionably organized auctions, of state assets in mining and agricultural industries ensued at superficially low prices from the government to the financial conglomerates.[28] In the aftermath, following the fiascos in the Czech Republic and elsewhere, the World Bank took a step back from the mass privatization approach, advocating a case-by-case method. Later on into the 2000s some attempts were made to restructure the ownership in some of the leading mining and steel enterprises, so as to recoup some of the lost state revenues. At that point, the role of state and state corporations would become pivotal in large-scale operations by the early 2010s.

Privatization and FDI

Back in the 1990s, there was initial strong resentment to foreign ownership. Much of the resistance was politically motivated: in the post-Soviet dominant world order, the popular platforms in CEE ran against yielding any further national assets to foreign influence.[29] However, as societies gradually opened up, sales to foreigners may have also led to rising foreign direct investment (FDI).

FDI has the potential to advance corporate governance and restructure reform in the privatization process. In fact, Estrin *et al.* (2009), find that privatization to foreigners resulted in rapid improvement in firms' performance. At the same time, they found less impressive performance in firms privatized by domestic owners. This is not too surprising, considering some evidence discussed above.

However, the obvious contradiction was that FDI tended to flow into the countries, industries, and enterprises that presented the highest potential for foreign investors. By definition, those firms needed less reorganization and the end result was missed opportunities for other sectors, with utilities sector enterprises being the safest bet in some smaller countries.

Hungary seemed to have found comfort with the notion earlier than others. In Kornai's assessment, Hungary initially followed the first option of gradual privatization. Breaking with the soft budget constraint, which pushed loss-making enterprises out of business, and consolidating the banking sector brought in significant participation of foreign capital. According to some estimates, consistently engaging foreign capital since 1990, Hungary's foreign participation in privatization peaked at approximately 68 percent as share of total in 1995, while for Bulgaria it was 70 percent, and Croatia 95 percent in the same year, and 72 percent for Poland in 1992 (as reported in Kalotay and Hunya, 2000). From the FSU, Estonia's example, aided by technical assistance from the German government, stands out as successful non-voucher privatization with foreign participation. Just as in Armenia, the role of the diaspora in Estonia would play a role in attracting investment through the transition and into more recent times (see Nellis, 2002 on Estonia).

Figure 7.6 offers a cross-country analysis contrasting average EBRD privatization index for the first ten years (based on each country's starting period, as in Table 7.2) to each country's average FDI as a share of gross investment for the same ten-year period. The privatization index is an average between small and large enterprise privatization as appeared in various EBRD reports. The higher the index, the more complete the reform is considered (see Table 7.4A and Table 7.5A of Appendix for guidance on scores interpretation).

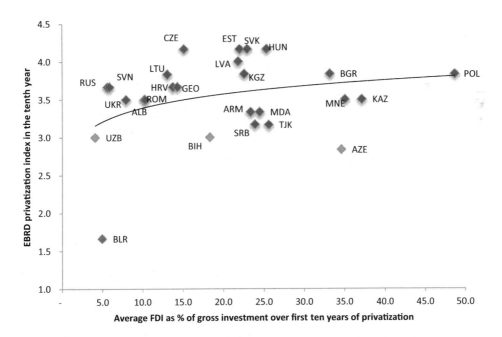

Figure 7.6 Privatization and foreign direct investment in the first decade.

Notes: privatization index is an estimated average of small and large enterprise privatization; time periods are different for each country and include the first ten years since privatization announcement (see Table 7.3); due to data limitations not all countries are included.

Sources: author's estimates based on the following: Privatization index is from EBRD (2017) and data on transition indicators; FDI is from UNCTAD World Investment Report 2017: Annex Tables

One conclusion that may be inferred from Figure 7.6 is that there is no consistent narrative to FDI volumes and success in privatization. Consider countries at and around the 25 percent average FDI share of gross investment threshold. Here, Armenia, Moldova, Serbia, and Tajikistan are contrasted with privatization super-achievers such as Estonia, Hungary, Latvia, and Slovakia (with the addition of Kyrgyz Republic).

At the same time, Poland, that seems to be leading the group as FDI magnet, scores at the levels of Georgia, Russia, and Ukraine on the average privatization index. The results may be puzzling, but there is one obvious story and that is of competition for FDI. Formerly members of the centralized common market, with the initiation of transition to market, each CEE and FSU economy has found itself to be on its own in the race to attract foreign exchange into the productive sectors of the economy.

Indeed, each has become "unhappy in its own way . . ."

Corporate governance

In terms of corporate governance and enterprise restructuring, Figure 7.7 offers a high-level comparison based on the EBRD index. The higher the index, the more successfully has the institutional basis for private business operations evolved (see Table 7.5A of the Appendix for definitions).

As Djankov and Murrell (2002) observe, corporate restructuring was most effective in the privatized enterprises operating in an institutionally advanced climate. Those would be the countries of CEE and the Baltics. Removal of soft budget constraints and introduction of property rights and contract laws, as the chronology from the EBRD reports attest, was the earliest and steadiest in those countries.

As in many previous comparisons, we find Central Asian countries and smaller FSU economies significantly lagging behind the top performers in CEE. The differences in performance, albeit accounting for any superficiality of an index, are visible even in the starting, 1994, positions. While a conventional reading of Figure 7.7 would put an emphasis on the almost perfect scores of the top tier group (those in the 3.5+ range), one should also consider, if we are to take the index as a guide, a relatively impressive improvement in scores for some countries starting at initially low scores.

These points are brought up in the recent colloquium hosted by *International Business Review* in 2015.[30] For example, consider countries rated 1 in 1994 and 2.5+ as of 2014. With the obvious exceptions of Russia and Ukraine, the remaining countries (Armenia, Georgia, Montenegro, and Serbia) fit the profile of small open economies. A common characteristic of that group, as our data throughout the book indicates, has been relative underdevelopment and strong dependence on the centralized economy. Their macroeconomic disruption was one of the most severe and recovery has been one of the slowest, as we noted before. In addition, military conflicts and natural disasters delivered further major destruction to the economy.

It is indeed then a significant achievement that small economies have been able to turn around at least to some extent, achieving improving scores in the World Bank's Doing Business survey (where Georgia was ranked eighth in the world—within a top ten of world economies on the ease of doing business ranking; DBS 2017).[31] This finding is further supported in Table 7.4A of the Appendix reporting on private sector share as percent of GDP by country. Based on the EBRD estimates, one can see a clear trend in private sector growth among some of the smallest (but determined?) transition economies with modest beginnings compared to their more affluent peers. The above amounts to a sober reminder to scholars

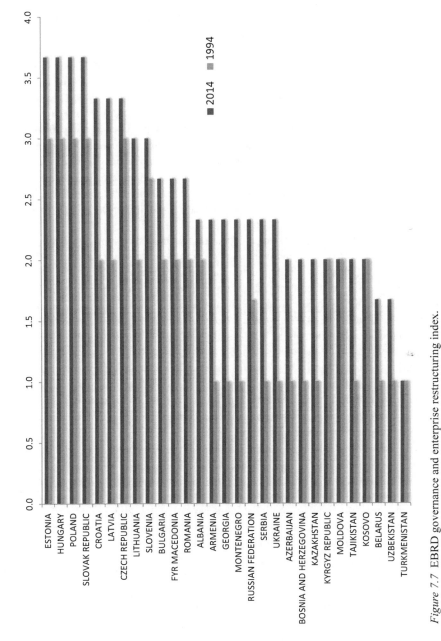

Figure 7.7 EBRD governance and enterprise restructuring index.

Source: EBRD Transition Reports and data on transition indicators, EBRD (2017)

and students of transition economics, to maintain focused attention on starting conditions and country context in cross-country comparisons and macroeconomic policy development.

Some unique and common lessons of privatization

We are obliged to mention few additional words to conclude our lengthy excursion into the modalities of privatization in the post-socialist transition economies. Privatization reform emphasized, unlike any other during the transition period, the uniqueness of each country's experience. However, some unique and common lessons could be drawn despite the variety of country approaches.

Privatization reform was instrumental to market transition in post-socialist CEE and FSU but it was not the only important factor. Domestic macroeconomic conditions, institutional base, political cycles, and cultural attitudes to private or foreign ownership played an important role. In many CEE economies, over time privatization largely delivered on its promise, as reported in the highest EBRD rankings and consistently growing shares of the private sector in the economy. With some successes in the FSU, the 1990s reforms laid the foundation for the growing private sector in the 2000s. Hence, establishing the culture of private entrepreneurship early on, which required speedy reform, would appear to be important in privatization reform there. Furthermore, in some cases in CEE (Hungary or Poland) and even in the case of Russia, centrally mandated privatization was not exactly an option: the de facto managers (especially in Russia's remote areas) were increasingly assuming greater control of the enterprises as the links with the administrative centers weakened.

In his early evaluation of the privatization process, Milanovic (1991) warned that effectively every method of privatization had its advantages and, much more dire than expected, disadvantages. In the absence of developed capital markets, external privatization may be too slow (hence our earlier question about the possibility of individual entrepreneurs mustering sufficient finance to buy out inefficient firms). Mass privatization through free distribution (vouchers and certificates) is prone to lead to concentration of economic power and revenue proceeds from sales. Manager–employee buyout schemes, while to some degree successful and eventually prevailing in many countries, did indeed result in social tensions, diverting the reforms process from its trajectory (e.g. consider, coalminers' strikes of the mid-1990s in Russia and other similar examples elsewhere).

In the end, the reformers came to the gradual realization that private ownership was not the end goal. Nor was it a sufficient condition for successful transition to a market economy. In their extensive survey, Estrin *et al.* (2009) find that privatization does not necessarily guarantee improved results and the type of owner matters. As Nellis (2002) observes, the FSU countries lacked the solid institutional capacity to enforce operational efficiency and prevent asset stripping of newly privatized enterprises. At the same time, those in CEE with a stronger tradition of market-like institutions, by virtue of direct sales (and spontaneous) privatization, created industries of concentrated ownership outside of existent institutional frameworks.

Still, privatization meant introduction of new laws on property rights and their enforcement; and development of private capital markets in the vacuum of post-socialist realities (in this context much attention has been given to the role of pension funds and mutual funds). Privatization also meant growth of an effective management class from within as well as adopting best practices of corporate governance under competitive market pressures. Much of that was unknown, unexplored; yet held much potential for the transforming societies.[32]

In hindsight, focusing on getting the "good owner" could have been prioritized as opposed to pushing through with privatization in an unprecedentedly short time period. Mass privatization could have also been coordinated with greater immersion in the process by the policy advisers from multilateral organizations to gain country-specific grounding. At the same time, attempts to repeat Southeast Asian miracles in CEE or the FSU would probably be inadequate, simply considering the varying starting industrial and institutional foundations, as well as political and development aspirations.[33]

Perhaps, Kornai (2000) put it best by saying that "[t]he transformation of society is not a horse race." In the case of Russia's privatization, advice that would hold for the FSU's European, Caucasus, and Central Asian economies, gradualism should have been a key phrase, as also argued in Arrow (2000). Over time, as the middle class emerged and the concept of property rights solidified, privatization could have been pushed further. In that, there is hidden a more important insight for reformers. Instead of contrasting shock therapy to gradualism, there has been a need for sustainability of achievements of the social transformation process.

The shock therapy debates

Rapid privatization, as with the aggressive push for wide market liberalization and most austere stabilization programs, was a pillar element in what became known as the shock therapy ("big bang") reforms package. The bulk of theoretical models and policy implications constituting the reforms on the ground shaped contemporary academic work and policy memos. To understand how shock therapy prevailed as the guiding policy we need to delve deeper into the genesis of the reform.

The practice and theory of shock therapy

Speaking about Poland in 1994, Jeffrey Sachs, one of the leading proponents of shock therapy reforms, emphasized the need for the country to move to "normal" capitalism modeled on Western Europe (Sachs, 1994, p. 267). He quoted Poland's Deputy Prime Minister Leszek Balcerowicz as saying that Poland was "too poor to experiment" (see Box 7.1). As such, shock therapy or aggressive and rapid implementation of free market transition reforms was, albeit with (some) pain, going to deliver the transformation in the shortest period of time possible.

While the term is now solidly attached to the experience of CEE and FSU economies in the 1990s, shock therapy was not new. In post-WWII macroeconomic policy, "shock therapy" was said to describe West Germany's reconstruction (PBS, 2003). Over a short period immediately after the Second World War, West Germany's government liberalized prices and private business activity, ushering in a market economy (of course, one must also account for the crucial factor of stability in the form of economic and political support from the European recovery effort discussed in earlier chapters). In more recent years, reforms fitting the general pattern of shock therapy prescriptions were tried in Latin America, at the time most notably in Chile in the 1970s and in Bolivia in the mid-1980s (PBS, 2003).[34]

On the theoretical front, the Polak model (Polak 1957, 1997) of macroeconomic prudence offered some clear technical guidance for open economy modeling. With all fairness, the Polak model has been the conceptual and analytical framework of much of the IMF's financial programming work across the world. Hernandez-Cata (1997), for example, offers an empirical analysis of austere macroeconomic stabilization, growth, and trade liberalization *à la* Polak. In the CEE/FSU narrative, the free market was to triumph and Hayek's prophecy on unsustainability of the socialist model had to be true (Hayek, 1935 or 2007).

Integral to the shock therapy-style open economy model was the emergence of a large number of private enterprises, in a typical theoretical, microeconomic sense of perfect competition. Once that happened, a watered-down interpretation of Polak's model would then balance domestic monetary policy (and inability to finance budget deficit) and external balance, as markets cleared. Competitive pressures would force participants to provide highest-quality output at optimally competitive prices. Inefficient firms, running up their costs, would eventually exit the market. At the same time, government spending is curtailed to avoid any potential crowding out in private markets and limit the probability of twin deficits.

With sweeping social and political transformations, unprecedented economic reforms were launched in CEE and the FSU. Much of the inspiration for rapid reforms came from strong belief in the promise of the free market (e.g. Sachs, 1995). Ironically, it seemed as if the post-socialist societies turned away from one ideology and immediately embraced another, its opposite, with equally strong fanaticism.

However, as explored elsewhere in this chapter, the political turnaround did not have the same immediate macroeconomic or social re-positioning as had been expected. It seemed to the reformers that pushing through with massive privatization and market liberalization would change the established order almost overnight. In some ways it did but not as theoretically predicted. Rooted in the socialist hierarchical structure of state ownership legacy, social relations persisted and under the pressure of reforms mutated into unmanageable distortions (see analysis by Åslund *et al.*, 1996).

The Washington Consensus

By the early 1990s, policies applied in one group of countries were argued to be applicable elsewhere provided conditions in one resembled those in the other. A list of economic reform measures had been worked out, dubbed the "Washington Consensus" (WC). The Polak model provided technical foundation for the conceptual design of the evolving framework. Articulated in an article by John Williamson, the consensus would become one of the most dominant models in economic development. Both Williamson (1993) and Rodrik (1996) describe how the WC emerged from policy reforms tried in the late 1980s in Latin American economies to its more general application in Southeast Asia and CEE/FSU.

As Rodrik (1996) states, there were two simultaneous developments: 1) a larger portion of the developing world was falling into a prolonged debt crisis; and 2) countries, in particular in Latin America, were scrapping what were, by then, becoming ineffective import substituting industrialization (ISI) policies. In the mid-1970s, Chile was the first in Latin America to open its economy and introduce market liberalization reforms. Macroeconomic stabilization and structural reforms ushered in a significant initial reduction in inflation and spike in economic activity.

Comparing Latin America's experience to Southeast Asia does not seem to be on par. If in Latin America much of the financing came through capital markets and sovereign loans, in Asia the sources were of multilateral and bilateral origin. Suffice to say that conditionality varied in both and inspired growth and development in the long run in one case (Asia) and stagnation and chaos in the other (Latin America).[35] Support for the

Washington Consensus was also found in foreign exchange-based stabilizations of Israel (1985), Mexico (1987), and Argentina (1991) that led to initial consumption booms.[36] Those, yet, again were some initial results and the difficulty would be to sustain them, as other Latin American economies followed suit. Sustaining the gains of reforms would prove to be a difficult task in an environment of underdeveloped capital markets. Unfortunately, history, evolutionary in nature, by the late 1990s and then through the 2000s would disprove advocates of fixed measures, upsetting some of the gains in the structurally weaker Latin American economies (e.g. the Argentinian debt crisis of 2000 and then later in the 2010s).

Post-WWII economic history and the flurry of publications in the economic development field (especially motivated by works of Chenery, 1975; Lewis, 1954; Rosenstein-Rodan, 1943; and others) may have provided sufficient clues on the effectiveness of economic policy in development as well as on which policies satisfied democratic criteria. In an effort to avoid any substantive digression in our discussion, we leave the debate around exact definitions of democracy to more qualified presentations. However, three aspects would seem relevant in the context of our discussion: rule of law; clearly defined property rights; and political pluralism.

As such, the Washington Consensus also implied some degree of broadly accepted principles of economic development and a common final destination. The latter was a fully-fledged market economy. Dissent was stashed away as marginally insignificant. Williamson (1993) identifies ten core characteristics of the WC, listed here in shorthand with minor clarifications as the topic has been explored extensively in the literature:

1 Fiscal discipline: budget deficits to be financed without inflation tax. Target primary surplus (i.e. excluding debt service) at certain percent of GDP.
2 Public expenditure: redirect public expenditure from administration, defense, subsidies, etc., towards healthcare, education, and infrastructure. These guarantee higher returns to the economy.
3 Tax reform: broadening the tax base. Improve horizontal equity. Effective taxation.
4 Financial liberalization: market determined interest rates and/or "sensible interim objective" as abolition of any preferential rates.
5 Exchange rates: unified exchange rate set at a competitive level to promote growth in non-traditional exports (essentially, free float).
6 Trade liberalization: removal of any quantitative restrictions on trade; scaling down tariffs.
7 Foreign direct investment: removal of any barriers to FDI. Allow foreign and domestic firms to compete on equal terms.
8 Privatization: actively privatize state enterprises.
9 Deregulation: abolish regulations that act as entry barriers to new firms moving into the market; or any competition barriers. Ensure all regulations comply with safety, environmental protection, and prudential financial supervision.
10 Property rights: secure property rights and supporting legal system.

The consensus in CEE/FSU

It did not take long for economists to develop WC-based policy advice and run country comparisons ranking against WC's ten principles. Alas, what mattered in the early 1990s CEE/FSU was a slogan: free market by all means! In their early analysis, Fischer and Gelb (1991) offered a concise summary, reminiscent of the shaping blueprint for the WC, of the main reform components in the post-socialist CEE and FSU on the way to a free market system:

1   Macroeconomic stabilization and control—tight fiscal and credit policies to reduce inflation and current account deficit were critical. Monetary overhang was to be resolved by means of radical currency reform, inflation, or raising interest rates to encourage investment in financial assets.
2   Price and market reform—implied, among others, trade liberalization at an "appropriate" exchange rate and a "rational price system." The underlying assumption was that price liberalization would necessarily lead to rapid increase in availability of consumer products of higher quality. Capital and labor markets were to be liberalized as well.
3   Enterprise reform—this was the privatization reform that would lead to efficiency gains of the private sector. Foreign ownership would lead to more transparent transactions and operational efficiencies. Free market competition should be promoted.
4   Role of state—there is no room for "all-encompassing" role in a market economy. Instead, the state should introduce broad-based taxes, social safety nets; reorient expenditure on education, healthcare, and infrastructure.

The four points above offer an indicative summary of the direction of the general transformation in the CEE/FSU. One could poke a number of holes in the list focusing on the CEE/FSU, for example capital markets had to be started from scratch; absolute liberalization of labor markets combined with asset-stripping privatization as functioning factories were brought to a standstill led to massive unemployment and social degradation. We leave those arguments outside of the present discussion as related examples are cited throughout the chapter and elsewhere in the book.

One of the most penetrating critiques, with the hindsight of time, and discussion of alternatives, comparing the CEE/FSU experience to China's, came from Roland (2001b) in his "Ten years after . . ." According to that analysis, not only was the Washington Consensus an erroneous blueprint to follow, but the results could have been more sustainable across every aspect of the reform if the evolutionary–institutionalist approach was followed. Instead, the predominant view was to remove old institutions and build new from the foundation up. This may have worked in societies with broader support for reforms, for example Hungary and Poland. Incidentally, those were also the nations that eventually returned to gradual steps in privatization and other reforms. In a sobering comment, Roland (2001b) explains how the common market (CMEA) collapse was not an exogenous shock as was the prevailing view, but an endogenous outcome of the complex intra-market members' interactions.

But back in the policy space of the mid-1990s, the common refrain was to generate winners to ensure sustainability of the reforms path. Unfortunately, the emerging "winners"—well-connected groups controlling much of the national financial and industrial capital—seemed to be more interested in asset expropriation than organic development of domestic enterprise. Furthermore, there was little incentive to enforce the new rules of the game.

And as one travelled further East (credit goes to Djankov and Murrell, 2002, for being one of the first to coin the phrase) things appeared more challenging. In the environment of open borders and globalization, the early business winners were focused on cashing out and moving abroad, hence giving up any pretense of a struggle to sustain newly emerging market economy institutions. Parallel to that, the 1990s saw an unprecedented rise in organized crime, permeating practically every sphere of economic activity in every post-socialist society.

Still, much of the academic research was fixated on select, early success stories. Among numerous other authors (see Box 7.3), Rodrik (1996) cited Poland and the Czech Republic, arguing that determined reform reduced, not intensified, short-term costs of transition.[37] Output collapse was largest in countries with the least extensive reforms, such as Ukraine. This is similar to the more recent view in Havrylyshyn (2007) articulating the "big bang" (shock therapy) approach.

Problems of distribution and economic equality were argued to be not short-term but long-term concerns; and in the long term as theory predicted, Pareto optimal distribution, in any case, would be achieved. Hence, let the reform run its course. Instead, problems in macro-economic capacity and growth were due to governments' indecisiveness in reforms implementation. Time should not have been wasted on trying to build a large coalition of reforms supporters (e.g. Sachs, 1995 or Balcerowicz and Gelb, 1995). The environment of high intellectual pressure shaping economic policy responses by CEE and the FSU was charged.

Alternatives?

There were alternatives to shock therapy, as many observed.[38] Experiencing some hiccups mid-way, economists began to address questions of reforms sequence, institutional development, structural capacity, and, importantly, speed of transformation measures were put in place. A debate between those advocating shock therapy and those arguing for gradual reform (gradualists) ensued. Turning to this subject, we need to move our discussion away from the vast array of complex and interlinked explicitly political questions. Roland (2000) offers an easy reference to the academic literature of the time (see Box 7.3).

Advocates of shock therapy, as has been already suggested, worried about rent-seeking and political reversals of the reform movement in case of delays. For them, market liberalization was primary to institutional reforms. Gradualists—one should also add Arrow (2000) to the group—were concerned about rising social costs and the lack of (and very different) institutional base in countries rapidly pursuing reforms. Kornai, in his works cited here, while a staunch supporter of the transition to the capitalist system, warned against rushed measures. The complexity of the social balance, which we have tried to explore in the earlier chapters in this book, was paramount and could not be assumed as just an exogenous distortion. A mixed approach: retaining some central control over the state sector, while the private sector was emerging seemed as plausible for, among others, Murell and Wang (1993).

Box 7.3

In his text titled *Transition and Economics: Politics, Markets, and Firms* Roland (2000) offers a clear guide to the early debates on shock therapy versus gradualism.

Among the *big bang* advocates—those proposing simultaneous and rapid reform (shock) were: "Lipton and Sachs (1990a), Åslund (1991), Berg and Sachs (1992), Boycko (1992), Murphy, Shleifer, and Vishny (1992), Sachs (1993), Frydman and Rapaczynski (1994), and Woo (1994)."

Gradualists emphasized the need for sequencing and gradual transition and included: "Svenjar (1989), Portes (1990, 1991), McKinnon (1991), Roland (1991), Dewatripont and Roland (1992a, 1992b, 1995), McMillan and Naughton (1992), Murrell (1992), Aghion and Blanchard (1994), Litwack and Qian (1998), and Wei (199[7])."

On the other hand, Kornai (199[1]), Blanchard *et al.* (1991), and Fischer and Gelb (1991) accepted the initial big bang approach with subsequent gradualism "along other dimensions."

Source: adapted from Roland (2000, p. 1)

In the case of Poland, Pereira *et al*. (1993) argued that reforms should not be coming from above and should not be disruptive measures. In essence, the authors find social dimensions of the "big bang" reforms lacking despite the proposal's "economic" elegance. Lack of such social dimension threatens sustainability of the short-lived "economic miracle."[39] Pereira (1993) also raises a concern over missing realization of cyclicality of the social and economic change across Latin America and Eastern Europe. This would turn out to be a prescient warning.

Sequencing of reforms offered an opportunity to achieve some balance, at least conceptually allowing for some degree of gradualism in implementing the new measures. Dewatripont and Roland (1992a, 1992b) offered some of the early theoretical models working in this direction. But while the state's gradual retreat from the economy is possible, the overall institutional bases of transparency, openness, and competitiveness were slow to be developed especially in highly centralized economies (e.g. see Dewatripont and Roland, 1996).

In his commentary, Popov (2000, 2007a) argued that those countries that had adopted a gradual or partial approach had been able to achieve more sustainable returns as opposed to those that rushed ahead. A critical aspect of that analysis was the emphasis on different starting conditions across the CEE/FSU region. Once adjusted for that, the speed of reform had negative correlation with output effects.[40] Time was needed for economies and societies, especially where distortions of the centralized system were deeply rooted, to adjust to the new, fragile, institutional framework. Havrylyshyn (2007) admits to the fact that in the decisive first years of reforms, policy advisers largely ignored the institutional development aspect of transition, in preference for economic rationale.

On the latter point, commenting on the early results from Central and Eastern Europe, Balcerowicz and Gelb (1995) argued that "radical is less risky" and warn not to "fine-tune" reforms at the start. In fact, it was "better to err on the tight side" than to attempt to develop more nuanced policy that would account for a country's initial conditions. Those views prevailed, again focusing on the technical aspects of the macroeconomic reform and leaving the softer, human transition, for a later time. However, the focus on achieving macroeconomic stabilization should still be seen as credible. This was necessarily so for countries that had crossed the point of no return following the launch of initial reforms. In that environment, assertive measures would seem to work best to overcome massive output collapses.

Grappling with explanations for the mid-term disappointments of shock therapy-style transition, Blanchard and Kremer (1997) advanced the concept of disorganization. The emphasis was on information asymmetries, which, as we have seen from the preceding review sections, had been widespread through transition. As such, abrupt liberalization led to disruption (collapse of the centralized market system). In their model, Blanchard and Kremer (1997) offer some initial rationale for gradualism by considering a temporary government subsidy to state firms, preventing immediate collapse. Sustaining companies on life support during transition is not a preferred policy option. However, effectively doing so, the economy gains time to gradually grow its competitive productive capacity, as subsidies eventually expire. This scenario, however, would be possible if there is no pressure on the government to push through quick privatization.

In reality, fiscal austerity and withdrawal, by means of privatization, from traditionally state-sponsored sectors was part of the early transition to market. Citing work on transition economies done by Coricelli (1997), Pirttila (2001) emphasizes the fact that as the state sector diminished, social and economic pressures exacerbated and fiscal revenues fell faster than expenditures. Therefore, deficits would initially be impossible to prevent in practice, going against the WC stabilization targets. These problems are amplified in conditions of shock therapy transition when state-owned assets cease to generate the necessary tax revenue and unemployment grows exponentially as firms shed labor.

Echoing those conclusions, Roland and Verdier (1999) raise problems of search frictions and relation-specific investment. Both essentially tell the story of transition: following disruption of the existent economy, there was a period of disorganization and chaotic activity. Some firms were privatized and new owners attempted to grow their businesses; others, while also privatized, were run to the ground in a large-scale asset-stripping phenomenon, from which no post-socialist economy was immune. Roland and Verdier (1999) make an important theoretical contribution to the macroeconomic liberalization debate, emphasizing on a microeconomic (firm) level the dangers of sudden collapse of established production links, fall in investment, and inability to raise new capital in the absence of functioning capital markets and credit contraction.[41]

Some conclusions on free market reforms

Now, with the benefit of hindsight and plurality of macroeconomic development experiences, we may try summing up this conceptual discussion on the academic and policy debates around transition in post-socialist Europe and the FSU. By the early 1990s, the belief in the socialist economic model was replaced with an equally, if not more, zealous belief in transitioning to a capitalist society. Common to the early approaches was the conjecture that socialism could be *revolutionarily* discarded and a new formation ushered in.[42] Paradoxically, the reformers' hubris was as much motivated by economic theory as by the dominant view of Karl Marx's "prediction" of successive replacement of one social formation by the other.[43] Following that logic, socialism that had been proven wrong was to be replaced by a new formation. However, even assuming such a replacement, the evolutionary aspects of social and economic development (e.g. see Chapter 2) were absent.

In his sharp critique of the transition period reforms, Stiglitz (2000, 2003) unleashes full-force against simplified interpretations of the Washington Consensus methodology and mediocre results of the early transition years. This critique stands in stark contrast with conventional views, for example Havrylyshyn (2007), on the success of the early reform movements. Still, Stiglitz's critique is a sober reminder of the problem of country-specific development policy and initial conditions, reviewed at length above.[44]

A relatively recent contribution to the substantiated critique of the radical reforms comes from Berend (2009). In his study focusing on Central European economies, Berend emphasizes the factor of structural differences. For example, Hungary followed a gradual path towards liberalization from the late 1960s, earning the country's membership in the General Agreement on Tariffs and Trade (GATT) by 1973, with up to 86 percent of imports liberalized (gradually, again) by 1991. At the same time, others rushed into liberalization in the early 1990s in the most abrupt fashion.

Aside from the speed of reform, what really mattered, as noted by Kornai (2000), was sustainability of the adjustment process. The late 1980s debates on the course of reforms across the CEE and FSU countries come to mind, as examples of a more holistic and sustainable approach. As Berend (2009) observes, the realization of strains of rapid *"overliberalization"* dawned upon local economists and quite soon Poland, Czech Republic, and Slovakia shifted to a more gradual pace to ensure some stability and sustainability of emerging market institutions. Unfortunately, this was more of an exception than a general case across post-socialist transition.

Importantly, in a heavily centralized political, social, and economic setting, the transition process from socialism to capitalism in CEE and the FSU did not adequately account for a coordinated exit of the state from the economy nor for any intermediate provisions to fill the vacuum in investment or social safety nets. And if the *perestroika* movement was inspired by Lenin's NEP and market socialism transformations in CEE, by the mid-1990s the interim results of the new spin of (now, free market) reforms were quite the opposite.

Conclusion

The 1990s ended with Russia's default of 1998. The crisis that also affected smaller FSU economies dependent on trade with Russia and large advanced economies with overextended investments became the turning point in the free fall of the transition economies. By the early 2000s, the majority of countries gained some, if not complete, control over their run-away privatization and factor-specific markets. The structural splits based on export performance were cemented. The state emerged as a more dominant and proactive agent in the still largely disorganized economies, gradually moving towards a symbiosis of private and public market system. Unfortunately, relative improvements in economic performance came at high human cost of transition, as discussed earlier.

In this chapter, we have attempted to narrate the critical events of the 1990s—the post-socialist transition decade. The challenge to compactly arrange all relevant topics in one accessible section required sacrificing the depth of some discussions. Yet, our goal was dual. First, we attempted to lay out the evidence in a transparent way, relying on multiple data sources. By now, the magnitude of the macroeconomic disruption should not escape anyone studying the CEE and FSU region even semi-seriously.

Second, in the much-contested discussion of macroeconomic policy alternatives we have tried to offer a brief, objective assessment maintaining balance between the big bang and gradualist point of views. It is hardly possible to disagree with the primacy of the human element in transition and, hence, the need for building a platform to proceed further in the reform. After all, was the economic transformation not launched for the purpose of attaining better living standards for the citizens of the countries involved? Furthermore, history is a fact that has taken place in a certain form and with given content. Despite wishful thinking for better outcomes, this chapter has attempted to discuss the free market reforms as they happened, relying on the wealth of literature on the topic.

Overall, two lessons emerge from the above analysis. First, there was no single pattern to post-socialist transition that could be considered as an optimal example. Once adjusted for the differences in initial conditions, a critical factor overlooked by early reformers and rarely brought up in our contemporary discussions, there was not much of a difference in the speed or effectiveness of reforms (e.g. work by Popov, 2000a and 2007).

The second conclusion rests upon the first. Discussion in our chapter should lead a curious reader to the realization of an immensity of social evolution currently ongoing in the post-socialist societies. In fact, our exploration in the book attests to that core point of social analysis. What that means for economic policy is quite simple: do not seek simple solutions. The experiences of the 1990s transformation now lay at the foundation of the post-socialist dynamic.

In a nutshell, society is a complex mix of history, culture, politics, and economic relations that are in constant dynamic movement. Therefore, even attempting a transition from one social formation to another, the latter cannot be viewed as the final resting point. And even if a common policy is tried across countries with no regard for the diverse initial phases, the speed of implementation may need monitoring and rebalancing; just as riding a bicycle downhill requires occasional squeezing of the brakes to maintain balance.

Alas, all that is easier said than done. The dynamic of the social reality at the time dictated its pace and direction of transformation. Neither foreign nor domestic economic advisers nor policy experts could foresee the massive change uncontrollably unfolding in front of them. Years passed before accumulated knowledge about the reforms process would begin to guide economists and policy makers.

In the next chapter, we endeavor to lift the veil on some critical elements of human transition. Specifically, Chapter 8 will discuss problems of social safety nets, poverty, income inequality, and labor migration during the 1990s market liberalization phase and into the 2000s. The story of human transition will continue in the concluding chapters.

Appendix

To capture the reforms progress, in its 1994 *Transition Report*, EBRD developed a system of indicators that, since adjusted, has helped track the progress of transition economies. The EBRD index, ranging from 1 to 4.5+ and not without its flaws, is one of the longest index measures on the market reforms according to general institutional change standards.

Table 7.4A Private sector share in GDP, %

Country	1989	1990	1991	1996	2001	2006	2010
Czech Republic	5.0	10.0	15	75	80	80	80
Estonia	10.0	10.0	10	70	75	80	80
Hungary	5.0	25.0	30	70	80	80	80
Slovakia	5.0	10.0	15	70	80	80	80
Albania	5.0	5.0	5	75	75	75	75
Armenia	10.0	10.0	30	50	60	75	75
Azerbaijan	10.0	10.0	10	25	60	60	75
Bulgaria	10.0	10.0	20	55	70	75	75
Georgia	10.0	15.0	15	50	60	70	75
Kyrgyzstan	5.0	5.0	15	50	60	75	75
Lithuania	10.0	10.0	10	70	70	75	75
Poland	30.0	30.0	40	60	75	75	75
Croatia	15.0	15.0	20	50	60	65	70
Latvia	10.0	10.0	10	60	65	70	70
FYR Macedonia	15.0	15.0	15	50	60	65	70
Romania	15.0	15.0	25	55	65	70	70
Slovenia	10.0	15.0	20	55	65	65	70
Kazakhstan	5.0	5.0	5	40	60	65	65
Moldova	10.0	10.0	10	40	50	65	65
Montenegro	na	na	na	na	na	na	65
Russia	5.0	5.0	5	60	70	65	65
Bosnia and Herzegovina	na	na	na	na	40	55	60
Serbia	na	na	na	na	na	na	60
Ukraine	10.0	10.0	10	50	60	65	60
Tajikistan	10.0	10.0	10	30	45	55	55
Uzbekistan	10.0	10.0	10	40	45	45	45
Belarus	5.0	5.0	5	15	20	25	30
Turkmenistan	10.0	10.0	10	20	25	25	25

Source: compiled from EBRD Transition Reports (various years)

Table 7.5A Selected EBRD transition indicators

Index value	Large-scale privatization	Small-scale privatization	Governance	Competition
1	Little to no progress	Little to no progress	Soft budget constraints dominate	No competition legislation and institutions
2	Comprehensive reform ready for implementation (some sales)	Substantial share privatized	Moderately tight credit and subsidy policy; lacking bankruptcy legislation enforcement	Competition policy legislation and institutions set up; some barriers to market entry lowered or enforcement action on dominant firms
3	Over 25 percent of state-owned and farm assets privatized or in the process	Comprehensive reform ready for implementation (some sales)	Significant and sustained actions to harden budget constraints and to promote corporate governance effectively	Substantial reduction of entry barriers and implementation of enforcement actions to reduce abuse of market power
4	Over 50 percent of state-owned and farm assets privatized or in the process + progress in enterprise governance	Complete privatization of eligible small companies	Substantial improvement in corporate governance, including minority holdings by financial investors	Significant enforcement actions to reduce abuse of market power. Competitive environment promoted
4+	Over 75 percent of state-owned and farm assets privatized or in the process + standards and performance of advanced industrial economies	Standards and performance typical of advanced industrial economies	Standards and performance typical of advanced industrial economies	Standards and performance typical of advanced industrial economies

Source: EBRD Transition indicators methodology, available online: www.ebrd.com/cs/Satellite?c=Content&cid=1 395237866249&d=&pagename=EBRD%2FContent%2FContentLayout

The index includes data on corporate governance, external market, privatization, and competitiveness. We summarize information on four indexes pertaining to our discussion in Table 7.5A. In general, the index has been quite influential in empirical and conceptual studies since the early transition.[45]

Notes

1 An official version of the song's video is available on YouTube: www.youtube.com/watch?v=n4 RjJKxsamQ.
2 Here, of course, we are referencing one of Churchill's famous statements on democracy, "it has been said that democracy is the worst form of Government except all those other forms that have been tried from time to time . . ." from one of his 1947 speeches in the House of Commons. 206–07 The

The 1990s free market reform   157

Official Report, House of Commons (5th Series), 11 November 1947, vol. 444, p. 207. Available online: http://hansard.millbanksystems.com/commons/1947/nov/11/parliament-bill#column_206.

3   There is no lack of literature on the subject. From the classics, Kornai's *The Socialist System* already mentioned earlier would be essential reading. A more recent political economy exploration is by Connolly (2013).

4   In their edited volume, Marelli and Signorelli (2010) offer a recent sample flavor of the economic reasoning that dominated academic and policy debates of the time.

5   Among the blogs, one the most prescient is Branko Milanovic's blog on global inequality with an often very specific critique of the post-socialist experience from the global perspective. Available online: http://glineq.blogspot.co.uk.

6   Among some of the early contributions, see Fischer and Gelb (1991), Gomulka (1992), Bruno (1992), Rodrik (1996), and others.

7   In their early econometric analysis Calvo and Coricelli (1993) find a significant role for enterprise financial credit (either via centralized or semi-centralized channels) becoming scarce as at least a partial contributing phenomenon to output collapse in Poland.

8   For terminology and recent analysis of transitional periphery from an international business perspective, see Wood and Demirbag (2015).

9   Regional aggregations are consistent with the UN Economic Commission for Europe (UNECE) report *Economic Survey of Europe* (2004). CIS stands for Commonwealth of Independent States, as defined earlier in Chapter 1.

10 On the problem of investment vacuum in the CIS context and challenges to balancing fiscal budget, see Gevorkyan (2011).

11 The main sources for Table 7.3 are EBRD (2000, 2001, 2002, 203, 2004). Also see official website: www.ebrd.com.

12 For one of the earliest and most convincing prescriptions on market reforms see Lipton and Sachs (1990), Bruno (1992), Fischer and Gelb (1991), and others.

13 For directional summaries, see Roland (2000).

14 In addition to the works already cited, consider analysis found in Havrylyshyn (2007) or Åslund *et el.* (2001).

15 As described in Lipton and Sachs (1990b, p. 293).

16 Practically every country has some type of restriction on foreigners' residential or agricultural land ownership. In many cases, e.g. Armenia, Bulgaria, Georgia, and Poland, the restriction can be circumvented by either attaining a residence permit or citizenship, or, as in Poland, by also providing evidence of strong personal and business ties with the country (e.g. Lavigne, 1999 on the subject).

17 See Adam (1999), chapter on privatization.

18 See Nellis (2002) for data and insightful discussion on privatization experiences in Poland, Czechoslovakia, and Russia. Also, Fischer and Gelb (1991) on state-owned enterprises estimates.

19 This idea is similar to the discussion on surplus value distribution found in Minasyan (1989).

20 For example, Kornai (1990).

21 Also see the seminal Djankov and Murrell (2002) paper analyzing literature on privatization in post-socialist transition. For a more recent attempt, see Estrin *et al.* (2009).

22 See Milanovic (2014b) for brief comment on the Coase theorem and implied logic in the context of post-socialist reforms.

23 For insightful recent discussions on privatization and its discontents, including post-early transition institutional underdevelopment and failures of the free market, see collection of studies in Dale (2011).

24 Restitution laws enacted or adopted: Albania (1993), Bulgaria (1992), Croatia (1997), Czech Republic (1991), Hungary (1995), Lithuania (1991), Romania (1995), Slovak Republic (1991), Slovenia (1991) – as reported in EBRD (1999). For East Germany see Box 7.2 and sources therein.

25 For details on privatization via restitution, see Bornstein (1997).

26 Incidentally, in Czechoslovakia, and subsequently elsewhere, the old practice of appointing enterprise managers returned in 1990 as more relevant in the early privatization effort.

27 See Svihlikova (2011) for a non-mainstream assessment of the privatization and reforms process in the Czech Republic.

28 An authoritative account of Russia's privatization process can be found in Nellis (1999, 2002) and Black *et al.* (2000). The latter paper is written by the principal participants and advisers to the privatization process and is peppered with first-hand accounts, some quite dramatic, of systematic disruptions to a fair privatization process across the CEE/FSU and Russia in particular.

29 See Adam (1999) on evidence from sales to foreign owners in the Czech Republic, Hungary, and Poland.
30 See special issue on transitional periphery in *International Business Review* Volume 24 (2015) and studies therein.
31 See analysis in Gevorkyan (2015) on Armenia's and Georgia's transformation since the early 1990s reforms.
32 For an extensive analysis on various aspects of privatization reform see the discussion in the World Bank's World Development Report (1996).
33 At the same time, the suggestion that the market alone may not be the panacea seems to hold some truth as argued in Amsden *et al.* (1998).
34 PBS (2003) provides a selection of brief thematic updates and interviews on the history of the reforms as well as experiences in Latin America and CEE/FSU.
35 An insightful guide on macroeconomic development policies and experiences across the world is the text by Agénor and Montiel (2008).
36 For a most piercing critique of the conventional view on Southeast Asian industrialization, see Amsden (2003).
37 Importantly, see Sachs' (1995) argument on preferences for "shock-therapy" reform in Russia as "the least cost and less risky form of stabilization" (p. 58).
38 See earlier comments in Roland (2001b). Also, an insightful commentary is found in Arrow (2000) on the preference for gradual transition over more than a decade.
39 For an in-depth analysis of various macroeconomic theories and policies, including from a post-Keynesian perspective, see Marangos (2004a).
40 Also see much later Popov (2013a) on experiences in Uzbekistan.
41 On the relation between credit contraction and output collapse, see Calvo and Coricelli (1993).
42 On the *revolutionary* bias of the transition reforms and immediate institutional vacuum, see Gaidar (2012).
43 Various observers commented on this issue. In particular, the disconnect is explicitly articulated in Minasyan (1989) as applied to the Soviet economy and in Foley (1986) as applied to Marx's political economy and its "predictions" in general.
44 For brief assessments of the transition period see an insightful colloquium in the *IMF's Finance and Development* issue dedicated to the Economies in Transition (2000), Vol. 37 N0. 3 www.imf.org/external/pubs/ft/fandd/2000/09/index.htm.
45 On discussion of the EBRD index of institutional change, see Weder (2001). Institutional reform in transition economies: how far have they come? *International Monetary Fund Working Paper*.

Part IV

The human transition

Still happening

8 Poverty, income inequality, labor migration, and diaspora potential

> An increase in the number of paupers does not broaden the market.
>
> Michal Kalecki, *Theory of Economic Dynamics*

Introduction

By now, it must be clear that there is a need to shift academic and policy perceptions from viewing the economies of Eastern Europe and the former Soviet Union as "a social experiment in the making" to a more appropriate alternative. However, it is equally difficult to simply come up with that "alternative" category. The use of the adjective "normal" as Branko Milanovic reminds us in one of his critiques (Milanovic, 2014c) is equally inadequate.[1] Instead, perhaps, we ought to first avoid labels that may be misleading given the diversity of experience we have covered so far. And second, it may instead be appropriate to rely on an inclusive macroeconomic development approach that is more reflective of evolving conditions. Such a methodological shift requires, of course, the acceptance of two obvious facts.

First, despite a profound social and economic transformation over the past two decades, in many countries of the region, the long-awaited post-socialist macroeconomic miracle, except for isolated cases, has largely failed to materialize. The first decade of transition led to a situation characterized by the World Bank as "jobless growth" (e.g. Mitra *et al.*, 2007) as despite high unemployment, growth was pushed by either rising productivity or infrastructure projects. Second, and subsequently, the macroeconomic development problems facing the newly sovereign economies require immediate resolution based on objective empirical assessments. One intriguing angle of analysis that may help explicate the two issues is a discussion of the economic potential of the diaspora in the context of massive labor migration, underdevelopment, and poverty alleviation as part of the region's broader macroeconomic development.

Since the liberalization reforms in the early 1990s, the diaspora has been theorized as a positive contributor to post-socialist economic and social transformation. In fact, poverty rates in transition economies might have been to some extent reduced through active involvement of the diaspora community through local humanitarian efforts, economic revival, politics, or social activities.[2] Such a model may be viable in particular for the resource-constrained, net importer, transition economies. However, diasporas are not monolithic entities that act uniformly—an insight often omitted in academic literature.

Deviating from the chronological structure of the preceding discussion, this chapter offers a comparative study of the CEE/FSU region, with an emphasis on the problems of labor migration and the diaspora role in development. We illustrate the limited institutional foundation for the reforms at the start and the influence of legacy policies on the ongoing institutional transformation. As such, this chapter also leads towards policy proposals involving relations between the home countries and their respective diasporas in the context of economic development, finance, labor migration, and soft engagement (e.g. health care, education, politics), gauging their effectiveness.

Poverty and income inequality

Although income inequality was present even under socialism (e.g. a gap existed between urban vs. rural wages), absolute poverty was quite uncommon. Moreover, despite disparities between the northern and southern FSU republics, income inequality diminished in the 1980s (e.g., Alexeev and Gaddy, 1993). Virtually everyone, up to 90 percent of the labor force, was in a wage-paying occupation in state-run enterprises (Milanovic, 1998).

Collapse of the state-funded welfare networks created a void in previously functioning support programs. By the early 1990s, poverty rates skyrocketed, inequality worsened, and the unemployment rate hit double digits, leading to a further deterioration in human welfare. Employment guarantees, universal (and free) education, healthcare, housing provisions, childcare, and other extensive social care programs for workers ceased to exist, as also did many state-led employment opportunities.

Personal income in the second decade of transition

In the aftermath of the first decade of transition, income levels declined beyond any expected estimates, as the World Bank effectively admitted in its 2000 report (World Bank, 2000).[3] Even in 2000, when by all estimations of early reform programs living standards should have recovered and exceeded pre-transition levels (e.g. as modeled in Hernandez-Cata, 1997), despite some progress, per capita incomes for the majority of the countries remained significantly depressed below 1989 levels, as Figure 8.1 illustrates. Adding the 2016 GDP per capita index data (the rhombuses in Figure 8.1), we note that even in more recent years there is still a substantial number of countries with income per capita levels below their pre-transition standards.

The stronger a particular country's relative pre-transition macroeconomic performance was in comparison with its post-socialist peers, the more difficult was the recovery challenge (as discussed in Chapter 7). This is where data for 2016 in Figure 8.1 for some of the countries might seem a bit surprising. Specifically, note the relative positions of such primary commodity exporters as Azerbaijan, Turkmenistan, and Uzbekistan for example. There, the 2016 GDP per capita index exceeds the 1989 levels by two or three times. While commendable, one must recall the problem with GDP per capita aggregation not reflecting relative distributions or economic structure idiosyncrasies (e.g. commodity-driven growth).

A glimpse at post-transition well-being

Some additional social indicators reveal a more nuanced story. Table 8.1 compares data on poverty and income inequality by country for early and more recent transition periods. While, overall, both income inequality and poverty rates have declined for the region and in sub-groups, individually there have been quite broad variations across countries. It is

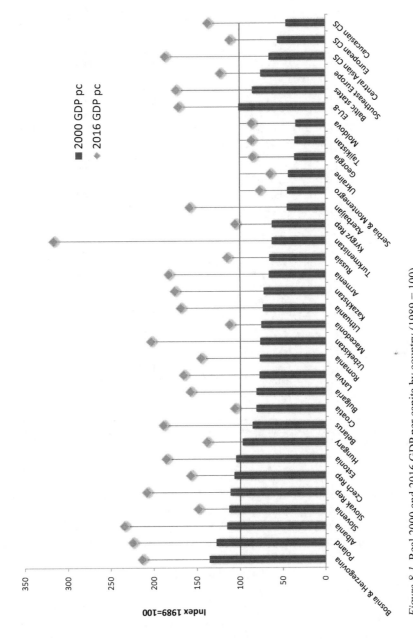

Figure 8.1 Real 2000 and 2016 GDP per capita by country (1989 = 100).

Source: author's calculations based on data from The Conference Board Total Economy Database (TCB, 2017)

Table 8.1 Selected social indicators of income inequality and poverty, period averages

Region	Country	GINI index		Poverty headcount ratio at national poverty lines (% of population)		Poverty headcount ratio at $3.10 a day (2011 PPP) (% of population)	
		1995–2005	*2006–2014*	*1995–2005*	*2006–2014*	*1995–2005*	*2006–2014*
EU-8	CZE	26.77	26.34	10.15	9.24	0.12	0.15
	EST	34.72	32.37		21.80	4.29	1.39
	HUN	28.89	28.51	14.70	13.63	0.44	0.28
	LTU	33.10	34.82	20.25	20.06	3.53	2.56
	LVA	34.62	35.81	21.45	21.74	5.02	2.32
	POL	33.59	33.17	17.32	17.25	3.02	0.55
	SVK	28.03	26.37	12.45	12.01	0.96	0.41
	SVN	27.57	24.69	11.90	13.13	0.12	0.04
Southeast	ALB	29.78	29.47	21.95	13.35	12.92	6.45
Europe	BGR	30.85	33.89	18.40	21.57	4.54	4.38
	BIH	32.01	33.45		18.05	0.79	0.44
	HRV	29.71	31.81		20.24	0.24	0.90
	MKD	36.28	43.35		24.83	8.64	8.53
	MNE	30.22	31.02	11.20	8.35	1.11	1.05
	ROM	29.91	33.23		23.04	19.68	10.19
	SRB	32.80	29.11		25.10	2.45	1.31
	XKX	30.10	29.88	38.73	34.63	15.01	9.39
European	BLR	29.77	27.71	26.48	6.60	14.91	0.35
CIS	MDA	37.28	31.62	28.17	20.98	48.18	5.48
	UKR	31.30	25.72	70.10	13.07	14.15	0.47
Russia	RUS	39.70	41.22	20.08	12.53	6.94	0.97
Caucasian	ARM	36.76	30.94	48.30	32.41	42.44	17.88
CIS	AZE	23.36	31.79	49.60	10.43	6.95	2.51
	GEO	39.98	40.87		18.12	37.70	34.00
Central	KAZ	33.15	28.27	38.84	8.08	20.40	2.06
Asian	KGZ	33.42	30.40		34.93	61.43	23.78
CIS	TJK	31.95	30.93		33.15	65.71	47.38
	TKM	40.77				69.14	
	UZB	37.27			14.55	83.42	

Sources: author's estimation based on data from WDI (2017) and World Bank's Poverty and Equity database. Available online: http://iresearch.worldbank.org/PovcalNet/index.htm

important to remember that reliable data for our set of countries and on the topics of social development, inequality, poverty, and others are quite scarce.

We rely mostly on data aggregated in the World Bank's World Development Indicators and databases as noted in sources. Milanovic (1998, 1999, 2012, and 2014a) and Wade (2004), among others, separately offer additional focused insights on the problems of poverty and inequality in the course of transition and worldwide (including issues with reliable data availability).

Indeed, the decline in overall poverty rates has been one of the most significant differences between the early transition period and more recent years.[4] Yet, here, again, we encounter a rather wide dispersion from approximately 8 percent (Kazakhstan and Montenegro) to 35 percent (Kyrgyz Republic and Tajikistan) of the population below national poverty lines in recent years. This also applies to the variation in rural and urban poverty rates across countries. For example, in 2000 Belarus reported 50 percent of the rural population as poor, while Kazakhstan saw 59.4 percent of the rural population as poor. Both had these statistics lowered by 2015 at 8.7 percent and 4.4 percent, respectively. Elsewhere, rural poverty has stubbornly oscillated near the 40 percent average since 2000 up until recent years (e.g. Kyrgyz Republic, Tajikistan, Uzbekistan), according to World Bank data.

Problems of urbanization

At the same time, Kosovo's urban poverty rates have declined from 46.6 percent in 2003 to the 2011 mark of 26.7 percent of the total urban population. In Armenia, urban poverty peaked at 35.7 percent in 2010 and came down to 30 percent in 2014. For underdeveloped economies, these are relatively high urban poverty rates.[5] Elsewhere, urban poverty rates varied from 23.2 percent in Tajikistan in 2015 to 1.3 percent in Kazakhstan for the same year. In passing, we note that another dimension contributing to urban poverty was a slight increase in an already relatively high share of urban population concentrated in the largest city for some countries.

As shown in Figure 8.2, the largest city urban population shares increased on average between the first transition decade and through the 2000s. Among the territorially smaller economies, Georgia, Albania, Armenia, and Moldova (in this order) have seen the largest increases. Among territorially larger or commodity exporter economies, the shares of urban population concentrated in key metropolitan areas went up in Kazakhstan, Russia, and Turkmenistan. Lithuania appears to be the only one in the EU-8 group with any significant increase in largest city concentration. Conventional views would point to signs of underdevelopment in the background of rising, large metropolitan concentrations.

One should recall the higher degree of urbanization in the CEE/FSU region (as discussed in Chapter 6) and the industrialization model that tended to have factories located in and around metropolitan areas. This point is also brought up in Berend (2009), pointing to the strong regional disparities between large metropolitan areas and provincial regions. This has been equally true for large countries (e.g. Russia's Moscow and St. Petersburg areas, Hungary's Budapest, Ukraine's Kiev, etc.) and in the smaller countries (e.g. Armenia's Yerevan, Latvia's Riga, Georgia's Tbilisi, etc.). In all these cases, the share of the largest city income in the overall national GDP often reached (and reaches) 50 and more percent. So, legacy played a role and as the reform bells rang and subsidies to agriculture (recall our earlier discussion) dried up, the CEE/FSU experienced a new phase of rural-to-urban migration.[6]

Income inequality and distribution

Even with relative successes in reducing absolute poverty a problem of worsening income inequality still remains. Gini coefficients reported in Table 8.1 help to further appreciate the severity of income inequality immediately after the launch of reforms and a decade after. Again, we observe wide within-sample variations despite the overall declining range. For example, some stand out with their Gini index of 40 in the second period (e.g. Georgia, Macedonia, Russia). Others report Gini coefficients below 30 (e.g. Belarus, Czech Republic, Kazakhstan, Serbia, and others) in the second period. This latter result is relatively close to the OECD average ranging between 30.2 in 2010 and 30.18 in 2014 (OECD, 2017). While for many countries both poverty and income inequality levels have come down, for some (in particular in Southeast Europe) there have been increases.

In his early analysis of the social costs of transition, Milanovic (1993 and 1998) focuses on the problem of middle-class hollowing out—a critical refrain that finds its affirmation in his

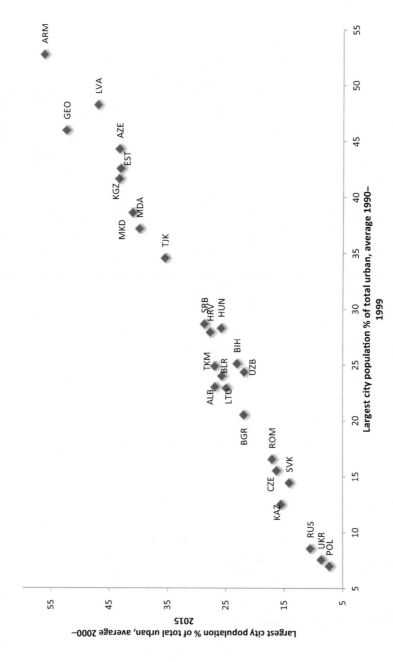

Figure 8.2 Largest city population as a share of total urban population, %.

Source: author's estimations based on data from WDI (2017)

more recent book on global inequality (Milanovic, 2016). Back in the transition economies, inequality increased sharply in the first five to six years, with the worst impacts in the FSU within the first years of liberalization and stabilization reforms. According to the estimates in Milanovic (1998), post-transition inequality coefficients were more dispersed compared to pre-transition. If anything, the economies of CEE and the FSU at the time proved an empirical observation that widening income inequality exacerbates the problem of poverty, often leading to absolute poverty (e.g. see high population shares of below the \$3.1 a day threshold in Table 8.1). Comparatively, the Central Asian countries have lived through some of the most unequal and impoverished years.

Some recent evidence on income distribution drives the point home. Figure 8.3 plots relative income distribution by income groups as of April 2017, based on the World Bank's Poverty and Inequality Database (WB, 2017) suggesting that, on average, up to 40.8 percent of total income (or consumption, as per source) is attributed to the top 20 percent of households across the sample. At the same time, only 7.8 percent of total income (or consumption) is held by the poorest 20 percent of households. In terms of country variations, Macedonia, Russia, Georgia, Bulgaria, Latvia, Poland, and Montenegro seem to stand out as those with the richest group's share ranging between 40–50 percent of national income.

This does not, however, in any way suggest that others may be significantly different. In fact, a closer look at the data in Figure 8.3 only reconfirms the intuition that the great income (and, in fact, wealth) redistribution of the transition period has happened, is real, and affected everyone. In that regard, it would be naive to make simplistic claims that one country's (region's) model of post-socialist transition and income distribution is in any way significantly superior in comparison to any others. Alas, the statistical evidence points to a sad convergence in high inequality and concentration at the top.

However, national inequalities globally have been on the rise, according to analysis in Milanovic (2016) and captured in his by now famous "elephant chart."[7] The phenomenon of middle-income group erosion may be a characteristic feature of the early 21st century for many countries. Though, overall (especially in Asia) income levels have risen, also contributing to eradicating extreme poverty, income and wealth inequality persist with varying degrees across the world.

Based on the 2015 *Life in Transition Survey*, EBRD (2016) finds that in self-assessments of income inequality "perceptions matter". And across the region's population there is reportedly a strong belief that income (and wealth) inequality levels have gone up despite over two decades of reforms. This may be due to the stark contrasts seen on streets by an average passer-by, as extravagant, glittering constructions of new office space and lavish residences rise up across the CEE/FSU countries. The perception may also be a reflection and reconfirmation of the conclusion of Figure 8.3 on disproportionate top-level income distribution.

Yet, an intriguing question that one might be asking is why are we seeing such startling high poverty and income inequality rates in the formerly socialist countries, where at EBRD's admission, pre-transition inequality levels were low, to begin with? At this point, the question remains mostly rhetorical. The dissolution of the old system of social welfare support without a functioning, viable replacement social contract had a negative effect on the social balance in the region. The new, capitalist, system emphasized individualism. The austerity programs of shock therapy necessitated removal of the old protection mechanism entrusting social welfare to the (still evolving) institutions of the free market.[8]

Worsening poverty, declining job prospects, and rising inequality, with the prospects of devastating military conflicts in some places, would now act as push factors for outward labor migration. In the latter case, temporary labor migration would often transform into

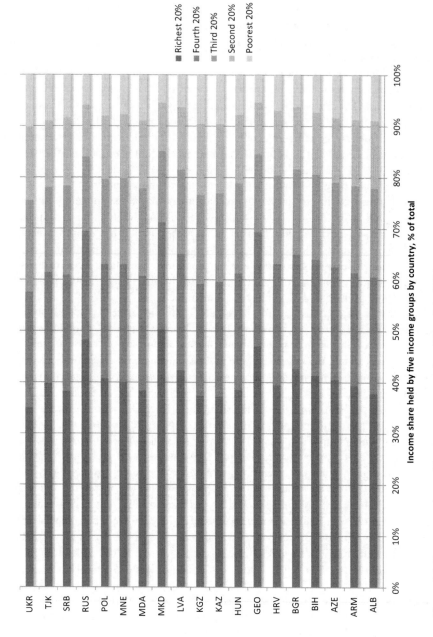

Figure 8.3 Percentage share of income or consumption, EE and the FSU.

Source: author's estimates based on WB Poverty and Equity database (2017). Available online: http://iresearch.worldbank.org/PovcalNet/index.htm

permanent settlement migration. The social pressures emerging in the early 1990s, were just the beginning of the massive social crisis that post-socialist nations are still coping with.

Labor migration

The preceding discussion inevitably brings us to the problem of human migration. The topic has regained its relevance in academic literature recently as the flows of labor migrants have remained high, the amount of monetary transfers (remittances) made by labor migrants from their host to their home economies has continued to rise, and the problem of migrants' adaptation to their new communities remains high on the agendas of the recipient (host) countries.

As a social phenomenon, migration was present in the socialist system. However, as with much else, migration flows on a large scale were centrally coordinated and constrained to CEE and the USSR separately (e.g. Heleniak, 2011 or Kaczmarczyk and Okólski, 2005). This was so in the case of international migration, within country movements, and rural-to-urban migration (despite the boost in the latter in the post-WWII period). With the market reforms of the early 1990s and opening of the borders and significant relaxation (if not abolition) of the old system, millions of people had gone on the move escaping severe poverty, limited job prospects, and, in some cases, military conflicts, and migration in and from the CEE/FSU region assumed new forms, goal, and structure.

Figure 8.4 offers an approximate estimate of the overall net flows of migrants. The data is based on cumulative net migration rates, in turn derived from the difference between immigrants and emigrants in each country in five-year frequencies, as reported by the World Bank. The data is shown as a percent share of the average population for the 1990s and 2000s.

Even with imperfect data, directional estimates show vast numbers emigrating between 1990 and 2012 from CEE/FSU: anywhere from 17 to 20 million people. Much of the initial migration was permanent in nature. Much of the later migration was temporary, labor migration. Early emigration from CEE countries was directed primarily towards Western Europe

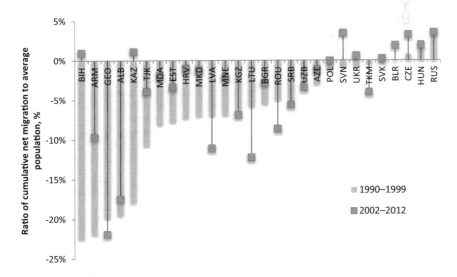

Figure 8.4 Ratio of cumulative net migration to average population by country and decade, %.

Note: data on net migration is available in five-year frequencies only (1992, 1997, 2002, 2007, and 2012).

Source: author's estimates based on WDI (2017)

and the UK, with some to the USA. Likewise, early emigration from the FSU economies was directed towards Russia as the main economic engine and, in relative terms, a promising beacon of political stability compared to the volatile and destructive system breakdowns in Central Asia and the Caucasus.

As nationalist topics dominated the early 1990s political agendas, massive population swaps along the ethnic lines gave rise to millions of forced migrants and refugees swelling economically fragile communities of the destination countries. For example, in the Balkans, the devastation from the civil war had a direct effect on migration from Bosnia and Herzegovina; ethnic Russians were on the move from Kazakhstan and elsewhere from Central Asia; people fled from conflicts and economic devastation in the Caucasus.

Noticeably, high net migration rates persisted from the smaller and structurally vulnerable economies. By the early 2000s, those began to reflect more temporary labor migration flows. For the smaller economies, the role of temporary labor migrants working elsewhere is significant, due to the high share of workers' monetary transfers in proportion to the country's GDP, as captured in Figure 8.5.

The share of remittances in the economy reached as much as 40% of GDP in Tajikistan during 2009–2015, 27.5% in Kyrgyzstan, 26.4% in Moldova, 17.5% in Armenia, 15.8% in Kosovo, 11% in Georgia and Bosnia & Herzegovina, and so on. Figure 8.5 plots the average remittance flows over the 2000–2015 period with details for pre- and post-global financial crisis of 2008 flows. From a macroeconomic perspective, such transfers raise concerns of capital outflow for the host country and domestic currency overvaluation in the recipient (home) economies.[9]

Total monetary transfers to the EE/FSU countries were estimated to reach approximately USD 73 billion in 2014, or roughly 13 percent of the world's remittances. From a development perspective, the shares of foreign exchange transfers targeted to specific dependent families in home economies are significant, capable of alleviating poverty considerably.

This view is confirmed in a World Bank Migration and Development Brief (WBMD, 2015) describing remittances as a stable source of external finance. Monetary transfers globally peaked in 2014 at USD 596 billion and have declined 3.6 percent in 2016, largely due to uncertainty in global economic pick-up complemented by political uncertainties in major labor migration host economies.[10] Out of those totals the countries of CEE/FSU received approximately 10 percent in 2016 (or USD 60.2 billion), a significant drop from the 2014 peak of USD 76.2 billion. Remittances to the CEE/FSU grew fastest between 2006 and 2007 at 38.8 percent for the year (all estimates based on data from the World Bank Migration and Remittances Data Portal; WB MR, 2017).

Khemraj and Pasha (2012) contend that remittances represent a constant and non-volatile inflow of foreign exchange. The authors suggest that for a broad sample of developing countries, this inflow may not be prone to sudden stops and reversals on an aggregate scale. In turn, this allows the recipient country's central bank to actively switch foreign exchange regimes. Recognizing the potential benefits, Chami *et al.* (2008), also raise concerns about the difficulties of managing macroeconomic effects of remittances and directing them towards sustainable development, in particular in small economies.

Although in general agreement, with the above, Gevorkyan and Gevorkyan (2012) also raise concerns about interruptions in flows due to host country business cycles and the effects that labor migration and remittance transfers may have on the home and host country's labor and capital markets and wage determination. Collectively, the three elements (remittances, labor market, and wage determination) form what the authors call a labor migration triad as a policy-guiding analytical framework.

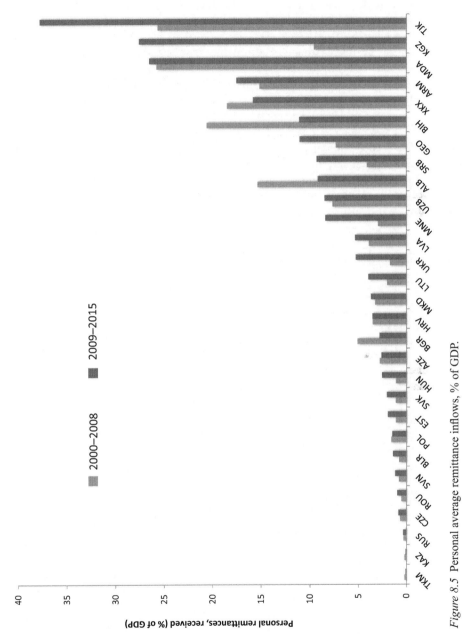

Figure 8.5 Personal average remittance inflows, % of GDP.

Source: author's estimates based on WDI (2017)

The direction of labor migration can also be traced by the largest origins of workers' remittance transfers. The smaller economies of the EE/FSU have a clear dependence on the Russian economy and its business cycle, as suggested by data in Table 8.2. According to the WB (2015), remittances to the region from Russia fell by an estimated 6.3 percent in 2014 (after an 11.1 percent increase in 2013). The EBRD (2009) estimated that remittances in hard currency from Russia to the Caucasus and Central Asian economies dropped 40 percent in 2015 with continued decline in 2016. In local currency, the decline was 30 percent and the Russian ruble 10 percent, suggesting a strong effect from the 2014 Russian currency devaluation.

Table 8.3 tells a story of the top ten largest losers in annual remittance growth, primarily as a result of the global financial crisis (GFC) and following Russia's currency devaluation in 2014. The first event is captured by a change in annual remittance volumes between 2008 and 2009, while the second is reflected in a drop in remittance volumes and values between 2014 and 2015 in percentage terms.

Countries that needed remittances the most have seen the largest drops in monetary transfer volumes right immediately after the global financial crisis (e.g. in Armenia, fall in receipts of 24%, in Tajikistan of 27%, and in Uzbekistan of 43%). The recent economic downturn in Russia—and corresponding job losses by immigrants—combined with the Russian ruble depreciation were responsible for this decline.[11]

Table 8.2 Top ten remittances senders to each CEE/FSU region, % of total

EU-8	Percent of total	Southeast Europe	Percent of total	European CIS	Percent of total
Germany	22%	Germany	16%	Russia	47%
United Kingdom	13%	Italy	11%	United States	7%
United States	11%	Turkey	8%	Italy	7%
Czech Rep*	6%	United States	7%	Germany	4%
Canada	5%	Serbia	7%	Ukraine*	4%
Austria	4%	Spain	6%	Kazakhstan	4%
Russia	4%	Croatia*	6%	Poland	3%
Slovak Rep*	3%	Switzerland	6%	Belarus*	3%
Ukraine	3%	Austria	6%	Uzbekistan	3%
Ireland	3%	Greece	4%	Israel	2%

Caucasian CIS	Percent of total	Central Asian CIS	Percent of total	Russia	Percent of total
Russia	60.3%	Russia	86.3%	Ukraine	31.1%
Ukraine	6.7%	Germany	4.3%	Kazakhstan	21.3%
Armenia*	6.5%	Kazakhstan*	2.2%	Germany	9.7%
United States	6.3%	Ukraine	2.1%	Belarus	6.2%
Uzbekistan	2.4%	Uzbekistan*	1.0%	Uzbekistan	5.3%
Germany	2.2%	Afghanistan	0.8%	United States	4.4%
Greece	2.2%	Belarus	0.5%	Tajikistan	2.2%
Kazakhstan	1.6%	United States	0.5%	Moldova	2.0%
France	1.3%	Azerbaijan	0.3%	Azerbaijan	1.6%
Turkey	1.1%	Tajikistan*	0.2%	Latvia	1.5%

Note: *including intra-region transfers; estimates do not add up to 100% since table shows top ten senders only; data as of April 2017.

Source: author's estimates based on data from WB MR (2017). Available online: www.worldbank.org/en/topic/migrationremittancesdiasporaissues/brief/migration-remittances-data

Table 8.3 Top ten remittances losers, % annual change

Country	Remittances loss after global financial crisis*	Country	Remittances loss after RUB devaluation**
Romania	−59.9%	Uzbekistan	−47.6%
Moldova	−36.5%	Turkmenistan	−46.7%
Turkmenistan	−32.4%	Belarus	−37.7%
Tajikistan	−31.3%	Lithuania	−35.0%
Uzbekistan	−31.1%	Tajikistan	−33.3%
Hungary	−30.7%	Azerbaijan	−31.2%
Armenia	−24.4%	Armenia	−28.2%
Poland	−22.0%	Georgia	−26.6%
Bosnia and Herzegovina	−21.7%	Moldova	−26.1%
Lithuania	−20.8%	Kyrgyz Rep	−24.8%

Note: *annual change between 2008–2009; **annual change between 2014–2015.

Source: WB Migration and Remittances Data Portal

Part of the problem, and a significant one, with remittances as a steady source of development finance, on top of dependence on the host economy's business cycles, is the inherent individuality of the ad hoc labor migration process. With some variations over time, the overall profile of a typical migrant has remained steady over the past two decades.[12] Typically, it is a male at prime working age often from a rural area, employed in the service sector of the next-largest economy (Russia for the small FSU states of Armenia, Georgia, Moldova, and Ukraine; and Western Europe for such EE countries as Bulgaria, Poland, Romania; e.g. WB [2015]). However, as the political situation in the home (source) countries stabilized, women joined the temporary labor migrants' ranks, either traveling as breadwinners or to reunite with families.

More recent trends reveal increasing diversity in skill sets of typical migrants. In the early transition years, permanent migration flows were mostly characterized by highly-skilled migrants, invoking the problem of "brain drain"—as a critical challenge exacerbating the underdevelopment position of smaller, structurally weaker economies. The less-skilled, with minimal professional training, migrants comprised the bulk of the temporary labor migration phenomena. Still, even more recent evidence suggests a growing trend of skilled temporary migration, for example via intra-company transfers as more foreign companies establish a presence in the small economy in search of low-cost but relatively skilled labor balance. The majority of these recently relocated migrants comprise a "new" diaspora, with strong active family and cultural ties to their country of origin.[13]

The new migrants' remittances, stemming from their income earned abroad, are usually relatively small sums of money sent on a regular basis with the aim of supporting their relatives in the home country. At the same time, the "new" migrants who return (return migrants) contribute their accumulated knowledge, skills, and entrepreneurial drive to their home communities. The phrase "earned income" is critical in distinguishing the qualitative origin of the transfers, as emphasized in Gevorkyan (2011) and presented empirically in Ratha and Mohapatra (2011). Elsewhere, Agarwal and Horowitz (2002) find altruism to be a critical driving factor behind remittance transfers to Guyana.

While the labor migration dynamic remains patchy, immediate impacts on the smaller FSU economies are significant. In this context, the smaller economies are at the greatest disadvantage relative to their "peers." In short, different countries require different solutions to their seemingly common problems, as poverty alleviation needs to be correlated with overall economic development improvement. This is where the diaspora thesis comes in as a possibly positive force of macroeconomic development for some CEE/FSU economies, consistent with a range of factors peculiar to transition.

Diaspora and economic development

Diaspora networks in the developing countries, which formed under the pressure of history or recent economic, social, and political turbulence, have long since been popularized as conduits of inclusive economic development, helping to combat poverty and promote job creation, transfering technology, knowledge, and best business practices. Clearly, there is concern over substantial population loss, furthering the brain drain. In fact, Bang and Mitra (2011) suggest a positive correlation between a country's higher institutional capacity and stronger incentives for higher-skilled workers to emigrate than for lower-skilled ones to do so, even in the presence of political stability—relevant factors in the EE and FSU region.

The first movers and the old vs. the new diaspora

Nevertheless, development literature has had particularly high hopes for the "first movers" and return migration's positive feedback (e.g., McGregor, 2014; Boly *et al.*, 2014; Gevorkyan & Gevorkyan, 2012; Ketkar and Ratha, 2010; and Freinkman, 2001). However, the practical difficulty of implementing the diaspora first-movers' vision requires a clear understanding of the nature of the relationship between the home country and the diaspora.

Focusing on remittances alone is not sufficient. As much as recent literature has focused on the labor migration aspect of the diaspora, the "new" diaspora aspect has gone largely unnoticed. Historically, these waves of outward migration from the EE/FSU have contributed to burgeoning diaspora networks abroad, reinvigorating altruistic motives of the "old" (dormant) groups. The latter represent established long-time citizens of the host countries to which either they or their ancestor emigrated some time ago. Still, the "old" retains nostalgic impulses to assist their distant countries of origin. Chander (2001) was one of the first to offer a comprehensive analysis of the altruistic motivations of the "old" diaspora towards their country of origin.

Conceptually, the "old" shares common ethnic or religious roots with the "new" diaspora. Often, the members of this "old" diaspora have cultural (and some tangible) ties with their birth country. Yet, in an environment of ever greater globalization, they are reinvigorated by the "new" diaspora and may develop further significant inclinations to take part in the development efforts of their ancestral home through humanitarian aid or other "soft" (e.g. educational, cultural exchanges) projects. By definition, the "old" diaspora makes up a more established and affluent entity. Because it has stronger institutional business leverage, the "old" diaspora's relationship with its country of historical origin (home) can result in more significant and systemic positive feedbacks to that country's development. This latter proposition is dependent on the effectiveness and strength of the individual country's diaspora–home link.

Based on national census data and other sources, we find that some countries in our sample have relatively sizable expatriate communities of the "old" and the "new" diasporas. That mainly pertains to Armenia, Bulgaria, Georgia, Moldova, Poland, Tajikistan, and Ukraine, with diaspora shares of up to 78% of the domestic population. They are scattered across the world because of a host of historical circumstances (Table 8.4). This accounting for the "old" diaspora is consistent with and adds to the earlier diaspora estimates elsewhere (e.g.

Table 8.4 Potential diaspora stock and geographical spread for some transition economies

Country	National mid-year 2008 population, in '000	Potential diaspora stock [estimated]	Diaspora spread by major countries
Armenia	2,969	5 mln – 10 mln	Russia, USA, Western Europe [France, UK], Middle East [Iran], Ukraine, Canada, other
Azerbaijan	8,178	2 mln – 4 mln	Russia, Ukraine, Georgia, Turkey
Belarus	9,686	2 mln – 3.5 mln	Ukraine, Latvia, Kazakhstan, Russia, USA, Canada, Australia
Bulgaria	7,263	2 mln – 10 mln	US, Canada, Germany, Moldova, Ukraine
Georgia	4,631	1.5 mln – 2 mln	Russia, Turkey, Ukraine, USA, other
Kazakhstan	15,341	4.5 mln – 5 mln	CIS, China
Kyrgyz Republic	5,357	0.5 mln – 0.7 mln	China, Kazakhstan, Russia, Tajikistan, Turkey and Uzbekistan.
Moldova	4,324	0.5 mln – 0.7 mln	Ukraine, Russia, Kazakhstan, Baltic states
Poland	38,501	15 mln – 16 mln	USA, Belarus, Moldova, Ukraine, Russia, Canada, West Europe, UK
Romania	22,247	8 mln	Moldova, Ukraine, USA, Spain, France, Germany, other
Russian Federation*	140,702	25 mln	Worldwide, mainly in CIS, USA, Europe
Tajikistan	7,212	0.6 mln – 5 mln	Russia, Uzbekistan, Iran, Middle East
Turkmenistan	5,180	2.5 mln – 3 mln	Russia, Iran, Iraq, Afghanistan
Ukraine	45,994	16 mln – 20 mln	Russia, Canada, USA
Uzbekistan	28,268	5.5 mln – mln	Tajikistan, Kyrgyzstan, Kazakhstan, Turkmenistan, Russia, Ukraine, Belarus, Lithuania, Afghanistan, Saudi Arabia, Turkey, Iran, China, India, Pakistan, Germany, USA, other

Note: see source for additional clarification.

Source: adapted from Gevorkyan (2011)

Heleniak, 2011, 2013). The statistics in Table 8.4 (while speculative and, certainly, subject to estimation bias) are also consistent with the World Bank and the UN (2014) DESA's Population Division (Migration Section), based on migration profiles by country.

We find confirmation of the above-established fact of diversity in destinations for the diasporas. Host economies (countries where expatriates settle) with established "old" diasporas tend to attract "new" migrants. In some cases, the determining factors may be the prospect of economic opportunity or geographic proximity to the country of origin. However, even in those cases, a new labor migrant (especially from home's rural areas) is driven to an area with an existing nucleus of compatriots (either old or new), as discussed in Gevorkyan and Gevorkyan (2012).

The distinction between the "old" and the "new" diasporas is critical for understanding any success or failure in the diaspora-driven development of the EE/FSU region. Diaspora studies often overlook a definitional problem implied by conceptual uniformity of the diaspora. Taking any ethnic, cultural, religious (or other) diaspora as a social monolith that *a priori* is altruistically interested in development of their country of origin is bound to lead to disappointment.

A dispersion?

Instead, the term *dispersion*—as in a widely scattered distribution of people, resources, ideas, and actions—more accurately characterizes the complex web of factional, political, business, and other divisions, interwoven with history of an expatriate community with some type of common background. Here, the inherent diversity of experiences, the *dispersion effect*, may act as a brake on development of the home economy as opposed to being an engine of it (Gevorkyan, 2011). As we reiterate below, to date, despite a wide range of mutual cooperation and joint projects with the countries of origin, diaspora involvement has not reached the levels anticipated at the start of the reforms' implementation in the post-socialist countries.

Although the representatives of the "old" and the "new" diasporas may share some abstract views of their historical home country on major strategic issues, their practical actions, ideas, and beliefs on other topics suggest some contradiction (Gevorkyan, 2015). The dispersion effect is real and points to the heterogeneity in political and other (religious, community, territorial origin) backgrounds.[14]

The divisions are even greater between the expatriate community and the countries of origin. The effect is exemplified in diverse efforts at involvement and the obvious lack of systematic institutional engagement aimed at the comprehensive development of those countries of origin, aside from various one-time humanitarian and cultural projects. For a detailed narrative of the different modalities in relations between the diasporas and their countries of origin in the EE/FSU, see Heleniak (2011, 2013). This brings us to a much-needed analytical assessment of the effectiveness of the diaspora networks in development and poverty alleviation in those countries of origin specifically.

Measuring diaspora's effectiveness

Temporary labor migration may make a positive contribution to poverty reduction through the transfer of regular remittances and skills (e.g., Gevorkyan and Gevorkyan, 2012; Heleniak, 2011, 2013; Agunias and Newland, 2012; Newland, 2010; Ratha and Mohapatra, 2011). If left to its own devices, the ad hoc temporary labor migration model is not a sustainable path to development or lifting the EE/FSU region out of poverty. Available data suggest that, after several rounds of temporary migration, breadwinners attempt to emigrate with their families, effectively cutting off the home economy from the financing based on remittances. As earlier cited studies suggest, continuous and sole reliance on remittances can erode the competitiveness of the domestic labor market, as the incentives to compete for jobs are over-taken by consumers' higher purchasing power.

Furthermore, only a handful of countries benefit from high (and consistent) inflows of remittances (see Figure 8.5). Dominance of a single source of remittance revenue calls into question the recipient country's sustainability and susceptibility to the sender's business cycle, a scenario that has played out in the EE/FSU region after the 2008–2009 crisis and following devaluation of the Russian ruble (Table 8.3). Aside from remittances, what other economic effects derive from diaspora communities?

Recent policy and academic publications explore the effects "beyond remittances" (e.g., Newland and Patrick, 2004) arguing that multiplier effects exist from diaspora-led foreign direct investment (FDI), technology transfers, philanthropy, tourism, political contributions, and cultural influences. For example, despite the limitations of data with respect to the impact of FDI from the diaspora, the evidence suggests that, in some economies with extended dias-pora networks, the "old" diaspora's active business involvement in the economy of the coun-try of origin has been critical to macroeconomic success (e.g., Armenia, Georgia, Poland, and Ukraine).

In Armenia, for instance, diaspora business networks are the source of over 60 percent of recent FDI and multinational enterprises (GIZ, 2011). Armenia (like Poland and Ukraine) has relied on its worldwide expatriate community for much of its large-scale business activ-ity (including tourism, mining, financial services, and information technology). Georgia's diaspora is young in terms of the phases of large-scale immigration that have contributed to the expatriate community formation.

For Georgia, large-scale migration began with dissolution of the USSR, whereas Arme-nia's Western diaspora has been in existence since, at least, the late 19th–early 20th century. In contrast to the Armenian diaspora, the Georgian diaspora is relatively small and lacks the proactive economic vibrancy in home–host country engagement (GIZ, 2011, 2012). But what type of diaspora-to-home involvement might be sufficient to guarantee a strong and lasting impact on poverty alleviation and does it depend on the diaspora's relative history?

At best, due to very scant data, there is no one conclusive answer. One could hypothesize, however. For instance, Figure 9.6 points to a clear mismatch between the incoming per capita external financial flows and GDP per capita for the full sample of the CEE and FSU econo-mies. We propose a new indicator for broadly defined external investment—a per capita sum of FDI and remittance inflows (on the vertical axis). Focusing only on the relatively recent, 2000–2015, period, that metric is compared to GDP per capita index for the same period, with 1989 taken as the base income.[15]

A quick glance at the pattern in Figure 8.6 is sufficient to reveal a somewhat contradic-tory story. We see some countries with relatively modest pre-transition recovery in GDP per capita with high inflows of combined external investments (e.g. Croatia, Hungary, or combined Serbia and Montenegro). Those are essentially the points above the trend line and right on or to the left and above of the average point. There are also those with strong per capita income growth but relatively weak external inflows. For the top performers, generally the EU-8 group (plus the new recent members), FDI flows play a greater role than remittances. To some extent this observation is also consistent with the fact that coun-tries with smaller income gains (bottom left from the average point) are seeing smaller per capita inflows.

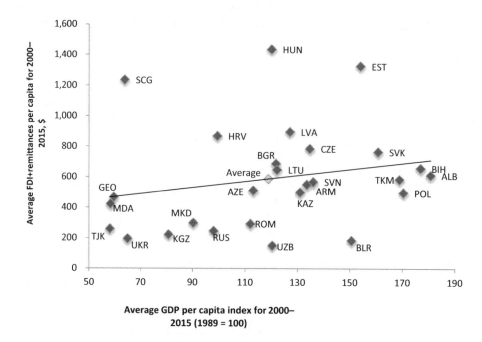

Figure 8.6 FDI and remittances per capita, 2000–2015, USD.

Note: see text for explanation of the vertical axis data.

Sources: author's estimates based on WDI (2017) and The Conference Board Total Economy Database (TCB, 2017)

However, Figure 8.6 presents a mixed set of evidence. What about those countries that may derive potential benefits from the larger diaspora, if estimates in Table 8.4 are any guidance? It appears those countries have not been able to attract significant levels of external investment at per capita levels. There are two concerns.

First, there are objective macroeconomic considerations with respect to the large-diaspora country's investment attractiveness. Entering the global capitalism stage, has also meant entering global competition for limited capital, which has proven to be a challenge to the emerging markets and the CEE/FSU group in particular (we review some of the related specifics in Chapter 10).

Second, the emerging economies may have been unable to fully mobilize the potential of their collective "old" and "new" diasporas. And if they have tried, the diaspora response has not been sufficient due to a host of factors. In the end, inability to secure sustained external financing either towards motivating domestic aggregate demand (remittances) or longer-term investment projects (via FDI) presents itself as a serious deterrent to the macroeconomic development models of the smaller EE/FSU economies.

In fact, perhaps the question may well be not so much about where to invest for diaspora or how resources are allocated in formal terms, but the inability to penetrate local markets. Over two decades since the transition reforms, the evolving local business networks are now actually competing with a potential diaspora capital. From the perspective of domestic firms, financial and project-driven investments from expatriates are viewed as competition rather than investment towards the country's development. The dynamic between the local and diaspora business networks requires a more careful analysis in a dedicated study.

Meanwhile, Heleniak (2011), Gevorkyan (2011), Newland (2010) and numerous other studies also see the need to go "beyond remittances" in their various policy proposals. A handful of countries (e.g. Armenia, Georgia, Moldova, Poland, Tajikistan, and Ukraine) have tried to put some such mechanisms in place. For example, Armenia (often touted as having the most organized diaspora, though the dispersion effect is applicable here) now has a range of development, education, humanitarian, philanthropic, and political projects involving individuals from the "old" and the "new" diasporas. On top of this, the country adopted a dual citizenship law (joined by a few, including Moldova and Kyrgyz Republic).

On the other hand, there is also a practice of "fuzzy citizenship" (Skrentny *et al.*, 2007) in reference to a semi-permanent residence status granted to the diaspora. For example, Poland has established a "card of the Pole" as a document that allows a Polish diaspora member to obtain a work permit, establish business in Poland, gain access to the country's educational system at no charge, and other benefits usually unavailable to foreign citizens (MFA, 2015). Other countries either initiate (as in the Polish model) or create conditions for expatriate entities to engage (as in the Armenian model) in economic and social activities (for a thorough review of the involvement of each diaspora with its country of origin, see Heleniak, 2011).

Constructing an index

The cumulative evidence so far points to two results: while some macroeconomic improvement is undoubtedly due to diaspora actions, there is, nevertheless, limited coordination in the diaspora-led initiatives due to the dispersion. The dispersion effect, of the scattered, unorganized, nature of such efforts, may be slowing potential economic progress. In contrast, if a country's fundamental macroeconomic and political environment is relatively predictable (i.e. the EU-8 countries), dispersion can have a positive effect, as the economy benefits from having a variety of medium- to long-term investment and cultural projects, in part driven by diaspora organizations.

Yet, for the most part, expatriate communities from the EE/FSU vary in terms of their involvement with their country of origin, depending on a variety of factors: (1) the distance between the expatriate's current country of residence and country of origin; (2) the relative age of the diaspora—defined as how long in history the diaspora has been in existence; (3) the political stability and macroeconomy in the country of origin; (4) the expatriate's legal status in the host country.

Clearly, those four factors are not exclusive and more research is needed with a country focus. Yet, based on the available data, we may attempt to construct a high-level index of home country to diaspora effectiveness. Much of the data comes from the earlier studies (e.g. Gevorkyan, 2011; Heleniak, 2011) and data publicly available for each country (e.g. official websites on diaspora or labor migration programs, specifying the scope and focus of involvement in each country), as well as data sources from Figure 8.6.

The index, appearing in Figure 8.7, ranges from 0 (least effective) to 5 (most effective), with some descriptive data assembled in Table 8.5A in the Appendix. As such, the following categories of home country to diaspora involvement with corresponding proposed scores are used to develop the index:

- Diaspora focus (OLD = 0.5; NEW = 0.5; NONE = 0)—a proxy indicator measuring a country's stated policy toward its (old or new) diaspora.
- Priority policy (Economic Development = 1; Identity, Cultural, Political = 0.5; NONE = 0)—a proxy for a country's stated objective for diaspora involvement.

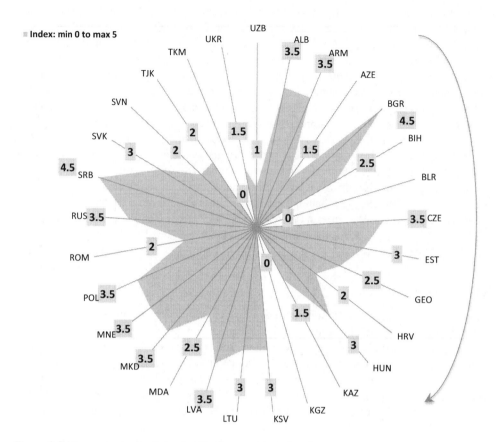

Figure 8.7 Home country-to-diaspora effectiveness approximation.

Sources: author's estimates based on WDI (2017), Heleniak (2011), and Gevorkyan (2011)

Economic Development implies active steps towards stimulating diaspora business activity in the country's development. Identity, cultural, and political categories refer to soft-power interactions with diaspora.

- Diaspora Institution (Ministry or Subministry = 1; Other = 0.5; NONE = 0)— proxy for existence and operation of a formal entity in charge of diaspora relations.
- FDI + Remit per capita variance from average (1 if positive and 0 if negative)— follows from the above analysis in Figure 8.6 and reports combined statistics' positive or negative variation from the average point by country.

For brevity, we omit individual country discussions, as some of the conclusions are self-evident from the presented evidence. Clearly, rankings in Figure 8.7 are subject to estimation errors and can only be treated as directional at best, as it is quite difficult to measure intensity of relationship between the diaspora and home country (e.g. case of Armenia with vast diaspora networks of generational layers of communities and case of Poland with practical steps towards engaging its recent expatriates). As the sample countries mature and develop more established infrastructure for relations with their diaspora, the rankings, undoubtedly, will change.

On paper, almost every country boasts some type of relationship with its diaspora community (e.g. ministry or high-profile regular gathering), through humanitarian projects, or through diaspora participation in public life in the country. Yet, the obvious conclusion at this point is the lack of a systematic large-scale institutionalized involvement of the diaspora in the macroeconomic development of its country of origin. A comprehensive plan that targets a multitude of macroeconomic development goals is still absent, despite variations in some countries (in particular, in humanitarian areas or one-time large investor projects). This reconfirms the much-needed country focus in development studies, and inadequacy of a "one-size-fits-all" model in the post-socialist transition.

We posit, then, that for the EE/FSU region and for the structurally smaller economies, specifically, there is still a great deal of room for more active diaspora involvement that may help promote overall macroeconomic development and bring down poverty rates. However, part of the problem might be in the interaction across diaspora and dispersion dynamics.

Some new and not so new policy proposals

Before concluding the present analysis, a few words are needed on policy proposals involving the diaspora that are aimed at poverty alleviation in the region. One of the proposals gaining support for the CEE/FSU has been the issuing of diaspora sovereign bonds. The proposal is often brought up as a potentially effective method of engagement between the economy in the countries of origin and their expatriate communities, a topic well covered in Chander (2001), Gevorkyan (2011), and Ratha and Mohapatra (2011), among others. This may soon become a reality, as even the smallest of the post-socialist economies have recently tapped international capital markets (e.g. Armenia and Georgia).

Alternatively, diaspora micro-loans to rural areas or diaspora business-funded basic income programs may be another method of proactive involvement. The volatility of global primary commodity supplies and prices exerts additional macroeconomic and financial pressure, exacerbating poverty in the smaller (commodity-exporting) countries. Hence, such diaspora micro-loans arrangements can be advantageous, in particular for post-socialist economies with a limited presence in global capital markets, limited FDI inflows, and a still evolving banking system.

Temporary labor migration can be coordinated via the diaspora regulatory mechanism (DRM), with remittances flowing to the Migration Development Bank (MDB) first introduced in Gevorkyan (2011), and Gevorkyan and Gevorkyan (2012).[16] Here, the blueprint (see Appendix Figure 8.9A) builds on the wealth of existing labor migration frameworks in advanced economies and elsewhere. To elaborate, consider the following.

The involvement of the "old" diaspora, without having to dedicate significant resources to the country of origin, is critical to the success of the DRM and MDB frameworks. Much activity takes place in the new country of residence, in which the "old" diaspora acts through organized recruitment agencies and diaspora centers help new migrants settle into the new environment and provide employment. In this way, the labor migration triad (host country labor displacement, capital transfers, and wage impacts), is balanced in a mutually beneficial way for all country participants.[17]

The Migration Development Bank

The MDB would be a financial conduit for a more streamlined (in contrast to ad hoc) transfer of remittance income. As funds flow into the bank, there would be opportunities for it to engage in development projects in infrastructure, poverty alleviation, education, and so forth, in the country of origin. The development focus would be driven by country specifics, targeting core regional underdevelopment problems and stemming the labor force exodus, with a broader positive effect on macroeconomic stabilization.

Funding for MDB projects would come from temporarily unclaimed deposits, bilateral state transfers, new direct loans, and borrowing from regional and international financial markets as well as by partially reinvesting earned interest. Further, a bilateral government deposit guarantee or active engagement of the multilateral development agencies in the MDB charter could mitigate some of the risks. Operational transparency could be gained by involving the "old" and the "new" diaspora members in a Diaspora Supervisory Board as a policy-setting and decision-making entity.

Establishing the MDB would also attract new diaspora investors who are hesitant to enter the market in the country of origin. For a non-diaspora investor, who is unfamiliar with local conditions but seeking portfolio diversification, MDB could be an alternative that would facilitate initial entry to the local market. For the host economies some of the funding could be directed towards better administration and regulation of the labor migration sector (e.g., financing diaspora centers, publications for labor migrants, and efficient fast-track immigration screening).

There is also scope for continuation of the "soft" aspect of relations between diasporas and their countries of origin, through exchanges in education, culture, business, and other areas. It is not difficult to envision cooperation on a joint strategic development project that would be long term and set macroeconomic development as its ultimate goal. Hence, the view of the dispersed diaspora business networks, as an alternative source for broader economic development and guarantor of financial stability remains viable.

Conclusion: diaspora model and social costs of transition

We have covered much ground in our discussion of various aspects of the social costs of transition. It is hardly possible to address every pressing detail on the topic in the confines of one study, and much less within one chapter. Still, building on the preceding discussions we have attempted to unveil in more broad strokes the magnitude of human deprivation and challenges to the earlier raised liveability concept endured in the early stages of transition to market. In the process, our discussion revolved around problems of poverty, income inequality, and migration in the post-socialist economies.

We found confirmation for the evident diversity in experiences across the post-socialist economies, individually and across regional groups. We then led our discussion to introducing the concept of diaspora. The potential for a powerful macroeconomic uplift from diaspora involvement towards development especially in the smaller countries, experiencing outward migration, could be the game-changing factor.

In the context of diaspora, the problem, of course, is whether the "giving back" momentum where it matters, may be sustained in a complex dynamic of globally redefined fundamental uncertainty. The diaspora's lack of consensus, the dispersion effect, and the lack of sustainable institutional arrangements with expatriate communities in their countries of origin have limited development that includes both sides. The effectiveness index in Figure 8.7, albeit at surface level, suggests there is room for improvement, which is approximated in a hypothetical model of diaspora engagement in Figure 8.8.

Consider four directions: 1) social and economic development; 2) business development; 3) political involvement; and 4) repatriation. The ideal outcome is the expatriate's

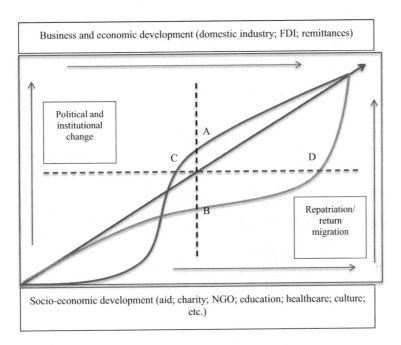

Figure 8.8 Diaspora model, social costs of transition, and development.

Source: author's approximation

community increasing movement along all four dimensions, along the diagonal 45-degree line. At the top of the horizontal axis runs a gauge for business and economic development, including industrial structure, FDI and remittance flows, and so on.

Socio-economic development (the social costs of economic reforms) is measured at the bottom of the horizontal axis (these include a range of "soft" development categories that often enough become critical to macroeconomic growth). Political and institutional improvements, moving up, are measured on the left-hand side of the diaspora model box and positive gains from repatriation and return labor migration are captured on the right-hand side of the box.

There are two scenarios, out of infinitely many, illustrated by the two curves deviating from the diagonal line (Figure 8.8). The deviations may be due to any range of factors, including issues emanating from lack of unity across the diaspora (i.e. dispersion). For example, outcomes A and B both achieve equal progress in social, business, and economic involvement but vary significantly on the measures of diaspora's political involvement in the home country's life and degree of repatriation. Similarly, points C and D correspond to the same levels in political and repatriation levels, while at the opposite ends of economic structure and social development. Scenarios for specific countries could be extended further, but the main point should be self-evident.

Figure 8.8 helps to capture the current concerns and, at the same time, offers some optimistic scenarios. Ultimately, the success of the diaspora networks in countries of origin is especially critical for development of the efforts against poverty and the survival of the smaller economies. It is in those post-socialist economies that are structurally weaker and geographically remote from key trade and industrial centers, where external pressures are particularly strong while the domestic market is weak and fiscal efforts may be insufficient due to budget constraints. Overcoming the dispersion effect, diasporas may potentially bring positive systemic changes to their countries of origin addressing the immensity of the human costs of post-socialist transformation. Harnessing that capacity would seem an important development policy milestone for a small country in a competitive global economy.

Appendix

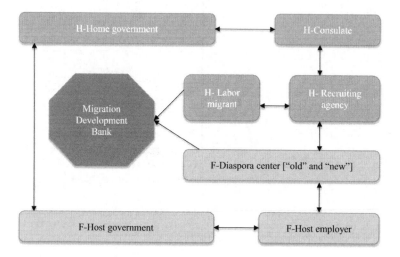

Figure 8.9A Diaspora regulatory mechanism and Migration Development Bank.

Note: see Gevorkyan (2011) for detailed discussion.

Sources: adapted from Gevorkyan (2011) and Gevorkyan and Canuto (2015)

Table 8.5A Home-diaspora development effectiveness matrix

Country	Country-to-diaspora focus	Country-to-diaspora priority	Diaspora Institution	FDI + Remit score
ALB	NEW	Econ	Sub ministry	1.00
ARM	OLD+NEW	Econ+Identity	Ministry	0.00
AZE	NEW	Identity	Other	0.00
BLR	NONE	NONE	No office	0.00
BIH	NONE	Identity	Sub ministry	1.00
BGR	OLD+NEW	Econ+Identity	Sub ministry	1.00
HRV	NEW	Identity	No office	1.00
CZE	OLD+NEW	Identity	Sub ministry	1.00
EST	OLD	Econ+Identity	No office	1.00
GEO	OLD+NEW	Identity	Ministry	0.00
HUN	OLD+NEW	Identity+Politics	Other	1.00
KAZ	NEW	NONE	Sub ministry	0.00
KSV	NEW	Econ+Identity	Ministry	0.00
KGZ	NONE	NONE	No office	0.00
LVA	OLD+NEW	Identity	Sub ministry	1.00
LTU	OLD+NEW	Identity	Other	1.00
MKD	OLD+NEW	Econ+Identity	Sub ministry	0.00
MDA	OLD+NEW	Econ+Identity	No office	0.00

Country	Country-to-diaspora focus	Country-to-diaspora priority	Diaspora Institution	FDI + Remit score
MNE	OLD+NEW	Identity	Sub ministry	1.00
POL	OLD+NEW	Econ+Identity	Sub ministry	0.00
ROM	NEW	Identity	Sub ministry	0.00
RUS	OLD+NEW	Econ+Identity	Sub ministry	0.00
SRB	OLD+NEW	Econ+Identity	Ministry	1.00
SVK	OLD+NEW	Identity	Other	1.00
SVN	OLD+NEW	Identity	Other	0.00
TJK	NEW	Econ	Other	0.00
TKM	NONE	NONE	No office	0.00
UKR	NEW	Identity	Other	0.00
UZB	NONE	NONE	Sub ministry	0.00

Notes: FDI_Remit pc score is 1 if country is above average and 0 if below, as per data in Figure 9.6. Data for Kosovo, Montenegro, and Serbia is based on WDI (2017) estimated separately.

Sources: author's estimates based on WDI (2017), Heleniak (2011), and Gevorkyan (2011)

Notes

1 In his blog entry Milanovic (2014a and 2014c) states that the transition-era output declines and social costs were far greater than conventionally assumed. As such, given the level of social development in pre-transition, a more significant recovery in key macroeconomic indicators, e.g. per capita output matching the OECD average, might be a necessary condition before the word "normal" can be used as a general description. For that matter, Åslund (2013) discussing market reforms in the case of Russia, appears to be more comfortable with the use of "normal" characterization.

2 Diaspora has played a direct role in poverty alleviation and has added a significant stimulus to economic development across a range of industries in Armenia—a country that is a classical case study of diaspora development oriented research (e.g. Gevorkyan, 2016).

3 For an in-depth analysis see the World Bank (2000) report issued at the time as social costs had become more evident and dire.

4 The observation is true either measured as a percentage of total population or by World Bank's $3.10 a day benchmark. For some guidance on the World Bank's international poverty lines see a blog entry by Ferreira *et al.* (2015).

5 For instance, the official poverty rate in New York City, net of various social transfers, in 2013 was 21.3 percent, putting significant strain on a city with a GDP of approximately USD 700 billion at the time, easily exceeding most CEE/FSU economies (CEO, 2013).

6 Hamilton *et al.* (2005) offer an insightful discussion on the problems of urban and metropolitan area development. They point to a range of categories among CEE/FSU cities (e.g. those in CEE focused on European integration compared to those ravaged by war or industrial desolation) as foundational characteristics in explaining differences in social and economic performance.

7 There has been no lack of commentary on the "elephant chart" and global inequality since Milanovic's original publication. PBS Newshour dubbed the graph as the "hottest chart in economics" (Solman, 2017).

8 See Adam (1999) on the social costs of transition and the distinction argument between socialist and capitalist systems.

9 For further clarification on the role of remittance transfers, see Ratha (2003).

10 See Gevorkyan and Canuto (2015) for a recent analysis of labor migration and remittance transfers in the case of CEE/FSU and Ratha (2003) on an early case for remittances in development finance.

11 In their dedicated analysis of problems of migration and development, WB (2017a) offer additional details on the effects of the Russian crisis on remittances flows to the Caucasus and Central Asia. In 2016, remittance flows to developing countries declined for the first time, primarily due to cyclical factors and weak economic growth in the largest host economies.

12 For analysis of typical migration patterns from small FSU economies see Gevorkyan *et al.* (2008).

13 See EBRD (2000) for an early discussion of the perils of labor migration as well as some additional detail on distribution of CEE/FSU migration by country destination.
14 See Gevorkyan (2016, 2013b) on the examples of dispersion concept in the case of the Armenian diaspora.
15 This is an already familiar GDP per capita index from our earlier exercises (consider, Figure 8.1).
16 For Russian language version, see Gevorkyan (2007).
17 See Gevorkyan and Gevorkyan (2012) for detailed discussion of the labor migration triad.

Part V

The roaring 2000s and the present

9   Contours of the new era post-transition economy

They are all different

Even the darkest night will end and the sun will rise.

Victor Hugo, *Les Misérables*

The character of the new millennium

In the societies of the post-socialist Europe and former USSR, the new century ushered in determined efforts to recover from the multiplicity of the 1990s shocks. The prevailing feeling was all about moving forward faster and steadier towards new economy, new social institutions. Emphasizing the critical element of diversity in the post-socialist experience, this chapter, attempts to logically extend the preceding narrative in the context of the first two decades of the new century. Broadly, four approaches conceptualize the emerging political economy in the region.

First, across the region there has been a clear emphasis on macroeconomic stabilization and key domestic growth drivers. Second, for some, becoming part of a bigger project, such as the European Union for the CEE countries, has held the promise of a path to progress and final categorical break with the socialist past. Third, as individuality (if not, nationalism) of each country continues to influence moods, doing things all alone becomes a matter of national pride. Introduction of local currencies in the FSU (while CEE economies had retained their national currencies through the Soviet era, the ruble was the only legal tender in the former USSR) was one of such proud moments, reasserting national sovereignty. And fourth, going their own way has also meant seeing the world's institutional and development practices, often making the best of those but also sometimes going only halfway.

This latter point is of special importance. In certain areas, for example financial, information and technology sectors, social safety and labor market reforms, efficient energy focus and environmental projects, and other areas of development, there has been significant progress in some CEE/FSU countries. This partly may have been due to the perfected policy design recommendations streaming from country offices of multilateral organizations. Partly, local attempts to comply with higher-standard institutional demands for global or regional integration played a role. Relying on strong human capital capacity and the remnants of a once strong technical sciences education system has also been touted in national development programs. Lastly, the post-socialist societies yearned for the best after the 1990s social and economic collapses. To some extent, one could find validation for Gerschenkron's (1962) "economic backwardness" view by observing the changes in the early 2000s and after the 2008 global financial crisis (GFC). Diversity again characterized post-socialist experiences.

After a false start in the 1990s, the post-socialist societies across the CEE/FSU map pushed for having all that capitalism could offer. The luxury veneer of the free market and accessibility to the previously unreachable consumer choices breathed revolution into every fiber of social structure. The nouveau riche culture began its steady rise. Everything was new and desirable, from high-end spending at newly built restaurants with invited French and Italian chefs, to luxury fashion spending, and more frequent trips abroad, and more. Of course, as the income inequality review in the previous chapter makes clear, luxury spending has not been the vocation of all. However, the mere possibility of tapping into that elite category of consumers has served its Veblen-esque purpose.

This new consumer society was quickly evolving, burgeoning, and, seemingly aiming to catch up with and, in some ways, to exceed the standards of the West. The latter had enjoyed those visible consumerist facets of a capitalist society for much longer, while the straitjacket socialist model denied them for many. The problem with this tendency, however, has been the conspicuous grotesqueness of the new shopping malls, entertainment programs, mass media propagation, sleek night lounges, designer clothes, and other attributes of modern consumer society mushrooming in the 2000s in the post-socialist context against a still fragile overall institutional basis.[1]

In this chapter, we offer a brief macroeconomic overview of the former socialist economies covering the period of roughly 2000 to early 2017. A separate section is devoted to the discussion of the financial and banking systems in the post-socialist region. We then direct our attention to the questions of regional economic integration, trade direction and foreign direct investment, and some assessment of business climate evolution in the CEE/FSU.

The "roaring" 2000s

The early 2000s marked a period of strong economic growth across all economies in the post-socialist CEE/FSU group. Long forgotten were the instability and uncertainty evoked by the Russian default of 1998 (see Box 9.1). Macro-stabilization appeared in sight. On the surface, it seemed as if warm, sunny days had finally arrived to replace the uncertainty of long, cold nights.

Looking again at the fundamentals in Figure 9.1, we plot average annual GDP growth by region. There is a clear, positive trend at the beginning of the 2000s. On average, growth was in the 6–7 percent annual range, with exceptionally high rates in the Caucasus, sustained strong growth in Russia and the Central Asian economies, and rising in the EU-8 group. Spurred on by strong exports and credit expansion, the early 2000s indeed had "roaring" growth as the pace picked up at the beginning but economies strained towards the end of the decade.

In fact, early in the decade, Goldman Sachs—the world's leading financial institution—in their assessment of the global economy at the start of the new century, added Russia to a select club of promising and fast-growing BRIC economies, along with Brazil, India, and China (O'Neill, 2001).[2] The World Bank in their in-depth analysis of the tiny Armenia, commenting on the economy's strong-paced, sustained growth, named the country a "Caucasian Tiger" by analogy to the "East Asian Tigers" (Mitra *et al.*, 2007).[3] Elsewhere, by 2004 eight CEE countries were brought into the European Union (EU)—Czech Republic, Estonia, Hungary, Latvia, Lithuania, Poland, Slovak Republic, and Slovenia. Bulgaria and Romania the EU in 2007.[4] It seemed as if the path to long-awaited prosperity was wide open and the promise of the 1990s free-market reforms was near. The pains and sacrifices of the 1990s may not have been in vain . . .

Alas, the 2008 global financial crisis (GFC) ended the positive trend with a sobering reminder of remaining structural deficiencies across the post-socialist range of countries.

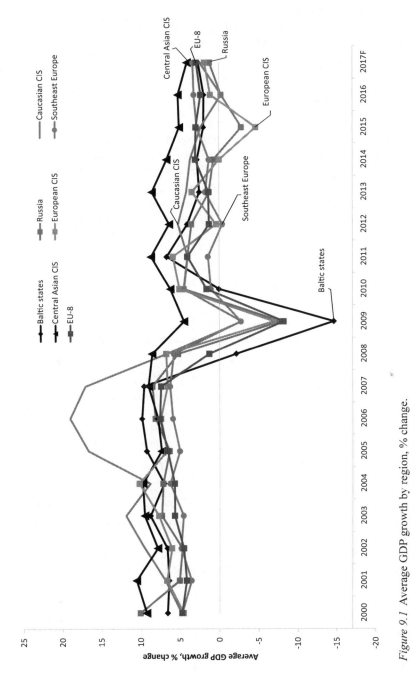

Figure 9.1 Average GDP growth by region, % change.

Note: Baltic States are also part of EU-8 group; F = forecast or preliminary data.

Source: author's calculations based on data from The Conference Board Total Economy Database (TCB, 2017)

Figure 9.1 shows a sharp decline in growth rates in 2009—the crisis year in the CEE/FSU (unlike 2008 in advanced economies)—and, in most cases, relatively quick recovery to positive rates but at levels below the pre-crisis averages. The next test of endurance would come at the end of 2014 (a visible dent in Russia's and European CIS, the latter largely due to the economic crisis in Ukraine; growth rates in Figure 9.1). Then, under the weight of recessionary pressures, declining commodity prices, and abrupt cuts to international trade and financial flows, the Russian economy contracted and the currency was devalued.

Before the global financial crisis

In more specific terms, much of the pre-2008 gains were driven by a combination of rising domestic private sector credit growth feeding into consumption, infrastructure investment, real estate spending, and, particularly for commodity exporters, a steady rise in crude oil and other primary commodity prices.[5] The period of the early 2000s was also characterized by improving fiscal balances, especially in the small CEE and net importer FSU economies. In addition, consistent with the countries' aims on global economy integration, capital accounts in CEE and the European FSU remained open to foreign exchange flows, which later intensified instability during the crisis.

Box 9.1

The Russian crisis of 1998 (also known as the Russian default of 1998)

The Russian crisis of 1998 was severe, deep, and for many, unexpected, despite the 1997 Asian crisis before. The Russian government defaulted on its debt (the GKOs and OFZs)* devaluing the currency as social costs mounted and some large commercial banks shut down. In a severe hit to domestic consumers, the currency dropped from 5 rubles per one USD before August 17 (date of default) to approximately 21 rubles by the end of September in 1998. Ironically, due to a combination of a more cash-based economy at the time and rise in export revenues as commodity prices began to increase, the economy returned to positive growth within a year (approximately 6% in 1999 and 10% in 2000).

The crisis spread beyond Russia. The smaller economies of the Caucasus and Central Asia were hit especially hard. Both were affected via the imports channel (as Russian imports dropped and suppliers demanded payment in hard currency). Commodity exporters (including declining steel production in Ukraine) experienced competitiveness shock as economies opened up to global markets, while Russia's commodity exports gained, helped by the weaker currency. Dependent on consumer goods and energy imports Belarus, Moldova, and Ukraine sustained losses to their currency values. The Baltics defended their currency boards with interest rate hikes and interventions; while the CEEs were mainly affected via capital market contagion effects as foreign capital pulled out.

Unexpectedly, both advanced and emerging markets experienced a drop in capital flows. Brazil (1999), Argentina and Turkey (2001) were in crisis shortly after Russia. And in the US a leading hedgefund, Long-Term Capital Management, that seemed to have made wrong bets tied to emerging and Russian markets, lost 50 percent of its capital, prompting a bailout orchestrated by the Federal Reserve Bank of New York.

The abruptness of the Russian default was obfuscated by economy's momentous return to positive growth in 1997 and hyperinflation containment. The Central Bank of Russia (CBR) kept the exchange rate pegged while speculative foreign capital saturated the high-yield GKO market, with frequent investor cash-outs. To calm the volatility, the CBR stepped in several times early in 1998 to defend the currency, before eventually letting it float in August. The next time a similar devaluation happened was in November 2014.

* GKO or *Gosudarstvennoye Kratkosrochnoye Obyazatyel'stvo*—a short-term treasury bill without coupon. OFZ or *Obligatsyi Federal'nogo Zaima*—a long-term treasury bond with coupon. The 1998 default was primarily on the GKOs.

Additional readings

Gilman, M. 2010. *No Precedent, No Plan. Inside Russia's 1998 Default.* Cambridge, MA: MIT Press.

IMF. 1999. *Russian Federation: Recent Economic Developments.* IMF Staff Country Report 99/100.

Pastor, G. and T. Damjanovic. 2003. The Russian financial crisis and its consequences for Central Asia. *Emerging Markets Finance & Trade*, 39(3): 79–104.

Poirot, C. 2001. Financial integration under conditions of chaotic hysteresis: The Russian financial crisis of 1998. *Journal of Post Keynesian Economics*, 23(3): 485–507.

For the primary commodity exporters (i.e. primarily the net exporters as defined in Gevorkyan [2011], Azerbaijan, Russia, Kazakhstan, Turkmenistan, Uzbekistan, and Ukraine) the years building up to late 2008 brought in surplus revenues from commodity exports. Commodity prices were on the rise, with crude oil peaking significantly above $100 per barrel in mid-2008 (Figure 9.2).[6] Much of that revenue was directed towards: a) build-up in foreign exchange reserves (a lesson learned from the 1997 Asian and 1998 Russian crises), b) domestic infrastructure spending, and c) sustained public spending, including restarting some social programs, curtailed during the lean 1990s.

Elsewhere, high domestic credit growth (e.g. CEE and the Baltics) was driven by Western European banks scrambling to carve out larger market shares by offering cheap credit.[7] Housing prices were rising sharply. Capital inflows, in particularly in CEE, were massive as lower labor costs in the destination economies coupled with lower global interest rates and relative stability of the early to mid-2000s guaranteed higher returns on investment for Western multinationals.

Still others, for example smaller FSU economies (Armenia, Georgia, Moldova), relied primarily on labor migrants' remittance transfers for consumption growth. Also in these countries, large idiosyncratic capital infusions from multilateral institutions or other external entities (such as significant infrastructure investments in Armenia, funded mainly by diaspora businessmen and complemented by the World Bank) amounted to almost 10 percent of GDP at the time. In these cases, high external deficits were incurred (earning them "net importers" designation) and borrowing in foreign currency (at lower rates than domestic, due to inflation and riskiness) became a norm. Gradually, the post-socialist economies were entering the international capital market, building up their external debt obligations.

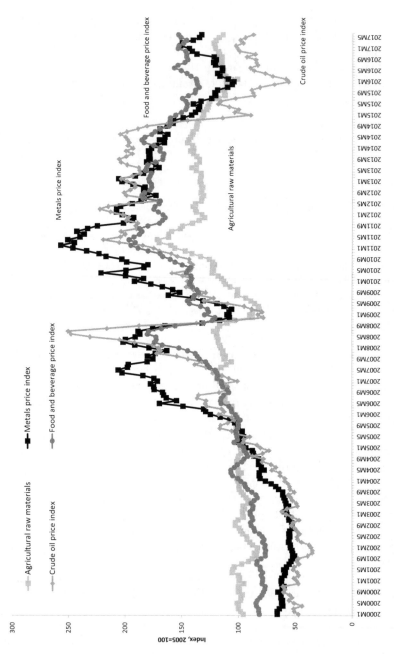

Figure 9.2 Primary commodity prices super-cycle of 2000s, index (2005 = 100).

Notes: as per IMF definitions, Metals index is based on copper, aluminium, iron ore, tin, nickel, zinc, lead, and uranium prices; crude oil index is a simple average of Dated Brent, West Texas Intermediate, and the Dubai Fateh prices; agricultural raw materials index includes timber, cotton, wool, rubber, and hides prices; Food and beverage index is based on processed food and beverage price indices.

Source: extrapolated from the IMF's Primary Commodity Prices database (IMF, 2017)

As the private sector expanded across the map, the pro-cyclical fiscal policy stance also improved in the years immediately before the GFC. Table 9.1 details recovery, in some cases strong, in the general government balances over a seven-year period between 2000 and 2007. As can be inferred from the table, a substantial number of the CEE/FSU countries have had their fiscal balances improved by three percentage points of GDP or more.

Two primary factors stimulated the improved fiscal policy stance across CEE/FSU: 1) rising tax (or direct) revenues from commodity exports (e.g. Russia and Kazakhstan) and 2) early tax-base consolidation (especially in the EU-8 countries).[8] Still, on average fiscal policy was pro-cyclical before the GFC as public expenditure increased sharply.

Table 9.1 General government balance, % of GDP

Country	2007	Change between 2007–2000	2009	2011	2013	2015	2016	2017F
Albania	−3.2	4.6	−6.6	−3.5	−5.2	−4.1	−1.7	−1.0
Armenia	−2.3	1.0	−7.7	−2.9	−1.6	−4.8	−5.6	−3.8
Azerbaijan	0.7	−1.6	8.3	11.7	1.0	−4.8	−1.4	−10.4
Belarus	−1.8	−2.1	−9.0	2.5	−2.8	−4.1	−4.6	−8.2
Bosnia and Herzegovina	0.2	4.8	−5.3	−2.7	−1.9	−0.2	0.0	−0.5
Bulgaria	3.1	3.7	−0.9	−1.8	−1.8	−2.8	1.6	−1.3
Croatia	−2.4	3.1	−6.0	−7.8	−5.3	−3.3	−1.5	−1.9
Czech Republic	−0.7	2.8	−5.5	−2.7	−1.2	−0.6	0.2	−0.2
Estonia	2.4	2.6	−1.9	1.1	−0.2	0.1	0.3	0.3
Georgia	0.8	2.8	−6.5	−0.9	−1.4	−1.3	−1.6	−1.4
Hungary	−5.1	−2.0	−4.6	−5.5	−2.5	−2.0	−1.8	−2.6
Kazakhstan	5.1	3.8	−1.3	5.8	4.9	−6.3	−4.4	−6.3
Kosovo	7.0	5.2	−0.6	−1.8	−3.1	−1.9	−1.5	−2.5
Kyrgyz Republic	−1.0	9.7	−1.5	−4.7	−3.7	−1.2	−4.5	−3.0
Latvia	0.6	3.1	−7.0	−3.1	−0.6	−1.5	−0.4	−1.2
Lithuania	−1.0	3.0	−9.3	−8.9	−2.6	−0.2	0.0	−0.6
FYR Macedonia	0.6	−1.8	−2.6	−2.5	−3.8	−3.5	−2.6	−3.3
Moldova	0.1	3.7	−6.4	−2.5	−1.9	−2.3	−2.1	−3.7
Montenegro	8.5	9.9	−6.7	−6.7	−4.5	−4.8	−5.3	−7.5
Poland	−1.9	1.1	−7.3	−4.8	−4.1	−2.6	−2.4	−2.9
Romania	−3.1	0.9	−7.1	−4.2	−2.5	−1.5	−2.4	−3.7
Russia	5.6	2.5	−5.9	1.4	−1.2	−3.4	−3.7	−2.6
Serbia	−0.9	−0.7	−3.6	−4.1	−5.3	−3.6	−1.3	−1.3
Slovak Republic	−1.7	10.3	−7.7	−3.9	−2.5	−2.7	−2.0	−1.8
Slovenia	0.3	1.5	−5.4	−5.5	−13.9	−3.3	−1.8	−1.5
Tajikistan	−5.5	0.0	−5.2	−2.1	−0.8	−1.9	−4.4	−2.5
Turkmenistan	3.9	4.4	7.0	3.6	1.5	−0.7	−1.3	−0.7
Ukraine	−1.9	1.3	−6.0	−2.8	−4.8	−1.2	−2.2	−3.0
Uzbekistan	4.6	7.1	2.5	7.8	2.4	−0.5	−0.3	−0.2
Caucasian CIS	−0.3	0.8	−2.0	2.7	−0.7	−3.6	−2.9	−5.2
Central Asian CIS	1.4	5.0	0.3	2.1	0.9	−2.1	−3.0	−2.5
European CIS	−1.2	1.0	−7.1	−0.9	−3.1	−2.5	−3.0	−5.0
Southeast Europe	1.1	3.3	−4.4	−3.9	−3.7	−2.8	−1.6	−2.6
EU–8	−0.9	2.8	−6.1	−4.2	−3.4	−1.6	−1.0	−1.3

Notes: regional items are simple average estimates for directional presentation only, based on country groupings as in earlier chapters. For consistency, Bulgaria, Croatia, and Romania are included as part of Southeast Europe, as before. F= forecast.

Source: data extrapolated from IMF World Economic Outlook (IMF WEO, 2017)

In a range of views on the pre-GFC fiscal changes, Rahman (2010), for example, suggests that CEE/FSU as a group made limited efforts to improve structural positions or to reduce public debt. For the majority, especially commodity exporters, surplus revenues from all sources (including some from privatization) fueled pro-cyclical expenditures. This result is somewhat confirmed in the analysis of primary surplus of the FSU economies in Gevorkyan (2011), when looking at the large net commodity exporters (e.g. Azerbaijan, Kazakhstan, Russia, Turkmenistan, Uzbekistan).[9] In those cases, surplus revenues allowed for larger public expenditure programs and sustained legacy social obligations for a longer period than elsewhere (e.g. in terms of pensions or healthcare coverage).

Where improved commodity prices did not play a major role, it appears that smaller, less endowed, economies following a less expansive growth pattern (e.g. Armenia, Bulgaria, Czech Republic, Estonia, Kyrgyz Republic) have had greater success (relative to their economies) in creating broader fiscal space. For the CEE (and specifically the EU-8 group), transfers related to the EU integration project added to the new member states' fiscal pro-cyclicality (e.g. Rosenberg and Tirpák, 2008). At the same time, Becker *et al.* (2010) suggest that while pro-cyclical, in the CEE region fiscal policy alone was not sufficient to offset pressures from credit growth and dependence on consumer imports.

Collectively, credit growth, commodity exports, and varying pro-cyclicality in public expenditure on top of remaining structural weaknesses in some countries led to a precarious situation in the CEE/FSU right before the GFC.

The global financial crisis

Summarizing some of the above observations and extending the analysis in Gevorkyan (2011), it is possible to advance at least five critical channels of the GFC propagation in the CEE/FSU transition economies:

1   Abrupt decline in commodity prices and losses in export revenues.
2   Currency pressures leading up to sharp depreciation or managed devaluation.
3   Overleveraging and liquidity dry-out in the banking system.
4   Build-up in public debt, including foreign currency denominated debt.
5   Ad hoc nature and sizeable declines in the volumes and values of labor migrants' remittance transfers.

The intensity with which each of the five channels mattered in every country largely depended on the specific economy's structure, its integration within the global markets, and direction of trade. Those specific aspects should be relatively accessible from the preceding discussions and additional facts presented below.[10] Figure 9.3 helps put the severity of individual countries' immediate losses from the crisis in perspective. The losses are measured as percentage change in GDP per capita (in PPP 2011) between 2008 and 2009.

Between 2008 and the end of 2009, Estonia, Ukraine, Armenia, Lithuania, and Latvia experienced the sharpest declines in income per capita. In the Baltics, where unemployment also soared and remained persistently high in the following quarters, the crisis was largely associated with the second and third channels from the above list and overexposure to West European (mainly, Scandinavian) banks. For Ukraine, the impact came through channel one, drops in steel and agricultural prices, channel four, and to some extent channel five. For Armenia and Moldova, it was primarily a steep decline in migrants' remittances undercutting

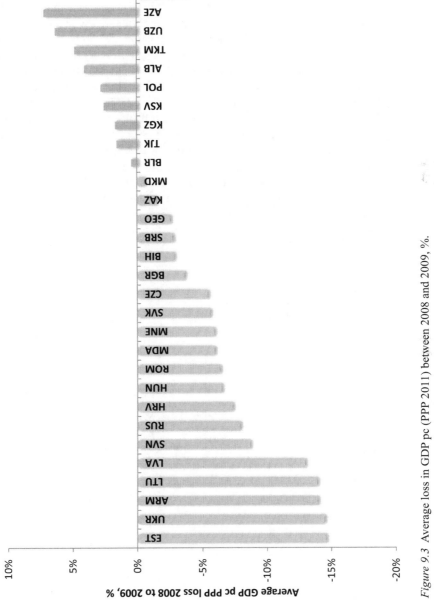

Figure 9.3 Average loss in GDP pc (PPP 2011) between 2008 and 2009, %.

Source: author's estimates based on WDI (2017)

domestic consumption, as well as aftershocks of business cycle declines in major trading partner economies (mainly Russia).

In fact, as observed elsewhere, in several cases (e.g. Armenia, Georgia, Moldova) there was a brief moment of reverse remittance flows: from home country to the host. To support labor migrants abroad, rather than returning home, the family provided a temporary reprieve. That helped migrant workers to remain in the host countries (primarily Russia, but also Kazakhstan) without risking potential employment opportunity losses, or, worse, forfeiting their ability to return to the host country due to immigration formalities (Gevorkyan, 2011).

Not all countries experienced severe declines in their income per capita, as seen in Figure 9.3. While some managed to weather the crisis with smaller output losses (those with positive changes in Figure 9.3), the three commodity-exporting nations (Azerbaijan, Uzbekistan, and Turkmenistan) posted gains over 5 percent to the preceding year. These countries, at the time, remained largely insulated from the big foreign capital flows stage. With market reforms partially implemented, much of the industrial and banking system's capacity was controlled by the official state, not easily accessible by foreign capital, except for the mining infrastructure industry that continued to receive investments and to grow.

Across CEE and FSU economies, several saw their current account balances worsen as exports sharply declined.[11] This can be seen in the post-crisis period analysis in Figure 9.4 (omitting the 2009 data points). Russia and Ukraine were the large casualties of the massive hiccup in the commodity cycle, which eventually came to an end towards 2013, when commodity prices reversed.[12] At the same time, the smaller Albania, Armenia, Belarus, Kyrgyz Republic, Moldova, and Tajikistan—among those that have seen current account worsening

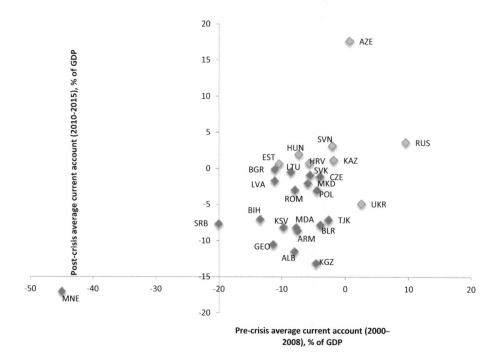

Figure 9.4 Current account as percent of GDP, pre- and post-GFC.

Note: the crisis year 2009 is omitted. Those with current account surplus in either period are in lighter tones.

Source: author's estimates based on data from WDI (2017)

in the post-crisis period to date—have also been cyclically affected by aggregate demand declines in their largest trade partner countries (either EU or Russia).

According to the estimates from ILO Stat (2017), the post-GFC (2009–2014) annual growth in the mean real monthly earnings of workers, was significantly slower than in the pre-crisis 2000–2008 period. The most precipitous declines in wage growth rates, between 10 and 19 percent, were among FSU economies (e.g. Uzbekistan with 18.5% loss, Georgia at 14.2%, Armenia 10.9%, and so on). The CEE economies, with the exception of Albania's positive growth of 1.7 percent and Serbia's decline of 13.6 percent, on average saw annual declines in real monthly wage growth on a smaller scale, between 0.6 and 8.7 percent.

Build-up in currency pressures forced sharp declines in the exchange rates of Czech Republic, Hungary, Poland, Romania, and Ukraine. In Russia, currency pressures were counterbalanced for a short period of time by running down international reserves (e.g. Gevorkyan 2011, 2012). In fact, international reserves losses were much broader, largely, affecting countries with fixed exchange rates or currency pegs the most.

The structural blueprint emerging from Figure 9.4 helps to draw an important conclusion from this discussion. The CEE/FSU world continues to be diverse and this variety is strengthening. The net exporters are the larger commodity producers (e.g. Azerbaijan, Kazakhstan, Russia, and Turkmenistan) and those in the CEE (alternatively, EU-8) are closely integrated in the West European supply chains (see discussion below). The net importers remain structurally weaker and smaller Armenia, Georgia, Moldova, and so on.

At the same time, Czech Republic, Poland, Slovakia and post-crisis Bulgaria, Latvia, and Lithuania are clustered at the balance line with increasing integration in the EU trade framework. The significance of this observation is conceptual and informative for policymaking. It appeals to the preference for a custom country-specific analysis and policy approach, rather than a debate on the speed, sequence, and pressure of reforms (a throwback to our discussion in Chapter 7).

Responses to the GFC

In a broader study on emerging markets, Llaudes *et al.* (2010) found that initial conditions played a role in determining the severity of the crisis impact and its propagation on a country-by-country case.[13] Logically, those with weaker fundamentals but with high financial and trade integration with other economies were affected the worst, in comparative terms. Those with sufficient fiscal space and high foreign reserve holdings were able to mitigate the immediate effects of the crisis.

The case of Russia (and to some extent, Kazakhstan and Ukraine), mentioned earlier, is illustrative of the international reserves factor. To defend its currency, the country spent up to 15 percent of 2008 GDP in foreign reserves.[14] That allowed some time to be gained, guiding the inevitable decline in the value of the domestic currency as foreign capital withdrew in a precautionary move. Of all the foreign capital inflows, Russia's losses were among the most substantial (e.g. Figure 9.7). Llaudes *et al.* (2010) found that on average emerging markets lost approximately 7 percent in GDP equivalent international reserves in the GFC aftermath.[15]

As part of the response to the GFC, across the CEE/FSU group there was strong initial fiscal accommodation (as the data in Table 9.1 help infer from widening fiscal deficits) and monetary stimulus to the extent that individual country capacities allowed. This was especially the case in the larger exporter nations. In some cases, the limitations to fiscal space were too obvious (e.g. in the weakest at the time, Armenia, Bulgaria, Georgia, Tajikistan).

Those would be the cases fitting a definition of "surviving the crisis on its own" found as a description of Bulgaria's efforts in the edited study by Bakker and Klingen (2012).[16]

The speed and extent of the recovery in many ways depended on pre-GFC fiscal positions (e.g. contrast Armenia to Romania 2007 to 2010 positions in Table 9.1; or Bulgaria to Hungary, etc.): the lower the fiscal deficit, the better were the chances for post-GFC recovery.[17] In fact, as a group, EU-8, largely pulled down by the Baltics, fared worse in rebuilding their fiscal balances immediately after the crisis. However, by 2016–2017 the situation has reversed as structural aspects of the EU-8 improved, while those of the FSU (with the exception of Russia) worsened in the years since the GFC.

Often, the structurally weaker economies opted for bilateral loans from larger trading partners (Russia in the CIS space, but also Kazakhstan in Central Asia, Sweden in the Baltics, and Germany in the CEE) or earmarked financing from multilateral institutions. More broadly, it helped to remain under the radar of the speculative financial flows at the time. However, as Figure 9.5 suggests such measures led to higher public debt to GDP ratios over time. For example, the debt to GDP ratio increased 67 percentage points for Ukraine, 52.9 for Slovenia, 45.5 for Croatia, 41.6 for Belarus, and somewhat less for others between 2006 and 2016 (also see Table A9.1 in the Appendix).[18]

Only in three cases did public debt to GDP ratio decline in that period for Kyrgyz Republic (by 14.1%), Uzbekistan (by 9.8%), and Kosovo (by 8.1%) as fiscal expenditure was cut. For others, ability to tap international markets in the post-GFC environment (e.g. Armenia and Georgia for the first time ever) offered an unprecedented opportunity to plug fiscal expenditure (or debt repayment) challenges, taking opportunity of global liquidity and lower borrowing costs, fueled by global investors' search for the yield.[19]

Elsewhere, as part of monetary accommodation, foreign currency support was procured via a range of agreements (swap and repo) between CEE and EU central banks (more on this below, see Box 9.2 on the Vienna Initiative, for example).[20] In addition, several countries appealed to the IMF for financial bailouts (Hungary was the first to pursue this line, Belarus, Bosnia and Herzegovina, Latvia, Romania, and Ukraine, followed shortly after). Clearly, IMF's support at the time was not cheap and austerity measures were put through. For example, Latvia had to raise taxes, reduce government salaries, and shed a large share of government employees (e.g. Åslund and Dombrovskis, 2011).[21]

Gradual recovery began in 2010, as can be inferred from Figure 9.1. However, the new growth rates, while positive, would remain below the pre-crisis average. Still, one of the critical characteristics of the post-crisis environment has been the emergence of strong central banks and proactive monetary policy, informed with peculiarities of the local banking and industrial system. That, in turn, in addition to overall macro-stabilization, has helped bring average annual inflation down from its pre-crisis average levels in the majority of the countries in the region (see Figure 9.6).

Inflationary pressures emanated from the structural component in the smaller economies, dependent on labor migrant remittance flows and from spillovers in resumed commodity price growth as can be inferred from Figure 9.2. For example, this was particularly relevant to post-crisis recoveries in Albania, Armenia, Belarus, Bulgaria, and Kyrgyz Republic. Inflation in the Baltic countries crept up in the immediate aftermath of the GFC as excise taxes went up sharply as part of fiscal consolidation (also in Belarus, Croatia, Hungary, Moldova, and Romania). Growth in residential real estate and the increasing popularity of mortgage-like loans fed into inflation in the larger economies, quickly spreading into smaller economies after initial delay. At the same time, the central banks have maintained a proactive stance in subduing inflation, as memories of hyperinflation of the 1990s remained fresh.[22]

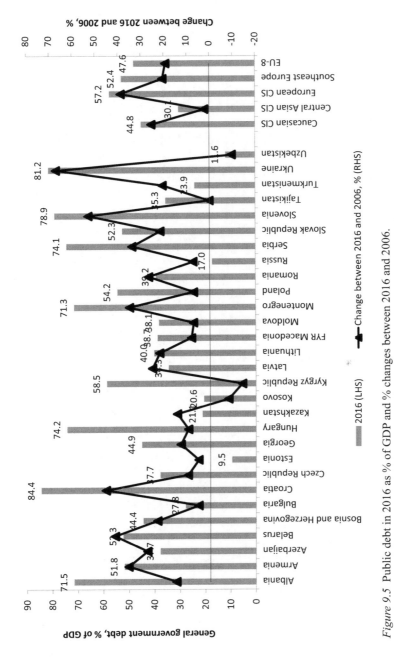

Figure 9.5 Public debt in 2016 as % of GDP and % changes between 2016 and 2006.

Notes: general government debt. Regional items are simple average estimates for directional presentation only, based on country groupings as in the earlier chapters. For consistency, Bulgaria, Croatia, and Romania are included as part of Southeast Europe, as before.

Source: data extrapolated from IMF World Economic Outlook (IMF WEO, 2017)

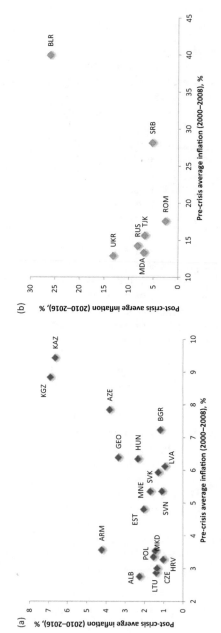

Figure 9.6 Average annual inflation pre- and post-GFC, %.

Note: the crisis year 2009 is omitted. Inflation estimate is WDI's "consumer price annual percent change." Two graphs are shown to accommodate for scale of presentation.

Source: author's estimates based on data from WDI (2017)

Another outcome of the crisis has been a significant rise in the services sector's value added as a share of GDP across the CEE and FSU. For example, according to data from WDI (2017), in Armenia, where a combination of hospitality, tourism, and financial services growth have speeded up in recent years, change in this indicator was the highest for the group (12.9 points), reaching up to 48 percent of GDP in the post-crisis (2010–2015) period. At the same time, manufacturing continued to decline making up only 31.6 percent of GDP. Latvia's more advanced services sector accounted for 72 percent of GDP (combination of export-related and financial services) in the post-crisis period. Turkmenistan reported the lowest share of services accounting for 28.5 percent of GDP, while industry share (natural gas exploration) accounted for 60 percent of GDP in the post-crisis period.

For the same period, the economies of CEE more integrated with the EU, reported higher services sector shares at over 60 percent of GDP, reflecting those countries' strong financial sector components. Across the post-socialist region, agriculture's value added hardly exceeded single digits, with the exception of Tajikistan (25.9%), Albania (21.9%), Armenia (20.4%) and Uzbekistan, Kyrgyz Rep, Kosovo, Turkmenistan, and Ukraine, ranging between 10 and 20 percent of GDP in the post-crisis period.

Consistent with earlier cited development literature, growth in the services sector is often seen as a sign of a country's further structural maturity. Whether this would turn out to be so in the countries where services now play a major role is open to debate. This recent development, clearly, represents a break with the socialist economic model, when heavy industry development was prioritized above others, as argued in earlier chapters. Clearly, there is ongoing adaptation to the competitive pressures of the global economy, as neither textbook nor previously tried economic models prove adequate.

The Russian crisis of 2014

Perhaps, the most unexpected event of the post-GFC period was the Russian recession of 2015–2016. Output contracted by approximately 3.7 percent in 2015 (EBRD, 2016), returning to positive growth after 2016 as can be seen in Figure 9.1. It is safe to say that one of the key triggers for Russia's turbulence was the structural characteristic of the economy influenced by sustained decline in the crude oil price in late 2013–early 2014—the ill-famed end of the commodity super-cycle. Unfortunately, the combined declines in the global demand for fossil fuels and of the price of crude oil, as competition tightened, occurred before Russia's private sector had a chance to fully recover from the GFC shocks.[23]

Added to the mix were quickly mounting geopolitical pressures and calamity in Ukraine (as political crisis erupted in late 2013). Ukraine's economy, not fully recovered from the earlier GFC and caught in political stalemate, contracted by 6.5 percent in 2014 and 10 percent in 2015 before returning to a moderate 2.3 percent growth in 2016, according to the underlying data in Figure 9.1. Obviously, modest recovery rates, while positive, are not sufficient to compensate for recent losses.

As the geopolitical environment worsened, a set of EU- and US-led international economic sanctions was imposed on Russia's economy in early 2014 cutting off paths to some of its exports (primarily in agriculture) and access to long-term conventional financing facilities. Russia reciprocated by banning agricultural imports and shifting the economy towards import substitution, primarily in the agricultural sector. This unprecedented, since the early 1990s, turnaround in geopolitical attitudes towards Russia inflicted many economic pains on local producers and consumers on both sides of the dispute.

The agricultural sector in those European countries with large shares of exports directed to Russia, now banned, was affected most directly (e.g. Bulgaria, Poland, Moldova, and also Finland and France to some extent lost access to a sizeable market). Other sectors were affected as well, including European manufacturers' plans for greenfield investment in Russia, the financial sector and capital markets opportunities, and others. Over time, the effects were felt on domestic economies, and the unanimity of views on sanctions in Europe began to fade as Italy, Hungary, Bulgaria, and a few others broke ranks requesting a revaluation of sanctions renewals. In Russia, the agricultural industry recovered and early indications by 2017 suggested growth as a result of import substitution strategy.[24]

The Russian ruble sustained immediate and severe pressures from external and domestic markets. The oil price dropped by an estimated 60 percent in the second half of 2014 and close to 80 percent by early 2016 in the international markets. Russia's currency exchange rate to the dollar dropped from 35 RUB in June 2014 to 56.3 RUB for one USD by the end of the year (CBR, 2017).[25] The pains fell on import-dependent average consumers who had to halve their consumption basket as wages did not keep up with import price-induced inflation, causing a prolonged adjustment in household spending patterns.

In one of the early academic analyses of the ruble's depreciation, Dreger *et al.* (2015) attempted to empirically articulate the pass-through mechanism from the oil price decline to the Russian currency. They found currency depreciation to be the primary cause for Russia's recession, while sanctions added conditional volatility. The ruble eventually came off managed peg and set to float in relation to other currencies. That signaled a major change in policy since the GFC period. As currency pressures escalated, the rationale for spending limited foreign exchange reserves to protect the peg faded.

In the first weeks of currency value decline in November–December 2014, a J curve-like effect was registered in the domestic consumer durables markets. Purchase orders were placed with deliveries stretching into June of 2015.[26] Those importers that had not revised foreign exchange rates in their pricing due to earlier contractual obligations incurred initial losses when ruble revenues were converted back to foreign currency.

Car dealerships (as well as electronics stores and others that traded imported goods with prices in rubles but pegged to the euro or the dollar at pre-depreciation exchange rate) had their inventory cleared out across the country within days in December of 2014 as consumers expected further deterioration (they turned out to be correct) in the coming year. Elsewhere, there was a drop in luxury travel from Russia to Europe and across the board tourism from Russia sustained initial declines (e.g. business flights declining 26 percent between Russia and France as reported in Grossbongardt, 2015).

Credit growth declined as the ruble's purchasing power dropped, combined with rising unemployment and a decline in real wages (as illustrated below). Capital outflows from Russia intensified through 2015 as uncertainty in the capital markets set in and investment projects were canceled while banks paid down their foreign debt obligations. In fact, Figure 9.7 offers a broad historical overview of combined banking and other private sector capital flows to and from Russia. For the most part, capital outflows dominated the trend. Instability periods of 2008 and 2014 recorded the highest outflows, with strong negative trends sustained since the first crisis.

By the second quarter of 2017, the Russian economy returned to growth. Capital outflows somewhat subdued, which the Bank of Finland's Institute for Economies in Transition (BOFIT) characterized as "a rather exceptional situation in recent years."[27] Preliminary estimates indicate an approximate $3 billion inflow in the second quarter of 2017. In the same report, BOFIT also reported on year-over-year recovery in Russian export earnings in the

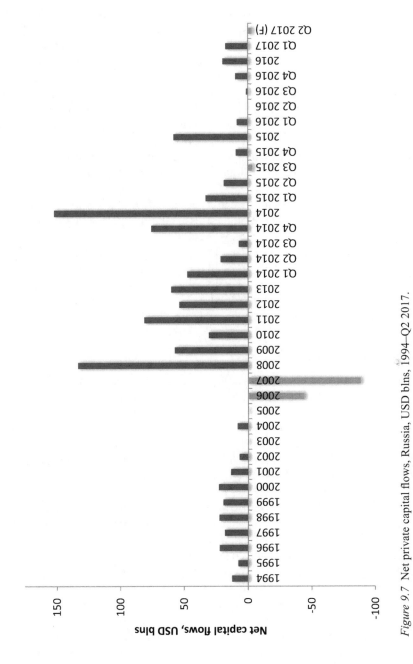

Figure 9.7 Net private capital flows, Russia, USD blns, 1994–Q2 2017.

Note: net capital inflows are marked with a (−) sign, outflows are (+). Combined banking and other private sectors data. F = preliminary estimate.

Source: based on data extrapolated from Central Bank of Russia online database (CBR, 2017).

second calendar quarter of 2017. This is further corroborated by evidence in other independent reports (Medetsky, 2016 and Buckley, 2017). Outpacing its US and EU rivals, Russia for the first time in decades became the largest wheat (grain) exporter globally.[28]

Rapid growth in wheat exports is also indicative of expanding and rising growth in the agricultural sector overall. Part of the success is due to the weaker currency and lower fuel and fertilizer prices. The first helps boost exports to the rest of the world (outside of the sanctions list, e.g. countries in Northern Africa) and the other two help keep production costs at lower levels. Helping overall growth are targeted government subsidies to farmers.[29]

While it is early to pass any judgment on whether the recent gains in Russia's agricultural and informational technology (IT) sectors are sustainable, there is no lack, so far, of opportunities for future growth. In agriculture, much depends on the ability of private farms to reinvest recent gains in capital funds and boost productivity facing strong domestic and export demand. At the same time, new opportunities may be in expanding agricultural production in the territories closer to the border with China as a complementary attribute to overall growth. In IT, the key is to be able to successfully bridge the gap between experimental designs and the mass consumer market.

Despite the objective pressure factors mentioned here, Russia is the leading economy in the region. There is much dependence on the Russian business cycle by the smaller net importer economies in a broader trade context, as well as it being a source of temporary employment for labor migrants, and important for the EU economies, primarily, in terms of energy markets. Within a relatively short period of time, Russia has experienced at least four severe economic deteriorations: 1) the economic collapse of the early 1990s, 2) the 1998 crisis, 3) the detrimental impacts of the 2008 GFC, and (so far) 4) the 2014–2015 recession and depreciation. It remains to be seen how the country pulls through this latest tribulation.[30]

A segway into broader conversation

The economic situation in Russia in 2014–2015 also impacted neighboring states. Particularly hard hit were the economies of the FSU via financial and currency crisis channels. Those in CEE sustained minor collateral shocks from the initial trade sanctions impacts. The declines in expected remittance values were significant in countries dependent on labor migration-related income, as reviewed in Chapter 8. Figure 9.8 plots the relative distribution of nominal depreciation over two periods (2013–2016 and 2014–2015), measured as percent change in local currency units (LCU) per one USD, based on official exchange rates reported in WDI (2017).

This is a broad view of annual averages. However, one can clearly see the severe degree of national currency depreciations in the immediate spillover from 2014 into 2015 and continued weakening in most cases through the end of 2016. In the latter case, comparison is made between average annual currency exchange rates of 2013 and 2016 to further emphasize the point of deep weakening in some of the FSU economies.

Trade and capital flows with Ukraine were most directly affected following the political crisis of 2014 with the effects extending into subsequent years. To sustain its economy, Ukraine relied on the IMF's support, with an approved package of $17.5 billion and approximately $9 billion of that received by mid-2017.[31] Due to its tight trade links with the Russian market prior to 2015, and declining international prices of steel (a commodity of export in Ukraine), Ukraine's currency, hryvna, came under pressure losing up to 80 percent of its value to the USD (Figure 9.8) and 62 percent in value to the euro between early 2014 and 2015.[32]

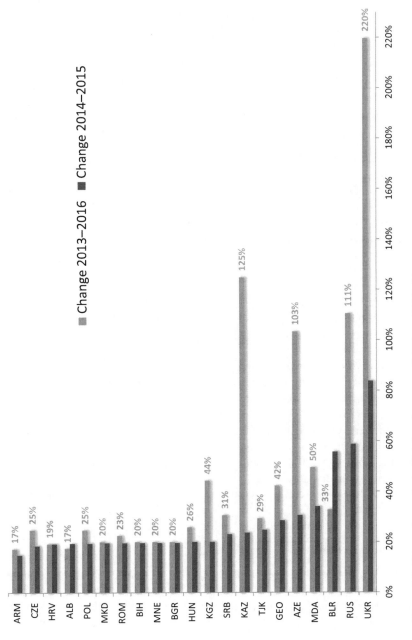

Figure 9.8 Change in nominal official exchange rate (LCU per USD), %.

Notes: change in annual averages of local currency units (LCU) per one USD. Some countries are omitted due to missing data.

Sources: author's estimates based on data from WDI (2017)

Elsewhere, declining primary commodity prices compounded initial spillover effects into domestic currency values via trade with Russia, and despite regional diversification. For example, Azerbaijan (despite strong trade links with Turkey) and Kazakhstan (but also Belarus) lost up to 30 to 50 percent of their currency value (against the USD) in late 2014–early months of 2015, with exacerbating losses in subsequent months. Armenia, Georgia, Kyrgyz Republic, and Moldova sustained sharp declines in the value of labor migrants' remittances, posting currency losses in the range of 15 to 35 percent between early 2014 and 2015 (e.g. Gevorkyan, 2017 and WB, 2015).[33]

However, another significant factor, for the latter group, has been the decline in the Russian consumer market and as such, drastic declines in smaller countries' exports to Russia.[34] Finally, a major factor for some of the smaller FSU states has been a risk of declining FDI inflows. However, in countries with a strong presence of Russia-based multinational corporations those risks may have been avoided (e.g. Armenia). In all the above cases, national central banks relied on a combination of international reserves sales (larger economies), raising interest rates, proactive foreign exchange interventions (e.g. repurchase agreements market in Armenia), and even some elements of capital controls (e.g. EBRD, 2016).[35]

In the Central European economies, the currency pressures spread via the foreign exchange market primarily to countries with flexible exchange rates (e.g. Hungary, Poland, and Serbia). However, those effects were quickly dissipated due to limited (by now) trade or financial links with Russia and the fact that contagion was localized primarily between Russia and Ukraine. We see in Figure 9.8 that nominal exchange rate losses were contained within the 18 to 20 percent range for the CEE economies.[36]

In their Transition Report, the EBRD (2016) foresee subdued growth in the region. Growth in Russia is expected to rise to 2.5 percent. That could have a tail-wind effect in strengthening growth in the Caucasus and Central Asia. Growth in the CEE economies is expected to remain positive as well. For Russia, according to an analysis by the World Bank (2017b), growth is to average around 1.3 to 1.4 percent between 2017 and 2019.[37]

The driving factors for the above growth projection would be established macro-stability and the sustained price of crude oil. This is coupled with expected strength in domestic demand and tighter fiscal policy rules, while raising productivity remains as one of the challenges to long-term growth.[38] However, for the entire CEE/FSU group much uncertainty remains. Defined by structural aspects of each economy, the uncertainty is topped mainly by idiosyncratic events in the global economy (e.g. rising protectionism, foreign exchange volatility, most recently from 2015 onwards, or spillovers from larger, e.g. EU, Russia, or China, regional economic deterioration).

We now proceed to review recent developments in the financial sector of the CEE and FSU.

Financial sector development

Within financial development in the post-socialist economies, transformation in the banking sector has been the most definitive and foundational. While there is much diversity in the fundamental macroeconomic characteristics of each economy in the CEE/FSU region, there are, actually, significantly more similarities in the banking sector development of these countries. Subsequent to the setbacks of the mid-1990s and after the 1998 Russian default, the majority of post-socialist countries have followed a shared path of setting up western-style banking. A somewhat uniform tendency, conditioned by the global nature of capital flows, has led to the emergence of a modern and comprehensive financial sector in many post-socialist societies. But the ascent has not been steady (e.g. Bonin *et al.*, 1998).

Three common trends have characterized the CEE/FSU experience through the present time. First, there has been the emergence of strong, national central banks. Second, has been the proliferation of private banking activity, mainly driven by foreign banks from Western Europe. And third, as a result, there has been strong growth in private domestic credit. The latter, in turn, fed into, but was also conditioned by, burgeoning domestic consumer and property markets across the CEE/FSU. A looming problem in that context has been the challenge of financial inclusion and credit accessibility.

How things were and gradual change

Prior to *perestroika*, with the exception of Yugoslavia, a monobank system was the banking model in the socialist economies. By definition, a monobank was a state-owned bank that was responsible for monetary emission and credit provision to the economy with all operations consistent with the broader national plan (e.g. the Five-Year Plan).[39] Effectively, a credit intermediation system, for all practical purposes, in its textbook view of competitive matching of borrowers and debtors, was non-existent at the time in the CEE/FSU.

The state bank allocated funds to each state-owned enterprise in accordance with the latter's estimated needs. According to some estimates, in 1980 in the FSU, state provided credit accounted for an average of 46 percent share of enterprises' working capital (Geraschenko *et al.*, 1982). At the same time, manufacturing enterprises' own resources accounted for 33 percent, for those in trade, 28 percent, and for those in agriculture, 22 percent of the overall estimated working capital financing in each sector.[40]

Special purpose entities, such as agricultural bank, foreign trade bank, and savings bank, also all state-controlled, coordinated planned enterprise activity in accordance with their sector designations. A savings bank provided opportunities for minimal consumer banking, typically in the form of long-term savings deposits. As the mid-1980s search for "new thinking" spiraled to proposals for macroeconomic overhauls, rivaling traditional socialist structures, realization of a need for a more robust, two-tiered (central and commercial) banking system evolved.[41]

By the early 1990s, the emerging banking sectors (and subsequent capital markets) were being built from scratch with no initial foundation for private banking. Hungary was the first to introduce banking sector reforms in 1987, followed in 1988 by Poland. And Yugoslavia had already been running a two-tier system. However, even in the latter case, the banking system operated within the enterprise self-management process. With the liberalization of the late 1980s, the majority of the CEE/FSU countries jumped on the bandwagon, going to the other extreme of monobanks: deregulation. The emerging banking environment often led to excesses in commercial banking activity in contrast to real economy needs.[42]

The reforms envisioned rising commercial banking in line with accepted conventional views of credit intermediation. Structural and institutional changes, supporting economic growth, were to drive increasing credit intermediation.[43] As Fries and Taci (2002) mention, most of the post-socialist economies followed the transformative blueprints provided by the IMF and WB (see discussion in Chapter 7 on shock therapy).[44] As applied to banking, the key requirements of the Washington consensus-like approach shifted pressure on to the state to introduce prudential regulation and bank supervision. Removing entry barriers for new private banks, liberalization of interest rates, credit facilitation, and currency convertibility topped the reformers' agenda.

The early banking crises

As the trinity of the 1990s reforms (liberalization, privatization, stabilization) pushed forward, the non-performing loans (NPL) to state enterprises mounted largely due to the problem of soft budget constraint mentioned earlier. Particularly, this was the case in Albania, Bulgaria, and Romania that had a slower pace of banking reform adoption (Fries and Taci, 2002). In Central Europe (Czech Republic, Hungary, Slovakia, etc.) and the Baltic countries, the process was relatively balanced. There, banking reform was somewhat consistent with the state's gradual withdrawal and expansion in private economic activity.

In the FSU, where the state's withdrawal from the economy was more abrupt (with the exception of parts of Central Asia), non-performing private sector loans and "one-night" banks were on the rise. The latter was characteristic of the early transition-era schemes by which firms (or banks) would be registered under false documentation and remain in existence for a very short period. Proliferation of low-capitalized private banks engaged in the "loans for shares" credits of privatization schemes, mentioned in Chapter 7, only added fuel to the fire of post-socialist transition vulnerabilities.

Throughout the 1990s, across the map, interest rates were rising (in the desperate efforts to offset hyperinflation) and non-performing loans were not being recovered. It did not take long for the first banking crises to rattle across the CEE/FSU. Table 9.2, based on data from Laeven and Valencia (2008, 2013), summarizes episodes of banking, currency, and sovereign debt crises in the CEE/FSU countries.[45]

Table 9.2 Banking, currency, and sovereign debt crises in CEE/FSU, 1980–2008

Country	Banking crisis				Currency crisis (year)	Sovereign debt crisis (default date)	Sovereign debt restructuring (year)
	Start	End	Fiscal costs (% of GDP)	Fiscal costs (% of financial assets)			
Albania	1994	1994	-	-	1997	1990	1992
Armenia	1994	1994	-	-	-	-	-
Azerbaijan	1995	1995	-	-	-	-	-
Belarus	1995	1995	-	-	1997, 2009	-	-
Bosnia and Herzegovina	1992	1996	-	-	-	-	-
Bulgaria	1996	1997	14.0	21.4	1996	1990	1994
Croatia	1998	1999	6.9	15.0	-	-	-
Czech Republic	1996	2000	6.8	9.2	-	-	-
Estonia	1992	1994	1.9	-	1992	-	-
Georgia	1991	1995	-	-	1992, 1999	-	-
Hungary	1991	1995	10.0	21.3	-	-	-
Hungary	2008	ongoing	2.7	3.3	-	-	-
Kazakhstan	2008	ongoing	3.7	7.5	1999	-	-
Kyrgyz Rep	1995	1999	-	-	1997	-	-
Latvia	1995	1996	3.0	10.1	1992	-	-
Latvia	2008	ongoing	5.6	5.2	1992	-	-
Lithuania	1995	1996	3.1	18.7	1992	-	-
Macedonia, FYR	1993	1995	32.0	-	-	-	-
Moldova			-	-	1999	2002	2002
Poland	1992	1994	3.5	13.7		1981	1994

Country	Banking crisis				Currency crisis (year)	Sovereign debt crisis (default date)	Sovereign debt restructuring (year)
	Start	End	Fiscal costs (% of GDP)	Fiscal costs (% of financial assets)			
Romania	1990	1992	0.6	-	1996	1982	1987
Russia	1998	1998	0.1	0.3	1998	1998	2000
Russia	2008	ongoing	2.3	6.6	1998	1998	2000
Serbia	-	-	-	-	2000	-	-
Slovak Rep	1998	2002	-	-	-	-	-
Slovenia	1992	1992	14.6	4.4	-	-	-
Slovenia	2008	ongoing	3.6	2.9	-	-	-
Tajikistan	-	-	-	-	1999	-	-
Turkmenistan	-	-	-	-	2008	-	-
Ukraine	1998	1999	0.0	-	1998, 2009	1998	1999
Ukraine	2008	ongoing	4.5	-	1998, 2009	1998	1999
Uzbekistan	-	-	-	-	2000	-	-

Notes: see source for additional details and definitions; blanks refer to data not available; "ongoing" in banking crisis end column is as of 2013. As per the source: "[f]iscal costs are defined as the component of gross fiscal outlays related to the restructuring of the financial sector. They include fiscal costs associated with bank recapitalizations but exclude asset purchases and direct liquidity assistance from the treasury" (Laeven and Valencia, 2013, p. 259).

Source: extrapolated from Laeven and Valencia (2008, 2013) and accompanying data file

According to Table 9.2, practically every CEE/FSU country went through a banking crisis in the 1990s, with some repeated episodes in 2008 (e.g. Latvia, Russia, Slovenia, Ukraine). In several cases, fiscal costs exceeded double digits, as share of GDP (e.g. Macedonia, Slovenia, Bulgaria, and Hungary). Macedonia's 1993 crisis was one of the top ten costliest in the world in terms of fiscal costs in percent share of GDP; while Latvia's 2008 crisis was the costliest in terms of output loss (102 percent of GDP) since 1970, as per Laeven and Valencia (2013).

In the early phases of banking industry development in CEE/FSU, the size of the financial sector was relatively small, bumping fiscal costs up further (as can be inferred from Table 9.2). In contrast, advanced economies with decades of private banking tradition, have deeper overall financial markets and lower costs when expressed as shares of financial sector, as per estimates in Laeven and Valencia (2013).[46] At the same time, currency and sovereign debt crises in transition seem to have coincided on many occasions with banking crises, which Laeven and Valencia (2013) refer to as twin or triplet crises.[47]

Foreign banks, foreign banks

As banking sector reforms advanced, the shares of foreign banks in each country varied with time. Based on EBRD data on foreign bank ownership, Table 9.3 shows changes in those shares in the year of 1998, Russia's financial crisis, right before the 2008 GFC, and a revised position as of the latest date available.

The majority of foreign banks were from advanced economies in Western Europe, transplanting established operational processes, technology, supervision standards, and customer service onto post-socialist fertile ground.[48] Expansion of foreign banks in the CEE and the Baltics has been stronger than in some FSU countries (with few exceptions, e.g. Armenia and Georgia). Geographical proximity to and prospects of EU membership played an important role in orienting the EU-8 economies towards necessary institutional adjustment and opening

Table 9.3 Foreign banks' ownership shares in CEE and FSU as % of total banking sector

Countries where foreign bank ownership increased after GFC				Countries where foreign bank ownership decreased after GFC			
Country	*1998*	*2007*	*2011 (or latest available)*	*Country*	*1998*	*2007*	*2011 (or latest available)*
Bosnia and Herzegovina	1.9%	93.8%	94.5%	Estonia	90.2%	98.8%	94.0%
Macedonia, FYR	11.4%	85.9%	92.4%	Slovak Rep	23.7%	99.0%	91.5%
Croatia	6.6%	90.4%	90.6%	Lithuania	50.7%	91.7%	90.8%
Czech Republic	26.4%	84.8%	90.6%	Albania	14.4%	94.2%	90.3%
Montenegro	16.9%	78.7%	89.7%	Georgia	19.3%	90.6%	87.2%
Hungary	59.2%	64.2%	85.8%	Romania	15.1%	87.3%	81.8%
Armenia	40.5%	49.0%	67.5%	Bulgaria	32.5%	82.3%	76.5%
Latvia	79.1%	63.8%	65.0%	Serbia	0.5%	75.5%	74.5%
Moldova	22.4%	24.8%	40.9%	Poland	17.4%	75.5%	69.2%
Slovenia	4.9%	28.8%	29.3%	Kyrgyz Rep	35.8%	58.7%	47.9%
Belarus	2.3%	19.7%	20.6%	Ukraine	9.2%	39.4%	38.0%
Azerbaijan	4.4%	7.5%	9.5%	Kazakhstan	18.9%	38.5%	19.2%
Tajikistan	70.2%	6.6%	6.6%	Russia	10.3%	17.2%	16.9%
Uzbekistan	2.7%	4.4%	4.4%				
Turkmenistan	1.3%	1.1%	1.2%				

Notes: foreign owned bank is defined as a bank with assets of foreign ownership greater than 50 percent of the bank's total assets. Figures for Azerbaijan and Montenegro for 1998 are as of 2000 and 2002, respectively; Uzbekistan 2007 and 2011 are as of 2004; figures for 2011 for Armenia and Lithuania are as of 2010; for Belarus, Czech Republic, and Turkmenistan are as of 2008; for Bosnia and Herzegovina are as of 2009.

Source: data extrapolated from EBRD (2017)

up to foreign capital. As mentioned earlier, the privatization process was open to foreign investors, including in the banking area (e.g. Poland). To some extent, such expansion also followed the manufacturing sector and foreign direct investment flows (FDI), which were higher in the CEEs within the immediate proximity of the European Union.

Undeniably, foreign banks brought to the region a range of opportunities. An assessment by IMF (2013) finds that foreign banks contributed to the declining incidence of banking crises, as operational practices improved and foreign banks were able to absorb local shocks. Gevorkyan and Semmler (2016) also find strong spillover effects from the European Monetary Union financial markets into the Central European EU-member states (e.g. Hungary and Poland), often solely based on financial factors and less so on macroeconomic trends.

Perhaps, most significantly, arrival of the foreign banks led to a strong rise in domestic private credit as captured in Figure 9.9. By 2008, European banks in their competitive push for Eastern Europe facilitated a watershed of capital flows. That, in turn, fueled speculative consumer demand and led to a rise in the property markets.

Yet, with rising domestic credit and rapid financial deepening, in the background of still maturing regulatory regimes, smaller CEE economies became quickly overexposed to fluctuations in the foreign financial flows. As global liquidity tightened, foreign banks curtailed credit provisions exacerbating the GFC impact on the smaller, mostly CEE, economies. Granted this move came with some lag (early 2009) after the pivotal moment of Lehman Brothers collapse in September 2008. Deleveraging was most significant across banks with weaker foreign parent balances and foreign loan growth fell by more than domestic credit

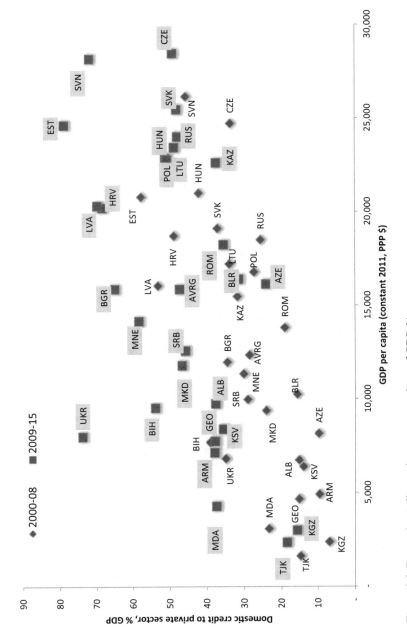

Figure 9.9 Domestic credit to private sector as share of GDP, %.

Source: author's estimates based on data from WDI (2017)

(IMF, 2013; Cull and Peria, 2013; and De Haas and Van Horen, 2013). The Vienna Initiative (Box 9.2) aimed to prevent disorderly retraction of foreign banks and largely succeeded in its goals of stabilizing the flows preventing widespread disruptions (with few exceptions, e.g. Latvia and Poland).

Box 9.2

The Vienna Initiative (VI)—launched in January 2009 in Vienna, Austria, brought together policymakers and representatives of the largest EU-based banks with business in Central and Eastern Europe, as well as multilateral institutions (IMF, EBRD, WB). By September 2008, foreign banks extended close to USD 970 billion to the CEE and Baltic countries, roughly 23 percent of the region's GDP. For some countries, notably Croatia, Estonia, Hungary, and Latvia, these exposures amounted to 60–80 percent of individual economies' GDP. Most of the systemically significant banks were foreign owned. So, any uncontrolled withdrawal would have wreaked havoc in the still fragile post-socialist economies. Unless contained with a multilateral agreement, with public sector guarantees, such overexposure risked throwing Eurozone economies off balance, as liquidity was drying up fast.

The VI set at least two practical goals. First, this was an effort to prevent massive uncoordinated pull-out from the CEE region by the European banks. Second, the VI sought guarantees from the private banks to maintain their exposure to the region, recapitalizing their subsidiaries as part of broader support from the IMF and European Commission. As a result, with banks' commitments, EU countries of origin in their turn guaranteed that any public support to the parent bank would not discriminate between domestic and foreign operations. Similar guarantees to the banking sector were given by the CEE host countries.

As the GFC subdued, the VI activity also diminished, but resumed in 2012 as "Vienna 2" at the time of the renewed Eurozone crisis. In late 2011, a severe credit crunch in the Euro area was combined with foreign banks deleveraging in the CEE. Those host economies where foreign banks played an instrumental role (systemic) were again affected the most. The result of the Vienna 2 was agreement on increased home–host country cooperation against abrupt deleveraging. To facilitate transparency and fully inform all stakeholders, the VI publishes Quarterly Deleveraging Monitors with the latest information on fund flows in the Eurozone and the CEE region with participation of active foreign banks.

Additional reading

See Vienna Initiative website for further details: http://vienna-initiative.com.
EBRD. 2012. *Vienna Initiative – Moving to a New Phase*. London: EBRD. Available online: www.ebrd.com/downloads/research/factsheets/viennainitiative.pdf.

Post-GFC challenges to banking sector growth

Following the GFC, domestic credit in the private sector resumed its growth (the 2009–2015 estimates in Figure 9.9). This time, banks have strived to reposition towards more domestic funding sources, as deposit volumes increased. Also, post-GFC commodity boom and accommodative monetary stance in the advanced economies helped CEE/FSU domestic banks attract funding from other sources. As such, a decentralized model of self-funded subsidiaries and domestic banks has emerged in the region (IMF, 2013).

It is instructive to note, in this context, a significant change in credit growth in several countries vis-à-vis their national economies (from Figure 9.9). For instance, note the significant changes in credit to GDP ratios for Ukraine (39 percentage points increase compared to the pre-crisis period), Bulgaria (30), Armenia (28.3), Montenegro (28.2), and so on, while GDP per capita in absolute terms did not change much. In some cases, relative change in GDP per capita was significantly less than a percent change in credit ratio (e.g. Croatia 19.5 percentage points change in credit to GDP compared to 8 percent relative change in GDP per capita). In relative terms, credit to GDP ratio growth significantly surpassed GDP per capita indicators.

It is difficult to justify much of the reported credit growth as fully "organic," applying modern terminology, in other words, being stimulated mainly by rising domestic economic activity.[49] One must also account for the growing factor of the ability of domestic banks to borrow in local and international markets and the remaining element of foreign subsidiaries' reliance on cheap financing from foreign parent entities. In addition, the EBRD (2015) raises the problem of non-performing loans (NPL) as credit soared across the region. The EBRD (2015) also confirms a global trend for the CEE/FSU that higher initial indebtedness (especially before GFC) has been closely associated with increasing NPL levels in relation to overall loans or a country's GDP. A rise in NPLs in turn may be slowing down private credit growth and firm-level investment. Decomposing those tendencies in relation to the needs of the real economy is beyond the scope of this study.[50] However, it is important to raise the concern about sustainability of credit growth, especially in the structurally weaker economies, early on. Some additional insights may be derived from regular monitoring reports conducted by domestic regulatory agencies and foreign banks active in the region.[51]

The above observations also lead us to the rising influence of independent central banks in the region.[52] In several countries, especially where the foreign exchange market is a crucial element of the financial system, central banks have assumed a market maker role (e.g. Gevorkyan, 2017). This implies a tightly monitored environment within national banking sectors and proactive policy stance by the monetary authority. Perhaps this is partially in compensation for the other extreme of a relatively regulatory-free ride in the years leading up to the GFC and speculative credit booms.

Much also depends on the chosen foreign currency exchange rate policy. In this case, the split between the CEE and FSU is further manifested by strong exchange rate regime preferences. The latter group leans towards a managed peg, which requires frequent interventions in the exchange market. And since much of the consumer credit, especially in housing mortgages, provided by commercial banks, is tied to the foreign exchange market there are instances of high dollarization (and euro-ization, especially in the CEE region) of retail deposits and loans.

On the latter point, Brown and Stix (2014) find that higher propensity for foreign currency deposits is in part due to a habit and in part driven by the volatility of the 1990s in the region. As such, consumers seek confidence by diversifying in more stable foreign currencies.[53] Luca and Petrova (2008) find that credit dollarization in transition economies is conditioned by domestic deposits dollarization and efforts of the banks to maintain currency-matched portfolios. On that, Temesvary (2016), also points to retail borrowers underpricing the exchange rate risk and the banking sector being over-cautious on that.[54] Collectively, in CEE/FSU, these findings suggest that there is yet much to be covered in fully independent national financial systems development. In the meantime, continued episodes of volatility in individual credit markets and currency pressures cannot be fully ruled out as CEE and the FSU (with relatively lower exposure in Central Asia) attempt to balance the real macro-economy and financial sector.

Related to the divergent tendencies in credit intermediation in the transition region, the EBRD (2016) report raises a problem of financial inclusion. According to the findings in that report, there has been significant increase in financial inclusion across the board, with some relative mismatches on more specific scales. For example, the EBRD (2016) finds evidence of a gender gap in the majority (including EU member) of countries as women-owned small businesses seem to be at a disadvantage when it comes to access to credit. To that end, the EBRD is actively engaged in some CEE countries in providing technical assistance and developing risk-sharing mechanisms to enhance opportunities in access to credit by women-led firms.

Another path of opportunity, as per the EBRD (2016) findings, could be the introduction of new financial products geared towards lower-income households. This would involve developing a framework that would rely on more traditional examples of collateral (e.g. tangible as opposed to financial assets), as the category of credit history gradually evolves in the region. These observations speak loudly of the ongoing financial deepening and recognizing the need for a gradual and regulated process is paramount to avoid the fiascos of the 1990s reforms.

As such, over time, and particularly in the first two decades of the new century, there has been growing sophistication in banking practices. It is a true testament of one of the most globalized industries, banking, how quickly the international norms and modes of operation are being adopted in the CEE/FSU region. Further regulatory harmonization is expected to continue as national economies integrate within international financial markets.[55] There is a lot more that could be said about the banking industry transformation in the CEE/FSU. However, we must move on.

It is still important to appreciate the fact that among several transformative novelties of the post-socialist transformation period, would be the emergence of modern categories of banking and credit that would instill a fundamental change in CEE/FSU societies. This observation then opens up the possibilities for discussion beyond just the local economy context, leading into trends of regional integration, foreign direct investment flows, and broader institutional change.

Regional integration and foreign direct investment

This sub-section offers a brief observation on the regional integration processes in the CEE and FSU as well as a discussion on evolving foreign direct investment and export exposure directions. There is no pretense at exclusive analysis here. However, the section raises some important objective points on the diversity of narratives in post-socialist integration dynamics.

Between the union and the union

Among many other aspects already covered in this chapter, the 2000s were also characterized by two important regional integration movements across formerly socialist societies. Both have had far-reaching economic, social, and political ramifications. The first concerned integration of some of the Central and Eastern European economies within the European

Union (EU). And the second, more recent, has been the emergence of the Eurasian Economic Union (EAEU) within the Commonwealth of Independent States (CIS). Ironically, both movements represented a transition from one union (Soviet) to another (either EU or EAEU) within a relatively short period since the demolition of the socialist bloc.

For the societies in Eastern Europe, the potential prospect of integration within capitalist Europe played an important role in breaking with the previous way of living during the 1990s transition.[56] Those early aspirations were built on both political (cutting ties with the socialist past) and economic (access to Western markets and consumer imports) foundations. For Western Europe, the goals for EU enlargement were also driven by political and economic factors, though more nuanced.

On the political side, Berend (2009) finds that some Western Europeans (e.g. UK and Denmark) saw the EU's eastward enlargement as a "brake against further and deeper integration" (p. 86). An expanding market would have a difficult time coordinating a common policy and instilling uniform regulation across all members, possibly leaving sufficient autonomy to more individualistic member states. On the economic side, Eastern Europe presented an opportunity of untapped consumer market with a relatively developed industrial base and high-skilled labor that was also relatively less expensive compared to Western European standards.

Be that as it may, but by mid-2004 the first eight CEE countries (the EU-8 we have referred to throughout the book), that is, Czech Republic, Estonia, Hungary, Latvia, Lithuania, Poland, Slovak Republic, and Slovenia, joined the EU. Bulgaria and Romania joined the union in 2007 and Croatia in 2013. Remaining countries have assumed either potential candidate or candidate status with prospects for future integration.[57]

Box 9.3

The Eurasian Economic Union (EAEU) – is an international organization that aims to deepen economic integration among its member states in the Eurasian region. As of 2017, the union includes Armenia, Belarus, Kazakhstan, Kyrgyz Republic, and Russia. Some of the other FSU countries have recently been accepted as either observers (Moldova) or potential new members (Tajikistan). The EAEU started as an idea for economic cooperation in 1994 and Eurasian Customs Union (in operation between 2010–2014), moving towards a single market agreement by 2012 (Belarus, Kazakhstan, and Russia) as the key elements of economic integration. The EAEU agreement was signed at the end of May 2014 and by 2015 Armenia and Kyrgyzstan joined the union. As a regional integration framework, the union facilitates free movement of goods, services, labor, and capital. The EAEU also maintains common policies in foreign trade, customs clearance, and anti-trust regulation.

With combined GDP in 2016 at an estimated USD4.4 trillion (PPP in 2016 $), the EAEU claimed approximately a 3.2 percent share of the global economy (according to the Total Economy Database estimates). The EAUE has a total population of about 180 million people. Roughly 93 million are economically active and 59.4 percent of the member countries' population has access to the Internet, as per the EAEU figures. Russia is clearly the leading economy in the group.

Similar to the European Union and its governing structures, the EAEU is governed by supranational entities (the Supreme Eurasian Economic Council and Eurasian Economic Commission). There have been preliminary suggestions for introduction of a single currency among the member states, though it is not clear if that would be replacing national currencies or a stand-alone unit of exchange within the union.

As a political and economic project, the EAEU's model is often contrasted to the European Union's attempts to link with the post-socialist states of the FSU (as mentioned in the text). For current EAEU members, while prospects of reaching affluent European consumers are tempting, competitive obstacles aside, much of the regional trade flows suggest stronger connection within the EAEU framework, e.g. Armenia's reliance on Russia for foreign trade and investments, as per UNCTAD trade partner data. For the smaller Armenia and Kyrgyzstan, the ability of labor migrants to find work in Russia or other member states is yet another advantage of the EAEU model. Nevertheless, the EAEU framework remains adaptive suggesting the final blueprint is yet to evolve contingent upon individual country's dynamics.

EAEU official website: www.eaeunion.org/?lang=en#about.

Additional reading

Tarr, D. 2016. The Eurasian Economic Union of Russia, Belarus, Kazakhstan, Armenia, and the Kyrgyz Republic: Can it succeed where its predecessor failed? *Eastern European Economics*, 54(1): 1–22.

Vinokurov, E. 2012. *Eurasian Integration: Challenges of Transcontinental Regionalism.* London: Palgrave Macmillan.

Of the current members, Estonia, Latvia, Lithuania, Slovak Republic, and Slovenia are also members of the European Monetary Union (Eurozone) with the euro as the official currency.[58] Finally, the EU through its Eastern Partnership program has signed association agreements with Georgia, Moldova, and Ukraine—a subject of much geopolitical controversy in recent years.

Another regional bloc emerging in the post-socialist space has been the Eurasian Economic Union. Some additional details on this new union are provided in Box 9.3. As a new regional entity that brings together the economies of Armenia, Belarus, Kazakhstan, Kyrgyz Republic, and Russia, the EAEU has a strong economic potential for growth. The key to sustained success would appear to be in achieving a balance across the labor, capital, and manufactured goods movements within the EAEU and maintenance of healthy trade relations with non-members (including advanced economies, EU, and China).

Commenting on EU integration, Berend (2009) also emphasizes the influence that the enlargement process has had on institutional change for the first candidates. To that end, EU integration has seriously accelerated institutional change in post-socialist Central and Eastern Europe. In turn, those that have had similar aspirations of becoming part of the EU (e.g. in the Balkans) have carefully been adjusting their regulatory systems and competition policies within EU confines. However, Berend (2009) stops short of declaring unequivocal improvement in living conditions across the board (in fact, his conclusion is quite the opposite).

This has also been true in the case of the FSU economies that see themselves as part of the bigger global economy and foster economic openness to the extent that there is interest from international investors. Nevertheless, as EBRD indicators and other indexes (discussed here and in the next chapter) suggest, progress across the CEE/FSU, while significant initially, has been more gradual in the post-GFC period.

Foreign direct investment and export exposure

Evidence on foreign direct investment flows in the CEE/FSU further corroborates the picture of diversity in the region (e.g. Figure 9.10 and Figures 9.11A and 9.11B). The CEE economies (EU-8 and later EU members) have benefited significantly by leveraging their pre-transition initial economic structures from the EU integration process. Massive FDI inflows into the region, especially in the first decade of transition before the GFC, facilitated further integration of these economies within global supply chains.

The pre-GFC ratios of FDI inflows to capital stock were especially high given the recovery from the 1990s economic activity slowdowns. In the post-crisis period, CEE countries continued to outperform the FSU group in terms of FDI stock to GDP shares as well. Notably, by that time domestic capital growth has rebounded and the FDI flows indicator has not exceeded pre-GFC values (with some exceptions in the Balkan countries, which due to objective reasons, as we commented earlier, had a later start in their economic reforms).

A range of financial flows and other assistance (including agricultural and infrastructure support) to CEE followed the initial phase of EU accession. In the immediate years, Berend (2009) reports that foreign companies assumed dominant shares of economic activity. By the mid-2000s, Central Europe (with Czech and Slovak Republics, specifically) became one of the world's fastest-growing auto makers, as German, Japanese, and US car makers relocated some of their assembly plants to CEE regions with up to USD 24 billion investment between 1995 and 2006. Manufacturing capacity of the automobile industry of the region that had been introduced during the import substituting industrialization phase under the socialist economy, has now been grown by several times as the new technology was brought in by foreign manufacturers.[59]

Elsewhere, in manufacturing, the countries with immediate geographical proximity to Germany have been the most successful. As a result, the CEE countries benefited from opportunities to generate comparative advantage in high-skilled manufacturing and began to integrate within the European (primarily German) supply chain (Rahman and Zhao, 2013). For the Baltics, it was mostly Swedish banks, while other countries had a more diverse mix, ushering in FDI projects and paving the foundation for broader institutional change across business and competition policies. Top banks from Austria, Netherlands, Germany, France, and Belgium, including some from the United States, were among the leading entities in announced greenfield FDI projects in the CEE/FSU region.[60]

The number of announced greenfield FDI projects has also been disproportionately larger in the CEE compared to the FSU economies (Figures 9.11A and 9.11B) with the exception of Russia. The latter benefited from a wide range of FDI projects in construction, retail, and banking, but also, importantly, in the mining and energy industry. In addition, according to UNCTAD (2017), between 2003 and 2016 (as per the available data) the total value of greenfield projects in FDI amounted to USD 179 billion or roughly 53 percent share of the total value. The second largest have been investments in Czech Republic (USD 25.1 billion or 7.4%) and Azerbaijan (USD 24.3 billion and 7.2% of total value). Poland received approximately USD 17.8 billion or 5.3 percent of the total share during the same period.

For the FSU economies, especially those in the EAEU, the role of Russian outward foreign direct investment has played an important role in stimulating the local energy, construction,

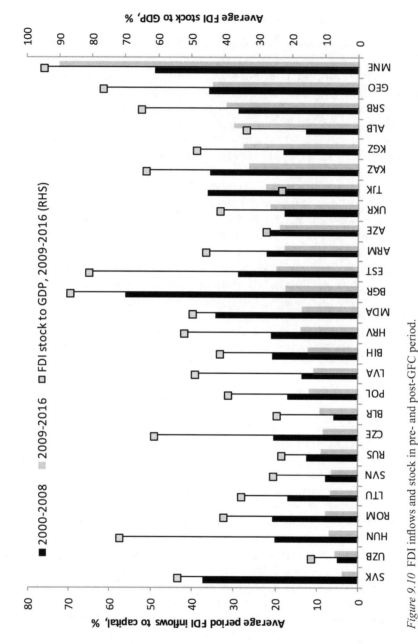

Figure 9.10 FDI inflows and stock in pre- and post-GFC period.

Notes: FDI inflows are percent share of gross fixed capital formation. FDI stock is a share of GDP. MKD and TKM are missing due to lack of FDI inflows data.

Source: author's estimates based on UNCTAD World Investment Report 2017, FDI/MNE database

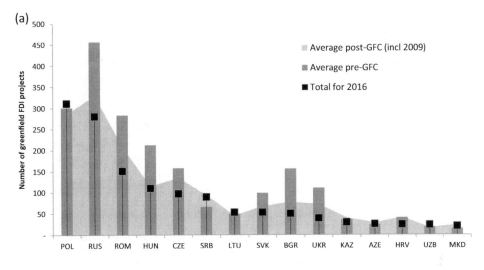

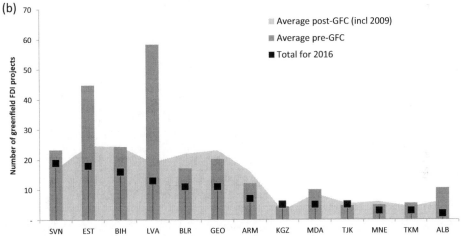

Figure 9.11 Average number of announced greenfield FDI projects, by destination, pre- and post-GFC.

Source: author's estimates based on UNCTAD World Investment Report 2017, FDI/MNE database. Two graphs are shown to accommodate for scale of presentation

and financial sectors. In the pre-crisis period, Russia's OFDI has also reached advanced economies and may be expected to resume growth as economic activity rebounds.[61]

However, as part of a common trend, the majority of the CEE/FSU countries saw both the number and the dollar values of their announced greenfield FDI decline precipitously in the post-GFC environment of sluggish growth and uncertainty. Some recovery was registered in the commodity-exporting nations, albeit too briefly, until the drop in commodity prices. In Russia, this dynamic was further exacerbated following the announcement of economic sanctions, mentioned earlier in this chapter.

It should then come as no surprise, following the above discussion and data compiled in Table 9.4, that much of Central and Eastern Europe (including the Baltic and Balkan countries) is closely integrated in trade with the European Union. In a way, this is a continuation of the pre-1990s trend by which those countries had maintained higher shares of foreign trade with Europe and advanced economies compared to the USSR republics at the time.

In addition to the quite visible direction of trade, Table 9.4 also tells a story of export exposure for each economy. The two major magnets for the remaining economies are the EU and Russia's consumer markets. With much reliance on single exports destination, smaller countries in the transitional periphery remain highly dependent on the major trading partner's business cycle. For example, note the high shares of the Russian and CIS market for Armenia, Belarus, Kyrgyz Republic, Moldova, Ukraine, and others when contrasted to those countries' respective export to GDP ratios to advanced economies and the EU. Similar observations apply to the EU-member post-socialist economies as well, with high dependence on trade with Western Europe (e.g. Czech and Slovak Republics, Slovenia, and the Baltics).

As such, any instability in the main exports destination economy translates as additional challenges to economic activity back home. Still, those in the FSU group largely remain

Table 9.4 Exports exposure index: direction of exports, 2000–2016 average percent of GDP

Country	Advanced economies		Emerging and developing economies			World
	Total	Euro area	Total	Russia	CIS	
Albania	9.6%	9.2%	2.3%	0.0%	0.0%	11.8%
Armenia	8.6%	4.8%	6.4%	2.4%	3.7%	15.2%
Azerbaijan	25.9%	19.3%	11.1%	1.6%	3.9%	37.0%
Belarus	17.3%	13.1%	35.0%	21.8%	27.8%	52.8%
Bosnia and Herzegovina	13.6%	12.0%	9.4%	0.1%	0.2%	23.4%
Bulgaria	25.0%	20.6%	16.4%	0.9%	2.1%	42.5%
Croatia	13.6%	11.7%	7.2%	0.4%	0.5%	21.0%
Czech Republic	51.8%	43.1%	12.6%	1.5%	2.4%	64.4%
Estonia	45.0%	27.3%	10.2%	4.3%	5.6%	55.9%
Georgia	3.8%	1.7%	9.5%	1.2%	5.9%	13.3%
Hungary	52.1%	41.1%	15.6%	1.7%	3.2%	67.7%
Kazakhstan	22.0%	14.5%	19.4%	4.6%	7.3%	41.5%
Kosovo	1.5%	1.0%	3.6%	0.0%	1.6%	5.0%
Kyrgyz Republic	10.4%	2.1%	17.4%	4.4%	11.2%	27.8%
Latvia	24.7%	16.1%	9.6%	4.2%	5.9%	34.5%
Lithuania	32.2%	20.6%	18.0%	7.3%	12.1%	50.3%
FYR Macedonia	22.0%	19.3%	14.1%	0.3%	0.5%	36.1%
Moldova	10.0%	7.5%	21.9%	9.1%	14.2%	32.0%
Montenegro	6.0%	5.2%	6.5%	0.2%	0.4%	12.5%
Poland	25.7%	18.4%	6.0%	1.3%	2.6%	31.8%
Romania	20.5%	16.6%	9.2%	0.5%	1.4%	29.8%
Russia	15.4%	10.4%	9.8%		3.2%	25.9%
Serbia	11.4%	9.7%	11.0%	1.2%	1.7%	22.4%
Slovak Republic	54.9%	36.9%	17.9%	1.9%	2.8%	72.8%
Slovenia	38.2%	31.8%	20.6%	2.2%	3.1%	58.8%
Tajikistan	13.3%	10.9%	21.0%	4.5%	8.1%	34.3%
Turkmenistan	4.5%	3.6%	23.5%	1.7%	11.1%	28.2%
Ukraine	11.3%	7.5%	28.2%	8.3%	12.1%	39.5%
Uzbekistan	4.9%	1.7%	14.2%	3.6%	7.8%	19.1%

Note: estimates reflect share of country exports by destination as a percent of country's GDP.

Source: author's estimates based on data from IMF Direction of Trade Statistics and World Economic Outlook (IMF WEO, 2017)

relatively weaker structurally and with still maturing financial markets. Such characteristics complicate any efforts to quick economic rebound in case of recession in the major exports' magnet country, as reviewed in the macroeconomic analysis above.

On a different dimension of regional integration and FDI attractiveness, the EBRD index of competition policy (Figure 9.12) seems to confirm the above trends. First, for the original EU-8 groups, the index was higher compared to the rest of the countries in the post-socialist region. One exception was Latvia that in 2000 matched Russia's 2.3. According to the latest data, after briefly reaching a value of 3.0 in 2011 and 2012, Slovenia's 2014 index dropped back to 2.7 as in 2000, showing little progress in its competition policy. As a group, however, by 2014 the EU-8 was ahead of the rest of the pack. Competition policy indicators improved significantly for Latvia, Estonia, Lithuania, and Poland.

The smaller economies in Southeastern Europe that joined the EU after 2007 (Romania, Croatia, Bulgaria) would come out second best according to this measure. Approaching an index of four, the EU-8 plus the three later members by 2014 were reaching EBRD's standards of strong competitive environment enforcement and curtailing market power abuse. This result comes with a notable exception in competition policy in Czech Republic and Slovenia.

An earlier report by the EBRD (2006) connects strong progress in competition policy with improvements in the financial markets and establishment of independent competition authority with the ability to enforce anti-trust regulation (Estonia). At the same time, lagging progress in competition policy is often explained by slow progress in removing barriers to entry, business climate change, and unclear state mandate views on the competitive environment (e.g. Czech Republic, Slovenia, but also Hungary and Slovak Republic).[62] Similar observations would be valid for the FSU countries, especially where foreign banks pushed the wave of institutional and business practice change further ahead.

The Global Competitiveness Report (GCR), produced annually by the World Economic Forum, provides a different angle on the CEE/FSU economies' integration into the world economy. According to the latest data in WEF (2017), the majority of post-socialist countries have seen their positions improved significantly between 2010 and 2017 (see vertical change in ranking axis in Figure 9.13).[63]

Significantly, Estonia has maintained its position in the top 30 globally competitive economies since at least the 2007 report. In 2017, Czech Republic regained its pre-GFC level as the 31st economy in the global ranking. These are quite noteworthy achievements for these two economies, considering a relatively wide dispersion of scores for the rest of the group. As any index measure, GCR appears to be also influenced by the economy's relative weight in global trade, as FSU commodity exporters show relatively decent scores. Finally, it is also important to note relative deterioration in competitive positions of three EU-member economies (Hungary, Slovenia, and Slovak Republic), despite a higher benchmark implied by regional integration. In those cases, institutional factors, unclear tax regulations, administrative overheads, and policy instability assume primary responsibility for pulling down overall scores.

We leave these observations here for now and connect with them again in the next, concluding, chapter. Suffice it to say that the competition policy index roughly coincides with the direction of the FDI flows and economic (as well as political) integration trends mentioned above. To some extent, CEE's enthusiasm for the new capitalist model that paved the way for adoption of a new institutional framework, was also backed by a more tangible push for a clearer marketplace as foreign subsidiaries moved into various relatively modern industrial sectors of the individual economies. Importantly, the reasons for either phenomenon

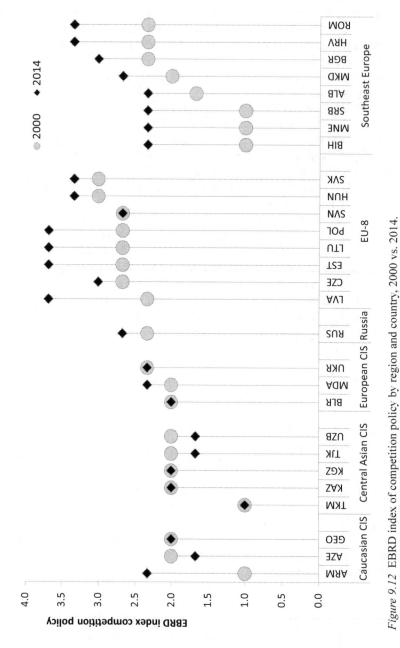

Figure 9.12 EBRD index of competition policy by region and country, 2000 vs. 2014.

Source: extrapolated from EBRD Transition Reports and EBRD data on transition indicators (EBRD, 2017)

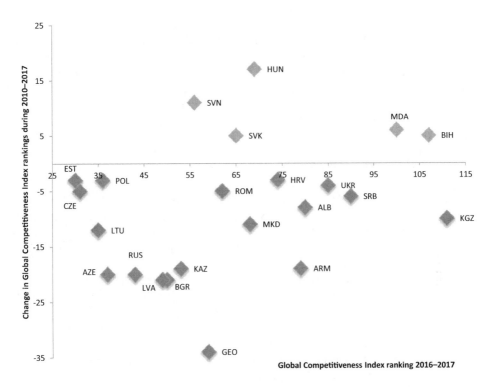

Figure 9.13 Global competitiveness index ranking in CEE/FSU.

Notes: ranking scale is from 1 to 138. Lower ranking indicates economy's stronger competitiveness as per the report methodology. Negative change between 2010 and 2017 represents relative improvement in the overall ranking position. Positive change (in lighter tone) indicates relative worsening in global ranking.

Source: author's estimates based on the Global Competitiveness Index Historical Dataset, World Economic Forum (WEF, 2017)

(enthusiasm for new institutions or increased FDI) remain categorically different across the 29 countries, as argued above.

Conclusion

This chapter may be the longest in our narrative of post-socialist societies but there is a reason for that. Covering the first two decades of the 21st century, the spectrum of questions that one could raise here is vast. The chapter has attempted to address some of the underlying factors along the region's macroeconomic, financial, and regional integration dimensions. Three immediate observations emerge as a result of this effort.

First, following the 1990s transition turbulence, the CEE/FSU economies experienced strong economic growth through the early 2000s. Much of that growth was conditioned on the catching-up factor for the lost decade, strong domestic demand, in turn fueled by rapidly expanding credit and rising commodity prices, helping commodity-dependent exporters, and initial signs of relative macroeconomic stabilization. It is the latter factor that will play a definitive role in each country's development in the years to come, affecting both economic structure and institutional change. In the post-GFC environment, unconditioned FDI flows have ended and it remains up to each individual economy to diversify its exports and work its way up the food chain within regional integration projects.

Second, in addition to uncovering structural weaknesses in each economy's development, the succession of macroeconomic crises in the CEE/FSU has also offered an opportunity, at least to some degree, to address those fragile aspects of each economy. Of course, one would be warned not to take this statement to an extreme vision of macroeconomic bliss. Yet, to the extent, for example, that currency and credit pressures led to outcomes approaching macroeconomic crises, the prudential regulatory framework in financial markets continues to evolve and some degree of financial stability is emerging across the map.

Somewhat structurally stronger in terms of industrial diversification and institutional integration, the economies of Central and Eastern Europe exhibit more visible immediate changes. At the same time, progress is more gradual in Southeastern Europe and parts of the FSU, where FDI flows have been relatively slower and integration with the international capital markets system is more modest. However, it is precisely these types of conditions that are forcing smaller countries on the so-called transition periphery to attempt daring steps in reforming their economies (e.g. Armenia's focus on the knowledge economy; or Georgia's bet on the growing tourism sector).

Finally, uncertainty and diversity will continue to characterize development patterns across CEE and the FSU, even despite the ongoing integration processes. In fact, dependence on the main exports' destination's business cycle, either for manufactured exports or, as in weaker smaller economies, for possibility for labor migrants' temporary employment, carries with it a blessing in disguise. Such realization remains as a guiding light in the small, open CEE/FSU economy development as the search for a post-transition path continues. Whichever political, cultural, and social drivers may take precedence in objectively changing macroeconomic conditions, the proliferation of diverse experiences across CEE/FSU is inescapable. And that observation offers some hope for a country-unique path to sustainable development in the post-socialist region.

Appendix

Table 9.5A General government debt across CEE/FSU economies, % of GDP

Country	2006	2008	2009	2011	2015	2016	2017F	Change between 2016 and 2006, %
Albania	56.7	55.1	59.7	59.4	73.7	71.5	68.6	14.8
Armenia	16.2	14.6	34.1	35.7	43.0	51.8	53.1	35.6
Azerbaijan	10.3	7.3	12.4	11.4	28.3	37.7	33.1	27.4
Belarus	10.7	20.2	32.2	53.9	53.0	52.3	58.0	41.6
Bosnia and Herzegovina	21.2	30.9	35.1	43.1	45.4	44.4	42.5	23.1
Bulgaria	22.8	14.7	14.6	14.4	25.6	27.8	24.5	5.1
Croatia	38.9	39.6	49.0	65.2	86.7	84.4	83.1	45.5
Czech Republic	27.9	28.7	34.1	39.8	40.3	37.7	36.0	9.8
Estonia	4.4	4.5	7.0	6.1	10.1	9.5	9.0	5.1
Georgia	32.0	31.2	41.0	36.5	41.4	44.9	45.5	12.9
Hungary	64.6	71.6	77.8	80.7	74.7	74.2	73.3	9.6
Kazakhstan	6.7	6.8	10.2	10.2	21.9	21.1	21.8	14.4
Kosovo	28.7	21.2	6.1	13.9	18.9	20.6	23.5	−8.1
Kyrgyz Republic	72.6	48.3	58.1	49.4	64.9	58.5	63.2	−14.1

Country	2006	2008	2009	2011	2015	2016	2017F	Change between 2016 and 2006, %
Latvia	9.2	16.2	32.5	37.5	34.8	34.3	33.7	25.2
Lithuania	18.0	15.4	29.0	37.3	42.5	40.0	38.9	22.0
FYR Macedonia	30.6	20.6	23.6	27.7	38.2	38.7	37.6	8.1
Moldova	30.9	19.3	29.1	24.1	38.5	38.1	40.2	7.2
Montenegro	36.3	32.1	41.4	48.6	69.3	71.3	74.3	35.0
Poland	47.2	46.6	49.8	54.1	51.1	54.2	54.6	7.1
Romania	12.5	13.4	23.3	33.9	39.4	39.2	40.6	26.7
Russia	9.8	7.4	9.9	10.9	15.9	17.0	17.1	7.3
Serbia	40.3	32.4	36.0	46.6	76.0	74.1	72.8	33.8
Slovak Republic	30.7	28.1	35.9	43.2	52.5	52.3	51.9	21.6
Slovenia	26.0	21.6	34.5	46.4	83.1	78.9	77.7	52.9
Tajikistan	35.3	30.0	36.2	35.5	33.9	35.3	48.5	0.0
Turkmenistan	3.3	2.8	2.4	10.0	19.4	23.9	21.9	20.5
Ukraine	14.3	19.7	34.1	36.9	79.3	81.2	89.8	67.0
Uzbekistan	21.3	12.7	11.0	9.1	10.3	11.6	13.2	-9.8
Caucasian CIS	19.5	17.7	29.2	27.9	37.6	44.8	43.9	25.3
Central Asian CIS	27.9	20.1	23.6	22.8	30.1	30.1	33.7	2.2
European CIS	18.6	19.7	31.8	38.3	57.0	57.2	62.7	38.6
Southeast Europe	32.0	28.9	32.1	39.2	52.6	52.4	51.9	20.4
EU-8	28.5	29.1	37.6	43.1	48.7	47.6	46.9	19.2

Notes: Regional items are simple average estimates for directional presentation only, based on country groupings as in earlier chapters. For consistency, Bulgaria, Croatia, and Romania are included as part of Southeast Europe, as before. F= forecast.

Source: data extrapolated from IMF World Economic Outlook (IMF WEO, 2017)

Notes

1 This discussion should naturally evoke parallels to Veblen's (1899) conspicuous consumption. To easily grasp the foundational weakness of maturing social institutions in the CEE/FSU, one may contrast examples mentioned here with our earlier discussion in Chapter 8 of the problems of poverty and income inequality. Still, one might argue that demand for luxury brands is stronger in Southeast Europe and in the countries of the FSU, though it is a somewhat subjective measure for now.

2 Also see discussion in Gevorkyan (2012) and Keohane (2011) on the accuracy and significance of BRIC's designation.

3 The symbolism with country–animal associations seems to be popular in the economic development field. For example, due to their rapid growth since the late 1950s, the East Asian Tigers (also referred to as Four Asian Dragons) were Hong Kong, Singapore, South Korea, and Taiwan, with an accompanying group of "Tiger Cub" economies (of Indonesia, Malaysia, the Philippines, and Thailand) in Southeast Asia. By the early 2000s, Ireland became known as the Celtic Tiger. In all of these cases, just as later in the CIS, and Armenia in particular, rapid export-driven or credit-fueled growth came to a halt in crisis-like situations. For additional references, see Amsden (2003), Kirby *et al.* (2002), World Bank (1993).

4 Croatia joined the EU in 2013. Because of this difference in timing in EU accession, which also reflects the difference in underlying economic models of the countries, we maintain our country grouping as per earlier chapters, i.e. EU-8, Southeast Europe, etc. More on integration movement in CEE and FSU appears below.

5 Recall our earlier discussion in Chapter 1 of commodity-dependent countries (CDCs). Similarly, an early analysis in Gevorkyan (2011) discusses net exporter versus net importer economies in the FSU based on external position and types of key exports.

6 Figure 9.2 reflects what in the financial media has become known as the commodity "super-cycle" of the two and a half decades since the mid-1990s and up to the mid-2010s. For additional discussions see Johnson and Sharenow (2013), Gevorkyan and Kvangraven (2016), and, already mentioned, Canuto and Cavallari (2012).

7 On the primacy of export-led and credit-led growth in the early 2000s, see also analyses in Bakker and Klingen (2012). Also, see Åslund (2007) for a general overview of post-socialist transformation progress.

8 Also, Rosenberg and Sierhej (2007) suggest that financial transfers connected with the EU integration process helped with pro-cyclical fiscal pressures in the EU-8 group.

9 Primary surplus can be defined as the current government expenditure less current revenue from taxes, excluding government debt interest payments.

10 We address the latter point of direction of trade in the section on regional integration and institutional changes later in this chapter. For a country-level overview of the GFC effects in the CEE/FSU, see analysis by the IMF economists in Bakker and Klingen (2012).

11 In the vast post-GFC literature there was no lack of search for reasons of decline in emerging markets' exports. For example, in Baldwin (2009) the emphasis is on global demand factors, such as loss in confidence and declining consumer spending and investment delays, as key determinants of decreased exports.

12 On commodity cycles, see Figure 9.2 detailing price fluctuations in the commodity markets.

13 This is consistent with our preceding observations in the CEE/FSU group.

14 That amounted to almost one half of overall reserves holding, dropping from USD 600 billion to a very rough estimate of USD 300 billion (e.g. Gevorkyan, 2011).

15 A detailed discussion of Russia's early strategy out of crisis is provided in Gevorkyan (2011). Also see chapters on the GFC in EBRD Transition Reports (EBRD, 2009 and EBRD, 2010).

16 For country-specific responses to the GFC see Bakker and Klingen (2012). The overall conclusion of that research points to the problem of build-up in vulnerabilities in Central and Eastern Europe (emerging Europe in the text) since the 1990s markets reforms, which is consistent with our earlier discussions (e.g. Chapter 7).

17 Of course, this is not to be taken as a universal statement, rather more as a trend.

18 One must also account for the effect of Ukraine's political and economic crisis between 2014 and 2016 as explanatory components for the country's higher public debt to GDP ratios.

19 On CEE/FSU, see Bakker and Klingen (2012). On broad emerging markets trends, see Garcia-Kilroy and Silva (2016), especially discussion on progression from foreign currency debt to local currency bonds, including in frontier markets. On some specifics of sovereign debt in sub-Saharan Africa, as an example of overall trend, see Gevorkyan and Kvangraven (2016) or Cassimon *et al.* (2016).

20 A summary analysis is found in Allen and Moessner (2010).

21 Also see Bakker and Klingen (2012) for a case-by-case analysis of IMF support to the CEE and some FSU economies in the post-GFC recovery.

22 Also see discussion in EBRD (2010).

23 In another study written before the 2014 crisis, we developed a case for Russia's growth potential driven by an increasing number of private sector self-financed firms that showed resilience during the crisis thanks to effective operational management and access to credit (Gevorkyan, 2012).

24 Academic literature on the topic of the Russian 2014 recession is still quite scant. Much of the immediate (and, in fact, rigorous) analysis comes from international business media. For example, just to give a taste of some reports, see Hille (2017), Buckley (2017), Grossbongardt (2015), Emmott and Baczynska (2016), and others.

25 According to analysis of the exchange rate data from CBR (2017).

26 This is supported by analysis of exchange rate pass-through in the cases of Russia and Ukraine found in Faryna (2016). Also see literature cited therein. In a study in the wake of the 2008 GFC, Bahmani-Oskooee and Hajulee (2010) addressed the problem of duality that devaluation may have on domestic investment. This would seem to be relevant in the case of Russia, considering capital outflows reported here and state-led recovery in the agricultural sector. Effectively, the latter action channeled needed financial support at the moment when RUB depreciation was eroding much of private sector profits.

27 See BOFIT's weekly updates for July 14, 2017 (BOFIT, 2017).

28 This is in contrast to the previous position of the USSR being a net importer of wheat (grain) since the 1960s.

29 Medetsky (2016) offers one of the early comparative reports on Russia's post-sanctions wheat export changes.

30 Writing before the 2014 crisis, a broad consensus of authors in a collective study by Alexeev and Weber (2013) offer a mixed, though hopeful, assessment of the economy's prospects. Much attention is drawn to the institutional reforms and structural aspects of the economy, weakened in successive macroeconomic crisis situations.

31 See summary of IMF's 2016 Article IV and the funds involvement with Ukraine at IMF's Country Focus page: www.imf.org/en/News/Articles/2017/04/03/na040417-ukraine-receives-imf-support-but-must-accelerate-reforms.

32 The loss to the EUR is estimated in Dabrowski (2015).

33 The World Bank's updates on labor migration and remittance flows provide timely reports from the field. A full archive of all publications is accessible online: www.goo.gl/xdaaLJ.

34 As estimated in Gevorkyan (2015) the effect was most profound in Armenia, compared to its neighbor Georgia, due to Armenia's high external exposure index and significant share of agricultural exports channeled to Russia.

35 For example, Gevorkyan (2017) looks at Armenia's implied dual-exchange rate target (Armenian dram to Russian ruble and Armenian dram to US dollar). In a relatively competitive banking sector, albeit with roughly 21 banks, the Central Bank is able to preemptively suppress any panic-like reactions in the foreign exchange market. That has helped maintain volatility in the market at relatively predictable levels, while maintaining inflationary targets at the same time.

36 This fact in itself speaks of significant reversal of the CEE's national economic policies and political preferences from the earlier pre-transition to more recent days.

37 See in depth analysis in the World Bank's May 2017 Russia Economic Report (World Bank, 2017b).

38 The World Bank finds Russia's fiscal spending as a share of GDP to be lower compared to OECD countries and EU members. Approximate spending on social protection accounted for 15% of GDP, education, health, and defense under 5%—all below other countries' averages.

39 For example, see Zwass (1979) on the mechanics of the typical Soviet banking system. Any operations requiring going through the banking system (i.e. non-cash transactions) were restricted to enterprises' needs for input components in production, not leaving much flexibility for setting business plans.

40 In individual sector breakdowns, trade received the largest share of state bank credit in 1980 (56.6% of working capital), agriculture the second largest (55.7%), and manufacturing the least at 50.2 percent, according to the data in Geraschenko *et al.* (1982).

41 See discussion in Barisitz (2007) on the monobank system and comparative analysis of the socialist banking process across countries.

42 For additional details on the history of the post-socialist banking system transformation see Bokros (2002) and Bonin *et al.* (1998). Also, see Steinherr (1997) for midway into reforms assessment of the banking reform and warning about disparity in the progress of legislative adoptions, but lacking implementation.

43 In their early analysis of the reforms process, Fischer and Gelb (1991) pointed out that before a sound banking system or open financial markets, the CEE/FSU had to address the problems of bad loans.

44 In fact, Schiffman (1993) rationalizes the benefits of adoption of the Western banking model in the FSU. The argument suggests that banks in the FSU would be able to arrange for financing from a range of diverse sources just as their peers in the West. However, the author emphasizes the need for enterprise restructuring, i.e. avoiding "soft budget constraint."

45 For the CEE/FSU, Laeven and Valencia (2008, 2013) studies cover the period through the 2008 GFC and immediately after.

46 The topic of financial deepening in emerging markets, and CEE/FSU economies, is central to the discussions in Canuto and Gevorkyan (2016).

47 For example, Semmler and Gevorkyan (2011) model a range of scenarios connecting banking sector factors with external pressures for small, open economies, with an emphasis on the central bank's international reserves management and exchange rate targets.

48 For example, see IMF (2013) on assessment of foreign banks' presence in the CEE and FSU.

49 See EBRD (2015) for a dedicated analysis of problems of financial sector development in the post-socialist transition region.

50 Impavido *et al.* (2013) attempt to address challenges of CEE banks' rebalancing from foreign sources of funding to other alternatives. The end result leads to much heterogeneity, even with the Central and Eastern European group, paving the way for more country-specific studies.

51 For instance, as part of its research segment Austria's Raiffeisen Bank International conducts regular analysis of the economic development progress and capital market changes in the CEE/FSU regions. See dedicated online portal: https://goo.gl/iJzDCF.

52 For example, see a colloquium on central banking in one of the special issues by the Bank for International Settlements (BIS, 2015).

53 Similar conclusions are raised in Gevorkyan (2011) and more recently in Gevorkyan (2017).

54 While directionally informative and important, panel studies often conceal nuanced individual country tendencies. Still, foreign currency denominated transactions in CEE/FSU are quite widespread despite the efforts of national monetary authorities to instill domestic currency discipline.

55 Banking can be said to be a truly global industry that instills common rules and practices across a diverse palette of nations. Perhaps the only other such universally global sector is soccer, as observed in Milanovic (2005).

56 One of the most authoritative and conclusive studies on the problems of post-socialist CEE integration with the EU is the one by Berend (2009).

57 The European Commission maintains an active website that allows one to check the current status of the accession process: https://ec.europa.eu/neighbourhood-enlargement/countries/check-current-status/.

58 Kosovo and Montenegro have adopted the euro as de-facto currency.

59 Recall our earlier discussion on the key impediment to growth of the socialist economic model being the inability to invest in and sustain a technological upgrade.

60 Rapid growth of foreign ownership in the banking sector and structural connections with the EU economy quickly, according to Barisitz (2009), led to evolution of pan-European microeconomic networks.

61 On Russia's OFDI activity see general discussion in Gevorkyan (2013a) and an instructive case study in Spigarelli (2011). For a broader overview of growing multinational enterprises in emerging markets, see Ramamurti (2009).

62 This would also be an opportune moment to remind our reader about the edited collection by Dale (2011) that raises critical concerns around uneven development in the post-socialist transition region, even in countries that are generally seen as success cases.

63 As a reminder, the GCR index is based on 12 key areas including institutional development, infrastructure, macroeconomics, health, and primary education progress as the basic requirements. The remaining eight pillars are organized within efficiency enhancers and innovation sub-groups (WEF, 2017).

10 Facing the present by knowing the past

It is harder to crack a prejudice than an atom.

Albert Einstein

Why the present

Perhaps one of the difficulties for a nation is to become content with its own history. This does not necessarily allude to the popular expression about being doomed to repeating one's history due to ignorance (although this matters, too). Instead, the difficulty is in the capacity to objectively accept the past and pragmatically seek balance in the present.

By the early 21st century, the post-socialist economies of Eastern Europe and the former Soviet Union are independent nation states. This is no small feat, as history reminds us. And at an abstract level, one might even view the future of the post-socialist countries to be well defined by two equally strong and widely shared desires.

First, there is a clearly articulated push for logically continued improvement in the nation's material well-being. In a more complex way, at an individual household level this translates into a fulfilling lifestyle supported by a stable and higher income. This would appear quite consistent with the basic microeconomic consumer preferences of a capitalist society. However, it also involves a range of macroeconomic policy measures and sustained achievements.[1]

Second, as the preceding chronicles might suggest, at a country level there is an inherent drive to remain politically and economically important on the world map in the age of globalization. This bodes well with the first, higher income, goal but also raises concerns for individual country competitiveness. And while the political aspects may find explanation in national sovereignty aspirations and incentives to elites, the competitiveness aspect is more complex from a perspective of macroeconomic sustainability and social development.[2]

In this last chapter of our journey, we draw a temporary concluding line to our narrative as we attempt to take stock of the present transformative dynamic in the region. Methodologically, this brief discussion connects with the model of socio-economic transformation (Figure 2.5) developed in Chapter 2. The reason why these are only "temporary" conclusions, is because of the inherent dynamic of the social history. As such, we proceed with an expectation of changing qualifying characteristics in the future. That is the reason why an objective assessment of the present, and not automatically the future, of the post-socialist world, is so much more critically important.

The macroeconomic (competitive) aspect

The macroeconomic, or competitive structure, aspect is the first element of the socio-economic transformation model derived in Figure 2.5. In this context, the upbeat tone of recent macroeconomic reviews of the region is welcome but can hardly be surprising.[3] Taking into consideration the extent of the 1990s abyss, current income levels do seem encouraging across the CEE/FSU palette. As we established in Table 7.1 and Figure 7.4, mid-way into reforms output fell up to 45 percent (as in Georgia) with greater declines in GDP per capita (even accounting for massive population losses).

As a reminder, the same analysis established that both total and per capita GDP declines were not the same for the group. For some in the CEE (especially the EU-8 countries), the losses were relatively small against the background of systemic collapses of some smaller FSU economies (e.g. see Figure 7.1 and Figure 7.2 for group-level contrasts). For those countries, losses in GDP growth ranged from as low as 8.9 percent (Slovenia) and as high as 32.1 percent (Latvia). This was still relatively low compared to the rest of the post-socialist economies. Losses in the 1995 GDP per capita compared to the 1989 levels (based on analysis in Figure 7.4) were equally small for EU-8 (e.g. 1% for Poland, 3% for Czech Republic as opposed to double-digit losses in the FSU).

Data imperfections and statistical discrepancies notwithstanding, the scale of the region's 1990s transformation is further illustrated in Figure 10.1. According to this representation, the combined CEE and FSU economies' share as of global economy fell from approximately 15 percent in 1980 to barely 6 percent in more recent years. Factoring out the scale of Russia's economy, combined the Caucasus, Central Asian, and European CIS economies make up 1.3 percent of the global economy today (compared to, albeit still modest but higher, 3 percent in 1980). Central and Eastern Europe's share in the world economy has declined from 4.1 percent in the 1980s to 2 percent in early 2010s with continued likelihood of decline.

Notably, the largest declines in the relative shares of economy size followed the 1990s systemic collapse (or transformational recessions, as Kornai, 1994 and Popov, 2013b, aptly illustrate) of the central planning model. However, there is also a visible decline following the 1980s, which may be attributed to the, largely endogenous, constraints on the socialist economic model to retain and reproduce the momentum of the post-WWII economic miracle in later years (Chapters 3 and 4).

As discussed in Chapters 5 through 7, this was primarily due to the inability to shore up sufficient investments towards innovative technology and reorient the economy to a qualitatively more competitive consumer goods production.[4] The endogeneity of the predominant model's constraints emanated from the growing complexity of the centralized plan system. Of course, as discussed in Chapter 6, that in turn had to withstand its ultimate test with the launch of the *perestroika* reforms. Unfortunately, the industrial balance, maintained through the plan system and common socialist market (the CMEA) was but all too fragile and the technological gap vis-à-vis the rest of the world continued to widen, exacerbating the industrial losses of the first decade of transition.[5]

To the extent that those gaps translate in today's macroeconomic conditions, Figure 10.2 provides an unambiguous conclusion. All the CEE and FSU economies, even those that are part of the selective regional (e.g. EU) or economic associations (e.g. OECD), seem to be significantly distanced from the benchmark levels of the industrialized economies (e.g. OECD average).

There is no doubt, of course, that per capita income recovery, reported in Figure 8.1, appears impressive and, hopefully, suggestive of sustained improvement over the coming years. However, subsequent progress would be a function of a host of external (global supply chain integration) and domestic (institutional development and industrial policy) factors that remain a subject of careful scrutiny by economists. For now, the results in Figure 10.2 suggest that the distance between the current income levels and prosperity, if one takes advanced economies' per capita incomes as such approximation, remains significant.[6]

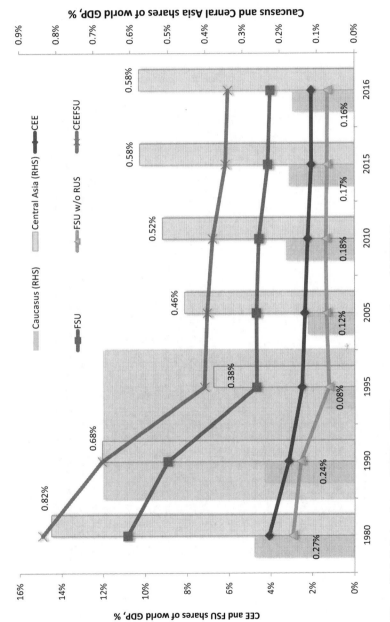

Figure 10.1 Relative shares of CEE and FSU country groups to the world GDP, %.

Notes: All country groups as per earlier definitions (see Chapter 1). Caucasus and Central Asia measured on the right-hand side axis; shaded area between 1990 and 1995 represents the period of initial market reforms.

Source: author's calculations based on data from The Conference Board Total Economy Database (TCB, 2017)

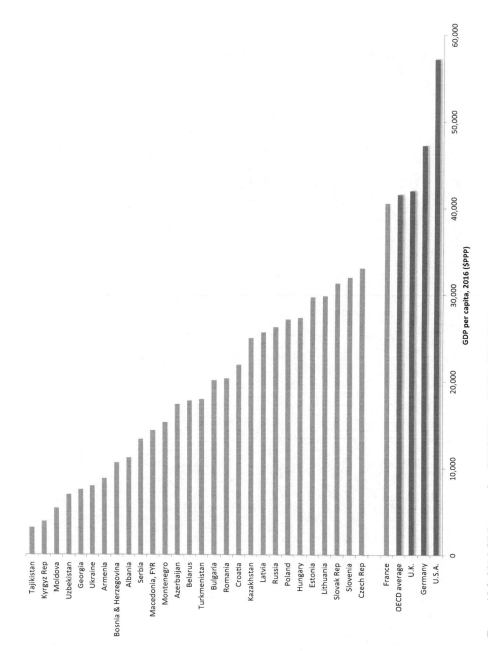

Figure 10.2 2016 GDP per capita: CEE/FSU *vs.* OECD, 2011 $PPP.

Sources: extrapolated from WDI (2017) and TCB (2017)

Evidence on foreign direct investment, another dimension towards economic growth and competitiveness, also suggests a concern. As was observed in Chapter 9 (e.g. Figure 9.10 and Figure 9.11) FDI flows to the region remain sporadic, uneven, and largely dependent on the country's integration with the global supply chain or its primary regional trading partner's external patterns. A recent, at the time of writing, report on expected record growth in private equity investment in Central European countries only reconfirms the sporadic nature of broader capital flows into the region (e.g. Shotter, 2017).[7] The effect of foreign flows on an individual economy's structure is then further obfuscated by larger trends of the global value chains (GVC) as multinational corporations seek resilient consumer markets and competitively attractive low costs of production, against the background of ongoing technological substitution (e.g. Milberg and Winkler, 2013).[8]

And yet, there is still another side to the economic change in the transition region. Despite their modest income positions in contrast to the global economy, Eastern Europe and parts of the FSU are placed fourth (following Western Europe, Asia Pacific, and North America) in the global rankings for estimates of the retail value of the luxury goods market.[9]

Slightly below the North American rate, the CEE/FSU luxury goods market is expected to grow at 4 percent CAGR between 2014 and 2019, claiming 4.7 percent (or USD 19 billion) of the global share in 2019. Most indicative, luxury goods advertising spending between 2017–2018 in CEE/FSU is expected to increase 10 percent, significantly outstripping planned increases in Latin America (5 percent) and North America (4 percent), with reportedly up to 6 percent declines elsewhere. The role of the Russian market in the CEE/FSU and global luxury market is undoubtedly large, but this is merely due to the economy's overall size compared to the smaller CEE and FSU states.

The trend, as Veblen-esque as it may be (mentioned in Chapter 9), is inescapably common across the post-socialist realm. Growth in the luxury segment is an advantage enjoyed by more affluent consumers and feeds into the earlier observations of unequal income distribution (e.g. Chapter 8; Table 8.1 and Figure 8.3) and uneven growth patterns across the CEE/FSU and within each individual country. This then brings us to the discussion of the second dimension of the socio-economic transformation: social welfare or human transition.

Human transition (again)

Among the immediate impacts of the 1990s macroeconomic transition on social welfare was visible worsening in the life expectancy at birth in CEE and FSU. Figures 10.3 and 10.4 summarize available data in a compact analysis. Consider the evidence in Figure 10.3 first. This shows that life expectancy in CEE/FSU dropped precipitously through the 1990s (on more detailed examination, specifically, in the first half of the decade) compared to the maximum life expectancy in the decade before, namely 1980–1989. The finding appears to hold for practically all post-socialist countries, with few exceptions.

Life expectancy at birth is a critical indicator of social well-being and is routinely brought up in cross-country comparisons. Its purpose is to inform research of challenges to sustained economic development, alerting to critical negative tendencies at social level.[10] As nutrition, access to healthcare services, hygiene, income, and a range of other factors improve, life expectancy typically rises as well. Indeed, as those factors improved, Ortiz-Ospina and Roser (2017) find that collectively the world has moved from equality in low life expectancy of the 19th century, to inequality of the 1950s, and to relative equality in more recent years but higher life expectancy levels.

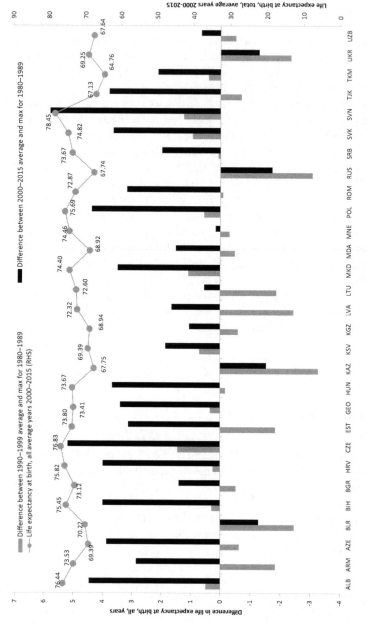

Figure 10.3 Life expectancy at birth in CEE/FSU, total, in relation to 1980s maximum and 2000–2015 average.

Note: left-hand side axis reflects difference in life expectancy years between a maximum value for the 1980–1989 and 2000–2015 average. Right-hand side (RHS) axis reports average life expectancy years over 2000–2015.

Source: author's estimates based on data from the WDI (2017)

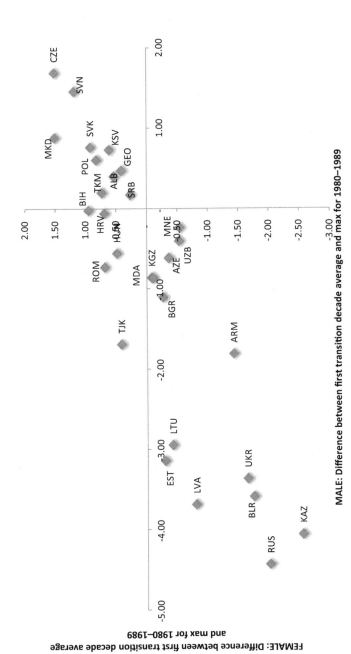

Figure 10.4 Life expectancy in CEE/FSU in the first transition decade vs. peak during 1980–1989, male and female, years.

Notes: difference in life expectancy years between a maximum value for the 1980–1989 and average values for 1990–1999. No change for Serbia, due to data limitations.

Source: author's estimates based on data from WDI (2017)

For the CEE/FSU the finding is indeed, relative. The highest average life expectancy value (in Slovenia—one of the developed economies within the former Yugoslavia—at 78.45 years), while higher than the world average (71.66) is still below industrialized nations 2015 level (e.g. U.S. at 78.74 and Germany at 81.09 years). Yet, in relative terms, the most recent indicators represent a gradual improvement of living conditions across CEE/FSU as life expectancy rebounds. As the other component of Figure 10.3 suggests, for the majority of the post-socialist nations the 2000s have recorded significant improvements, compared to the 1980s. Exceptions to this positive trend have been Belarus, Kazakhstan, Russia, and Ukraine.

In those countries, the economic aftershocks of the reforms era and deterioration in health-care systems are still being felt.[11] In Russia, perhaps the most indicative (and researched) case, mortality rates due to disease and a range of unnatural causes among working-age men outpaced those among women (e.g. Notzon *et al.*, 1998).

Corroborating analysis in Figure 10.3, for example, Figure 10.4 shows a decline of 4.44 years for male life expectancy in Russia between the average 1990s and maximum value during the 1980s. This was the highest in its group across post-socialist economies. Kazakhstan recorded the second highest decline in male life expectancy for the same period (4.06 years). For brevity, we refrain from delving into much further detail behind the variations across the post-socialist space and such significant declines. Problems of social under-development, common to the region and varying in intensity across countries, have been the subject of intense scrutiny since the early days of reforms (e.g., Blanchard, 1997; Mikhalev, 2003; Milanovic, 1993, 1999; Popov, 2011; etc.).

Continuing with the living conditions theme, EBRD (2016) empirically confirms that people born during their country's transition (specifically, the initial, price liberalization years) are at least 1.1cm shorter than those born before or approximately five years after the initial reforms. Usually, variations in average height reflect the economic conditions (abundance if high, deprivation if shorter) in the first years of a child's life.

As such, combined with our earlier observations on life expectancy, this finding on average height speaks clearly about significant deterioration in living conditions during the initial reforms years and elevated pressures of psychological stress in the background of systemic disruptions of economic institutions and social capital depletion.[12] As conditions improved in the post-socialist economies, according to EBRD (2016), the next generation has grown taller—a positive finding in the CEE/FSU development context.

Table 10.1 adds a different assessment perspective of the state of human development and gender development in the post-socialist economies. Intended to capture a symbiosis of the earlier discussed metrics reflecting a long and healthy life (life expectancy), knowledge (years of schooling), and decent standard of living (income per capita), the Human Development Index (HDI), which ranges from 1–188 on the global scale, is reflective of the diversity across the CEE/FSU.

The HDI ranking of post-socialist countries is easily interpreted vis-à-vis the rest of the world. Three of the CEE countries are included in the world's top 30: Slovenia, Czech Republic, and Estonia. The remainder of the transition sample is almost equally split between 13 countries in the 31 to 69 ranking range and the remaining 12 below the 70th rank. Many Central Asian countries are ranked at the bottom of the list, with EU-8 showing better scores and mixed evidence for FSU and other remaining CEE economies.

Data for the Gender Development Index (GDI), mostly reflecting improvements across the palette, adds to the results in the HDI columns of Table 10.1. Here again, the EU-8 countries are relatively ahead of the rest of the pack (the closer the index value to 1 the smaller the gap

Table 10.1 Human and Gender Development Indexes in CEE/FSU, select years

Country	HDI Rank (2015)	Human development index (HDI)			Gender Development Index (GDI)		
		2000	2010	2015	2000	2010	2015
Slovenia	25	0.82	0.88	0.89	0.99	1.01	1.00
Czech Rep	28	0.82	0.86	0.88	0.97	0.97	0.98
Estonia	30	0.78	0.84	0.87	1.03	1.04	1.03
Poland	36	0.78	0.83	0.86	0.99	1.01	1.01
Lithuania	37	0.76	0.83	0.85	1.02	1.04	1.03
Slovak Rep	40	0.76	0.83	0.85	1.00	0.99	0.99
Hungary	43	0.77	0.82	0.84	0.98	0.99	0.99
Latvia	44	0.73	0.81	0.83	1.04	1.04	1.03
Croatia	45	0.75	0.81	0.83	0.96	0.99	1.00
Montenegro	48	0.74	0.79	0.81	0.94	0.95	0.96
Russia	49	0.72	0.79	0.80	1.03	1.02	1.02
Romania	50	0.71	0.80	0.80	0.97	0.99	0.99
Belarus	52	0.68	0.79	0.80	1.02	1.03	1.02
Bulgaria	56	0.71	0.78	0.79	0.98	0.99	0.98
Kazakhstan	56	0.69	0.77	0.79	1.00	1.01	1.01
Serbia	66	0.71	0.76	0.78	0.95	0.97	0.97
Georgia	70	0.67	0.74	0.77	0.94	0.95	0.97
Albania	75	0.66	0.74	0.76	0.94	0.96	0.96
Azerbaijan	78	0.64	0.74	0.76	0.95	0.95	0.94
Bosnia and Herzegovina	81	0.70	0.71	0.75	0.92	0.93	0.92
Macedonia, FYR	82	n/a	0.74	0.75	n/a	0.80	0.95
Armenia	84	0.64	0.73	0.74	0.95	1.00	0.99
Ukraine	84	0.67	0.73	0.74	0.99	1.01	1.00
Uzbekistan	105	0.59	0.66	0.70	n/a	n/a	0.95
Moldova	107	0.60	0.67	0.70	0.98	1.01	1.01
Turkmenistan	111	n/a	0.67	0.69	n/a	n/a	n/a
Kyrgyz Rep	120	0.59	0.63	0.66	0.96	0.96	0.97
Tajikistan	129	0.54	0.61	0.63	0.91	0.92	0.93

Notes: "n/a" data not available; data for 2000 for Bosnia and Herzegovina is as of 2005; for Montenegro as of 2003. HDI ranking closer to 1 is indicative of a country's strong progress in human development.

Source: extrapolated from the UNDP Human Development Report (2016). Available online: http://hdr.undp.org/en/2016-report

in HDI indicators between women and men).[13] While GDI paints a relatively positive picture across longevity, education, and income levels for women in the transition countries, there are deeper structural alterations to the gender balance ongoing since the transition reforms.

Focus on the challenges to the changing role of women in the post-socialist world has been high on the agenda of researchers and policymakers.[14] In a consolidated analysis across the CEE and international data, Metcalfe and Afanassieva (2005) find that the share of women in management roles across transition countries has been gradually eroding.[15] The finding stands in particular contrast to the socialist-era emphasis on gender equality and women participation in the labor force. For some countries, the declines in female labor force participation has been quite significant and has remained relatively low compared to the total indicator (e.g. Table 10.2 for the early transition and more recent indicators).

More specifically, Metcalfe and Afanassieva (2005), separately with other commentators (e.g. Welter *et al.*, 2006), conclude that the breakdown in the socialist-era social guarantees

Table 10.2 Labor market indicators in CEE/FSU, 1990 and 2015

Country	Labor force participation, all		Labor force participation, female		Total unemployment, all		Youth unemployment	
	1990	*2015*	*1990*	*2015*	*1995*	*2015*	*1995*	*2015*
Albania	64.1	50.3	53.2	40.3	21.3	17.3	38.7	32.7
Armenia	60.2	63.3	50.3	54.9	18.0	16.3	37.9	37.2
Azerbaijan	60.9	65.0	52.9	61.9	6.5	4.7	15.1	14.3
Belarus	67.2	60.8	60.3	54.5	6.5	6.1	13.4	12.9
Bosnia and Herzegovina	44.5	46.1	31.5	34.4	25.0	30.3	51.0	66.9
Bulgaria	58.8	54.2	54.9	48.6	15.9	9.8	32.1	22.2
Croatia	57.1	52.3	46.6	46.4	9.3	16.1	24.0	43.8
Czech Rep	60.8	59.4	51.7	51.1	4.0	5.2	7.7	13.0
Estonia	69.2	61.9	63.0	55.5	9.7	5.9	14.1	11.3
Georgia	63.7	67.1	54.6	57.3	16.1	12.3	36.0	29.8
Hungary	54.8	54.0	46.2	46.4	9.9	7.0	17.5	18.2
Kazakhstan	69.8	71.2	62.3	66.1	11.0	5.6	12.2	5.1
Kyrgyz Rep	66.0	62.9	58.4	49.4	9.2	8.2	16.6	14.6
Latvia	69.0	60.4	62.6	54.4	19.0	9.8	34.7	14.8
Lithuania	66.4	59.1	59.4	53.9	17.5	9.5	32.6	17.6
Macedonia, FYR	55.1	55.9	43.0	43.9	31.5	26.9	52.4	49.4
Moldova	67.2	42.0	61.1	38.8	6.8	5.0	15.2	15.6
Montenegro	53.5	48.9	44.5	42.0	19.3	18.2	35.5	37.5
Poland	63.4	56.9	55.3	49.1	13.3	7.4	30.5	19.9
Romania	59.2	55.9	51.6	47.6	8.0	6.9	20.4	23.1
Russia	67.2	63.5	59.5	56.6	9.4	5.8	18.7	15.0
Serbia	55.3	51.5	43.9	43.4	13.4	19.0	29.6	45.2
Slovak Rep	66.1	59.5	59.6	51.4	13.1	11.3	24.7	25.2
Slovenia	53.8	57.5	47.8	52.2	7.2	9.3	19.3	16.7
Tajikistan	66.7	68.5	58.1	59.4	12.2	10.9	18.3	16.8
Turkmenistan	60.2	62.0	46.4	47.3	n/a	n/a	n/a	n/a
Ukraine	62.8	59.1	56.1	52.2	5.6	9.9	12.3	23.1
Uzbekistan	59.3	61.8	46.1	48.3	11.2	10.1	21.0	19.8

Notes: "n/a" data not available; series included are Labor force participation rate (% ages 15 and older); Labor force participation rate, female (% ages 15 and older); Youth unemployment rate (% of labor force ages 15–24); Total unemployment rate (% of labor force).

Source: extrapolated from the UNDP Human Development Report (2016). Available online: http://hdr.undp.org/en/2016-report

of employment, state assistance with childcare and healthcare services, education, and other non-waged provisions, was a definitive factor for many CEE countries where share of women in labor market was relatively high during Soviet times.

With the onset of the capitalist social and economic tendencies, the share of non-waged provisions either precipitously declined in some countries (e.g. Albania, Belarus, Bulgaria, Estonia, Kyrgyz Republic, Latvia, Lithuania, Moldova, Montenegro, Poland, Romania, Russia, Slovak Republic, and Ukraine) or remained relatively stable to its 1990s value in other countries. And while at first it is tempting to seek explanation for gender disparities in societies where traditional family roles and customs have persisted even through Soviet times, intensifying recently (i.e. Central Asia), as alluded to in UNDP (2007), the problem of gender disparity seems to be more pervasive and quite heterogeneous than might be suggested by cursory analysis of the post-socialist geography.

For example, Velluti (2014) in the analysis of Hungary and Poland—where transition to the capitalist system began much earlier than elsewhere—finds that, along with legacy factors, gender equality in the CEE countries suffers from a similar set of socio-economic determinants as the older European Union member states. Specifically, membership in the EU has yet to result in improved, broader, and beyond the socialist model's legacy, opportunities to women and as such, of itself adoption of the new capitalist norms, has not necessarily unequivocally guaranteed improved gender outcomes. Elsewhere, an early case study (McCarthy *et al.*, 1997) documented successes of women entrepreneurs in Russia early in the transition period. Apparently, in the void of the receding socialist welfare state the new institutional framework emerges as a comprehensive and complex web of contemporary cultural, social, gender, and macroeconomic external and internal pressures.

Finally, on employment trends, Table 10.2 draws concerns around sustained high unemployment rates in structurally weaker post-socialist economies. Those rates, persistent as they are, are further exacerbated by equally high youth unemployment rates. In addition, vulnerable employment (unpaid domestic or part-time work) remains relatively high across the region. According to the available data (UNDP, 2016) only a handful or countries reported vulnerable employment at below 10 percent of total employment (e.g. Estonia at 5.7%, Hungary at 5.8%, Russia at 6%, and Lithuania at 9.8% in 2013 and 2014). The highest values were reported in Georgia at 59.8 percent and Albania at 58.1 percent of total employment in 2013.

Naturally, there is a clear connection with a country's level of macroeconomic development. It should be possible to correlate countries with stronger income growth, from earlier discussions, with evidence in Table 10.2 with those with lower unemployment rate (comparing CEE and FSU horizontally in each column). Yet, results on youth unemployment and vulnerable employment suggest there are still deep structural problems remaining affecting all former socialist economies.

What is striking, in particular, about youth unemployment, is the increase between 1995 and 2015 rates in some of the countries with stronger income growth, for example, some in the EU-8. A possible explanation alludes to the breakup in the legacy guarantees of either the education path or job prospects of the pre-transition era. In more recent years, FDI-driven demand for specialized skills, competition in the domestic labor markets, and uneven patterns of economic growth result in fewer opportunities for the youth in guaranteed employment. The effects of sluggish growth on youth employment would appear to be common across the post-socialist spectrum and in advanced European economies.[16] As reviewed in Chapter 8, lack of opportunities for employment at home has also served as a push factor for outward labor migration from structurally weaker (but also relatively stronger, e.g. Poland) economies.

Institutions

On the third pivot of the socio-economic transformation model, the institutional aspect, one is reminded of our discussion on gradualism in Chapter 7 and some observation on competitiveness towards Chapter 9. To clarify, our focus is specifically on business climate-related institutional development, which encompasses entrepreneurial, social, macroeconomic, and administrative factors of the CEE/FSU transformation. It is worth remembering in this context that among others, Gaidar (2012) discussed the gradual nature of new institutions' evolution as old, collapsing structures were replaced. In other words, newly emerging social and business institutions lacked foundational tradition in the majority of the post-socialist economies. Overburdened with macroeconomic crises, volatile politics, and muted side turns of the development path, in many CEE/FSU countries new institutions have been slow to evolve and solidify. The adaptation to the new, post-socialist system—whatever it is called— is gradual and unsteady, as the dynamic self-regenerating process of new social norms and business practices takes hold. And so, it has been a process of transformation rather than transition.

Data presented in Figure 10.5 and further detailed at country level in Figure 10.6 (a–f) offers a recent snapshot from the World Bank's Doing Business Survey (DBS, 2017). The rankings are well-known in the literature on international business and institutional development and often serve as an initial guide to cross-country comparisons. We see that in terms of Ease of Doing Business in Figure 10.5 (measured on the left-hand side), the majority of countries are stacking up relatively clearly within the top 40 ranking out of a total 190 as per the DBS (2017) survey. The record on Starting a Business indicator is a bit patchier, with variations depending largely on country-specific administrative hurdles. Notably, this indicator is particularly high for some in the EU-8 group (e.g. Lithuania, Poland, Czech Rep, Slovenia) but relatively low for such countries as Armenia, Macedonia FYR, Estonia, Georgia, and others.

This is where the subjectivity of each country's case comes into play, as can be gleaned from Figure 10.6 (a–f). As some countries outperform on one measure, they tend to underperform on others. Bypassing individual country discussion of evidence in Figure 10.6 (a–f) due to space constraints, we note a diversity of development model patterns clearly illustrated in the variety of the results here. It is equally important to note that constructing objective institutional measures is a notoriously difficult task and any such results should be taken with caution. Yet, data assembled in Figure 10.6 (a–f) remain directionally helpful for country-specific studies and some cross-country comparative work.

In the context of our discussion, assuming economic liberalization takes place, as the vacuum created by the retreat of the state is gradually filled with new market institutions, more solid economic structures may evolve (e.g., Popov, 2011). This seems to coincide with a general trend over a longer historical period, as seen in Putterman (2013). Havrylyshyn and van Rooden (2003) stress pragmatic structural reforms to achieve sustainable growth in transition in addition to institutional change. Varying aspects of the above-listed measures have been tried (and tested) in the EE/FSU over the past two decades.

In the context of gradual institutional change of the post-socialist economies, North's definition of institutions as "the rules of the game in a society" (North, 2004, p. 3) captures the essence of the real question about the type of institutions emerging in CEE/FSU. Facing such a multitude of post-socialist experiences, it would then be somewhat appropriate to bring into discussion a categorization that might guide the way through the diversity of social and economic experiences across countries.

The ideology of socialist system ended with the breakup of the Soviet Union in 1991 and, as such, contemporary literature focuses on another variety: "varieties of capitalism" arrangements (e.g. Lane, 2007; Hall and Thelen, 2008; Myant, 2016). Jackson and Deeg (2008) warn over simplistic interpretation of institutional dynamics. Joining the chorus of a growing number of publications, they raise the need for "country-specific configurations" instead of "bundles" of economic systems views.

More substantively, North's (1991, 2004) view of society at a given time as the outcome of an evolving web of accumulating institutional tendencies is suggestive of country-specific change. There may be still some convergence at surface level, e.g. notional direction of transition towards capitalism. However, extending the logic further, one necessarily ascends to

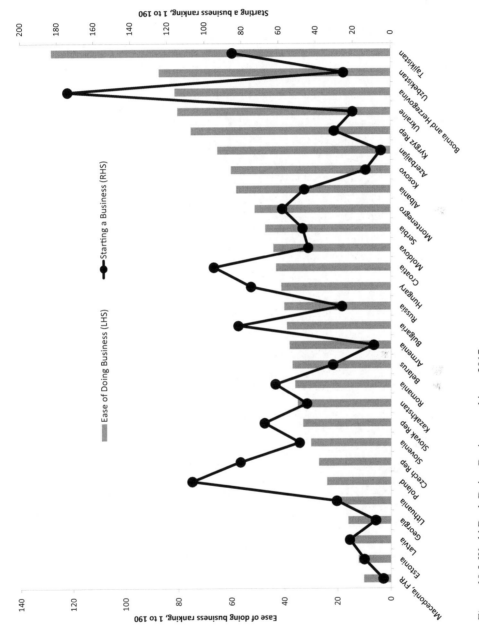

Figure 10.5 World Bank Doing Business rankings, 2017.

Source: extrapolated from the World Bank Doing Business Database, WB (2017c). Available online: www.doingbusiness.org

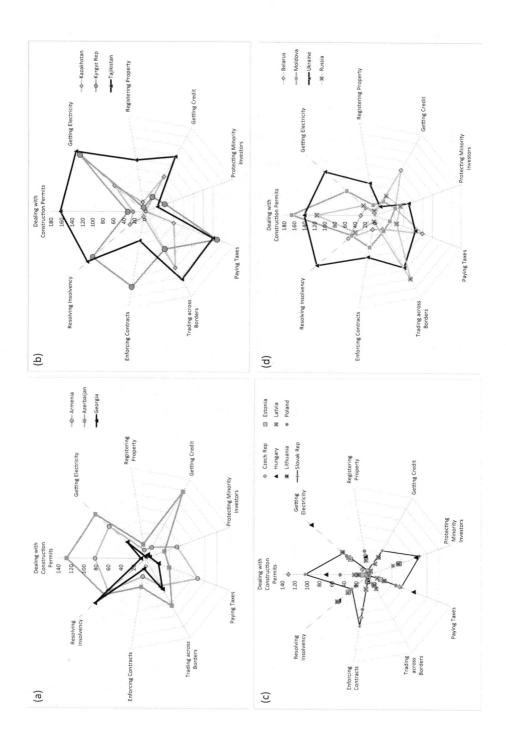

(a)

Dealing with Construction Permits

Getting Electricity

Registering Property

Getting Credit

Protecting Minority Investors

Paying Taxes

Trading across Borders

Enforcing Contracts

Resolving Insolvency

◆ Armenia
■ Azerbaijan
▲ Georgia

(b)

Dealing with Construction Permits

Getting Electricity

Registering Property

Getting Credit

Protecting Minority Investors

Paying Taxes

Trading across Borders

Enforcing Contracts

Resolving Insolvency

◆ Kazakhstan
● Kyrgyz Rep
▲ Tajikistan

(c)

Dealing with Construction Permits

Getting Electricity

Registering Property

Getting Credit

Protecting Minority Investors

Paying Taxes

Trading across Borders

Enforcing Contracts

Resolving Insolvency

◆ Czech Rep
▲ Hungary
✕ Lithuania
— Slovak Rep
■ Estonia
✕ Latvia
◆ Poland

(d)

Dealing with Construction Permits

Getting Electricity

Registering Property

Getting Credit

Protecting Minority Investors

Paying Taxes

Trading across Borders

Enforcing Contracts

Resolving Insolvency

◆ Belarus
■ Moldova
▬ Ukraine
✕ Russia

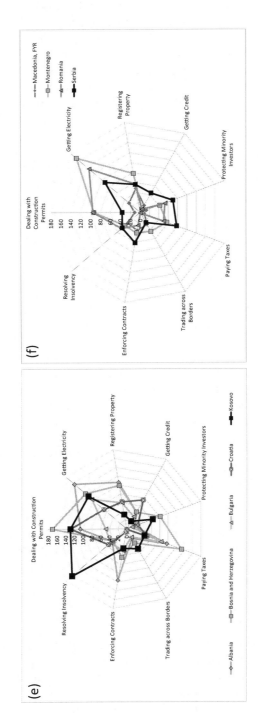

Figure 10.6 Word Bank Doing Business Report country-specific indicators, 2017.

Source: extrapolated from the World Bank Doing Business Database, WB (2017c). Available online: www.doingbusiness.org

the transformational aspects of the varieties of capitalism discussions of established frameworks (e.g. Hall and Soskice, 2001) in the case of transition economies (Myant, 2016).

Broadening the discourse, Puffer *et al.* (2015) also raise the "varieties of communism" when assessing individual risk-taking. In their findings, the authors allude to a more nuanced mix of motivations for risk-taking rather than just broad institutional context, which then informs a range of entrepreneurial behavioral outcomes in post-socialist transition. Elsewhere, McCarthy and Puffer (2016) discuss how "institutional voids on individuals in emerging markets" may affect individuals (by focusing on Russia as an example) to pursue opportunities in more proactive ways elsewhere. Often, such opportunities evolve into resumed connections with the home country.

Attention to the unique institutional characterizations in CEE/FSU and nuanced individual country experiences since the early 1990s then informs contemporary understanding of consistent outcomes that characterized the socialist economic model, as reviewed in Chapter 6. Namely, while at the surface level there was a notional socialist economic model, variations at the country level were many and often superseded any centrally administered initiatives (e.g. consider contrasting with the rest of the group efforts in self-management and market socialism in Hungary, Yugoslavia and Poland, discussed earlier).[17]

Even with a new system, whichever the classification, gradually taking over, legacy institutions persist. Turning to the work of Douglas North again (North, 1991 or 2004) one finds that institutional transformations require significant amount of time for a technological change to occur. In the post-socialist space, as Hare (2001) and Popov (2011) confirm, the relevance of the legacy institutions declines with time as pressure from new production methods and social changes intensify.

A direct outcome of the controversies of the early transition years has been the emergence of shadow economies in the CEE/FSU region. The complexity of the phenomenon was and continues to be conditioned by a host of specific country-level cultural, historical, and objectively macroeconomic factors. In his analysis of the Soviet experience, with a case study of Armenia, Mikaelian (2016) finds that the weakening economic structure through the 1990s paved the way for the shadow economy's growth. As the official state was weakening to combat informality, the society relied more on informal transactions. The research on shadow economies in the CEE/FSU is quite broad, as authors attempt to rationalize through the emerging patterns of capitalism across transition in real time.[18]

There is one relevant conclusion that may be derived on the basis of the above and that is one of continuous, non-linear, and multivariate institutional transformation. The success of the CEE/FSU countries collectively and individually, pulling out of the abyss of the 1990s destruction, requires appreciation. As such, it remains to be seen, with much hope, if a gradualist, country-specific approach, may deliver on forming a sustained framework for a productive and fulfilling social and business development.

Finding a place in the present

In a recent empirical study, Djankov *et al.* (2016) argue that economic transition in the post-socialist economies has reached a successful conclusion, while on a psychological level, there still remains "the happiness gap." The gap refers to the difference between quality of life perceptions among residents in the CEE/FSU and those in the peer group of European countries that were neither part of the socialist system nor experienced the brunt of the 1990s reforms.

For its part, EBRD (2016) adds that despite the difference, the gap is in fact narrowing. This may be a positive finding, perhaps, reflective of improving living standards and rising incomes across the regional palette. At the minimum, this finding suggests convergence at society's perceptions. However, the EBRD report also acknowledges, that the narrowing gap might not just be due to improved CEE/FSU living standards but, perhaps, more so, due to declines in the quality of living across the advanced economies, especially in the post-GFC macroeconomic uncertainty. Notably, the younger generation in the transition economies, that has largely escaped the difficulties the older generation faced in the 1990s, appears to be relatively satisfied with life, despite challenges to the labor market discussed above.

While the path of the long journey of the societies of Eastern Europe and the former Soviet Union is relatively known, the destination seems to be unknown. This need not be taken in a pessimistic way. Connecting the three pivots of the socio-economic transformation model of Figure 2.5, we have illustrated the developments across the macroeconomic, institutional, and human elements in the post-socialist region. The sacrifices those nations have experienced are not easily measured. However, there remains hope that experience to date, informing economic and social research and policy, may have a positive contribution to the still-shaping transition societies. The true living tendency of the post-socialist transformation, as the quote by Georg Hegel given in Chapter 2 reminds us, is yet to be fully comprehended for the journey is still ongoing.

We dedicated a substantial portion of this study chronicling social and economic history of the region starting in what today may seem the distant past and gradually moving the discussion to the present. In the process, we discussed macroeconomic evidence and commented on divergent patterns of transition, including among the countries of the same geographical or economic aggregation. The intention of those discussions has been to help with the realization of why past experiences and legacy social constructs have such immense influence over the present direction in the CEE/FSU political economy.

There is no lack of opinion, supported by empirical and theoretical analysis, as to whether or not the macroeconomic and institutional gains of the post-socialist transition may be sustained. However, attention, more appropriately perhaps, may also be directed towards realization of the type of societies that have evolved across the CEE/FSU mosaic. The change in the political and economic system was not peaceful. Across the map, military conflicts remain dormant.

Collectively, such traumatic experiences, from economic volatility to political cycles, have formed the new societies of each of the countries in the region. Now, almost three decades since the transition, each society continues the search for its unique development path, as our narrative illustrates. Kolodko (2007) raises these concerns in the context of globalization, implying that at some point soon a choice would need to be made at each society's level on the direction in which their country is moving and the latter's integration in the global construct.

For its part, this book has attempted to address the economic history of the post-socialist CEE and FSU countries from an objective perspective. We have shown how throughout history this region has been the subject of much volatility, either political or economic. Moreover, in more modern times, despite those efforts at conscious separation from the previous models, some legacy norms and categories continue to play a role. Institutional change, which we recall from the previous discussions, largely occurring on barren foundations, has been gradual at best in some countries.

That, in turn, raises questions about sustainability of the new era economic models. Our discussion of a range of social and economic development problems has attempted to shed more light on the immense degree to which the lasting impact of the 1990s transformation has not been even across the countries of the region. The human element is integral and remains definitive if one is to attempt to assess the structure of the post-socialist society. As such, studying the post-socialist economies of the CEE and FSU requires what Albert Einstein thought to be quite difficult: overcoming a prejudice. In this region, cracking the (economic research) prejudice requires an economist to open up to a range of opinions and perspectives, but most importantly, to recognize the need for a country-unique approach informed by history.

Part of our initial discussions, in Chapters 1 and 2, where early attempts to rationalize the conceptual views of CEE/FSU economic history and free-market reforms, revolved around the meaning of the terms transition and transformation as applied to describe the 1990s switch from socialist economic model to capitalism. For all practical purposes, evidence amassed in this study, should be convincing enough to support the view of endogenously transformational tremors along the three pivots of the model of socio-economic transformation introduced in Figure 2.5 at the beginning of our conversation.

Indeed, the outcomes on the ground are dynamic, mixed, and ever-changing. There is hardly any settled equilibrium as the post-socialist world remains in motion through its history embodying the unity of contradiction of the multiplicity of social development challenges, institutional adaptations, and emerging economic production modes.

In fact, one could suggest that it really no longer matters as much if the "transition" per se is considered to be over. The modern societies of CEE and FSU live in the present, albeit significantly informed and influenced by past experiences. With evidence and discussions assembled in this volume, we have attempted to establish the historically deeply-rooted socio-economic living tendencies of the post-socialist region and a categorically transformative nature of the 1990s reforms that form the context of the region's present.

Of the future

If the process of free market transition in Eastern Europe and the former Soviet Union meant a switchover to a perfected vision of higher living standards then, for the most part, as evidence shows, with minor exceptions, it is yet to materialize. Perhaps, as some argued, a country-specific gradual approach to the 1990s reforms from the very start might have achieved a more encouraging outcome. Yet, history has been made. Almost three decades since the transition reforms, dynamic outcomes of the post-socialist transformation have piled up on top of the decades of societies and economies in motion prior to that.

In the context of the three-pronged model of socio-economic transformation (introduced in Chapter 2), the CEE/FSU experience has been unique to each country's nuanced set of macroeconomic, institutional, and social components. Some countries, as we saw in the earlier discussions, have done better than others. Explanations varied across a wide range of policy and economic structure options. Clearly, there is minimal homogeneity in post-socialist transition. As social relations, deeply-rooted in a country's traditions and political economy, evolve they also diverge from theoretical blueprints. This dialectical transformation seems to be guiding the societies of Eastern Europe and the former Soviet Union on increasingly varying, individual development paths.

There remains an even greater factor to social advancement. Significantly, unlike the goals of the socialist decades and unlike the aspirations of the early free-market reforms era, there appears to be no finite destination to today's transformational journeys. What seems to be emerging in the post-socialist space of CEE and FSU is a type of mixed construct embracing elements of both socialist and capitalist economic models. How exactly that may play out is left to speculative views of the formerly socialist societies' future. The challenge for them now remains to ensure a clear and sustainable present.

Notes

1 For example, see Berend (2009) on select Central European countries in a comparative analysis to Western European economies.

2 On the subject of incentives to elites we recall the insightful study by Bavel (2016). On globalization and political tendencies in CEE/FSU, see Estrin *et al.* (2009).

3 For example, EBRD (2016). For most recent summary analysis see World Bank's portal for Country Program Snapshots for the Europe and Central Asia region. Available online: www.worldbank.org/en/region/eca/brief/country-program-snapshots.

4 For references, see discussions within earlier chapters, but in particular Voyno (2017) for the most recent empirical confirmation.

5 In more recent years, as Dutta *et al.* (2015) report, some post-socialist countries have seen strong improvements in their global information and communication technology rankings. In particular, Estonia, where software for one of the world's most popular virtual communications applications was developed (Skype, 2017), in 2015 ranked 22 out of 143 countries in the World Economic Forum Networked Readiness Index. Other countries in CEE/FSU ranked above 30 and more in the 40–70 range (the lower, the worse). Elsewhere, Armenia (e.g. Kuriakose, 2013) is reported to have strong innovative capacity, introducing up to 3 percent of global innovative products (e.g. PicsArt application) and in Russia (e.g. Gevorkyan, 2013c), the information technology sector benefited from state-sponsored contracts providing a strong boost to homegrown technology and research activity. However, on the scale of the global economy, as the Dutta *et al.* (2015) ranking suggests, there is still much to be covered.

6 Atoyan (2010) offers an empirical analysis of divergent macroeconomic development paths in the CEE/FSU region. In short, three channels to growth sustainability are emphasized: 1) export-led growth; 2) domestic financial deepening; 3) proactive macroeconomic policies aimed at shoring up capital flows and investment in tradable sectors.

7 The latest report alludes to the occasional capital inflows to Central Europe, rather than a more sustained pace. In that regard, CEE and FSU fit the overall patterns of capital flows to emerging markets (e.g. Canuto and Gevorkyan, 2016; IIF, 2016).

8 In their study, Milberg and Winkler (2013), articulate the problem of an individual country's adaptations in the global economy as the GVC's dynamic supersedes national macroeconomic development, with individual corporate profit-led development.

9 Data on luxury goods market trends is from Bloomberg (2017a, 2017b) obtained via Statista online database.

10 For a broad country-level comparative analysis of significance of life expectancy and other human development factors, based on the latest data, see Ortiz-Ospina and Roser (2017).

11 On the challenges to health systems in some FSU countries, see analysis by Rechel *et al.* (2013).

12 On the connection between economic conditions and a person's height, see indicative studies cited in the EBRD (2016) *Transition Report*, e.g. Almond (2006), Case (2004), Case and Paxson (2010), Duflo (2003), etc.

13 For details on estimation and interpretation of HDI and GDI results, see UNDP (2016).

14 For example, see a collection of studies in UNDP (2007) and regular policy updates from UN Women at www.unwomen.org.

15 For more on the topic of varying roles of female entrepreneurship, see Welter *et al.* (2006).

16 For example, see analysis of youth unemployment in Europe by Banerji *et al.* (2014).

17 For instance, Lane (2007) attempts to assess and emphasize country-specific factors, something that was omitted at the most crucial time of the reforms launch, and that can help develop a more informed understanding of the CEE/FSU transformation.

18 Schneider *et al.* (2010) develop CEE/FSU ranking of the size of shadow economies, with some in the EU-8 reporting greater formality than some in the FSU, in particular in the Caucasus and Central Asia. Contributing to the emergence of the shadow economies have been inconsistently heavy taxation, lapses in governance, and other negative institutional externalities. Separately, Henig and Makovicky (2017) edited a colloquium on the "economies of favor" across the post-socialist spectrum. Such transactions permeate both formal and informal economic spaces with multifaceted variations and manifestations across countries.

References

Abalkin, L. 1999. *Ekonomicheskie vozzrenia i gosudarstvennaya deyatel'nost' S.Y. Witte.* [Economic views and state activity of S.Y. Witte]. Moscow: Russian Academy of Sciences – Institute of Economics.

Acemoglu, D. and J. Robinson. 2012. *Why Nations Fail: The Origins of Power, Prosperity, and Poverty.* New York: Crown Business.

Adam, J. 1999. *Social Costs of Transformation to a Market Economy in Post-Socialist Countries.* New York: Palgrave MacMillan.

Aganbegyan, A. 1990. Perestroika. In Eatwell, J., M. Milgate, and P. Newman (eds) *Problems of the Planned Economy.* New York and London: W. W. Norton & Co. pp. 1–12.

Agarwal, R. and A. Horowitz. 2002. Are international remittances altruism or insurance? Evidence from Guyana using multiple-migrant households. *World Development,* 30(11): 2033–2044.

Agénor, P.-R. and P. J. Montiel. 2008. *Development Macroeconomics.* 3rd ed. Princeton, NJ: Princeton University Press.

Aghion, P. and O. Blanchard. 1994. *On the Speed of Transition in Central Europe.* NBER Macroeconomics Annual. Cambridge.

Agunias, D. R. and K. Newland. 2012. *Developing a Road Map for Engaging Diasporas in Development.* Washington, DC: Migration Policy Institute.

Alexandrov, B. 1949. The Soviet currency reform. *Russian Review,* 8(1): 56–61.

Alexeev, M. and S. Weber. 2013. *The Oxford Handbook of the Russian Economy.* Oxford: Oxford University Press.

Alexeev, M.V. and C.G. Gaddy. 1993. Income distribution in the USSR in the 1980s. *Review of Income and Wealth,* series 39(1): 23–36.

Allen, W.A. and R. Moessner. 2010. Central bank co-operation and international liquidity in the financial crisis of 2008–9. *BIS Working Paper No* 310.

Almond, D. 2006. Is the 1918 influenza pandemic over? Long-term effects of in utero influenza exposure in the post-1940 U.S. population. *Journal of Political Economy,* 114(4): 672–712.

Amsden, A. H. 2003. *The Rise of "The Rest": Challenges to the West from Late-Industrializing Economies.* Oxford University Press.

Amsden, A., J. Kochanowicz, and L. Taylor. 1998. *The Market Meets Its Match: Restructuring the Economies of Eastern Europe.* Cambridge, MA: Harvard University Press.

Arrow, K. 2000. Economic transition: Speed and scope. *Journal of Institutional and Theoretical Economics (JITE)/Zeitschrift für diegesamte Staatswissenschaft,* 156(1): 9–18.

Åslund, A. 2013. Russia's economic transformation. In Alexeev, M. and S. Weber (eds) *The Oxford Handbook of the Russian Economy.* Oxford: Oxford University Press.

Åslund, A., 2007. *How Capitalism Was Built; The Transformation of Central and Eastern Europe, Russia, and Central Asia.* Washington: Peterson Institute for International Economics.

Åslund, A. 1991. Principles of privatization. In L. Csaba (ed.) *Systemic Change and Stabilization in Eastern Europe.* Aldershot: Dartmouth. pp. 17–31.

Åslund, A. 1988. The new Soviet policy towards international economic organizations. *World Today*, 44(2): 27–30.

Åslund, A. and V. Dombrovskis. 2011. *How Latvia Came Through the Financial Crisis.* Washington, DC: Institute of International Economics.

Åslund, A., P. Boone, and S. Johnson. 2001. Escaping the under-reform trap. *IMF Staff Papers*, 48 (Special Issue): 88–108.

Åslund, A., Boone, P., Johnson, S., Fischer, S. and Ickes, B.W. 1996. How to stabilize: Lessons from post-communist countries. *Brookings Papers on Economic Activity*, 27(1): 217–314.

Atoyan, R. 2010. Beyond the crisis: Revisiting emerging Europe's growth model. IMF Working Paper 10/92.

Bacon, E. and M. Sandle (eds). 2002. *Brezhnev Reconsidered.* New York: Palgrave Macmillan.

Bahmani-Oskooee, M. and M. Hajulee. 2010. On the relation between currency depreciation and domestic investment. *Journal of Post Keynesian Economics*, 32(4): 645–660.

Bakker, B. and Klingen (eds). 2012. *How Emerging Europe Came Through the 2008/09 Crisis: An Account by the Staff of the IMF's European Department.* Washington, DC: IMF.

Balcerowicz, L. and A. Gelb. 1995. Macropolicies in Transition to a Market Economy: A Three-Year Perspective. *Proceedings of the World Bank Annual Conference on Development Economics 1994.* Washington, DC: World Bank. pp. 21–44.

Baldwin, R. 2009. *The Great Trade Collapse: Causes, Consequences and Prospects.* London: Centre for Economic Policy Research.

Banerji, A., Saksonovs, S., Lin, H., and R. Blavy. 2014. *Youth Unemployment in Advanced Economies in Europe: Searching for Solutions.* IMF Staff Discussion Note SDN/14/11.

Bang, J.T. and A. Mitra. 2011. Brain drain and institutions of governance: Educational attainment of immigrants to the US 1988–1998. *Economic Systems*, 35: 335–354.

Bank for International Settlements (BIS). 2015. What do new forms of finance mean for EM central banks? *BIS Papers No 83.* Available online: www.bis.org/publ/bppdf/bispap83.htm accessed August 15, 2017.

Barisitz, S. 2009. Banking transformation 1980–2006 in Central and Eastern Europe – from communism to capitalism. *South-Eastern Europe Journal of Economics*, 2: 161–180.

Barisitz, S. 2007. *Banking in Central and Eastern Europe 1980–2006: From Communism to Capitalism.* London: Routledge.

Bavel, Bas van. 2016. *The Invisible Hand? How Market Economies Have Emerged and Declined Since AD 500.* Oxford: Oxford University Press.

Becker, T., D. Daianu, Z. Darvas, V. Gligorov, M. Landesmann, P. Petrovic, J. Pisani-Ferry, D. Rosati, A. Sapir, and B. Weder di Mauro. 2010. Whither Growth in Central and Eastern Europe? Policy Lessons for an Integrated Europe, *Bruegel Blueprint No. 11.*

Berend, I. 2009. *From the Soviet Bloc to the European Union.* Cambridge: Cambridge University Press.

Berend, I. T. 1996. *Central and Eastern Europe, 1944–1993: Detour from the Periphery to the Periphery.* Cambridge: Cambridge University Press.

Berg, A. and J. Sachs. 1992. Structural adjustment and international trade in Eastern Europe: The case of Poland. *Economic Policy*, 14:117–174.

Bernard, L., Gevorkyan, A.V., Palley, T., and W. Semmler. 2014. Time scales and mechanisms of economic cycles: A review of theories of long waves. *Review of Keynesian Economics*, 2(1): 87–107.

Bilandzic, D. 1986. *Jugoslavija Poslieje Tita, 1980–1985.* Zagreb: Globus.

Black, B., R. Kraakman, and A. Tarassova. 2000. Russian privatization and corporate governance: What went wrong? *Stanford Law Review*, 52: 1731–1808.

Blanchard, O. 1997. *The Economics of Post-Communist Transition.* Oxford: Oxford University Press.

Blanchard, O. and M. R. Kremer. 1997. Disorganization. *Quarterly Journal of Economics*, 112(4): 1091–1126.

Blanchard, O., R. Dornbusch, P. Krugman, R. Layard, and L. Summers. 1991. *Reform in Eastern Europe.* Cambridge, MA: MIT Press.

Bloomberg (via Statista). 2017a. Retail value of the luxury goods market worldwide from 2014 to 2019, by region (in million U.S. dollars). www.statista.com/statistics/487381/retail-value-of-the-global-luxury-goods-market-by-region/ (accessed August 26, 2017).

Bloomberg (via Statista). 2017b. Compound annual growth rate (CAGR) of the luxury goods market worldwide between 2014 and 2019, by region. www.statista.com/statistics/487444/cagr-of-the-global-luxury-goods-market-by-region/ (accessed August 26, 2017).

Blum, J. 1971. *Lord and Peasant in Russia: From the 9th to the 19th Century.* Princeton, NJ: Princeton University Press.

BOFIT. 2017. *Weekly Review 2017/28. BOFIT.* Available online: www.bofit.fi/en/monitoring/weekly/2017/vw201728_2/.

Bokovoy, M.K., J.A. Irvine, and C. S. Lilly. 1997. *State-Society Relations in Yugoslavia, 1945–1992.* New York: Palgrave Macmillan.

Bokros, L. 2002. Financial sector development in Central and Eastern Europe. In Winkler, A. (ed.) *Banking and Monetary Policy in Eastern Europe: The First Ten Years.* New York: Palgrave MacMillan. pp. 11–40.

Boly, A., N.D. Coniglio, F. Prota, and A. Seric. 2014. Diaspora investments and firm export performance in selected sub-Saharan African countries. *World Development,* 59: 422–433.

Bonin, J.P., K. Mizsei, I. P. Szekely, and P. Wachtel. 1998. *Banking in Transition Economies Developing Market Oriented Banking Sectors in Eastern Europe.* Edward Elgar.

Bornstein, M. 1997. Non-standard methods in the privatization strategies of the Czech Republic, Hungary and Poland. *Economics of Transition,* 5(2).

Bornstein, M. 1961. The reform and revaluation of the ruble. *American Economic Review,* 51(1): 117–123.

Borodkin, L., B. Granville, and C.S. Leonard. 2008. The rural/urban wage gap in the industrialization of Russia, 1884–1910. *European Review of Economic History,* 12: 67–95.

Boughton, J.M. 2012. *Tearing Down Walls: The international Monetary Fund 1990–1999.* Washington, DC: IMF. Available online: www.imf.org/external/pubs/ft/history/2012/index.htm.

Boughton, J.M. 2001. *Silent Revolution: The International Monetary Fund 1979–1989.* Washington, DC: IMF. Available online: www.imf.org/external/pubs/ft/history/2001/.

Boycko, M. 1992. When higher incomes reduce welfare: Queues, labor supply and macroeconomic equilibrium in socialist economies. *Quarterly Journal of Economics,* 107: 907–920.

Brada, J. 1988. Interpreting the Soviet subsidization of Eastern Europe. *International Organization,* 42(4): 639–58.

Brahmbhatt, M., O. Canuto, and E. Vostroknutova. 2010. Natural resources and development strategy after the crisis. In O. Canuto and M. Giugale (eds) *The Day after Tomorrow: A Handbook on the Future of Economic Policies in the Developing World.* Washington, DC: World Bank.

Brandt, L. and T.G. Rawski. 2008. *China's Great Economic Transformation.* Cambridge: Cambridge University Press.

Brenke K. 2014. Eastern Germany still playing economic catch-up. *DIW Berlin—Deutsches Institut Economic Bulletin,* 4(11): 6–23.

Brown, A. 2009. *The Rise and Fall of Communism.* London: The Bodley Head.

Brown, M. and H. Stix. 2014. The Euroization of Bank Deposits in Eastern Europe. *Swiss Institute of Banking and Finance. Working Papers on Finance No. 2014/12.* Available online: https://papers.ssrn.com/sol3/papers.cfm?abstract_id=2551729 (accessed August 20, 2017).

Bruno, M. 1992. Stabilization and reform in Eastern Europe: A preliminary evaluation. *International Monetary Fund Staff Papers,* 39(4): 741–777.

Brus, W. 1990. Market socialism. In Eatwell, J., M. Milgate, and P. Newman (eds) *Problems of the Planned Economy.* New York and London: W. W. Norton & Co.

Brus, W. 1986a. Postwar reconstruction and socio-economic transformation. In M.C. Kaser and E.A. Radice (eds) *The Economic History of Eastern Europe 1919–1975, Vol. II.* Oxford: Clarendon Press. pp. 564–641.

Brus, W. 1986b. 1953 to 1956: the 'thaw' and the 'new course.' In M.C. Kaser and E.A. Radice (eds) *The Economic History of Eastern Europe 1919–1975, Vol. III*. Oxford: Clarendon Press. pp. 40–69.

Brus, W. 1986c. 1966 to 1975: Normalization and conflict. In M.C. Kaser (ed.) *The Economic History of Eastern Europe 1919–1975, Vol. III*. Oxford: Clarendon Press. pp. 139–249.

Buckley, N. 2017. Russian agriculture sector flourishes amid sanctions. Financial Times online edition (April 19): www.ft.com/content/422a8252-2443-11e7-8691-d5f7e0cd0a16.

Bukharin, N. 1925. O novoj ekonomicheskoj politike i nashikh zadachakh [On the New Economic Policy and Tasks Before Us]. Report to the Moscow Party activist organization (April 17, 1925). Available in Russian online: www.magister.msk.ru/library/politica/buharin/buhan008.htm.

Calvo, G.A. and F. Coricelli. 1993. Output Collapse in Eastern Europe: The Role of Credit. *Staff Papers – International Monetary Fund*, 40(1): 32–52.

Campbell, D'A. 1993. The World War II experience in the United States, Great Britain, Germany, and the Soviet Union. *The Journal of Military History*, 57(2): 301–323.

Canuto. O. and A.V. Gevorkyan. 2016. Tales of Emerging Markets. Huffington Post (Aug 6). Available online: www.huffingtonpost.com/otaviano-canuto/tales-of-emerging-markets_b_11367712.html.

Canuto, O. and M. Cavallari. 2012. Natural Capital and the Resource Curse. *Economic Premise; No. 83 (May)*. Washington, DC: World Bank.

Case, A. 2004. Does money protect health status? Evidence from South African pensions. In D. Wise (ed.) *Perspectives on the Economics of Aging*. Chicago, IL: University of Chicago Press. pp. 287–312.

Case and C. Paxson. 2010. Causes and consequences of early-life health. *Demography*, supplement to 47(1): S65–S85.

Cassimon, D., Essers, D., and K. Verbeke. 2016. The changing face of Rwanda's public debt. *Working Paper #14*. Belgian Policy Research Group on Financing and Development.

Central Bank of Russia (CBR). 2017. Foreign Currency Market database. Available online: www.cbr.ru.

Chami, R., A. Barajas, T. Cosimano, C. Fullenkamp, M. Gapen, and P. Montiel. 2008. *Macroeconomic Consequences of Remittances*. Washington, DC: International Monetary Fund.

Chander, A. 2001. Diaspora bonds. *New York University Law Review*, 76: 1005–1099.

Chenery, H. B. 1975. The structuralist approach to development policy. *American Economic Review*, 65(2): 310–316.

Chernyshevsky, N.G. 1886. *What is to be Done?* New York: Thomas Y. Crowell & Co. (English translation; Russian original published in 1863). Available online: https://archive.org/details/cu31924096961036.

Chobanyan, A., and Leigh, L. 2006. The competitive advantages of nations. Applying the Diamond model to Armenia. *International Journal of Emerging Markets*, 1(2): 147–164.

Connolly, R. 2013. *The Economic Sources of Social Order Development in Post-Socialist Eastern Europe*. Abingdon: Routledge.

Conquest, R. 2008. *The Great Terror: A Reassessment*. Oxford University Press.

Crump, L. 2015. *The Warsaw Pact Reconsidered: International Relations in Eastern Europe, 1955–1969*. Oxford: Routledge.

Cull, R. and M. S. Martinez Peria. 2013. Bank ownership and lending patterns during the 2008–2009 financial crisis: Evidence from Latin America and Eastern Europe. *Journal of Banking & Finance*, 37(12): 4861–4878.

Dabrowski, M. 2015. It's not just Russia: Currency crises in the Commonwealth of Independent States. *Bruegel Policy Contribution*, Issue 2015/01.

Dale, G. 2011. *First the Transition, then the Crash*. London: Pluto Press.

Davies, R.W. 1998. *Soviet Economic Development from Lenin to Khrushchev*. Cambridge: Cambridge University Press.

Davies, R.W. 1991. *From Tsarism to the New Economic Policy: Continuity and Change in the Economy of the USSR*. Ithaca, NY: Cornell University Press.

Davies, R.W. 1980. *The Socialist Offensive: The Collectivization of Soviet Agriculture*. London: Macmillan.

De Haas, R. and N. Van Horen. 2013, Running for the exit? International bank lending during a financial crisis. *Review of Financial Studies*, 26(1): 244–85.

Demoskop Weekly. 2014. Pervaya vseobwaya perepis' naseleniya Rossijskoj Imperii, 1897g. (First general population census of the Russian Empire, 1897) Available online: http://demoscope.ru/weekly/ssp/rus_sos_97.php?reg=0 (accessed: September 6, 2014).

Desai, P. 1986. Is the Soviet Union subsidizing Eastern Europe? *European Economic Review*, 30(1): 107–116.

Dewatripont, M. and G. Roland. 1996. Transition as a process of large-scale institutional change. *Economics of Transition*, 4(1): 1–30.

Dewatripont, M. and G. Roland. 1995. The design of reform packages under uncertainty. *American Economic Review*, 85: 1207–1223.

Dewatripont, M. and G. Roland. 1992a. Economic reform and dynamic political constraints. *Review of Economic Studies*, 59: 703–730.

Dewatripont, M. and G. Roland. 1992b. The virtues of gradualism and legitimacy in the transition to a market economy. *Economic Journal*, 102: 291–300.

Djankov, S., Nikolova, E., and J. Zilinsky. 2016. The happiness gap in Eastern Europe. *Journal of Comparative Economics*, 44(1): 108–124.

Djankov, S. and P. Murrell. 2002. Enterprise restructuring in transition: A quantitative survey. *Journal of Economic Literature*, 40(3): 739–792.

Dreger, C., J. Fidrmuc, K. Kholodilin, and D. Ulbricht. 2015. The ruble between the hammer and the anvil: Oil prices and economic sanctions. *BOFIT Discussion Papers 25/2015*.

Duflo, E. 2003. Grandmothers and granddaughters: Old-age pensions and intrahousehold allocation in South Africa. *World Bank Economic Review*, 17(1): 1–25.

Durgin, F. Jr. 1962. The Virgin Lands Programme 1954–1960. *Soviet Studies*, 13(3): 255–280.

Dutta, S., T. Geiger, and B. Lavin. 2015. *The Global Information Technology Report 2015.* Geneva: World Economic Forum.

Eichengreen, B. 2008. *The European Economy since 1945: Coordinated Capitalism and Beyond.* Princeton, NJ: Princeton University Press.

Eichler, G. 1986. The debt crisis: A schematic view of rescheduling in Eastern Europe. In *East European Economies: Slow Growth in the 1980s, Vol. 2, Foreign Trade and International Finance*, Selected Papers Submitted to the Joint Economic Committee, Congress of the United States, March 28. pp. 192–209.

Ellman, M. 1990. Socialist planning. In Eatwell, J., M. Milgate, and P. Newman (eds) *Problems of Planned Economy*. New York: W.W. Norton & Co. pp. 13–21.

Elrich, A. 1967. *The Soviet Industrialization Debate, 1924–1928.* Cambridge, MA: Harvard University Press.

Emmott, R. and G. Baczynska. 2016. Italy, Hungary say no automatic renewal of Russia sanctions. Reuters (March 14). Available online: http://uk.reuters.com/article/uk-ukraine-crisis-eu-idUKKCN0WG1B4.

Ericson, R. 1991. The classical Soviet-type economy: Nature of the system and imlications for reform. *The Journal of Economic Perspectives*, 5(4): 11–27.

Estrin, S. 1991. Yugoslavia: The case of self-managing market socialism. *The Journal of Economic Perspectives*, 5(4): 187–194.

Estrin, S., J. Hanousek, E. Kocenda, and J. Svenjar. 2009. The effects of privatization and ownership in transition economies. *Journal of Economic Literature*, 47(3): 1–30.

European Bank for Reconstruction and Development (EBRD). 2017. *Economic Data.* Available online: www.ebrd.com/what-we-do/economic-research-and-data/data.html

European Bank for Reconstruction and Development (EBRD). 2016. *Transition Report 2016–2017: Transition for all: Equal opportunities in an unequal world.* London: EBRD.

European Bank for Reconstruction and Development (EBRD). 2015. *Transition Report 2015–2016: Rebalancing finance.* London: EBRD.

European Bank for Reconstruction and Development (EBRD). 2010. *Transition Report 2010: Recovery and reform.* London: EBRD.

European Bank for Reconstruction and Development (EBRD) 2009. *Transition Report 2009: Transition in crisis?* London: EBRD.

European Bank for Reconstruction and Development (EBRD). 2008. *Transition Report 2008: Growth in transition.* London: EBRD.

European Bank for Reconstruction and Development (EBRD). 2004. *Transition Report 2004: Infrastructure.* London: EBRD.

European Bank for Reconstruction and Development (EBRD). 2003. *Transition Report 2003: Integration and regional cooperation.* London: EBRD.

European Bank for Reconstruction and Development (EBRD). 2002. *Transition Report 2002: Agriculture and rural transition.* London: EBRD.

European Bank for Reconstruction and Development (EBRD). 2001. *Transition Report 2001: Energy in transition.* London: EBRD.

European Bank for Reconstruction and Development (EBRD). 2000. *Transition Report 2000: Employment, skills, and transition.* London: EBRD.

European Bank for Reconstruction and Development (EBRD). 1999. *Transition Report 1999: Ten years of transition.* London: EBRD.

Faryna, O. 2016. Exchange rate pass-through and cross-country spillovers: Some evidence from Ukraine and Russia. BOFIT Discussion Papers 14/2016.

Ferreira, F., D. Jolliffe, and E. Pryoz. 2015. The international poverty line has just been raised to $1.90 a day, but global poverty is basically unchanged. How is that even possible? The World Bank Blog. Available online: http://blogs.worldbank.org/developmenttalk/international-poverty-line-has-just-been-raised-190-day-global-poverty-basically-unchanged-how-even.

Fischer, S. 1994. Russia and the Soviet Union then and now. In Blanchard, O. J., K.A. Froot, and J. D. Sachs (eds) *The Transition in Eastern Europe, Vol. I.* Chicago, IL: University of Chicago Press.

Fischer, S. and A. Gelb. 1991. The process of socialist economic transformation. *The Journal of Economic Perspectives,* 5(4): 91–105.

Foley, D. 1986. *Understanding Capital: Marx's Economic Theory.* Cambridge, MA: Harvard University Press.

Foreign Trade Statistics. 1991. *Foreign Economic Relations of the USSR in 1990. [Vneshnie ekonomicheskie svyazi SSSR v 1990 g. Statisticheskij sbornik].* Moscow: Finansy i Statistika.

Foreign Trade Statistics. 1987. *Foreign Trade of the USSR in 1986. Statistical compilation. [Vneshnya torgovlya SSSR v 1986 g. Statisticheskij sbornik].* Moscow: Finansy i Statistika.

Foreign Trade Statistics. 1982. *Foreign Trade of the USSR for 1922–1981. [Vneshnya torgovlya SSSR 1921–1981].* Moscow: Finansy i Statistika.

Freinkman, L. 2001. Role of the diasporas in transition economies: Lessons from Armenia. Paper presented at the 11th annual meeting of the ASCE. Retrieved from http://papers.ssrn.com/sol3/papers.cfm?abstract_id=2401447/.

Fries, S. and A. Taci. 2002. Banking reform and development in transition economies. European Bank for Reconstruction and Development. Working paper No. 71.

Frydman, R. and A. Rapaczynski. 1994. *Privatization in Eastern Europe: Is the State Withering Away?* London: Central European University Press.

Fukuyama, F.1993. The modernizing imperative. *The National Interest,* 31: 10–18.

Gaidar, Y. 2012. *Russia: A Long View.* (trans. Antonina W. Bouis). Cambridge, MA: MIT Press.

Gaidar, Y. 2003. The inevitability of collapse of the socialist economy. In Gaidar, Y. (ed.) *The Economics of Russian Transition.* Cambridge, MA: MIT Press.

Garcia-Kilroy, C. and A. C. Silva. 2016. Post-crisis lessons for EME capital markets. In A.V. Gevorkyan and O. Canuto (eds) *Financial Deepening and Post-Crisis Development in Emerging Markets: Current Perils and Future Dawns.* New York: Palgrave MacMillan.

Geraschenko, V., O. Lavrushin, and A. Kazantsev. 1982. *Organizatsiya i Planirovanie Kredita (Organization and Planing of Credit).* Moscow: Finansy i statistika.

German Agency for International Cooperation (GIZ) 2011. Current situation of the diaspora connected FDIs in Armenia. Yerevan: GIZ Private Sector Development Program South Caucasus.

German Agency for International Cooperation (GIZ) 2012. The Georgian diaspora study. Tbilisi: GIZ Private Sector Development Program South Caucasus.

Gerschenkron, A. 1962. *Economic Backwardness in Historical Perspective.* Cambridge, MA: Belknap Press of Harvard University Press.

Gerschenkron, A. 1952. An economic history of Russia. *The Journal of Economic History*, 12(2): 146–159.

Gerschenkron, A. 1947. The rate of growth in Russia: The rate of industrial growth in Russia, since 1885. *The Journal of Economic History*, 7 (Supplement: Economic Growth: A Symposium): 144–174.

Getty, J.A., G. T. Rittersporn, and V. N. Zemskov. 1993. Victims of the Soviet penal system in the pre-war years: A first approach on the basis of archival evidence. *The American Historical Review*, 98(4): 1017–1049.

Gevorkyan, A.V. 2017. The foreign exchange regime in a small open economy: Armenia and beyond. *Journal of Economic Studies*, 44(5): 781–800.

Gevorkyan, A.V. 2016. Development through Diversity: Engaging Armenia's New and Old Diaspora. *Migration Information Source* (March 23): www.migrationpolicy.org/article/development-through-diversity-engaging-armenias-new-and-old-diaspora.

Gevorkyan, A.V. 2015. The legends of the Caucasus: Economic transformation of Armenia and Georgia. *International Business Review*, 24(6): 1009–1024.

Gevorkyan, A. V. 2013a. Russia's economic diversification potential: The untold story? *International Business: Research, Teaching and Practice*, 7(1): 9–33.

Gevorkyan, A.V. 2013b. Armenian diaspora. In I. Ness and P. Bellwood (eds) *The Encyclopedia of Global Human Migration.* Oxford: J. Wiley & Sons; Blackwell.

Gevorkyan, A.V. 2013c. Russia – industry profile: Information technology. In *Encyclopedia of Emerging Markets.* 1st ed. Farmington Hills, MI: Gale, Cengage Learning: 316–322.

Gevorkyan, A.V. 2012. Is Russia still a BRIC? Some observations on the economy and its potential for diversification. *Challenge*, 55(6): 88–116.

Gevorkyan, A.V. 2011. *Innovative Fiscal Policy and Economic Development in Transition Economies.* Oxford: Routledge.

Gevorkyan, A.V. 2007. Voprosy regulirovaniya vremennoj trudovoj migracii. (On regulation of temporary labor migration). *Voprosy Ekonomiki*, 9: 147–149.

Gevorkyan, A. V. and Kvangraven, I. H. 2016. Assessing recent determinants of borrowing costs in Sub-Saharan Africa. *Review of Development Economics*, 20(4): 721–738.

Gevorkyan, A. and W. Semmler. 2016. Macroeconomic variables and the sovereign risk premia in EMU, non-EMU EU, and developed countries. *Empirica*, 43(1): 1–35.

Gevorkyan, A.V. and O. Canuto. 2015. *Toward a migration development bank for transition economies.* Huffington Post (June 2). Available online: http://tinyurl.com/pq7okdb.

Gevorkyan, A.V. and A. Gevorkyan. 2012. Factoring turbulence out: Diaspora regulatory mechanism and Migration Development Bank. *International Migration*, 50(1): 96–112.

Gevorkyan, A.V., Ar.V. Gevorkyan, and K. Mashuryan. 2008. Little job growth makes labor migration and remittances the norm in post-Soviet Armenia. Migration Information Source: www.migrationinformation.org/Feature/display.cfm?id=676.

Gilman, M. 2010. *No Precedent, No Plan. Inside Russia's 1998 Default.* Cambridge, MA: MIT Press.

Goldsmith, R. 1961. The economic growth of tsarist Russia, 1860–1913, *Economic Development and Cultural Change*, 9(3): 441–475.

Gomulka, S. 1992. Polish economic reform, 1990–91: Principles, policies and outcomes. *Cambridge Journal of Economics*, 16(3): 355–372.

Gorbachev, M. 1987. *Perestroika: New Thinking for Our Country and the World.* New York: Harper & Row Publishers.

Grand, J. le. and S. Estrin. 1989. *Market Socialism.* New York: Oxford University Press.

Granville, J. 2004. *The First Domino: International Decision Making During the Hungarian Crisis of 1956.* College Station, TX: Texas A&M University Press.

Gregory, P. 1994. *Before Command.* Princeton, NJ: Princeton University Press.

Gregory, P. R. and R. C. Stuart. 1986. *Soviet Economic Structure and Performance.* New York: Harper & Row.

Grossbongardt, H. 2015. Russia sanctions stall Europe's business aviation market. Aviation Week Network (May 5). Available online: http://aviationweek.com/ebace-2015/russia-sanctions-stall-europes-business-aviation-market.

Grossman, G.1990. Command economy. In Eatwell, J., M. Milgate, and P. Newman (eds.) *Problems of Planned Economy.* New York: W.W. Norton & Co. pp. 58–62.

Gvozdetskij, V.L. 2005. Plan GOERLO. Mify i Real'nost' [The GOERLO Plan: Myths and Reality], *Nauka i Zhizn'*, Vol. 5. Available online: www.nkj.ru/archive/articles/5906/.

Hall, P.A. and K. Thelen. 2009. Institutional change in varieties of capitalism. *Socio-Economic Review*, 7: 7–34.

Hall, P. A. and D. Soskice (eds). 2001. *Varieties of Capitalism: The Institutional Foundations of Comparative Advantage.* Oxford: Oxford University Press.

Hamilton, F.E.I., K.D. Andrews, and N. Pichler-Milanovic. 2005. *Transformation of Cities in Central and Eastern Europe: Towards Globalization.* New York: United Nations University Press.

Hare, P. 2013. Institutions and transition: Lessons and surprises. *Society and Economy*, 35(1): 1–24.

Hare, P. 2001. Institutional change and economic performance in the transition economies. Paper prepared for the UNECE Spring Seminar, Geneva.

Harrison, H. 2014. Untangling 5 myths about the Berlin Wall. *Chicago Tribune* (Nov 2). www.chicagotribune.com/news/opinion/commentary/ct-myths-berlin-wall-fall-reagan-east-west-perspec-1102-20141031-story.html#page=1.

Harrison, H. M. 2003. *Driving the Soviets up the Wall: Soviet-East German Relations, 1953–1961.* Princeton, NJ: Princeton University Press.

Harrison, M. 2011. The Soviet Union after 1945: Economic recovery and political repression. *Past & Present*, 210(6): 103–120.

Harrison, M. 2008. Prices in the Politburo, 1927: Market equilibrium versus the use of force. In Gregory, P. and N. Naimark (eds) *The Lost Politburo Transcripts.* New Haven, CT: Yale University Press.

Harrison, M. 2002. Economic growth and slowdown. In Bacon, E. and M. Sandle (eds) *Brezhnev Reconsidered.* New York: Palgrave Macmillan. pp. 38–67.

Harrison, M. 1996. *Accounting for War: Soviet Production, Employment, and the Defence Burden, 1940–1945.* Cambridge: Cambridge University Press.

Harrison, M. 1991. The peasantry and industrialization. In R.W. Davies (ed.) *From Tsarism to the New Economic Policy: Continuity and Change in the Economy of the USSR.* Ithaca, NY: Cornell University Press. pp. 104–126.

Harrison, M. 1985. *Soviet Planning in Peace and War, 1938–1945.* Cambridge: Cambridge University Press.

Harrison, M. 1980. Why did NEP fail? *Economics of Planning*, 16(2): 57–67.

Harvey, D. 2012. *Rebel Cities: From the Right to the City to the Urban Revolution.* Brooklyn, NY: Verso.

Havrylyshyn, O. 2013. Is the transition over? A definition and some measurements. In Hare, P. and G. Turley (eds) *Handbook of the Economics and Political Economy of Transition.* London: Routledge.

Havrylyshyn, O. 2007. Fifteen years of transformation in the post-communist world: Rapid reformers outperformed gradualists. *CATO Institute Development Policy Analysis No.4.*

Havrylyshyn, O. and R. van Rooden. 2003. Institutions matter in transition, but so do policies. *Comparative Economic Studies*, 45(1): 2–24.

Havrylyshyn, O. and T. Wolf. 1999. Determinants of growth in transition countries. *Finance and Development*, 36(2): 12–15.

Hayek, F.A. 2007. *The Road to Serfdom: Text and Documents.* Chicago, IL: University of Chicago Press. Available online: https://mises.org/library/road-serfdom-0.

Hayek, F. von (ed.). 1935. *Collectivist Economic Planning: Critical Studies on the Possibilities of Socialism.* London: Routledge & Sons.

Heleniak, T. 2013. Diasporas and development in post-communist Eurasia. Migration Information Source. Retrieved from www.migrationpolicy.org/article/diasporas-and-development-post-communist-eurasia/.

Heleniak, T. 2011. Harnessing the diaspora for development in Europe and Central Asia. MIRPAL Discussion Series. Washington, DC: World Bank.

Henig, D. and N. Makovicky (eds). 2017. *Economies of Favour after Socialism.* Oxford: Oxford University Press.

Hernandez-Cata, E. 1997. Liberalization and the behavior of output during the transition from plan to market. *IMF Staff Papers,* 44(4): 405–429.

Hewett, E.A. 1988. *Reforming the Soviet Economy: Equality Versus Efficiency.* Washington, DC: Brookings Institution.

Hewett, E. A. 1974. *Foreign Trade Prices in the Council for Mutual Economic Assistance.* Cambridge: Cambridge University Press.

Hille, K. 2017. Back to the land: Russia's farming transformation. Financial Times online edition (August 11): www.ft.com/content/b5115324-7c8e-11e7-ab01-a13271d1ee9c#comments.

Holzman, F. 1991. Moving toward ruble convertibility. *Comparative Economic Studies,* 33(3): 3–64.

Hovannisian, R. 1971. *The Republic of Armenia, Vol. 1.* Los Angeles, CA: University of California Press.

IAEA. 2006. *The Chernobyl Forum: 2003–2005.* Austria: International Atomic Energy Agency.

Ickes, B. W. 2001. Dimensions of transition in Russia. In Granville, B. and P. Oppenheimer (eds) *The Russian Economy in the 1990s.* Oxford: Oxford University Press.

Impavido, G., H. Rudolph, and L. Ruggerone. 2013. Bank Funding in Central, Eastern and South Eastern Europe Post Lehman: a "New Normal"? *IMF Working paper 13/148.* Washington, DC: International Monetary Fund.

Institute of International Finance (IIF). 2016. July 2016 EM Portfolio Flows Tracker and Flows Alert. Available online: www.iif.com/publication/portfolio-flows-tracker/july-2016-em-portfolio-flows-tracker-and-flows-alert.

International Labour Organization (ILO). 2017. ILO Stat. Available online: www.ilo.org/global/lang—en/index.htm.

International Monetary Fund (IMF). 2017. IMF's Primary Commodity Prices database. Available online: www.imf.org/external/np/res/commod/index.aspx.

International Monetary Fund (IMF WEO). 2017. *IMF World Economic Outlook (2017).* Washington, DC: IMF.

International Monetary Fund (IMF Direction of Trade). 2017. IMF Data. Available online: www.imf.org/en/Data.

International Monetary Fund (IMF). 2013. *Financing Future Growth: The Evolving Role of the Banking System in CESEE.* Washington, DC: International Monetary Fund.

International Monetary Fund (IMF). 1999. *Russian Federation: Recent Economic Developments.* IMF Staff Country Report 99/100.

Jackson, G. and R. Deeg. 2008. Comparing capitalisms: Understanding institutional diversity and its implications for international business. *Journal of International Business Studies,* 39(4): 540–561.

Janos, A. 1996. What was communism: A retrospective in comparative analysis. *Communist and Post-Communist Studies,* 29(1): 1–24.

Johnson, N. and G. Sharenow. 2013. Is the Commodity Supercycle Dead? PIMCO Viewpoint Paper (September), Newport Beach, CA. Available online at: www.pimco.com.

Kaczmarczyk, P. and M. Okólski. 2005. International migration in Central and Eastern Europe: Current and future trends. Paper presented at the United Nations expert group meeting on international migration and development, New York, 6–8 July. Available online: www.un.org/esa/population/migration/turin/Symposium_Turin_files/P12_Kaczmarczyk&Okolski.pdf (accessed July 10, 2017).

Kalotay, K. and G. Hunya. 2000. Privatization and FDI in Central and Eastern Europe. *Transnational Corporations,* 9(1): 39–66.

Kal'yanov A. and G. Sidorov. 2004. Kak prozhit' v Rossii? (How to Live in Russia?). Tula, Russia: Tula State Pedagogical University.

Kennan, G. F. 1947. The Sources of Soviet Conduct, (originally published under pseudonym "X"), Foreign Affairs (July): 852–868. On the Truman Doctrine see, for example, History Channel's online summary available: www.history.com/this-day-in-history/truman-doctrine-is-announced.

Keohane, D. 2011. Goldman Sachs: BRICs in 2050. FT.com, December 7. Available online: www.ft.com/content/937ba4d9-563b-3a69-b6b7-2b339dea124c#axzz1i17iiZ8z/.

Ketkar, S. and D. Ratha. 2010. Diaspora bonds: Tapping the diaspora during difficult times. *Journal of International Commerce, Economics and Policy*, 1(2): 251–263.

Khemraj, T. and S. Pasha. 2012. Analysis of an unannounced foreign exchange regime change. *Economic Systems*, 36:145–157.

Khrushchev, N. 1956. Secret Speech Delivered by First Party Secretary at the Twentieth Party Congress of the Communist Party of the Soviet Union, February 25, 1956. Full text in English available: http://legacy.fordham.edu/halsall/mod/1956khrushchev-secret1.html.

Kirby, P., L. Gibbons, M. Cronin. 2002. *Reinventing Ireland: Culture, Society, and the Global Economy.* London: Pluto Press.

Kolodkog, G. 2007. The great post-communist change and uncertain future of the world. In Estrin, S., G. W. Kolodko, and M. Uvalic (eds) *Transition and Beyond: Essays in Honor of Mario Nuti.* New York: Palgrave MacMillan. pp. 278–297.

Kontorovich, V. 1993. The economic fallacy. *The National Interest*, 31: 35–45.

Kontorovich, V. 1986. Discipline and growth in the Soviet economy. *Problems of Communism*, 34(6): 18–31.

Kornai, J. 2001. The Role of the State in a Post-Socialist Economy. Leon Koźmiński Academy of Entrepreneurship and Management (WSPiZ) and TIGER, Distinguished Lectures Series n. 6. Available online: www.tiger.edu.pl/publikacje/dist/kornai.pdf.

Kornai, J. 2000. Making the transition to private ownership. *Finance & Development*, 37(3). Online: www.imf.org/external/pubs/ft/fandd/2000/09/index.htm.

Kornai, J. 1994. Transformational recession: The main causes. *Journal of Comparative Economics*, 19(1): 39–63.

Kornai, J. 1992. *The Socialist System: The Political Economy of Communism.* Oxford: Oxford University Press.

Kornai, J. 1991. *The Road to a Free Economy: Shifting from a Socialist System—The Example of Hungary.* New York: W. W. Norton & Company.

Kornai, J. 1990. *The Road to a Free Economy. Shifting from a Socialist System. The Example of Hungary.* New York: W. W. Norton & Company.

Kornai, J. 1979a. Resource-constrained versus demand-constrained systems. *Econometrica*, 47(4): 801–819.

Kornai, J. 1979b. *Economics of Shortage.* Amsterdam: North Holland Press.

Kornai, J., E. Maskin and G. Roland. 2003. Understanding the soft budget constraint. *Journal of Economic Literature*, 41(4): 1095–1136.

Kotz, D.M. and F. Weir. 2007. *Russia's Path from Gorbachev to Putin: The Demise of the Soviet System and the New Russia.* London: Routledge.

Kotz, D. and F. Weir. 1997. *Revolution From Above: The Demise of the Soviet System.* Oxford: Routledge.

Kowalik, T. 1990. Central planning. In Eatwell, J., M. Milgate, and P. Newman (eds) *Problems of Planned Economy.* New York: W.W. Norton & Co. pp. 42–50.

Kuriakose, S. 2013. *Fostering Entrepreneurship in Armenia.* Washington, DC: World Bank.

Laeven, L. and F. Valencia. 2013. Systemic banking crises database. *IMF Economic Review*, 61(2): 225–270.

Laeven, L. and F. Valencia. 2008. Systemic banking crises: A new database. *IMF Working Paper No. 08/224.*

Lampe, J.R., Prickett, R.O., and Adamovic, L.S. 1990. *Yugoslav–American Economic Relations Since World War II.* Durham, NC: Duke University Press.

Lane, D. 2007. Post-state socialism: A diversity of capitalisms? In D. Lane and M. Myant (eds) *Varieties of Capitalism in Post-Communist Countries.* New York, NY: Palgrave MacMillan.

Lange, O.1936. On the economic theory of socialism. *Review of Economic Studies*, 4(2) 331–347.

Lapidus, G. 1991. State and society: Towards emergence of civil society in the Soviet Union. In Dallin, A. and G. Lapidus (eds). *The Soviet System in Crisis: A Reader of Western and Soviet Views.* Boulder: Westview Press. pp. 130–150.

Latsis, O. 1988. The problem of the rate of growth in socialist construction. *Problems of Economic Transition*, 31(4): 73–95.

Lavigne, M. 1999. *The Economics of Transition: From Socialist Economy to Market Economy.* 2nd ed. New York: Palgrave MacMillan.

Lees, L. M. 2010. *Keeping Tito Afloat: The United States, Yugoslavia, and the Cold War, 1945–1960.* University Park, PA: The Pennsylvania State University Press. p. 234.

Lenin, V.I. 1921 (1965). Novaya ekonomicheskaya politika i zadachi politprosvetov [The New Economic Policy and the tasks of the Political Education Departments]. *Lenin's Collected Works*, 2nd English Ed. Moscow: Progress Publishers. Vol. 33: 60–79.

Lenin, V.I. 1911 [1974]. "The Peasant Reform" and the Proletarian-Peasant Revolution. In *Lenin's Collected Works*, Vol. 17, pp. 119–128. Moscow: Progress Publishers. Available online: www.marxists.org/archive/lenin/works/1911/mar/19.htm.

Lewis, A. W. 1954. Economic development with unlimited supplies of labour. *The Manchester School*, 22(2): 139–191.

Linz, S.J. (ed.). 1985. *The Impact of World War II on the Soviet Union.* Totowa, NJ: Rowman & Allanheld.

Lipton, D. and J. Sachs. 1990a. Creating a market economy in Eastern Europe: The case of Poland. *Brookings Papers on Economic Activity*, 1990(1): 75–147.

Lipton, D. and J. Sachs. 1990b. Privatization in Eastern Europe: The Case of Poland. *Brookings Papers on Economic Activity*, 2: 293–341.

List, F. 1841. *The National System of Political Economy.* Various editions.

Litwack, L.F. 1980. *Been in the Storm So Long: The Aftermath of Slavery.* New York: First Vintage Books Edition.

Litwack, J. and Y. Qian. 1998. Balanced or unbalanced development: Special economic zones as catalysts for transition. *Journal of Comparative Economics*, 26(1): 117–141.

Llaudes, R., F. Salman, M. Chivakul. 2010. The impact of the great recession on emerging markets. *IMF Working Paper 10/237.*

Loth, W. 2004. The origins of Stalin's note of 10 March 1952. *Cold War History*, 4(2): 66–88.

Luca, A. and I. Petrova. 2008. What drives credit dollarization in transition economies? *Journal of Banking & Finance*, 32(5): 858–869.

The Maddison Project. 2013. The Maddison Project online database. Available online: www.ggdc.net/maddison/maddison-project/home.htm.

Marangos, J. 2004a. A post-Keynesian approach to the transition process. *Eastern Economic Journal*, 30(3): 441–445.

Marangos, J. 2004b. *Alternative Economic Models of Transition.* Burlington, VT: Ashgate.

Marelli, E. and M. Signorelli (eds). 2010. *Economic Growth and Structural Features of Transition.* New York: Palgrave Macmillan.

Marrese, M. and J. Vanous. 1983. *Soviet Subsidization of Trade with Eastern Europe: A Soviet Perspective.* Berkeley: University of California, Institute of International Studies.

Marx, K. 1867 [2003]. *Capital: A Critique of Political Economy, Vol.1, The Process of Capitalist Production.* Reprint. New York: International Publishers.

Marx, K. and F. Engels. 1985. *Collected Works, Vol. 41.* New York: International Publishers.

Maskin, E. 1996. Theories of the soft budget-constraint. *Japan and the World Economy*, 8: 125–133.

Mau, V. 2003. The logic and nature of the Soviet economic crisis. In Gaidar, Y. (ed.) *The Economics of Russian Transition.* Cambridge, MA: MIT Press.

Mau, V. 1996. *The Political History of Economic Reform in Russia 1985–1994.* London: CRCE.

McCarthy, D.J. and S. Puffer. 2016. Institutional voids in an emerging economy from problem to opportunity. *Journal of Leadership & Organizational Studies*, 23(2): 208–219.

McCarthy, D.J., Puffer, S., and A. Naumov. 1997. Partnering with Russia's new entrepreneurs: Software Tsarina Olga Kirova. *European Management Journal*, 15(6): 648–657.

McGregor, J.A. 2014. Sentimentality or speculation? Diaspora investment, crisis economies and urban transformation. *Geoforum*, 56: 172–181.

McKinnon, R. 1991. *The Order of Economic Liberalization.* Baltimore: John Hopkins University Press.

McMillan, J. and B. Naughton. 1992. How to reform a planned economy: lessons from China. *Oxford Review of Economic Policy,* 8: 130–143.

Medetsky, A. 2016. Russia becomes a grain superpower as wheat exports explode. Bloomberg (Oct 6). Available online: www.bloomberg.com/news/articles/2016-10-06/russia-upends-world-wheat-market-with-record-harvest-exports.

Medvedev, R. 2008. *Sovetskij Souz. Poslednie gody zhizni. Konets sovetskoj imperii (Soviet Union. Last years of life. The end of the Soviet empire).* In Russian. Moscow: AST.

Metcalfe, B.D. and M. Afanassieva. 2005. Gender, work, and equal opportunities in Central and Eastern Europe. *Women in Management Review,* 20(6): 397–411.

Mikaelian, H. 2016. *Shadow Economy in Armenia.* Yerevan: Caucasus Institute. (In Russian.)

Mikhalev, V. 2003. *Inequality and Social Structure During the Transition.* New York: Palgrave Macmillan.

Milanovic, B. 2016. *Global Inequality: A New Approach for the Age of Globalization.* Cambridge, MA: Belknap Press.

Milanovic, B. 2014a. For whom the wall fell: A balance-sheet of transition to capitalism. Globalinequality blog: http://glineq.blogspot.com/2014/11/for-whom-wall-fell-balance-sheet-of.html.

Milanovic, B. 2014b. The Coase theorem and methodological nationalism. Online blog entry: http://glineq.blogspot.com/2014/12/coase-theorem-and-methodological.html.

Milanovic, B. 2014c. Four tricks used by Shleifer and Treisman to convince you that the transition was a success. Blog entry (November 5). Available online: http://glineq.blogspot.com/2014/11/three-tricks-used-by-shleifer-and.html.

Milanovic, B. 2012. Global income inequality by the numbers: In history and now. World Bank Policy Research Working Paper WPS6259.

Milanovic, B. 2005. Globalization and goals: does soccer show the way? *Review of Political Economy,* 12(5): 829–850.

Milanovic, B. 1999. Explaining the increase in inequality during transition. *Economics of Transition,* 7(2): 299–341.

Milanovic, B. 1998. *Income, Inequality, and Poverty during the Transition from Planned to Market Economy.* Washington, DC: The World Bank.

Milanovic, B. 1993. Social Costs of the Transition to Capitalism: Poland, 1990–91. World Bank Policy Research Paper #WPS1165.

Milanovic, B. 1991. Privatization in post-communist societies. *Communist Economies and Economic Transformation,* 3(1): 5–39.

Milberg, W. and D. Winkler. 2013. *Outsourcing Economics: Global Value Chains in Capitalist Development.* Cambridge University Press.

Minasyan, A.M. 1989. *Until When? [Do kakix por? Logika "Kapitala" Marksa i sovremennoe obwestvoznanie].* Rostov-na-Donu: Rostov State University.

Ministry of Foreign Affairs – Republic of Poland (MFA). 2015. Card of the Pole. Retrieved from: www.msz.gov.pl/en/foreign_policy/polish_diaspora/card_of_the_pole/.

Mises, L. von. 1951. *Socialism: An Economic and Sociological Analysis.* New Haven: Yale University Press. Available online: https://mises.org/library/socialism-economic-and-sociological-analysis.

Mises, L. von. 1920. Economic calculation in the socialist commonwealth. In Hayek, F. von (ed.) 1935. *Collectivist Economic Planning: Critical Studies on the Possibilities of Socialism.* London: Routledge & Sons. pp. 87–130.

Mitra, S., Andrew, D., Gyulumyan, G., Holden, P., Kaminski, B., Kuznetsov, Y. and Vashakmadze, E. 2007. *The Caucasian Tiger: Sustaining Economic Growth in Armenia.* Washington, DC: World Bank.

Moon, D. (2002) Peasant migration, the abolition of serfdom, and the internal passport system in the Russian empire. In D. Eltis (ed.) *Coerced and Free Migration.* Stanford: Stanford University Press.

Murrell, P. 1992. Evolution in economics and in the economic reform of the centrally planned economies. In C. Clague and G. Raisser (eds) *The Emergence of Market Economies in Eastern Europe.* Cambridge, UK: Blackwell. pp. 35–53.

Murell, P. and Y. Wang. 1993. When privatization should be delayed: The effect of communist legacies on organizational and institutional reforms. *Journal of Comparative Economics*, 17(2): 385–406.

Murphy, K., A. Shleifer, and R. Vishny. 1992. The transition to a market economy: pitfalls of partial reform. *Quarterly Journal of Economics*, 107: 889–906.

Myant, M. 2016. Varieties of Capitalism in post-socialist countries. In J. Holscher and H. Tomann (eds) *Palgrave Dictionary of Emerging Markets and Transition Economics: Insights from Archival Research.* New York: Palgrave MacMillan. pp. 133–152.

Najarian, L. M., Goenjian, A. K., Pelcovitz, D., *et al.* 1996. Relocation after a disaster: Posttraumatic stress disorder in Armenia after the earthquake. *Journal of the American Academy of Child and Adolescent Psychiatry*, 35(3): 374–383.

Nellis, J. 2002. *The World Bank, Privatization and Enterprise Reform in Transition Economies: A Retrospective Analysis.* Washington, DC: The World Bank.

Nellis, J. 2001. Time to rethink privatization in transition economies? In O. Havrylyshyn and S. Nsouli (eds) *A Decade of Transition: Achievements and Challenges.* Washington: IMF. p. 170.

Nellis, J. 1999. *Time to rethink privatization in transition economies?* International Finance Corporation discussion paper IFD 38.

Newland, K. 2010. *Diasporas: New Partners in Global Development.* Washington, DC: Migration Policy Institute.

Newland, K. and E. Patrick. 2004. *Beyond Remittances: The Role of Diaspora in Poverty Reduction in their Countries of Origin.* Washington, DC: Migration Policy Institute.

North, D. 2004. *Institutions, Institutional Change and Economic Performance.* Cambridge, UK: Cambridge University Press.

North, D. 1991. Institutions. *Journal of Economic Perspectives*, 5(1): 97–112.

Notzon, F.C., Y.M. Komarov, S.P. Ermakov, C.T. Sempos, J.S. Marks, and E.V. Sempos. 1998. Causes of declining life expectancy in Russia. *The Journal of the American Medical Association*, 279(10): 793–800.

Nove, A. 1993. *An Economic History of the USSR: 1917–1991.* 3rd ed. Penguin Books.

Nove, A. 1986. *The Soviet Economic System.* 3rd ed. London: Allen and Unwin.

Nove, A. 1964. *Was Stalin Really Necessary?* London: George Allen & Unwin.

NYC Center for Economic Opportunity (CEO). 2013. CEO Annual Report 2012–2013. Available online: www1.nyc.gov/assets/opportunity/pdf/ceo_annual_report_2012–2013_web.pdf.

OECD. 2017. OECD Inequality online database. Available online: www.oecd.org/social/inequality.htm.

OECD 2006. "A. Eastern Europe and Former USSR", in The World Economy: *Volume 1: A Millennial Perspective and Volume 2: Historical Statistics.* Paris: OECD Publishing.

OECD. 1990. *OECD Economic Surveys: Yugoslavia 1990.* Paris: OECD.

O'Neill, J. 2001. Building better global economic BRICs. Goldman Sachs Global Economics Paper, No. 66 Available online: www.goldmansachs.com/our-thinking/archive/building-better.html.

Ofer, G. 1987. Soviet economic growth: 1928–1985. *Journal of Economic Literature*, 25(4): 1767–1833.

Ofer, G. 1976. Industrial structure, urbanization, and the growth strategy of socialist countries. *Quarterly Journal of Economics*, 90(2): 219–244.

Ortiz-Ospina, E. and M. Roser. 2017. Global Health. Published online at OurWorldInData.org. Available online: https://ourworldindata.org/health-meta/.

PBS. 2003. Commanding heights: shock therapy on PBS. PBS.org. Available online: www.pbs.org/wgbh/commandingheights/shared/minitextlo/ufd_shocktherapy.html.

Pasternak, B. 1991. *Doctor Zhivago.* New York: Pantheon Books.

Pastor, G. and T. Damjanovic. 2003. The Russian financial crisis and its consequences for Central Asia. *Emerging Markets Finance & Trade*, 39(3): 79–104.

Pennington, R. 2010. Offensive women: Women in combat in the Red Army in the Second World War. *The Journal of Military History*, 74(3): 775–820.

Pereira, L.C.B. 1993. Economic reforms and cycles of state intervention. *World Development*, 21(8): 1337–1993.

Pereira, L.C.B., J.M. Maravall, and A. Przeworski. 1993. *Economic Reforms in New Democracies: A Social Democratic Approach.* Cambridge: Cambridge University Press.

Perovic, J. 2007. The Tito-Stalin split: A reassessment in light of new evidence. *Journal of Cold War Studies*, 9(2): 32–63.

Petrick, M., J. Wandel, and K. Karsten. 2013. Rediscovering the Virgin Lands: Agricultural investment and rural livelihoods in a Eurasian frontier area. *World Development*, 43: 164–179.

Petrova, N.K. 2016. Sovetskie zhenwiny v gody Velikoj Otechestvennoj vojny. In Petrov, Y.A. *Velikaya Otechestvennaya – izvestnaya i neizvestnaya: istoricheskaya pamyat' i sovremennost'*. Moscow: Russian Academy of Sciences. Available online: http://rusrand.ru/spring/sovetskie-jenschiny-v-gody-velikoy-otechestvennoy-voyny.

Piketty, T. 2014. *Capital in the Twenty-First Century*. Cambridge, MA: Belknap Press.

Pirttila, J. 2001. Fiscal policy and structural reforms in transition economies: An empirical analysis. *Economics of Transition*, 9(1): 29–52.

Poirot, C. 2001. Financial integration under conditions of chaotic hysteresis: The Russian financial crisis of 1998. *Journal of Post Keynesian Economics*, 23(3): 485–507.

Pokrovskii, M.N. 1934. *Russkaya istoriya s drevnejshikh vremen* [Russian history from ancient times]. Moscow: gos. Socialno-ekon. Izd-vo.

Polak, J. 1997. The IMF monetary model at forty. IMF Working Paper No. 97/49.

Polak, J. 1957. Monetary analysis of income formation and payments problems. *IMF Staff Papers*, 6: 1–50.

Popov, V. 2013a. An economic miracle in the post-Soviet space: How Uzbekistan managed to achieve what no other post-Soviet state has. *PONARS Eurasia Working Paper*. Washington, DC: The Institute for European, Russian and Eurasian Studies.

Popov, V. 2013b. Transformational recession. In Alexeev, M. and S. Weber (eds) *The Oxford Handbook of the Russian Economy*. Oxford: Oxford University Press.

Popov, V. 2011. *The Strategies of Economic Development*. Moscow: Moscow State University Press.

Popov, V. 2007a. Shock therapy versus gradualism reconsidered: Lessons from transition economies after 15 years of reforms. *Comparative Economic Studies*, 49: 1–31.

Popov, V. 2007b. Shock therapy versus gradualism: The end of the debate (explaining the magnitude of the transformational recession). *Comparative Economic Studies*, 42(1): 1–57.

Popov, V. 2007c. Life cycle of the centrally planned economy: Why Soviet growth rates peaked in the 1950s. In Estrin, S., G. W. Kolodko, and M. Uvalic (eds) *Transition and Beyond: Essays in Honor of Mario Nuti*. New York: Palgrave MacMillan. pp. 35–57.

Popov, V. 2000. Shock therapy versus gradualism: The end of the debate (explaining the magnitude of transformational recession). *Comparative Economic Studies*, 42: 1–57.

Portes, R. 1991. The path of reform in Central and Eastern Europe: An introduction. *European Economy*, Special Issue, 2:3–15.

Portes, R. 1990. Introduction to economic transformation of Hungary and Poland. *European Economy*, 43:11–18.

Prebisch, R. 1959. Commercial policy in underdeveloped countries. *American Economic Review*, 49(2): 251–73.

Puffer, S. M., Banalieva, E. R., McCarthy, D. J. 2015. Varieties of communism and risk-taking propensity of Russian entrepreneurs. *Academy of Management Annual Meeting Proceedings*, 2015(1): 1–1. 1p.

Putterman, L. 2013. Institutions, social capability, and economic growth. *Economic Systems*, 37: 345–353.

Rahman, J. 2010. Absorption boom and fiscal stance: What lies ahead in Eastern Europe? *IMF Working Paper No. 10/97*.

Rahman, J. and T. Zhao. 2013. Export performance in Europe: What do we know from supply links? *IMF Working Paper No. 13/62*. Washington, DC: International Monetary Fund.

Ramamurti R., Singh J. 2009. *Emerging Multinationals in Emerging Markets*. Cambridge: Cambridge University Press.

Ratha, D. 2003. Workers' remittances: An important and stable source of external development finance. *Global Development Finance*. World Bank.

Ratha, D. and S. Mohapatra. 2011. Preliminary estimates of diaspora savings. Migration and Development Brief 14. Migration and Remittances Unit World Bank (February 1).

Rechel, B., Roberts, B., Richardson, E., Shishkin, S., Shkolnikov, V. M., Leon, D. A., Bobak, M., Karanikolos, M., and M. McKee. 2013. Health and health systems in the Commonwealth of Independent States, *The Lancet*, 381(9872): 1145–1155.

Rodrik, D. 2004. Getting Institutions Right. CESifo DICE Report 2/2004.

Rodrik, D. 1996. Understanding economic policy reform. *Journal of Economic Literature*, 34(1): 9–41.

Roland, G. 2001a. The political economy of transition. *William Davidson Working Paper Number 413*.

Roland, G. 2001b. Ten years after . . . transition and economics. *IMF Staff Papers*, 48(special issue): 29–52.

Roland, G. 2000. *Transition and Economics: Politics, Markets, and Firms.* Cambridge, MA: MIT Press.

Roland, G. 1991. Political economy of sequencing tactics in the transition period. In L. Csaba (ed.) *Systemic Change and Stabilization in Eastern Europe*, 47–64. Aldershot: Dartmouth.

Roland, G. and T. Verdier. 1999. Transition and the output fall. *Economics of Transition*, 7(1): 1–28.

Rosefielde, S. 2010. *Red Holocaust.* Oxford: Routledge.

Rosenberg, C. B. and M. Tirpák. 2008. Determinants of foreign currency borrowing in the new member states of the EU. IMF Working Paper No. 08/173.

Rosenberg, C. B. and R. Sierhej. 2007. Interpreting EU funds data for macroeconomic analysis in the new member states. IMF Working Paper No. 07/77.

Rosenstein-Rodan, P. N. 1943. Problems of industrialization of Eastern and South-Eastern Europe. *The Economic Journal*, 53(210/211): 202–211.

Rosser, J.B. and M.V. Rosser. 1997. Schumpeterian evolutionary dynamics and the collapse of the Soviet-Bloc socialism. *Review of Political Economy*, 9(2): 211–223.

Roth, K., and Kostova, T. 2003. Organizational coping with institutional upheaval in transition economies. *Journal of World Business*, 38: 314–330.

Sachs, J. D. 1995. *Russian Federation – Russia's Struggle with Stabilization: Conceptual Issues and Evidence.* Washington, DC: The World Bank.

Sachs, J.D. 1994. Shock Therapy in Poland: Perspectives of Five Years. The Tanner Lectures on Human Values. Delivered at University of Utah on April 6 and 7, 1994.

Sachs, J. 1993. *Poland's Jump to the Market Economy.* Lionel Robbins lectures. Cambridge, MA: MIT Press.

Sakwa, R. 1999. *The Rise and Fall of the Soviet Union, 1917–1991.* Oxford: Routledge.

Schiffman, H. 1993. The role of banks in financial restructuring in countries of the former Soviet Union. *Journal of Banking and Finance*, 17: 1059–1072.

Schneider, F., A. Buehn and C. E. Montenegro. 2010. Shadow economies all over the world: New estimates for 162 countries from 1999 to 2007. *World Bank Policy Research Working Paper 5356.*

Sebetsyen, V. 2009. *Revolution 1989: The Fall of the Soviet Empire.* New York City: Pantheon Books.

Semmler, W. and A.V. Gevorkyan. 2011. Sailing out of crisis emerging markets style: blending fiscal-monetary rules, nominal targets, and debt dynamics in some transition economie. In J. A. Batten and P. G. Szilagyi (eds) *The Impact of the Global Financial Crisis on Emerging Financial Markets.* Emerald Group Publishing Limited. pp. 155–195.

Sen, A. 1999. *Development as Freedom.* New York: Anchor Books.

Shatalin S., Petrakov, N, Yavlinskiy, G., Aleksashenko, S., Vavilov, A., Grigoriev, L., Zadornov, M., Martynov, V., Mashits, V., Mikhajlov, A., Fedorov, V., Yarygina, T., and Yasin, E. 1990. *Perexod k rynku.* Moscow: EPIcentr. Available online: www.yabloko.ru/Publ/500/500-days.pdf.

Sholokhov, M. 1941. *And Quiet Flows the Don.* New York: A. A. Knopf.

Shotter, J. 2017. *Investors pile into central Europe.* FT.com online edition (Aug 24). Available online: www.ft.com/content/f9da5b20-88b1-11e7-8bb1-5ba57d47eff7.

Sinn, Hans-Werner. 2000. EU enlargement, migration, and lessons from German unification. *German Economic Review*, 1(3): 299–314.

Skrentny, J.D., S. Chan, J. Fox and D. Kim. 2007. Defining nations in Asia and Europe: A comparative analysis of ethnic return migration policy. *International Migration Review*, 41(4): 793–825.

Skype. 2017. Welcome to Estonia, Silicon Valley with a moat. Available online: www.microsoft.com/en-us/stories/skype/skype-chapter-2-welcome-to-estonia.aspx.

Snowden, E. 1920. *Through Bolshevik Russia.* London: Cassell and Company, Ltd. Available online: https://archive.org/details/throughbolshevik00snowuoft.

Solman, P. 2017. The hottest chart in economics, and what it means. *PBS Newshour.* Available online: www.pbs.org/newshour/making-sense/hottest-chart-economics-means/.

Spence, M., P.C. Annez, and R. M. Buckley (eds). 2009. *Urbanization and Growth.* Washington, DC: The World Bank.

Spigarelli, F. 2011. The international expansion of Russian enterprises. Looking at Italian targets. *European Scientific Journal*, 10(March): 27–53.

Spufford, F. 2010. *Red Plenty.* Minneapolis, MN: Graywolf Press.

Statistics of the CMEA. 1986. *Statistical Yearbook of the CMEA 1986 [Statisticheskij ezhegodnik stran chlenov SEV 1986].* Moscow: Finansy i Statistika.

Steinherr, A. 1997. Banking reforms in eastern European countries. *Oxford Review of Economic Policy*, 13(2): 105–125.

Steininger, R. 1990. *The German Question: The Stalin Note of 1952 and the Problem of Reunification.* New York: Columbia University.

Stibbe, M. and K. McDermott. 2006. *Revolution and Resistance in Eastern Europe: Challenges to Communist Rule.* New York: Bloomsbury Publishing PLC.

Stiglitz, J. 2012. *The Price of Inequality: How Today's Divided Society Endangers Our Future.* New York: W. W. Norton & Company.

Stiglitz, J. 2003. *Globalization and its Discontents.* W. W. Norton & Company.

Stiglitz, J. 2000. Whither reform: Ten years of transition. In B. Pleskovic and J. Stiglitz (eds) *Annual World Bank Conference on Economic Development.* Washington: World Bank. pp. 27–56.

Svenjar, J. 2001. Transition economies: Performance and challenges. William Davidson Working Paper Number 415.

Svenjar, J. 1989. A framework for the economic transformation of Czechoslovakia. *PlanEcon Report*, 5(52): 1–18.

Svihlikova, I. 2011. The Czech Republic: Neoliberal reform and economic crisis. In Dale, G. (ed.) *First the Transition, then the Crash.* London: Pluto Press.

Swain, G. and N. Swain. 1993. *Eastern Europe since 1945.* London: Palgrave Macmillan.

Tagliabue, J. 1982. Payments Reported by Poland. *The New York Times* (January 13). Available online: www.nytimes.com/1982/01/13/business/payments-reported-by-poland.html.

Tarr, D. 2016. The Eurasian Economic Union of Russia, Belarus, Kazakhstan, Armenia, and the Kyrgyz Republic: Can it succeed where its predecessor failed? *Eastern European Economics*, 54(1): 1–22.

Taubman, W. 2004. *Khrushchev: The Man and His Era.* W. W. Norton & Company (reprint).

Temesvary, J. 2016. The drivers of foreign currency-based banking in Central and Eastern Europe. *Economics of Transition*, 24(2): 233–257.

Thatcher, I.D. 2002. Brezhnev as leader. In Bacon, E. and M. Sandle (eds) *Brezhnev Reconsidered.* New York: Palgrave Macmillan. pp. 38–67.

The Conference Board (TCB). 2017. *Total Economy Database (Adjusted version)*, May 2017. Available online: www.conference-board.org/data/economydatabase/.

UNCTAD World Investment Report 2017, FDI/MNE database. Annex tables. Available online: http://unctad.org/en/Pages/DIAE/World%20Investment%20Report/Annex-Tables.aspx.

UNCTAD. 2015. *The State of Commodity Dependence 2014.* New York: United Nations. Available online: http://unctad.org/en/pages/PublicationWebflyer.aspx?publicationid=1171 (accessed December 15, 2016).

UNDP. 2016. Human Development Report. Available online: http://hdr.undp.org/en/2016-report.

UNDP. 2007. Development & Transition: Gender in Transition. Bratislava and London: UNDP Bratislava Regional Centre and the London School of Economics and Political Science.

UN ECE (UNECE). 1999. Economic Survey of Europe 1999, No. 1. New York and Geneva: United Nations. Available online: www.unece.org/ead/ead_ese.html.

UN ECE (UNECE). 2004. Economic Survey of Europe 2004. New York and Geneva: United Nations. Available online: www.unece.org/ead/ead_ese.html.

United Nations, DESA-Population Division, and UNICEF. 2014. Migration profiles—Common set of indicators. Retrieved from http://esa.un.org/MigGMGProfiles/indicators/indicators.HTM#europe/.

United Nations. 1955. *Copy of the Treaty of Friendship, Co-operation, and Mutual Assistance.* UN Treaty Series, No 2962. Available online: https://treaties.un.org/doc/Publication/UNTS/Volume%20 219/volume-219-I-2962-Other.pdf.

Vainshteyn, A.L. 1972. Цены и ценообразование в СССР в восстановительный период 1921–1928. [Prices and price formation in the USSR in the recovery period], Moscow: Nauka.

Vainshteyn, A. 1929. K kritike pyatiletnego perspectivnogo plana razvertyvaniya narodnogo khozyastva SSSR [On the critique of the five-year plan for development of the USSR economy]. *Ekonomich-eskoe obozrenie,* 7: 64–65.

Veblen, T. 1899. *The Theory of the Leisure Class.* Available online: www.gutenberg.org/files/ 833/833-h/833-h.htm.

Velluti, S. 2014. Gender regimes and gender equality measures in Central Eastern European Countries post-accession: The case of Hungary and Poland. *Journal of International and Comparative Social Policy,* 30(1): 79–91.

Vinokurov, E. 2012. *Eurasian Integration: Challenges of Transcontinental Regionalism.* London: Palgrave Macmillan.

Von Hagen, J., R.R. Strauch, G. B. Wolff. 2002. East Germany: Transition with unification: Experiments and Experiences. *ZEI Working Paper,* No. B 19–2002.

Vonyo, T. 2017. War and socialism: Why Eastern Europe fell behind between 1950 and 1989. *The Economic History Review,* 70(1): 248–274.

Voznesensky, N. 1947. *Soviet Economy During the Second World War.* Moscow: International Publishers.

Wade, R. 2004. Is globalization reducing poverty and inequality? *World Development,* 32(4): 567–589.

Walko, J. W. 2002. *The Balance of Empires: United States' Rejection of German Reunification and Stalin's March Note of 1952.* Boca-Raton, FL: Universal-Publishers.

Ward, C. J. 2001. Selling the "Project of the Century": Perceptions of the Baikal-Amur Mainline Railway (BAM) in the Soviet Press, 1974–1984. *Canadian Slavonic Papers/Revue Canadienne des Slavistes,* 43(1): 75–95.

Weder, B. 2001. Institutional reform in transition economies: How far have they come? IMF Working Paper 01/114. Washington, DC: International Monetary Fund.

Wei, S.-J. 1997. Gradualism vs. big bang: Speed and sustainability of reforms. *The Canadian Journal of Economics,* 30(4b): 1234–1247.

Weintraub, R.M. 1977. Eastern Europe's foreign debt soaring. *The Washington Post.* (January 9). Available online: www.washingtonpost.com/archive/business/1977/01/09/eastern-europes-foreign-debt-soaring/3f3cc356-9a83-428d-9b07-105c0dd05a5d/?utm_term=.10669b81d03f.

Welter, F., Smallbone, D., and N. Isakova. 2006. *Enterprising Women in Transition Economies.* Burlington, VT: Ashgate Publishing Co.

Williamson, J. 1993. Democracy and the 'Washington Consensus.' *World Development,* 21(8): 1329–1336.

Witte, S.Y. 1921. *The Memoirs of Count Witte, translated and edited by A. Yarmolinsky.* Garden City, NY: Doubleday, Page & Co.

Woo, W. 1994. The art of reforming centrally planned economies: Comparing China, Poland, and Russia. *Journal of Comparative Economics,* 3: 276–308.

Wood, G. and M. Demirbag. 2015. Business and society on the transitional periphery: Comparative perspectives. *International Business Review,* 24(6): 917–920.

Woodhead, L. 2013. *How The Beatles Rocked the Kremlin: The Untold Story of a Noisy Revolution.* New York: Bloomsbury USA. Also available as documentary: www.imdb.com/title/tt1515155/.

World Bank (WB). 2017a. *Migration and Development Brief 27. Special Topic: Global Compact on Migration.* (April). World Bank.

World Bank (WB). 2017b. *From Recession to Recovery: Russia Economic Report (May).* Washington, DC: The World Bank.

World Bank (WB). 2017c. Poverty and equity. WB Poverty and Inequality Database. Retrieved from http://povertydata.worldbank.org/poverty/region/ECA/.

World Bank, World Bank Doing Business Database (DBS). 2017. Available online: www.doingbusiness.org.

World Bank, World Development Indicators (WDI). 2017. World Development Indicators. Online Database. Retrieved from: http://databank.worldbank.org.

World Bank Migration and Development Brief (WBMD). 2015. *World Bank Migration and Development Brief*. World Bank (April 13, 2015).

World Bank (WB). 2015. *Migration and Remittances Recent Developments and Outlook.* Migration and Development Brief 25 (October). World Bank.

World Bank (WB). 2000. *Making Transition Work for Everyone: Poverty and Inequality in Europe and Central Asia.* Washington, DC: The World Bank.

World Bank (WB). 1996. *World Development Report 1996.* Washington, DC: World Bank.

World Bank (WB). 1993. *The East Asian Miracle: Economic Growth and Public Policy.* New York: Oxford University Press.

World Bank Migration and Remittances Data Portal (WB MR). 2017. Available online: www.worldbank.org/en/topic/migrationremittancesdiasporaissues/brief/migration-remittances-data.

World Economic Forum (WEF). 2017. *The Global Competitiveness Report 2016–2017.* Available online: http://reports.weforum.org/global-competitiveness-index/ (accessed August 20, 2017).

Zajonchkovskij, P.A. 1968. *Otmena krepostnogo prava v Rossii* [Abolition of serfdom in Russia]. Moscow.

Zaleski, E. 1980. *Stalinist Planning for Economic Growth, 1933–1952.* Chapel Hill: University of North Carolina Press.

Zauberman, A. 1964. *Industrial Progress in Poland, Czechoslovakia and East Germany, 1937–1962.* London: Oxford University Press.

Zwass, A. 1989. *The Council for Mutual Economic Assistance: The Thorny Path from Political to Economic Integration.* Armonk, NY: M.E. Sharpe.

Zwass, A. 1979. *Money, Banking, and Credit in the Soviet Union and Eastern Europe.* London: M.E. Sharpe.

Index

500 Days Program 114–115

academia, Soviet Union 63
Adenauer, Konrad 77
'advantages of backwardness' 69, 189
aggregate demand (AD) 17, 178, 199
aggregate supply (AS) 17
agriculture: Decree on Land 44; early capitalism
    41–42; emancipation of the serfs 38–39;
    industrialization 47–48; New Economic
    Policy 45–46; *perestroika* reforms 103; post-
    war recovery 61, 62–63, 78–79; Russian
    crisis (2014) 204, 206; Russian Revolution
    (1905) 42; Scissors Crisis 46–47; socialist
    economic model 95
Albania 74, 199
anti-bolshevik movement 43
Armenia 111, 177

backwardness, economic 69, 189
Baikal Amur Mainline (BAM) 103–104
bailouts 86–87, 200–201
Balcerowicz Plan 127–128
Bank of Finland's Institute for Economies in
    Transition (BOFIT) 204–206
banking: bailouts 86–87, 200–201; early
    crises 210–211; foreign banks 211–214;
    monobank systems 209; *perestroika*
    reforms 109; post-financial crisis 215–216;
    privatization 141
Berend, Ivan. T. 73, 75, 100, 153, 217–219
Berlin Wall: Central and Eastern Europe
    73–78; construction 78; economic context
    37; fall of 78, 119; new world order
    107–112
big bang reforms (shock therapy) 18–19,
    147–154
Bloody Sunday 42
Bolshevik Party 43–45
Brest-Litovsk treaty 43
BRIC economies 190–192
Bukharin, Nikolai 47–48
Bulgaria 82, 210

capital flows 101, 192, 204–206, *205*, 212, 235
capitalism, varieties of 242–246, 248
capitalist economies: Berlin Wall 78; early
    capitalism 39–43; historical context
    11; inevitability of transition 21–26;
    transformation 3–4, 20–26; *see also* free-
    market economics
Caucasus: geography and history 6–11;
    landlocked 26; Leninst state 43; migration
    170; remittances 172; *see also* transitional
    periphery
censorship 23, 107–108
Central Asia: credit markets and currency
    pressures 216; geography and history 6–11;
    gender 240; income inequality 167; labor
    productivity 104; landlocked 26; migration
    170; remittances 172; urbanization 96–97; *see
    also* transitional periphery
Central and Eastern Europe (CEE): Berlin Wall
    73–78; common market 81–85; free-market
    economics 123–130; geographical context
    4–8; historical context 8–11; post-World
    War II 72, 78–81, 87–88; trade 85–87;
    transformation 3–4, 12–13
central planning: end of plan 118–120; prices
    68–69, 110; Soviet-type 64–69; *see also*
    socialist economies; state
Central Planning Board (CPB) 99
Central Statistical Administration 66
Chernobyl disaster 111
Churchill, Winston 72
Civil War, Russian 43, 44–45
Coase theorem 140
Cold War 72–78
collective responsibility 39
collectivization 48, 50, 53–54, 61–62,
    64, 79
COMECON *see* Council for Mutual Economic
    Assistance (CMEA)
commodity exporters, countries 8, 162,
    192–196, 223
common market 81–85, 129–130; *see also*
    European Union

Commonwealth of Independent States (CIS) 6, 119–120, 124–129, 217
communism, varieties of 73–78
Communist Information Bureau 74
community, collective responsibility 39
competition policy 223–225
competitive structure 231–235
compulsory education 49, 105
consumer goods *see* goods production
consumption: macroeconomic challenges 114; *perestroika* reforms 103
contemporary context 189–190, 225–227; economic development 7, 7–8, **13**, 190–192, 231–235; financial crisis (2008) 196–203; financial sector development 208–216; foreign direct investment 219–225; future of 248; human transition 235–241; institutions 241–246; macroeconomics 231–235; regional integration 216–219; roaring 2000s 27–28, 190–196; Russian crisis (2014) 203–208; understanding history 231, 246–248
cooperatives, *perestroika* reforms 109
Corn Campaign 63
corporate governance, privatization 144–146
Cossack Hosts 44
Council for Mutual Economic Assistance (CMEA) 81–85, 128, 129
credit growth 192–193, 204, 212–216
crisis *see* financial crisis (2008); Russian crisis (2014)
Czechoslovakia: Council for Mutual Economic Assistance 81–83; fall of Berlin Wall 119; privatization 141; shock therapy 150–151

debt bailouts 86–87, 200–201
Decree on Land 44
Decree on Peace 44
demographics: urbanization 41–42; World War II 56–59
dialectics: Berlin Wall 73–78; transition 29–32
diaspora, human transition 174–185
diaspora regulatory mechanism (DRM) 181
dispersion effect 176, 179
diversity of CEE/FSU group 9–11, 136–137
Doing Business Survey 144, 242–245

early capitalism 39–43
earthquake, Armenia 111
East Germany: Council for Mutual Economic Assistance 81–83; fall of Berlin Wall 119; market socialism 99–100; reunification process 136–137; Soviet Union 76–77
economic accounting 109, 112
economic development: contemporary context 7–8, 13, 190–192, 231–235; financial crisis (2008) 196–199; growth rates *27–28*, 27–29; historical context 37–51; human transition

130–133; post-financial crisis 215–216; post-war recovery 59–61, *60*; privatization 141; Russian crisis (2014) 203–208; socialist economic model 91–98; transformation 18–21; transition 124–129; *see also* macroeconomics
education: academia 63; graduate employment 116; mandatory 49, 63; *perestroika* reforms 105
elephant chart 167
emancipation, serfs 38–39
employment: contemporary context 239–241; financial crisis (2008) 196–198; graduates 116; Soviet economy 55–56; *see also* labor
Engels, Friedrich 38
enterprise reform 12, 17, 24, 150
Estonia, privatization 143
Eurasian Economic Union (EAEU) 6, 217–218
European Bank for Reconstruction and Development (EBRD): conceptualizing the reform 134–135; financial inclusion 216; foreign direct investment 223–225; human transition 238; income inequality 167; index system 155–156; living standards 235–238, 246–247; privatization 140–141, 144
European Union (EU) 6, 216–217, 218–219, 221–223, 241
Eurozone 218
evacuation, World War I 57, 58
exchange rate 116, 199, 204, 206–208, 215

financial crisis (2008): contemporary context 196–203; before the crisis 192–196; responses to 199–203; social movements 23
financial inclusion 216
financial sector development 208–216
first movers 174–175
Five-Year Plans: pre-World War II 54–55; socialist economies 49; Soviet-type economy 68
forced savings 56, 62
foreign direct investment (FDI): contemporary context 208, 219–225, 235; post-financial crisis 219–221; privatization 142–144
former Soviet Union (FSU): free-market economics 123–130, 136; geographical context 4–8; historical context 8–11; human transition 238; privatization 142; transformation 3–4, 12–13; *see also* Russia, history of
free-market economics 154–156; conceptualizing the reform 134–137; historical context 11; human transition 130–133; privatization 138–147; shock therapy 147–154; transition 122–130; *see also* capitalist economies

FSU *see* former Soviet Union
future of transition economies 248

Gaidar, Yegor 91–92, 118
GDR *see* East Germany
gender, World War II 56–57
Gender Development Index (GDI) 238–240
geographical context: Central and Eastern
    Europe 4–8; former Soviet Union 4–8;
    Germany 219
Georgia 177
Germany, post-financial crisis 219; *see also* East
    Germany; West Germany
Gerschenkron, Alexander 32, 41, 69, 189
Gini coefficients 165–167
glasnost 107–108
global financial crisis *see* financial crisis (2008)
global value chains (GVC) 68
globalization 174, 247
goods production: contemporary context 235;
    forced savings 56; industrialization 100;
    macroeconomics 232, 235; *perestroika* reforms
    103–105, 106–107, 110; socialist economic
    model 95; Soviet-type economy 67–68
Gorbachev, Mikhail: *perestroika* reforms 21–22,
    24, 107, 108; Soviet Union dissolution
    117–119
Gosbank 66
Goskomtsen 65
Gosplan 64–65
Gossnab 65
Gosstroi 65
gradualism 151–153
graduates, full employment 116
Great Patriotic War 56; *see also* World War II
Great Purge 54–56

happiness gap 246–247
Hegel, Georg Wilhelm Friedrich 31
historical context: importance of understanding
    231, 246–248; socialist economies 37–51;
    Soviet Union 8–11; *see also* Russia, history of
Human Development Index (HDI) 238–239
human transition 161–162; contemporary
    context 235–241; diaspora 174–185;
    income inequality 162–169; labor migration
    169–174; life expectancy 20–21, 235–238;
    macroeconomics 130–133; policy proposals
    181–182; poverty 162–169; transition
    economies 11–12
Hungarian Uprising 75–76
Hungary: bailouts 86; Council for Mutual
    Economic Assistance (CMEA) 81–83; market
    socialism 101–102; privatization 138, 143;
    self-management 75–76
hyperinflation 116, 119, 128–129

IMF: debt 86–87; financial crisis (2008) 200,
    206; transition 123, 128
import substituting industrialization (ISI)
    92–93
income inequality 162–169
independence, historical context 9–10
industrialization: *perestroika* reforms
    103–104; post-war recovery 78–80;
    socialist economies 40, 47–49, 93–95;
    Soviet-type economy 67; *see also* goods
    production
inequality, human transition 162–169
inflation: financial crisis (2008) 200, 202;
    hyperinflation 116, 119, 128–129
institutions 20–21, 241–246
Investment Privatization Funds 141
'iron curtain' 72

J curve 204

Kazakhstan 57, 63
khozraschet system 109, 112
Khrushchev Nikita 62, 77
Khrushchev Thaw 62, 64
kolkhoz framework 48, 58, 61, 79
Kornai, Janos 98, 139
kulaks 45–46, 48

labor: human transition 169–174; *perestroika*
    reforms 109; *see also* employment
Lange, Oskar 98–99
Latin America, shock therapy 148–149
legal context, *perestroika* reforms 109
Leninist State: New Economic Policy 45, 47;
    Russian Revolution 43–44, 50; socialist
    economies 43–45
liberalization 29, 115, 123, 138, 147–153, 161
life expectancy 20–21, 235–238
living standards: contemporary context
    235–238, 246–248; income inequality 130,
    162; industrialization 48, 85; *perestroika*
    reforms 112, 116, 123, 154; urbanization 95;
    West and East Germany 119, 137
likbez 44
Long-Term Capital Management 192

macroeconomic stabilization 123, 128, 138, 150,
    189
macroeconomics: Balcerowicz Plan 127–128;
    contemporary context 231–235; human
    transition 130–133; *perestroika* reforms
    112–118; socialist economic model 93–97;
    transformation 20, 22–23
manager–employee buyouts (MEBO),
    privatization 138–140, 146
mandatory education 49, 105

market economies *see* capitalist economies
market socialism 98–107
Marshall Plan 78–79
Marx, Karl 38, 110, 153
Marxism and Marxian economics 26–27, 44, 102
migration: Berlin Wall 78; diaspora 174–185; human transition 169–174; post-war recovery 63
Migration Development Bank (MDB) 181–182
Milanovic, Branko 138, 146, 161, 165–167
monetary systems: New Economic Policy 45–46; *perestroika* reforms 115–116; post-financial crisis 215–216; Russian crisis (2014) 204–206, 207; Russia's post-war recovery 61, 64; *see also* prices
monobank systems 209
multinational enterprises (MNEs) 68

New Economic Mechanism (NEM) 101
New Economic Policy 45–47
non-performing loans (NPL) 210
North, Douglas 242, 246
nuclear disaster, Chernobyl 111

October Revolution *see* Russian Revolution (1917)

Pareto efficiency 18–19, 31, 151
perestroika reforms: conceptualizing 107–108; economic context 37; inevitability of transition 21–26; macroeconomics 112–118; pre-1985 102–103; world order shaken 107–112; *see also* reform
planned economies *see* socialist economies
Polak model 147–148
Poland: bailouts 86; Council for Mutual Economic Assistance (CMEA) 81–83; political economy 76; privatization 138; shock therapy 150–151; also see *Solidarność*
political context: Eastern Europe 73–78; *perestroika* reforms 107–112; post-World War II 72–73
post-socialist economies: historical context 3, 8–11; human transition 162–169, 181, 182, 183–184; *see also* contemporary context
Potsdam Agreement 72–73
poverty 162–169
Poznan, Poland 76
present *see* contemporary context
prices: central planning 68–69, 110; *perestroika* reforms 115–116; shock therapy 150; subsidy debate 83–85; *see also* monetary systems
privatization 115, 135–136, 138–147, 149
privatization voucher 140–143
production *see* goods production

public debt, financial crisis (2008) 200–201

reform: conceptualizing 134–137; historical context 10–11; inevitability of transition 21–26; totality of 26–29; *see also perestroika* reforms; transition
regional integration 216–219, 223
remittances, labor migration 169–174, 177–179
rent seeking 25, 151
resource curse 8
restitution 140
roaring 2000s 27–28, 190–196; *see also* contemporary context
Romania 39, 82, 84, 86, 93, 119, 210
Russia, history of: 1861–1917 37–51; post-war recovery 59–64, 70; pre-World War II 54–56; Soviet-type economy 55–56, 64–69; war economy 56–59; *see also* former Soviet Union (FSU); Soviet Union
Russian Civil War 43, 44–45
Russian crisis (2014) 203–208
Russian default (1998) 192–193
Russian Revolution (1905) 42
Russian Revolution (1917) 43–44, 50

Sachs, Jeffrey 147
sciences, Russia 63
Scissors Crisis 46–47
self-management 75–76, 98–102, 110
serfs, emancipation 38–39
services sector 203
shadow economies 114, 246
shock therapy 18–19, 147–154
social context *see* human transition
social movements, financial crisis (2008) 23
socialism, varieties of 73–81
socialist economic model 91–98
socialist economies: allure of early capitalism 39–43; Berlin Wall 78; Central and Eastern Europe varieties 73–78; collectivization 48; emancipation of the serfs 38–39; end of plan 118–120; Five-Year Plans 49; happiness gap 246–247; historical context 37–51; industrialization 40, 47–49; inevitability of transition 21–26; Leninist State 43–45; market socialism 98–107; New Economic Policy 45–47; post-World War II 78–81; Soviet-type 55–56, 64–69; transformation 3–4
soft budget constraint (SBC): enterprise reform 17; human transition 130; market socialism 99–100; non-performing loans 210; *perestroika* reforms 105–107
socio-economic transformation, model of 29, 31–32, 231, 235, 241, 247–248

Solidarność (or Solidarity), movement 78, 86, 102
sovereignty, historical context 9–10
Soviet Union: East Germany 76–77; historical context 8–11; post-war recovery 59–64; pre-World War II 54–56; trade 85–87; war economy 56–59; *see also* former Soviet Union; Russia, history of
Soviet Union dissolution 10–11, 117–119
Soviet-type economies 55–56, 64–69
speed of reform *see* shock therapy
stabilization, macroeconomic 123, 128, 138, 150, 189
stagnation 105–106
Stalin, Joseph 48, 62, 74–75, 77
Stalin Note 77
standardization 104
state: inevitability of transition 22–23, 24–25; market socialism 101–107; prices 68–69, 110; shock therapy 150; Soviet-type economy 64–69
State Planning Committee 64–65
state-owned enterprises 12, 17, 24, 109, 150
structural transformation, Russia 54–55
subsidy debate 83–85
sustainability, socialist economic model 98

taxation: collective responsibility 39; financial crisis (2008) 195–196, 200; New Economic Policy 45–46; transformation 20; Washington Consensus 149; World War II 58
Thatcher, Margaret 139
Tito, Josip Broz 74–75, 101
trade: Central and Eastern Europe 85–87; European Union 221–223; free-market economics 129–130; post-financial crisis 219, 222–223; Washington Consensus 149
transformation: to capitalist economy 3–4, 20–26; inevitability 21–26; pre-World War II 54–56; terminology 15–16; totality of 26–29; vs. transition 16–19
transformational recession 232
transition: dialectics 29–32; free-market economics 122–130; human 130–133; inevitability 21–26; shock therapy 147–154; terminology 11–12, 15–16; vs. transformation 16–19
transition economies: geographical context 4–8; historical context 8–11; social context 11–12; trends 3–4
transitional periphery 30, 124, 130, 222, 226
transportation, early capitalism 40
Truman Doctrine 72

Ukraine 64, 144, 206; *see also* Chernobyl disaster
Ulbricht, Walter 76–77
unemployment 196–198, 240, 241
United Kingdom, privatization 139
urbanization 41–42, 49, 95–97, 165
USSR *see* Soviet Union

Veblen's conspicuous consumption 190, 235
Velvet Revolution 111–112
Vienna Initiative 214
Virgin Lands, campaign 63, 103

War Communism 44–45, 47
war economy 56–59; *see also* World War II
Warsaw Pact 75–76, 76–77
Washington Consensus 17–18, 148–150, 153
well-being *see* human transition
West Germany: reunification process 136–137; shock therapy 147
World Bank: Doing Business Survey 144, 242–245; financial crisis (2008) 200; income inequality 162; privatization 144–146; remittances 170; transition 123, 128
World War I 37, 43
World War II 54–59, 69, 72

Yeltsin, Boris 117–119
youth unemployment 240, 241
Yugoslavia 74–75, 93, 100–101, 119